Gastrofascism and Empire

FOOD IN MODERN HISTORY: TRADITIONS AND INNOVATIONS

Series Editors:
Peter Scholliers
Amy Bentley

This new monograph series pays serious attention to food as a focal point in historical events from the late eighteenth century to present day.

Employing the lens of technology broadly construed, the series highlights the nutritional, social, political, cultural, and economic transformations of food around the globe. It features new scholarship that considers ever-intensifying and accelerating tensions between tradition and innovation that characterize the modern era. The editors are particularly committed to publishing manuscripts featuring geographical areas currently underrepresented in English-language academic publications, including the Global South, particularly Africa and Asia, as well as monographs featuring indigenous and underrepresented groups, and non-western societies.

Published:
Food and Aviation in the Twentieth Century: The Pan American Ideal, Bryce Evans (2021)
Feeding the People in Wartime Britain, Bryce Evans (2022)
Rebellious Cooks and Recipe Writing in Communist Bulgaria, Albena Shkodrova (2022)
Globalization in a Glass: The Rise of Pilsner Beer through Technology, Taste and Empire, Malcolm Purinton (2023)
Apples and Orchards since the Eighteenth Century: Material Innovation and Cultural Tradition, Joanna Crosby (2023)
A History of Bread: Consumers, Bakers and Public Authorities since the 18th Century, Peter Scholliers (2024)
The Moral and Market Economies of Bread: Regulation and Reform in Vienna, 1775–1885, Jonas M. Albrecht (2024)

Gastrofascism and Empire

Food in Italian East Africa, 1935–1941

Simone Cinotto

BLOOMSBURY ACADEMIC
LONDON • NEW YORK • OXFORD • NEW DELHI • SYDNEY

BLOOMSBURY ACADEMIC
Bloomsbury Publishing Plc, 50 Bedford Square, London, WC1B 3DP, UK
Bloomsbury Publishing Inc, 1359 Broadway, New York, NY 10018, USA
Bloomsbury Publishing Ireland, 29 Earlsfort Terrace, Dublin 2, D02 AY28, Ireland

BLOOMSBURY, BLOOMSBURY ACADEMIC and the Diana logo are trademarks of
Bloomsbury Publishing Plc

First published in Great Britain 2024
This paperback edition published 2025

Copyright © Simone Cinotto, 2024

Simone Cinotto has asserted his right under the Copyright, Designs and Patents Act, 1988, to be identified as Author of this work.

For legal purposes the Acknowledgments on pp. viii–xiii constitute an extension of this copyright page.

Cover image © Mondadori Portfolio / Getty Images

Archival photographic content in collaboration with Archivio Luce in Rome

All rights reserved. No part of this publication may be: i) reproduced or transmitted in any form, electronic or mechanical, including photocopying, recording or by means of any information storage or retrieval system without prior permission in writing from the publishers; or ii) used or reproduced in any way for the training, development or operation of artificial intelligence (AI) technologies, including generative AI technologies. The rights holders expressly reserve this publication from the text and data mining exception as per Article 4(3) of the Digital Single Market Directive (EU) 2019/790.

Bloomsbury Publishing Plc does not have any control over, or responsibility for, any third-party websites referred to or in this book. All internet addresses given in this book were correct at the time of going to press. The author and publisher regret any inconvenience caused if addresses have changed or sites have ceased to exist, but can accept no responsibility for any such changes.

A catalogue record for this book is available from the British Library.

A catalog record for this book is available from the Library of Congress.

ISBN: HB: 978-1-3504-3683-1
PB: 978-1-3504-3687-9
ePDF: 978-1-3504-3684-8
eBook: 978-1-3504-3685-5

Series: Food in Modern History: Traditions and Innovations

Typeset by Newgen KnowledgeWorks Pvt. Ltd., Chennai, India

For product safety related questions contact productsafety@bloomsbury.com.

To find out more about our authors and books visit www.bloomsbury.com and sign up for our newsletters.

Contents

List of Illustrations vi
Acknowledgments viii

Introduction 1

Part I   Imperial Gastronomies: Bioimperialism, Ethiopian Resistance, and the Itineraries of Food

1   Ethiopian Foodways and Italian Foodways: Frameworks of an Imperial Culinary Encounter 23

2   Fascist Bioimperialism in East Africa: Mass Colonization as Transplantation of Seeds, Breeds, and Farming Hands 33

3   Establishing the Fascist Food System in East Africa: The Imperial Mobility of Italian Food and the Ethiopian Struggle for Food Sovereignty 55

Part II   Colonial Gastronomies: Food Apartheid, Intercultural Practices of Taste, and the Senses

4   Forbidden Commensality in a Supremacist Society: Food and Racial Segregation in Italian Ethiopia 87

5   Liminal Colonial Gastronomies: Ethiopian-Italian Food Encounters in the Interstices of Segregation 125

6   The Empire of the Senses: Food Tastes, Disgusts, and Identities in Italian Ethiopia 173

Conclusion: Fascist Colonial Crops and the Legacies of the Empire of Food 199

Notes 241
Bibliography 279
Index 291

Illustrations

1. La Molisana *Abissine* Pasta — 3
2. Italian troops distributing grain to inhabitants of a captured village on the northern front, during the Second Italo-Ethiopian War, November 10, 1935 — 4
3. Ad for Amaro Ramazzotti, Gino Boccasile, 1937 — 15
4. A prickly pear vendor breastfeeds her baby at the Harar "indigenous" market, May 8, 1936 — 16
5. Two Ethiopian women carrying a *mesob*, the Harari basket used for storing *injera*, April–May 1936 — 26
6. Two village women make dough seated on a mat, northern Ethiopia, April–May 1936 — 27
7. Children of Bari d'Etiopia being served spaghetti for lunch — 38
8. A tractor pulls ahead in a field, Ethiopian peasants plow on the side in an Italian settlement, Harar region, 1937 — 39
9. Italian soldiers have lunch in an army camp during the offensive in northern Ethiopia, February–March 1936 — 43
10. "Here's the Somali Banana! A Delicious and Nutritious Fruit." Ad for Società Anonima Banane Italiane (SABI—Italian Bananas Company), artist unknown, 1934 — 44
11. "The Somali Banana: The Fruit of Health." Ad for Società Anonima Banane Italiane (SABI—Italian Bananas Company), Alfredo Cavadini, 1934 — 47
12. Ad for Azienda Monopolio Banane (AMB—Banana Monopoly Agency), Gianni Li Muli, 1950 — 48
13. Ad for Lloyd Triestino, Gino Boccasile, 1937 — 61
14. Ad for L'Acqua dell'Impero (Mineral Drinking Water of the Empire) — 62
15. The severed head of Hailu Chebbede in a cookie box, Kerem, northern Ethiopia, September 24, 1937 — 73
16. Ethiopian troops and an allied Australian officer pose with their rifles as two soldiers cook a meal at an unspecified location in Ethiopia, February 18, 1941 — 74
17. A *spaccio* (informal grocery store) in a construction camp, October 1935 — 97
18. Italian supermarket in Addis Ababa, October–December 1936 — 98

19	The Addis Ababa market in the central Arada neighborhood, close to Saint George's Cathedral, *c.*1934	113
20	The "rationalized" Merkato Ketema, which Italians opened in the "native city" in northwest Addis Ababa, early 1937	114
21	*Askaris* of the Italian colonial army on their route to enter Addis Ababa butcher a camel, April–May 1936	137
22	Ad for Amaro Ramazzotti, Gino Boccasile, 1937	138
23	Italian soldiers peruse fruits at the Harar "indigenous" market, May 8, 1935	154
24	An Italian soldier offers canned food to a group of Ethiopians, April 26–May 5, 1936	155
25	Ad for Caramella San Giacomo, Luciano Bonacini, 1936	179
26	Three Oromo and two Italians capture a crocodile in southeastern Ethiopia near the Somali border, April–May 1936	180
27	Oromo farmers harvesting coffee in a plantation, while an Italian man looks on, southwestern Ethiopia, 1937	214
28	Bar Impero in Addis Ababa, 1938	215
29	Ad for Cacao Perugina chocolate powder, Federico Seneca, *c.*1930	231
30	Ad for Banane Perugina chocolates, Federico Seneca, *c.*1930	232
31	"I Am Coffee!" Ad for Bricco brand coffee blend, Gino Boccasile, 1939	235
32	"The Best Coffee Surrogate." Ad for Moretto brand coffee blend, Gino Boccasile, *c.*1939	236

Acknowledgments

I've had a lot of help!!!

I deeply apologize in advance to the many I'm going to forget while I hastily write these notes. The list of amazing people who critically contributed to the making of *Gastrofascism and Empire (G&E)* is incredibly long. One thing I know for sure is that it needs to begin with the editor, scholar, and friend without whom this book would literally not be in your hands. As per my previous book of exactly ten years ago, *The Italian American Table: Food, Family and Community in New York City*, it was the dedicated, exceptionally skilled, and professionally impeccable editorial work of Robert Oppedisano that shaped this book in every good feature it possesses. Errors and omissions remain, of course, entirely my own. Bob not only curated my English prose but also dramatically improved the text stylistically, as a reflection of his elegant literary taste. He made the book *G&E* so much better than the original manuscript was, and I'm eternally indebted to him.

The editors of the book series "Food in Modern History: Traditions and Innovations" at Bloomsbury—Amy Bentley (New York University) and Peter Scholliers (Vrije Universiteit Brussel)—are two food history giants who created and shaped the field since the mid-1990s through their scholarship, as well as their leadership in professional associations and academic journals. The fact that Amy and Peter immediately demonstrated their interest in *G&E* the moment I proposed it was thus truly heartening. I thank them so much for their trust in me.

My editors at Bloomsbury—Global and World History Acquisition Editor Maddie Smith (née Holder) and Editor Megan Harris—were of great assistance and support throughout. I really appreciate their keenness at listening and understanding my needs and idiosyncrasies, their excellent communication style, and their general enthusiasm for the project from beginning to end. The three anonymous reviewers Maddie and Meg lined up were also extremely helpful, providing different sets of insightful comments and constructive criticisms.

The help I received from so many sources was also critical on an emotional level, as the time when I wrote this book was admittedly the most painful and despairing I had ever lived through. Three of the most important and beloved people in my life passed away while *G&E* was in the making. All of them read portions of the manuscript, giving me, as always, much encouragement and love, but didn't live to see the completion of this book. (I'm crying.)

Maurizio Vaudagna was my mentor, my sterling example of what an academic should be like, my model of human being, and my dearest friend. I simply owe him everything. He found me when I was a long-haired guy in a punk rock band and asked me if I was interested in pursuing a career in research, as he apparently loved my BA thesis (because of that I still revere theses as life-changing experiences and often remind my students of Umberto Eco's adagio, "Your thesis is like your first love: it will be difficult to forget"). Since then, every minute spent with Maurizio was a priceless lesson learned. He taught me ALL my firsts—from how to work in an archive to how to organize a conference—and to this day, every time I'm in doubt of what to do, I think of what Maurizio would have done in that circumstance. A brilliant historian of comparative and transnational welfare states between Europe and the Americas, Maurizio was a tireless and magnificent cultural organizer. Prizing the collaborative dimension of research over anything else in academia, he facilitated the internationalization of numberless Italian, European, and US historians, actively creating a scholarly space for the study of transatlantic relations. I benefited from the networks he so skillfully created in a million ways and times; for example, when, as a fresh doctoral student, he shipped me to Columbia University, where I learned from historians of the caliber of Eric Foner, Alice Kessler-Harris, Mae Ngai, and the late Alan Brinkley, all Maurizio's friends. Although he had retired, he was still a superb intellectual, a stunningly beautiful man, and the most lovely and interesting person to be around, full of ideas, plans, and projects for the future. I miss him dearly every single day.

A few months before Maurizio, I had lost my best friend Gerald J. Meyer. Jerry and I met because of our common passion for the history of East Harlem, Italian immigration and life in New York City, and New Deal-era politics and programs, which he superbly expressed in his multi-edition biography of radical politician Vito Marcantonio (1902–1954). In the 1970s and 1980s, Jerry had been a leader in the struggle for keeping the New York City public university system accessible to minority and working-class students—notably at CUNY Hostos Community College, the school where he taught for thirty years—and continued in his enthusiasm and talent to organize people with the political-cultural group he created in the late 1990s, the Vito Marcantonio Forum. Jerry was my New York family. Together we went to innumerous conferences, concerts, dinners, and walks in the park, exploring the city and talking. He was so generous and so incredibly smart, so easy to adore. With him I lost such a big part of me and even much of my capacity to remember, as, since he passed away, memories seem to slip and fade like fine sand through the fingers of my hands.

Nothing, though, had prepared me to the loss of Valeria de Carli, my first wife and mother of my children. Valeria was the most independent, strongest, and bravest women I ever met. Together, in our early thirties, she and I delved into making family, self-taught each other parenting, and partnered raising the most wonderful children we could have ever dreamt of having. I was just blessed to have her as a loving companion on this most beautiful journey, and she was just a fantastic mom. Her brutal, untimely, and unfair passing was the saddest thing that happened to me in my entire life and has left me agonized, devastated, and desperate.

In the face of these tragedies, many great friends and colleagues helped me complete this book and make it so much better than would have been without their generous support, which included having me at their universities to introduce my research and discuss it with highly qualified audiences. US and international relations historian Mario Del Pero invited me to present my work in progress (specifically what would become Chapters 2 and 3 of *G&E*) at the London School of Economics–Sciences

Po International History Seminar. Mario, discussant David Motadel of LSE, and the participants in the seminar offered many excellent insights, for which I'm very thankful.

Canada Research Chair in Cultural History and Analysis at the University of Toronto Daniel E. Bender—with whom I partnered for organizing international conferences, coediting the volume *Food Mobilities: Making World Cuisines* (2023), and having memorable dinners across Italy and North America—invited me to talk about this book project at the University of Toronto History Department. (I'm indebted to Dan for many other reasons.) Among the participants in that talk, offering thought-provoking comments, was Donna R. Gabaccia. The amount and extent of the incredibly generous support Donna provided me with in the past twenty-five years—starting with line-editing my entire PhD dissertation when I was not her student, and she had absolutely no obligation to do that—equals her stature as one of the greatest historians of our times. Her work on migration history, gender and intimacy history, and food history shaped my scholarship in every possible way, as I have shamelessly tried over and over to imitate (without not even coming close) the brilliance of her research and the felicitousness of her writing. The affection, respect, and gratitude I have for Donna are unlimited and boundless.

Stanley Ulijaszek invited me to the seminar *Coffee and (New) Foodways in East Africa*, part of the UBVO Michaelmas Workshop, at the University of Oxford. Some of the text and ideas in the paper I presented on that occasion—"The Caffeinated Empire: Coffee and Gastrofascism in Italian East Africa"—are scattered through Chapters 2, 3, 5, and especially the Conclusion of this book. I'm also grateful to the seminar's organizer Sabine Parrish (City University of London) and, among the participants, coffee historian Jonathan Morris (University of Hertfordshire).

Jakob Klein invited me to the University of London SOAS to talk about *G&E* to an exciting audience of BA and MA students asking many great questions, under the joint aegis of the SOAS Food Studies Centre and the Centre for Migration and Diaspora Studies—a relation originally created with Parvathi Raman, whom I also thank very much.

For the launch event of the Italian version of this book at the University of Gastronomic Sciences in Pollenzo (UNISG), I had just the perfect panel, with two amazing discussants. Ferdinando Fasce (University of Genoa) is indisputably one of Italy's best historians, very well known internationally for his studies on US history, labor history, and the history of consumer culture and advertising in transatlantic perspective. Like Maurizio and Donna, Nando has been a perennial source of inspiration and the object of my countless attempts at imitation through all these years. He is also a dearest friend, to whom I owe the world; his massively smart reading of the Italian version of *G&E* is only the latest in a long series of gifts I received from him. I greatly admire Roberta Pergher's (Indiana University) work on Italian borderlands and colonialism during fascism. Learning that she favored the publication of *G&E* was, therefore, of tremendous encouragement. I thank her so much for the close and insightful reading of the Italian book and suggestions on how to improve this English edition. The moderator of the panel was Gabriele Proglio, my younger but so well-published, competent, and dynamic colleague at UNISG, with whom I am coauthoring a food history textbook (forthcoming). Gabriele's work is in many areas of study that are central to *G&E*—postcolonial Italy, the representation of food and race in popular culture, and the space of food in the experience of mobile people—and I benefited very much from the many conversations with him on these topics.

Historian David Gentilcore, from whom I borrowed most of the ideas about food history as history of taste packed into this book, extended a kind invitation to talk about the history of water in Italian East Africa (discussed especially in Chapters 3 and 6 of *G&E*), at the seminar series he coordinates at the University of Venice Cà Foscari. Graziella Parati, a professor of Italian literature and language, comparative literature, and women's and gender studies, whose work on migrations and diasporas in Italy is fantastic, trusted *G&E* to be good before it was even published and invited me to Dartmouth College for a book talk, which was supposed to be the first in a US book tour I planned to organize. I thank her very much for this.

Eugenia Paulicelli (CUNY Graduate Center) and David Ward (Wellesley College) encouraged me to publish an earlier article, "The Fascist Breadbasket: Food, Empire, and Modernity in Italian East Africa, 1935–1941," from the *G&E* research in the *Journal of Modern Italian Studies* (*JMIS*). John A. Davis (University of Connecticut) was an incredibly supporting editor, helping me successfully complete the task in record time. I also want to thank the two anonymous reviewers of the *JMIS* for providing many useful comments, and the independent scholar Patrizia Sambuco for writing a very useful review on the Italian version of this book (for the *JMIS*).

A new book is a great opportunity to thank amazing colleagues with whom I had not only the honor to collaborate for several years but also the most unique privilege to become friends. I was so lucky to have the chance to discuss *G&E*, halfway in the making, with the great American Jewish, US immigration, and food historian Hasia Diner. With Hasia, since we met at a conference on immigrant entrepreneurship at the University of Maryland in 2012, we organized two international conferences and edited a collection on the global history of Jewish food cultures, *Global Jewish Foodways: A History* (2018). Hasia helped me in innumerable ways all these years—inviting me several times to New York University as a visiting scholar—and all the time we had spent together, working or chatting, was nothing less than lovely and inspiring. We discussed this book over dinner in Italy, and she filled me with a lot of encouragement and great ideas.

It is equally a great pleasure to wholeheartedly thank Carl Ipsen. Carl and I have been working on many joint projects—from a documentary video on food activism between the United States and Italy to study-abroad programs—ever since he graciously invited me to teach at Indiana University for a semester in 2017. His outstanding work on historical demography, twentieth-century Italian social history, and food history was of tremendous inspiration for this book. Not least, Carl accepted to be my best man at my wedding and was the best best man a groom could possibly have on his side at such a momentous time.

I am so fortunate to know personally some of the most distinguished scholars in Modern Italian History, from whom I gathered many of the ideas and much of the support I used for this book. I'm heavily indebted to Patrizia Dogliani (University of Bologna) and her work on fascism and antifascism, Emanuela Scarpellini (University of Milan) and her work on Italian food history and consumer culture in the interwar years, and Ruth Ben-Ghiat and her work on Italian fascism, colonialism, and film. To Ruth, then the Chair of the Department of Italian Studies at New York University, and Stefano Albertini, Director of Casa Italiana Zerilli-Marimò, I owe my appointment as Tiro a Segno Visiting Professor in Italian American Culture at New York University in 2008–9. Ruth and Stefano made my experience of teaching graduate and undergraduate courses unforgettable and my overall stay an absolute ball.

My take at the representation of food and Black bodies in 1930s Italian advertising in this book's Conclusion owes an enormous lot to Karen Pinkus (Cornell University). Karen kindly accepted my invitation to deliver a fascinating talk about regenerative agriculture and soil from historical, critical, and theoretical perspectives at my university, and I took advantage of that meeting to seek her advice on the topic of the Black body in advertising she so dexterously explored in her work. I also owe much to Marco Armiero's (University of Stockholm) analysis of fascist environmentalism and Tiago Saraiva's (Drexel University) discussion of the use of agrobiotechnologies by fascist powers in their efforts at empire-making.

I want to thank my colleagues, friends, and teachers in food studies, whose inspiration is to be found at every corner of this book: Jeffrey Pilcher, Krishnendu Ray, David Sutton, Cindy Ott, Raj Patel, Paul Freedman, Massimo Montanari, Alberto Capatti, Jayeeta Sharma, Marion Nestle, Fabio Parasecoli, Elizabeth Zanoni, Peter Todd, Rafia Zafar, Anne Meneley, Andreas Weber, Robert Valgenti, and Valentina Peveri.

G&E is in many ways a book on one of *Italy's Many Diasporas* (Donna Gabaccia, 2000), and most of what I know about the subject I learned it from and together with my community of Italian American studies scholars: Stanislao Pugliese, Laura Ruberto, Joseph Sciorra, Nancy Carnevale, John Gennari, Fraser Ottanelli, Jennifer Guglielmo, Richard Juliani, Linda Reeder, Teresa Fiore, Fred Gardaphé, Marcella Bencivenni, Martino Marazzi, Giorgio Bertellini, Stefano Luconi, John Paul Russo, and James Periconi; through the catalyst of John D. Calandra Italian American Institute under the leadership of Anthony Julian Tamburri; and the journal *Italian American Review* (current editor David Aliano). I also want to thank at this point my much-esteemed reference scholars of Puerto Rican Studies and New York City history, Aldo A. Lauria Santiago (Rutgers University) and Mark D. Naison (Fordham University). I look forward to being in touch with them very soon: my next two books—one a decade and the other more than a decade in the making—are both US immigration histories.

Back at home in Italy, I want to thank Carlo Petrini, president of UNISG and founder of Slow Food. Kudos to the current president of Slow Food, Edie Mukiibi, who was an (amazing) student of the master's program in World Food Studies I coordinate at UNISG.

My former graduate student Elisa Cionchi did the research on the issues of *La Cucina Italiana* as her final assignment for my class on history of food cultures, which I used in the Conclusion. I thank her in appreciation.

So many thanks to the staff of the Interlibrary Loan Office at Indiana University Bloomington's Wells Library. The service they provided was beyond excellent. I could have never conducted research on such a disparate set of sources without their invaluable help and competence.

Thank you so much also to Patrizia Cacciani at the Archivio Luce in Rome for granting the permission to reproduce many photographs from their extensive and indispensable archives in this book.

My grandmother Maria Spinelli and godmother Anna Spinelli lived as young women through the events this book talks about. They experienced dictatorship, Fascist Party-sponsored home economics classes, and the "cuisine of sanctions." They saw young men getting drafted and leaving for Ethiopia. As rural migrants from the Italian South to Turin, they worked at several industrial jobs as teenagers, including in a candy and chocolate factory, before turning into "ethnic entrepreneurs" as fruit and vegetable vendors at the local open market, rain or shine. To a great extent they raised me; I spent all my holidays and summers with them, being around at the market and in their kitchen, until I was eleven or twelve. Only many years later I realized how much they taught me about how it feels to be a migrant, how important it is to cook and eat good food together, and love in general.

Talking about love, this book is dedicated to the dearest people of my life, who live in my heart and for whom I live. My wife Yara Ferreira Clüver is my soulmate and the love of my life. Yara, I cherish all the time we've been together and can't wait for so many more adventures with you. Thank you for being so amazing. My wonderful children, Ferdinando and Cristina, are the joy of my life. Ferdi and Cri, you make me so proud and happy always and I love you so very much, with all my heart.

Introduction

In early 2021, a heated dispute, largely conducted on social media, involved the Italian pasta company La Molisana, which had launched an advertising campaign to promote "historical pasta shapes," including a shell-shaped form called *Abissine* (Abyssinian women) (Figure 1). The text accompanying the glossy image of pasta packages left little doubt about what kind of history the product would evoke:

> In the Thirties, Italy would celebrate the age of colonialism with new pasta formats: *Tripoline, Bengasine, Assabesi,* and *Abissine*. Of strong *littorio* [the fascist symbol of the bundled axe] taste, abroad the name *Abissine* becomes Shells, that is, *conchiglie*. They have a soft, welcoming shape, cup-like, the outside is ridged and coarse, but the inside is smooth, velvety; ideal for fresh, natural sauces. We love them because they look compact and perfect like small female jewels.[1]

Some observers, including Laura Boldrini, a member of the Chamber of Deputies, quickly criticized the positive reference to fascist Italy's imperialist experience in Africa. The ad, Boldrini and others argued, was obviously aimed at Italian nostalgia for a past of national greatness that seemed to deny the realities of aggression, mass violence, and exploitation.[2] For critics like Boldrini, La Molisana's marketing drew on and reinforced a widespread Italian sense of exceptionalism, a sentiment that set Italy favorably apart from other European colonial powers and a feeling still prevalent in popular memory.[3]

Conservative media reacted loudly to the critics. They saw in the criticism of Boldrini and others an excess of political correctness that created a misleading attack on a blameless, and basic, feature of Italian identity—food, in particular pasta. According to conservatives, attacking a pasta name was both comical and disturbing, a sign of the "dominant political climate" of cancel culture. They stressed, also, that La Molisana's family owners were politically left-leaning and had agreed to withdraw the campaign; they portrayed the family as victims of political correctness.[4]

Almost regardless of the political reactions it fueled, the Molisana controversy managed to shed fresh light on a dynamic central to the Italian colonial past in East Africa—the deep connection between food and the fascist imperial project. Prime

Minister and fascist leader Benito Mussolini (1883–1945) had made his plans clear to Italians. Waging a war to defeat and occupy the independent kingdom of Ethiopia would create, alongside older Italian colonies of Eritrea and Somalia, an Africa Orientale Italiana (AOI—Italian East Africa) that would become "Italy's granary," an abundant "Empire of Food." In Mussolini's vision, whole communities of farmers and their families would be transplanted from impoverished Italy to colonize a land, Abyssinia, that would produce a bounty that local people, described as inherently lazy and incompetent, could not.

This large-scale migration of Italian pioneers would also transfer Italy's emerging agricultural and husbandry technologies that had already been proven successful in the Total Reclamation (1924) of such unproductive areas as the Pontine Marshes between Rome and Naples and in the Battle for Wheat campaign of 1925. The grand Ethiopian plan was foremost a demographic-nutritional one for achieving food autarchy (self-sufficiency and independence from imports) that could support a young and expanding population. Echoing the rhetoric of the Battle for Wheat, the most important product of the new Empire in East Africa would be wheat. After all, the Ethiopian highlands were said to be the original site of the domestication of many cereal varieties and the ideal place to grow the Italian wheat for bread and for the pasta "with a fascist taste" of La Molisana (Figure 2).

The Empire of Food would not only produce the calories, packed in grain, needed to fuel the growth of the "great proletarian nation" but also enrich the national diet and expand international trade by transforming exotic "colonial" products—coffee and bananas—once imported from other European empires into purely Italian products. Thanks to the infusion of "Italian labor," occupied Ethiopia would Italianize the growing of valuable subtropical crops. Fascist bananas grown in Italian Somalia could easily improve the national diet and replace costly imports from the United States' de facto colonies in Central America. In the same way, coffee, the main Ethiopian export before 1935, was to become a domestic staple for Italians, who were buying it with dollars from the world's main producer, Brazil.[5]

The La Molisana advertisement played with the appeal of another kind of consumption, one linked to eating. The ad's reference to *Abissine*/Abyssinians that/whom "we love because they look compact and perfect like small female jewels" referred to the Italian men, soldiers and settlers, who had invaded Ethiopia: their military victory would be a sexual conquest through the consumption of Black female (and sometimes male) bodies. In the advertisement, *Abissine*/Abyssinians "have a soft, welcoming shape, cup-like, the outside is rough, and the inside is smooth" that look like vulvas of hypersexualized colonized women, "ideal" for welcoming the "fresh juices" of conquering Italians.

The many opportunities for sexual consumption created by colonialism were the major incentive for Italian men to join the expedition. Leo Longanesi (1905–1957) commented that

> rapidly, Italians came to believe that in Ethiopia there will be work for everyone so they won't have to emigrate anymore. But the decisive argument for the Italian youth are the postcards with the portrayals of naked Abyssinians. No one had ever seen such turgid and pointy breasts. Southern Italians, especially, couldn't wait to leave.[6]

In the most popular imperial war song and most popular fascist song of all, *Faccetta Nera* (Pretty Blackface, 1935), notions of race and gender shaped the imaginary of Ethiopian food, culture, and landscape. Italian men lived the invasion of Ethiopia through the lens of what Anne McClintock called pornotropics—the gendered definition of colonial lands as "virgin," inhabited by inferior or invisible indigenous subjects and ready to be "penetrated" by White soldiers and colonists, where sexualized indigenous women were to be "conquered," tasted, and enjoyed.⁷ The sexualized advertisement of La Molisana captures the tone of Italian food advertising in the 1930s. During this period, the most celebrated illustrators, such as Gino Boccasile (1901–1952) and Federico Seneca (1891–1976), consistently used food to portray African bodies and landscapes, linking the consumption of colonial food to the consumption of the colonized other, intersecting the pleasure of the senses—sexual and gastronomic—in a colonial world of boundless consumption.⁸

The sexual appeal of the Italian adventure was only slightly restrained by the Fascist Racial Laws (1937) aimed at repressing *meticciato* (miscegenation). These laws permitted relations between Italian men and Black women only for sexual, nonsentimental, and nonreproductive purposes. They did not condemn prostitution but strictly forbade intimacy or an affective relationship of a conjugal nature, or one resembling marriage. Consequently, conviviality between Ethiopians and Italians in the privacy of domestic spaces was unlawful. At the same time the segregation of public

Figure 1 La Molisana *Abissine* Pasta. Collection of the Author.

In the early days of 2021, the pasta manufacturing company La Molisana launched a new pasta product, *Abissine* (Abyssinian women, in Italian). The name of the pasta shape—and especially the text of the accompanying advertising, which openly celebrated the memory of the fascist war and invasion of Ethiopia and the creation of the Italian Empire in East Africa—raised controversy. The pasta firm eventually apologized and withdrew the product from the market.

Figure 2 Italian troops distributing grain to inhabitants of a captured village on the northern front, during the Second Italo-Ethiopian War, November 10, 1935. Courtesy of Getty Images.

Wheat was supposed to be the most important prize of the construction of the fascist empire in East Africa: Mussolini and his colonization planners wanted to transform Ethiopia into Italy's breadbasket. In reality, as colonization plans faltered, for all the duration of the occupation, thousands of tons of wheat were imported from Italy every year for the occupation army's rations and baked as bread for settlers' consumption.

spaces made the interracial use of restaurants, cafes, bars, food stores, and markets a crime. Places of food production, processing, and consumption were separated. In the colonizers' cities, they were central, clean, and rational, while in the towns and quarters of the colonized, they were dirty, unsafe, and malodorous. As Frantz Fanon noted in *The Wretched of the Earth*, Italian Ethiopia resembled

> a compartmentalized world. The settlers' town is a strongly built town, all made of stone and steel. It is a brightly lit town; the streets are covered with asphalt, and the garbage cans swallow all the leavings. The town belonging to the colonized people is a world without spaciousness. It is a hungry town, starved of bread, of meat, of shoes, of coal, of light.[9]

Finally, by noting that, because of their "strong [fascist] taste," "abroad the name *Abissine* [will be changed to] Shells, that is, *conchiglie*," La Molisana touched on another important theme, the nationalist victim complex. Even today, while a pasta called *Abissine* might have some marketing value in Italy, its colonial and racist connotations abroad would likely lead to a consumer boycott. The 2013 international boycott launched against the pasta firm Barilla, for example, followed an interview in which a company executive made homophobic-sounding remarks.[10] For export, La Molisana would have to rename *Abissine*—unfortunately, the ad seems to suggest—into the politically neutral, but lackluster, Shells.

This need to suppress any link to the Italian "experience" in Africa is a reminder of the widespread international disapproval in 1935 of Italy's attack on Ethiopia. The Italian invasion and occupation destabilized the world order and was the first major international incident leading up to World War II. The global Black community mobilized against the aggression toward the last independent African state, the Ethiopian Empire.[11] On May 12, 1936, at the League of Nations in Geneva, the exiled Emperor Haile Selassie I (1892–1975) denounced Mussolini's aerial use of prohibited chemical weapons, earning Italy the distinction as the first country ever prosecuted by international courts for chemical warfare. Generals Rodolfo Graziani (1882–1955) and Pietro Badoglio (1871–1956) were later added to the United Nations list of war criminals. As a sanction, the League of Nations declared an embargo of Italian manufactured goods, raw resources, and machines, forcing a regime of rationing. Italy's deepening food crisis—restrictions, severe scarcity, and a collapse of domestic food security—transformed the fascist adventure in the Horn of Africa into a massive effort for survival.

Fascist propaganda mobilized Italian support for the occupation of Ethiopia as essential to Italy's food security and independence, and as a rebuff to the crippling embargo imposed by world powers. The caption "ITALIAN WHEAT" on the package of La Molisana's *Abissine* seems to guarantee not just quality and traceability but also an autarkic pedigree: pasta made from durum wheat grown in Italy, presumably by Italian farmers, and safe from "external enemies" such as globalization. The branding is also a symbolic response to the supranational power of EU agricultural policies and to immigrants from the Global South—and former European colonies—"returning" as a menacing wave.

The controversy over the marketing of *Abissine* sheds valuable light on the long-term consequences of the Ethiopian-Italian culinary encounter in which pasta played a key role. Today, Ethiopia is one of the largest pasta-consuming countries in the world. Its love for pasta is one legacy of the occupation (1935–41) that survives the bitter memory of Italy's short-lived, unfinished, and brutal rule.[12] Recent rural development cooperation programs between Italy and Ethiopia have boosted the production of Ethiopian pasta made from locally grown durum wheat, making "Italian" pasta a full-fledged presence in the Ethiopian foodscape.[13]

The culinary culture born in the Ethiopian-Italian encounter has also circulated within the global Ethiopian diaspora. The food magazine *Taste* featured a detailed report on Ethiopian lasagna, the classic dish Ethiopian American immigrant women make for their family's Sunday dinner.[14] In interviews, immigrant women acknowledged that lasagna helps them recreate their Ethiopian "home" in the United States even while serving as a reminder of Italian colonialism. Ethiopian women, who disproportionately suffered the physical violence of Italian aggression, played a paramount role in the war of liberation, fighting alongside men as both soldiers and auxiliaries (cooks).[15] As a layered assemblage of pasta sheets filled with ingredients from local traditions, lasagna offers diasporic Ethiopians an opportunity to craft a version different from any other lasagna—and from its original Italian sources.[16] In its postcolonial invention, Ethiopian lasagna recalls its origins in the forced encounter with Italian invaders and in the resistance that helped drive them out. The ingredients reference those culinary encounters: a sparing amount of cheddar and shredded mozzarella cheese contrasts with the generous sprinkling of *berbere*—the hot spice blend ubiquitous in Ethiopian cooking; and, in some versions, the substitution of Italian flour and egg pasta sheets with *injera*, the spongy flat sourdough made from fermented teff, the small-grain cereal native to the Ethiopian highlands. Cuisines—or "ingredients, their procurement and use in cooking, styles of cooking, and the social context of the presenting and consuming of cooked food"—are the products of "two factors: dominant political cultures, such as empires, and cultural exchange."[17] By that definition, then, Ethiopian lasagna exemplifies how cuisines are created and invested with political meaning.[18]

Gastrofascism and Empire explores the politics of food, migration, and race that fascist Italy established in Ethiopia between 1935 and 1941. It examines the circulation of foodstuffs, food practices, and food meanings in and out of Italian East Africa during the five-year occupation created by the Italo-Ethiopian War of 1935–6. After the dethroning of Emperor Haile Selassie I, and with Mussolini's proclamation of empire on May 11, 1936, fascist Italy consolidated Ethiopia and its older colonies of Eritrea and Somalia into Africa Orientale Italiana, boasting that Italy had finally found its "place in the sun."

Gastrofascism and Empire looks at the important role food played in this history of imperialism and anti-imperialism, colonialism and anti-colonial struggle. Part One describes the fascist ideology of demography (the political uses of population) and racism, the political uses of modern bio- and agrotechnology, and the effects on African physical and human landscapes. Part Two shows how, as racist laws made the sharing of food between Ethiopians and Italians illegal both in private homes and in public spaces, there, nonetheless, emerged an active Ethiopian-Italian colonial food exchange and from it a distinctive hybrid cuisine and taste in the corners of segregated worlds.

Imperial Gastronomies: Discourses and Biopolitical Practices of Colonial Gastrofascism

Chapter 1 discusses Ethiopian food cultures and cuisines at the time of the Italian invasion in 1935. Chapter 2 shows that the fascist project of settler colonialism in East Africa consisted in redirecting Italian surplus rural labor from its traditional path of international emigration to colonial settlements designed to transform Ethiopia into "Italy's granary." The new African breadbasket would help feed the expanding population of Italians in a strong, self-sufficient fascist state. Ethiopian resources would be essential for building a new Italy. Because it lacked the natural resources necessary for international competition—oil, gas, and coal—Ethiopian resources would be essential for building a new Italy largely through a growth in population made possible with foods produced on conquered African lands.

The grand fascist plan failed utterly. Not only did the new empire never come close to nourishing thousands of multiplying Italian bodies, but the colonial war and the economic sanctions of the League of Nations degraded the Italian diet so much so that when it entered World War II in June 1940, Italy faced critical, and worsening, food insecurity. However, the "valorization" of Ethiopia—as the extraction of its food resources was labeled—was extremely ambitious for the time, especially in its comprehensive redesign of African life.

The transfer to East Africa of advanced biotechnologies for the breeding of high-yielding plants and animals and the transplantation of Italians as settler-farmers should have developed a successful "demographic colonization." At the ideological heart of the plan was the construction of Ethiopians as racially inferior, and their agriculture as inherently primitive, inadequate, and irrational. There would be no question, then, about forcibly transforming traditional Ethiopian society through experimental model settlements and modernized, racially segregated cities and towns. The goal was the overall replacement of Ethiopian biodiversity and cultural diversity with Italian agriculture, husbandry, and civilization, in European models of intensive agriculture and husbandry that would radically reshape East Africa. Concurrently, demographic colonialism was to discipline African bodies and society with the introduction of European food, cuisine, and table manners.

As shown in Chapter 3, building a modern infrastructure to transport food and other goods was central to the fascist plan. A comprehensive network of roadways was to be the "backbone" of an extensive system for delivering fresh Ethiopian food to the metropole and global markets. The new roads were also to feed the projected millions of Italian settlers in East Africa and connect Ethiopia's outlet on the Indian Ocean to the Mediterranean Sea, securing a large, protected Italian commercial space.[19]

In the challenging geography of Ethiopian highlands and lowlands, this ambitious effort absorbed a disproportionate amount of financial and human capital, paradoxically competing for resources against the project of mass colonization it was supposed to enable. Adding to the irony, the motorized network also ended up doing what it was not originally meant to. Instead of creating food self-sufficiency throughout the East African Empire, it stuttered and flailed. For their part, Italian settlers—most of them living in cities and working in construction, transportation, and trade rather than in farming—instead enjoyed the surprising availability of imported food as a reward for migrating to Africa. Their dependence on imported foods was a strategic element in the making of an Italian Ethiopia.[20]

Also discussed in Chapter 3 is the fight of the armed Ethiopian Resistance (in Amharic *arbegnoch*, patriots; among Italians, *shifta*, Amharic for rebels or outlaws) to reclaim food sovereignty. Organized at the end of the Italo-Ethiopian War, the resistance attacked Italian settlements throughout the occupation. The movement understood the critical importance of the mobile food system the invaders had created and made the destruction of Italian food security its principal objective with constant attacks on trains, convoys, and settlements. When Italy entered World War II in June 1940, Ethiopian partisans joined forces with British colonial troops from Kenya and

Sudan, defeating Italian armies by the spring of 1941. Even more vividly than the military defeat, the demise of the fascist food system demonstrated to settlers the utter failure of demographic colonization as well as the power of the anti-colonial forces it had unleashed. In the end, Ethiopians regained possession of their own land and their own food sovereignty.

The understudied case of Italian East Africa offers intriguing examples of food imperialism and new perspectives on the interconnected movements of foods, culinary practices, and bodies in the working of empires. In this book, the exploitation, inequality, and environmental impact of the global food system and its use of food in racist and xenophobic discourses is described as gastrofascism.[21]

A rich scholarly literature has documented the ways in which early modern and modern empires, such as the Spanish, Portuguese, British, French, and Ottoman, were powerful engines of the circulation of people, plants, seeds, animals, germs, foods, and foodways. In the imperial project of extracting wealth from subjugated lands and peoples, colonizers transplanted their preferred food plants and animals as well as husbandry practices to the empire's peripheries, reworking landscapes, biodiversity, and social systems in the process.[22] From the arrival of Europeans in the Americas in 1492, modern empires created a global market for specialized products (spices, cane sugar, coffee, chocolate, tea, bananas, pineapples, or avocados, for example) aimed at privileged consumers in capitals from Madrid and Lisbon and London to New York. Europeans brought seeds, expertise, and processing practices to cultivate tropical and subtropical fields. They created an enslaved, indentured, or low-wage migrant labor force. They turned lands that supported village life into plantations and reduced countries to subaltern players in a global crop economy.

At the same time, colonizers sent back to the metropole and other parts of the empire the "exotic" products they encountered. In native markets and in the kitchens of local elites, they identified exploitable foods and culinary resources. The colonization of native plants like potato, corn, manioc, cocoa, tomatoes, peppers, peanuts, and pineapples in the Americas changed the world's cuisines and fueled the population growth of the nineteenth and twentieth centuries with abundant cheap calories. Extracting wealth from the food of colonies required new transportation infrastructures, capitalist trading systems, and industrial technologies.[23] Modern empires absorbed local food markets under a multinational capitalist umbrella, began globalizing the world's diet, and instrumentalized food for the benefit of capital and state power.[24] As Karl Marx would put it, modern empires made all that was solid about food melt into air.

For fascists of the 1930s and 1940s the link between food and empire was clear.[25] Fascists made Italian food sovereignty central to their political agenda and its ideology of nativism, racism, and aggression. Barely paying lip service to the "civilizing" benefits its conquests were supposed to bring, fascists instead were intent on destroying the food sovereignty of newly colonized subjects, sometimes to the point of genocide, to make space for their own settlers and the food they would produce to nourish the expanding Italian realm.[26]

Italian colonialism in Ethiopia stands out in three ways: (1) its use of modern technologies of violence and exploitation, (2) the planned migration of thousands of Italian farmers and families as settlers, and (3) the organized state racism that defined it all. And however much it might have sought to reclaim a glorious Roman imperial legacy or to distract its citizens from a deepening economic crisis, Italy's main motivations for the occupation of Ethiopia were rooted in demography, biopolitics, and food sovereignty. Food lay at the core of the goal of a new "organic national community," imagined as a vigorous collective body purified of racial, cultural, and social toxins.

By all accounts, fascism enforced no other policies more strongly than those aimed at achieving food self-reliance (*autarchia alimentare*, food autarchy). These policies were first applied at home by converting agriculture to the production of calorie-rich grains, reclaiming and improving underused lands, and developing highly resistant and productive seeds and animal breeds. East Africa was then defined as a natural and valuable extension of these national farmlands, ready to be taken from a people deemed inferior.[27]

Fascist food policies were shaped in an uneasy balance between a powerful cult of tradition and a fascination with modernity and technology.[28] On the one hand, the regime celebrated Italian rural civilization and the patriarchal family as the foundation of the state. Accordingly, cities were deemed dangerous incubators of political conflict and moral degradation and, with low fertility rates, serious threats to demographic security. The regime passed special laws to counter internal migration and push back against urbanization. Mussolini's ideas about population were rooted in racial Darwinism—to the Duce, the fight against declining Italian birthrates was "a question of life or death" in the battle against growing hordes of Africans and Asians. Without greater fertility, "the civilization of the White man was destined to perish."[29] Mussolini's ideas about food were predictably productivist and anti-Malthusian. Food possessed quantitative *and* qualitative value—it was the material basis of the fascist politics of numbers, while its ideological value drew on "tradition" and its "defense."[30] Along with pronatalism and the "fear of the modern," fascism promoted its own image of rural life—the ideal, as Antonio Gramsci (1891–1937) identified, of an Italian peasantry free from any trace of social conflict or poverty.[31] And among all aspects of peasant culture, or *la civiltà contadina*, the rich patrimony of regional and local foodways was by far the one most assertively celebrated.

To turn foodways into political weapons, fascists launched an unprecedented program to document and disseminate a great variety of "traditional" recipes from across the country. The first edition of the *Guida Gastronomica d'Italia* (Culinary Guide to Italy, 1931) was the prototypical modern culinary guide, not simply identifying but also *creating* local foods. Each chapter was dedicated to a region and its distinctive pastas, cheeses, cured meats, vegetables, sauces, sweets, and wines. The "Guide" linked food and place on the Italian map, inviting tourists to explore the country while enjoying its culinary treasures at the source. It also rallied Italians to take pride in the traditions created by generations of dedicated farmers and to "Buy Italian."[32]

The founder and life-long editor of the monthly magazine *La Cucina Italiana* (1929–), the committed fascist Umberto Notari (1878–1950), published chapters of the *Guida Gastronomica* as accounts of imagined journeys through a unique Italian countryside, while the Ente Nazionale Italiano per il Turismo (ENIT— National Tourist Board) hired the artist Umberto Zimelli (1898–1972) to draw the *Carta delle specialità gastronomiche delle regioni italiane* (Map of Principal Italian Regional Culinary Specialties), dotted with representative local foods. The program most effective in mobilizing rural Italians around food, place, and identity was the establishment of *sagre*—festivals celebrating local specialties that today remain popular attractions— and, for wine, *feste dell'uva* (grape festivals).[33] These politically charged festivities were replicated in Ethiopia and Italian East Africa, with tourist itineraries showcasing the histories, geographies, ethnic cultures, and foodscapes of the new empire.[34]

The new food festivals and celebrations paid special attention to peasant women as mothers and wives responsible for social reproduction, cultural preservation, and the transmission of local traditions. The regime organized those most neglected and excluded from the polity—married and elderly peasant women—in leisure-time associations such as Massaie Rurali (Rural Housewives). The local Massaie Rurali clubs travelled from the countryside to Florence, Milan, or Rome, parading in front of fascist leaders or members of the royal house, dressed in village costumes and carrying baskets of the best of their *paesi*, from gleaming peppers to giant asparagus. Before their move to Ethiopia as settlers, rural women were taught agricultural techniques, housework practices, and "colonial cooking" in programs jointly organized by the Fascist Party, Fasci Femminili (Fascist Women's Organization) and the Istituto Fascista dell'Africa Italiana (Fascist Institute for Italian Africa).[35]

These ideologies of rural traditionalism and idyllic pastoralism were in fact modern tools for nation-building and mass mobilization. But fascism also needed to *explicitly* endorse modernity as central to its political project. The cult of speed and steel, best articulated in the arts by Futurism, fetishized railroads, ocean liners, and aviation in the Ethiopian adventure. With this passion for the new, fascists would impose modern food technologies to make Italy self-sufficient at home and, with the acquisition of Ethiopia, in the empire.[36]

Among the earliest, most comprehensive, and lasting policies were those aimed at achieving total food sovereignty. The Battle for Wheat called for converting all Italian agriculture to the intensive production of wheat and other cereals as reliable sources of calories. Italians were asked to revere wheat bread as the most Italian of all foods, the staff of life, the sacred body of Christ shared in patriarchal family communion. The vast Integral Land Reclamation campaign sought to turn unused or unproductive rural areas into farmlands and then relocate peasants from overpopulated areas to new model agrotowns. These programs, destined to generate exports to colonies in Africa, were supported by state-sponsored research in high-yield, pest-resistant, and hybrid varieties of wheat, rice, and corn.[37] The programs mobilized leading geneticists, among them Nazareno Strampelli (1866–1942). Already well known for his experimentation with "elite" wheat varieties, Strampelli joined the Fascist Party in 1925 and became the life-long director of the Istituto Nazionale di Genetica per la Cerealicoltura (National Institute of Genetics for Cereal Crops). Strampelli and his Istituto oversaw the testing of new wheat varieties, such as the popular *Ardito*, *Mentana*, and *Quaderna*, and the implementation the self-sufficiency program. Following Nikolai I. Vavilov's (1887–1943) concept of centers of origin for cultivated plants, fascist scientists saw Ethiopia—one of the earliest sites of cereal domestication—as a particularly promising location for developing new strains.[38] Vividly promoted by popular images of golden Italian wheatfields and large, well-fed peasant families, food connected two major planks of fascist ideology: rural, pronatalist anti-modernism and hypermodern, aggressive, racist expansionism. The conquest of Ethiopia and East Africa provided optimal testing grounds for manipulating food, plants, animals, and humans through the most advanced biotechnologies available.[39]

In another research center, the Istituto Agronomico per l'Oltremare (Overseas Agricultural Institute) chemists, botanists, zootechnicians, and other scientists studied the development of tropical ecosystems through Italian agrotechnologies. Founded in 1904, the institute was incorporated in 1938 as Istituto Agronomico per l'Africa Italiana (Agricultural Institute for Italian Africa) under the direction of Armando Maugini (1889-1975), an agronomist from Italy's earlier colonization of Libya. Maugini's institute was to train technical personnel, study the agriculture of Italian colonies, and promote their "valorization."[40]

The institute's journal, *Agricoltura Coloniale* (Colonial Agriculture), was just one of many publications studying the potential of Ethiopia. Massive research and new knowledge from the Italian scientists fascism had enlisted was put at the service of the politics of colonial agriculture, striving to demonstrate that Ethiopia, unlike other Italian colonies, could become the "overseas granary" needed to support the growth of a "great proletarian nation" ready to join the club of the world's superpowers.

Previous attempts at developing agricultural settlements in the older, poorer colonies of Eritrea, Libya, and Somalia had been disappointing. Eritrea had been imagined as a prime destination for Italian farmers since its establishment as a colony in 1890. Senator Leopoldo Franchetti (1847-1917) envisioned recreating the sharecropping system of Central Italy, complete with entire families and communities of peasant farmers. As governor (1897-1907), Ferdinando Martini (1840-1928) turned confiscated land into state agricultural property and encouraged the rural deployment of technologies and trained personnel. However, by the mid-1930s successes remained elusive. Because its Italian farmers were never provided with necessary resources, Eritrea played a negligible role in securing food sovereignty.[41]

The colony of Libya was established in 1911 but did not become an agricultural asset until its bloody "pacification" in the early 1930s. In fact, the comprehensive *Piano dei ventimila* (20,000 Settlers' Scheme—the number of Italian farmers scheduled to migrate to northern Africa) did not start until 1937. This, the most important initiative of Governor Italo Balbo (1896-1940), was to complement a similar plan for Ethiopia.[42]

Somalia, instead, provided a model for what could be accomplished with another form of colonialism—the agroindustrial plantation system employing native labor. Italian ventures in Somalia's Shebelle River Valley, such as Village Duke of Abruzzi and Jenale, had already achieved some success growing tropical crops. But Mussolini, who dismissed the British model of plantation colonialism in favor of his *colonialismo di popolamento* (demographic colonization), did not encourage private capital to establish large plantations in Ethiopia.[43]

The Italian experience in its older colonies was mostly one of failure and offered the new project in Ethiopia few practical lessons. Only Eritrea provided any logistical advantage—as the base from which to invade Ethiopia. In Eritrea, local *Askaris* (predominantly Eritrean, but also Somali and Ethiopian) were enlisted as colonial troops. *Askaris* offered not only their bodies for battle but also their knowledge of Abyssinian terrain, populations, and available food resources.[44]

The same technology Italian armed forces used in the war against Ethiopia was later employed to create the Empire of Food, replacing by massive force a "primitive, inferior, and unproductive" Ethiopian agriculture. As Haile Selassie I testified to the League of Nations in 1936: "At the time of the operations for the encircling of Makalle, sprayers were installed on board aircrafts so that they could vaporize, over vast areas of territory, a fine, death-dealing rain. Soldiers, women, children, cattle, rivers, lakes and pastures were drenched continually with this deadly rain."[45]

Italian aircraft sprayed mustard gas, outlawed in 1925 by the Geneva Convention, on women, children, crops, livestock, and waters. In January 1936, frustrated by the progress of his armies, Mussolini considered starting a "total biological war" against Ethiopia; his aviator son Vittorio (1916–1997) had enjoyed burning "entire villages and fields of durra [sorghum]" from the sky.[46] The biological and technological war against Ethiopia was seen as a struggle of modernity against darkness, civilization against barbarism with the goal of expanding the borders of Italian life—plants, nonhuman animals, humans—overseas, in African territory.

Colonial Gastronomies: Racism, Food Exchange, and Practices of Taste

In the early twentieth century, positivist anthropology identified two Italian "races"— the Alpine and Celtic race of northern Italians and the Mediterranean, Levantine race of "dark" southern Italians; and in Ethiopia, predominantly Christian Abyssinians were classified as non-Black, non-African Semites.[47] After the attack on Ethiopia, however, the official divide between southern and northern Italian "races" conveniently disappeared: now, all Italians were fully White, and all Ethiopians fully Black. After the alliance with Adolf Hitler in 1937, racism became foundational to Italian fascism. The declaration *Manifesto degli scienziati razzisti* (Manifesto of Racist Scientists, widely known as *Manifesto della razza* or Manifesto of Race, July 14, 1938) and, finally, the anti-Semitic Racial Laws of September 18, 1938, installed a supremacist agenda in order to establish a fully Aryan "Italian race."[48]

In 1940, the magazine *La difesa della razza* (The Defense of the Race) dealt with the term *bonifica* in its double meaning of agrarian colonization and racial purification. In the article "*La nuova razza nell'Agro Redento*" (The New Race in the Redeemed Land), Giorgio Almirante (1914–1988) argued that "it will be a radiant day for Italy, when the Total Reclamation Authority of Ethiopia will be founded."[49] Notably, after 1937, physical contacts between Italians and Africans, which prefascist colonial culture had largely tolerated, became the ultimate danger to Italian racial health.[50]

Ethiopian plants, animals, and food were also racially redefined. Fascist scientists organized animal breeds and plants into superior and inferior organisms, based on their adaptability. The controlled breeding of animal species for human consumption, like the political controls on human sexuality, was designed to protect and advance the master race. In Italian, *razza* still means both (human) race and (animal or vegetal) strain.

As Chapters 4, 5, and 6 document, racism affected food in all its dimensions—from an engineered agriculture and a racially defined commensality to racial signposts in sensing the other. Racism underwrote the entire fascist project, where Italians—not Africans—would farm the rich lands as laborers, a role historically marked with the stigma of slavery. How could the invasion and exploitation of Ethiopia by Italian farmer-soldiers be a civilizing mission? And how could Italian settlers remain superior while performing "Black" labor?

The leading Italian scholar of Ethiopia, Carlo Conti-Rossini (1872–1949), explained in a 1935 essay that only Italian rule could promote development, since local populations were hopelessly unprepared.[51] In *Africa Italiana* (Italian Africa), the quasi-scientific journal of the Fascist Institute for Italian Africa, Lidio Cipriani (1892–1962), one of the authors of *The Manifesto of Race*, argued for the primacy of *rural* modernization because "natural causes, increasingly more acute, prevent African peoples to even begin developing an agriculture satisfying anything more than their basic necessities."[52]

In the *Corriere della Sera*, journalist Ciro Poggiali (1892–1955) reinforced Cipriani's argument.

> Who cultivates these luxurious fields? Where are the farmers? One drives for one-hundred miles and does not see one. Every now and then one can spot some negroid women bent over teff plants, lazily weeding out the bad weeds that threaten the harvest. No effort whatsoever is put in preparing the soil, helping vegetation, preserving it from parasites, regulating the waters. There are so few farmers at work, and so many tramps.[53]

Poggiali noted that "a cob of corn is enough to feed a native, a dirty pond to quench his thirst."[54]

The racist plan for Ethiopia was also heavily gendered. Italian women settlers were vital in taming Italian men, checking their aggressive sexuality and establishing stable families. Italian women were also in charge of the Ethiopians, mostly men, who worked as their servants, and trained before leaving for Africa to straighten out "lazy" and "childish" Ethiopians. Alba Sartori Felter (1897–1991) questioned "why have the indigenous people in all our empire continued to degrade themselves while they could have been healthy and wealthy by tending this marvelously fertile land?"[55]

To colonists, Ethiopia offered vast opportunities only Italians could fully realize.[56] Ironically, although European scientists had long studied Ethiopia, by the time of the occupation, colonizers still knew remarkably little about the landscapes, resources, and cultures around them. By force of racism, ignorance, or arrogance, Italians imposed mass evictions and internal displacements, restricted access to common lands, deforested wilderness, and introduced invasive species, while still unable to accomplish what they were sent to do.[57]

The mass migration of proletarian, jobless, and landless Italians exacerbated the racist character of settler colonialism, and because farm labor on this scale seemed a threat to Italian Whiteness, a system of agricultural apartheid was deemed necessary.[58] Watching shirtless Italians toiling under the sun, Ethiopians regularly commented that "Italians brought their White slaves with them."[59] Suddenly, the usual boundaries between class and race were not so clear, and the confusion threatened to "damage [Italians'] prestige as rulers."[60] A British observer noted that "the idea of making Italians work in road construction appears incomprehensible to the Ethiopians, who call the workers 'White Gurages'—individuals of subject populations, who traditionally fetch food and water in Addis Ababa."[61]

In response, Mussolini famously proclaimed that "in order to preserve the empire, the Ethiopians must hold the concept of our superiority as absolutely clear and overwhelming." He blamed Italians in Ethiopia for a dangerous "lack of racial dignity," especially by mingling with Ethiopians. "When [the Amhara] saw that the Italians went around in rags worse than theirs; that they lived in tukuls; that they abducted their women, etc., they said: 'This is not a race that brings civilization,' and they rebelled."[62]

Migrant farmers, Poggiali insisted, "must be sure before leaving that the faraway land they are moving to is just another fatherland for them, where their standard of life must be higher, not lower, than at home; where, among inferior people, they must excel materially, never to provide a show of poverty, deprivation, malnutrition."[63] These were the most suspect category of settlers: working by necessity alongside "indigenous people," they were required to resist any camaraderie.[64] Since most Italian laborers could not be trusted to comply with racist prohibitions, racial segregation was imposed. Among the few exceptions were Italian homes, where Ethiopians worked as servers.

Racism and segregation determined the framework for Ethiopian-Italian food exchanges. Earlier empires like the Spanish, Portuguese, British, and French had always functioned as "kitchens" of intercultural food exchanges, incorporating new tastes in traditional diets and leading to culinary inventions. Colonies became private markets for such European foods as salt pork, molasses, dried cod, cornmeal, cassava, and beans that ensured a healthy manpower. Military and mining camps, plantations, missions, restaurants, home kitchens, and dining rooms were principal sites for food exchanges. Native servants who shared their traditions, skills, and ideas with their European masters were in turn instructed in the standards of nutrition, hygiene, and domesticity that signaled racial superiority. Metropole-educated native elites, women and men in interracial marriages or forms of concubinage, merchants, soldiers, missionaries, travelers, and tourists were also key players in this culinary interchange. And the response of colonized people, from adaptation to resistance, created the countercolonial cuisines that have always been markers of identity for diasporic peoples.[65]

Italian East Africa provides a somewhat exaggerated example of classic food imperialism. Part Two of this book illustrates how in Ethiopia food crossovers arose in and survived racial segregation, and how gastronomic innovations were birthed in the liminal spaces of colonialism, racism, and sexism.

Chapter 4 shows how in segregated Ethiopia, public places for food preparation and consumption were the most strictly controlled. Interracial commensality at the household table was a crime, and restaurants and cafés were zoned to minimize opportunities for Italians and Ethiopians to interact closely as equals; the sharing of food, plates, or touches at the table was prohibited.

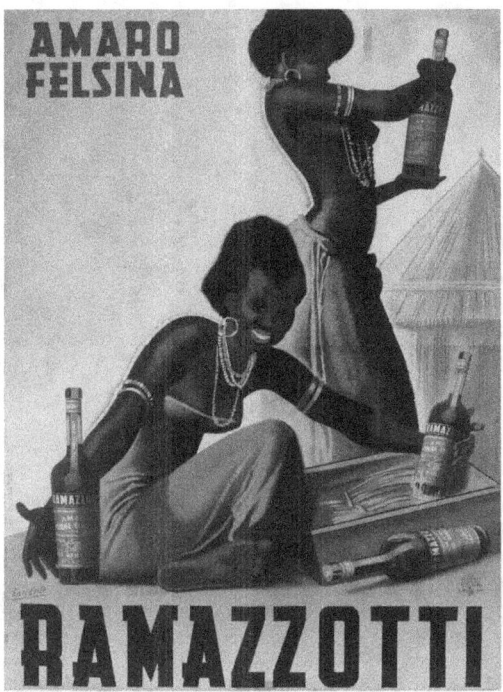

Figure 3 Ad for Amaro Ramazzotti, Gino Boccasile, 1937. Courtesy of Collezione Salce, Catalogo generale dei Beni Culturali.

Responding to, and fostering, the young male imaginary linking the conquest of African lands to the sexual conquest of African women, late 1930s Italian advertising fetishized colonial food products while commodifying the Black female body as a product of the empire and linking food and sexual consumption. As this ad suggests, on the one hand, the intraimperial circulation of the goods of mass consumerism taught Italian consumers about their entitlement as "imperial shoppers"; on the other hand, it was a tool to impress and "civilize" the colonized in the "superior" culture of the colonizer.

The preoccupation with eating together was driven by fear of miscegenation. To prevent the practice of *madamato*—the temporary, nonbinding marriages between Italian men and native women common in Eritrea—from taking hold in Ethiopia and producing mixed-race children (*meticci*), imprisonment and repatriation faced Italian men participating in mixed unions with some degree of intimacy. Prostitution might have been tolerated and even encouraged, but interracial marriage, concubinage, and love were criminal offenses.[66] In these cases, moreover, the sharing of food was linked frequently to affection and sexual intimacy.[67]

Still, as Chapter 5 illustrates, food moved freely between colonizers and the colonized. *Askaris* helped Italian soldiers collect or steal food from villagers and taught them how to use local ingredients. Italians often portrayed *Askaris* as loyal savages, and many became familiar with Italian food in army kitchens.

Italian women were trained to deal properly with their servants, and for many women, it was the first time they had at their disposal a staff of any kind. A special

Figure 4 A prickly pear vendor breastfeeds her baby at the Harar "indigenous" market, May 8, 1936. Courtesy of Archivio Luce.

The hypermodern character of the Italian aggression and attempt at colonizing Ethiopia is also revealed by the massive efforts at documenting, with photographs and films, every aspect of life in the invaded country. The photographers and filmmakers of Archivio Luce's Reparto Africa Orientale (East Africa Unit) documented Ethiopian foodways so as to produce a narrative mixing anthropological inquiry, exoticism, revulsion at the African Other's primitivism, curiosity, attraction, and disgust.

emphasis was placed on food: shopping, cooking, and creating meal plans and etiquette protocols that defined domestic roles. The incorporation of African spices and fresh local foods purchased at the "indigenous market" were the most visible features of an Italian-Ethiopian cuisine being born in the daily interactions between Italian housewives and Ethiopian servants (Figure 4).

Similar interactions took place in the Italian roadside and urban restaurants that Ethiopians could not patronize but where they could work as busboys or dishwashers, often paid in food. In their ambitious plans for modernizing Ethiopian cities, Italian architects were careful to separate new, sanitized, Italian marketplaces from traditional "native markets."[68] Complete racial separation was never fully realized, however, and in many open markets and food stores, "Ethiopian" (locally grown) and "Italian" (imported) foods were regularly bartered, bought, and sold by vendors and customers of many ethnicities, including Armenians and Greeks.

Many Italian men who found themselves out of work, in trouble with the law, or otherwise marginalized ended up living with an Ethiopian woman, and sometimes her children, in an Ethiopian community. In colonial slang, these men were called *insabbiati* (literally "lost in the sands," or living apart as pariahs).[69] For some Italian men, poverty and alienation led them to interracial marriages, families, and households. There, in a private domestic space, meals prepared and eaten together were the cornerstone of family life and social reproduction.[70] In these homes, Ethiopian women cooks followed the Ethiopian Christian Orthodox prescription that children assume the religion and the identity of the father. In homes where the father was an *insabbiato*, children were raised Roman Catholic and in the Italian culinary tradition whether or not the father was present.[71] Foods from such blended traditions, such as Italian-Ethiopian ravioli on Sunday or *panettone* at Christmas, were passed down through generations.

Food exchanges were a form of gastrodiplomacy in the banquets that Italian authorities and Ethiopian potentates enjoyed as political power plays. The menus depended on whether Ethiopian leaders were Christian Orthodox or Muslim and on the status of the diners, but every banquet, however formal, was an often-surprising exploration of different ways of eating.

Italian men and Ethiopian sex workers almost invariably shared each other's food. Under the occupation, with the killing of Ethiopian men, the destruction of local communities, and an abundance of Italian men, many Ethiopian women resorted to sex work, which Italian policies encouraged as one of the few permitted cross-racial relationships. In Addis Ababa alone, as many as 1,500 prostitutes worked to satisfy the demands of 57,000 Italian men.[72] Prostitutes often worked in public houses where they served *tej* (honey wine) and *tella* (Ethiopian beer), and when sexual encounters took place in a woman's tukul (a traditional round mud hut), coffee was served and food was sometimes shared.[73]

Food was regularly exchanged during travels through the colony. Italian officers, soldiers, and settlers, women and men, told of journeys fueled by Ethiopian food. Familiarity with the other's foods and foodways, from *injera* to spaghetti, *berbere* to prosciutto, *tej* to canned tomatoes, was an essential sense-making tool. As Chapter 6 shows, these cross-cultural food encounters produced entire smellscapes, gastrogazes, and tasteoramas.

In Italian Ethiopia, racism created a politics of the body like that found in other African and Asian colonies. But Italian fascism differed: it understood racism as the foundation of the imperial enterprise, not a consequence of it. Imposed from outside and above, racial segregation was enforced regardless of the desires, values, or needs of its settlers. In reconfiguring the racial status of Italy by colonizing Ethiopia, fascists viewed Italian and Ethiopian foodways in physiological/racial terms and aggressively controlled all culinary contacts.

Imaginary Gastronomies: Italian Representations of African Food, Landscapes, and Bodies

The Empire of Food generated a massive catalogue of representations of Ethiopian food, ecologies, and people. In cookbooks, food magazines, advertising, museum exhibits, textbooks, tourist guides, newsreels, documentaries, and even boardgames and postage stamps, Italian media created a powerful national discourse on African foods and bodies.

Because of the demise of the empire at the outbreak of World War II, relatively few products of the Italian-Ethiopian culinary exchange reached Italy. However, African landscapes, food, and African-Italian cuisines populated the Italian imagination. Photography, film, journalism, advertising, and other media created an enormous portfolio of imagery and narrative to serve political functions: mapping the land and life of Ethiopian peoples, convincing Italians to love the empire for the abundance it would provide, and establishing an idealized African other in vivid portrayals of Black bodies, landscapes, and foodways. These images of alterity, as seen today in the La Molisana pasta controversy, remain among the most influential legacies of Italian colonialism—for current Italian identity and the continuing racialization of Black food and bodies.

Inaugurating the opening in Rome of Cinecittà, the world's second largest film studio (1937), Mussolini declared that "Cinema," the most modern mass media, was also "the most powerful weapon." Istituto Luce (L'Unione Cinematografica Educativa— Educational Film Company, 1924) was the fascist organization for propaganda films and documentaries. By the mid-1930s, it produced dozens of theatrical newsreels about Ethiopia. They offered aerial tours of landscapes that would, in Italian hands, provide the agricultural bounty of the future and celebrated the technologies of mobility, destruction, and killing that Italian armies would use to produce it.[74]

Italian media assiduously covered the advance of Italian armies in Ethiopia and its exploitation for food. In propaganda movies such as *Il cammino degli eroi* (The Path of the Heroes; Corrado D'Errico, 1936), *Sulle orme dei nostri pionieri* (In the Footprints of Our Pioneers, 1936), and *La fondazione della nuova Addis Abeba* (The Foundation of the New Addis Ababa; Giovanni Martucci, 1939), the spectacle of Italian tanks rumbling across Ethiopia were followed by triumphant scenes of tractors tilling new farmland.[75]

In other media, African products and African bodies became desirable objects of mass consumerism, while the death and destruction inflicted on African peoples remained invisible (Figure 3). Cookbooks and food magazines such as *La Cucina Italiana*, for example, looked at colonial food from many angles, but always in the service of consumption, actual or metaphoric. They presented colonial food as examples of the success of imperial expansion in enriching the Italian diet but also as something to be approached with suspicion, as in the case of *wat* (*zig'ni*) or *injera*.

The use in advertising of food from the colonies was widespread. Advertisements for coffee and chocolate (the former, Ethiopia's most valuable crop; the latter, targeted for growth on new plantations) used Black bodies to signify the Blackness of the products.[76] Coffee most clearly stood for Italian Africa, but also for a mysterious Muslim world that had sent it to Europe, and for the European slave plantations in Latin American colonies. Coffee meant privilege: in Italy's White African cities, colonists drank it from China cups with silver teaspoons, seated at outdoor cafés in a spectacle of superiority.[77]

For Italians, while growing abundant supplies of wheat on White-run farms was the primary purpose of colonialism, native crops like coffee and chocolate figured prominently in the roles assigned to non-White bodies. In late 1930s Italian advertising, Black bodies were associated with coffee or chocolate in an interplay of color, texture, and substance.[78] Advertisements suggested a fantasy of "eating the Other," of consuming them sexually in an aura of pleasure built on unequal relations of power.[79] The idea that eating could be both gastronomic and sexual was illustrated in advertisements for bananas—long associated with Black bodies—emphasizing the fruit's phallic shape and its nature as food fit for primates.[80]

Civilized taste often meant consuming the exotic, the savage, and the wild in order to satisfy the White body (Figure 3).[81] As Chapter 6 details, Italian discourses did not always assign colonized bodies to the domain of the primitive; they also expressed attraction and the desire to swallow or penetrate the other.[82]

In *Black Skin, White Masks*, Fanon argued that colonial structures reproduced themselves through culture and psychology.[83] Italian-Ethiopian and Ethiopian-Italian cuisines were material and cultural constructions that circulated between Italy and Africa and throughout multiethnic Ethiopia. The cuisines born in colonialism articulated both a resistance to the food of the other and, at the same time, a broad culinary convergence along the edges of racist society.

The fascist fantasy of demographic colonialism predicted a massive movement of settlers whose labor would feed the metropole. In the case of bananas, for example, new technologies of refrigeration would allow ordinary Italians to enjoy what had once been the prerogative of the few: tropical food "fresh" from the plantation. Neither dream came true. The ambitious transportation infrastructure built to enable demographic colonization and the marketing of highly desired Ethiopian foods moved products, settlers, soldiers, men and women workers, and the seeds, plants, and animals to reconfigure a conquered land. Ironically, the new highways and railroads also brought in vast amounts of food made in Italy, allowing settlers to enjoy the material privileges of Whiteness.

The history of food in Italian East Africa is always, of course, the history of invaded and colonized people, and in resistance their struggles to reclaim their foodways. Although relatively brief, Italian colonialism was a violent interruption of the relationship between Ethiopians and their foods, the "highest form of alienation," as Fanon argued. "For a colonized people the most essential value, because the most concrete, is first and foremost the land: the land which will bring them bread and, above all, dignity."[84] For Ethiopians, decolonization meant taking back what the Italian food system had commodified, desacralized, marginalized, and often simply obliterated.

In Maaza Mengiste's award-winning novel *The Shadow King*, set during the Italian invasion, reclamation of the national "land" and "bread" from the bloody hands of the colonizer is the center of the narrative. Among the Ethiopian women in arms fighting the Italians who raped their land and bodies, there is one unnamed, one simply addressed as "the cook." Among the women soldiers *The Shadow King* rescues from oblivion, the cook suffered so much that she is nameless. She is also the quietest, but also the most daring, uncompromising, and ancestrally wise, a peasant prophet. She finds her voice and talks back with the food she sources, prepares, and feeds to her comrades. As a gesture of return to her land, the cook refuses to prepare any Italian food, particularly its greatest symbol of empire—pasta.[85]

The case of Italian imperialism in East Africa from 1935 to 1941 illustrates the practices and consequences of "classic" gastrofascism—the political complex of food nativism, state-sanctioned food sovereignty, and demographic agrarian colonialism. It also illuminates how those narratives and policies are relevant today. They are observable in global right-wing food neonationalism, which embeds racism, xenophobia, and exploitation in the love of roots and traditions, whether in rural landscapes and traditional economies or the centrality of workers, mothers, and children. The Ethiopian Italian/Italian Ethiopian cuisine created under occupation represents the convergence of many movements and mobilities, propelling the story of foods, practices, and meanings forward to the present. The controversy surrounding La Molisana's *Abissine* pasta today has roots in Mussolini's plans to turn East Africa into vast farmlands to feed the fascist dream of national self-sufficiency and global power.

Part I

Imperial Gastronomies: Bioimperialism, Ethiopian Resistance, and the Itineraries of Food

1

Ethiopian Foodways and Italian Foodways: Frameworks of an Imperial Culinary Encounter

At the time of their colonial encounter in the mid-1930s, Ethiopian and Italian cuisines were developing products from their respective processes of nation-building; they were projects aimed at combining foods from different regional, ethnic, and religious cooking traditions into a unified and distinctive identity, especially for their small but politically influential middle classes.

The distinctive development of Italian and Ethiopian national cuisines was based on political and historical differences. A discernibly Italian taste developed, albeit only among élites, within a century-long political domination of foreign powers, which shaped very different culinary patterns around the principal city-states, their courts, marketplaces, traditions, and local biodiversity, from Rome to Naples, Florence to Milan, Palermo to Turin, and Bologna to Venice. At the time of political unification and the birth of the nation-state in 1861, established Italian cuisine was, by any definition, a postcolonial one with no capital of taste, such as Paris, and the haute cuisine it defined had been in nineteenth-century France.

Ethiopia presented a very different case. Its cuisine was largely the expression of an imperial, hegemonic influence of an ethnic group, the Amhara and their allies Tigrayans—Semitic and Christian populations that together formed an Abyssinian cultural core. As fragmented as it was, nineteenth- to twentieth-century Ethiopia could be divided into two great civilizations: the civilization of teff in the center and the north, and the civilization of *ensete* in the south. Teff is the grain used to prepare *injera*, the thin flatbread baked on a stone grill that forms the staple source of carbohydrates in the diet of Amhara and Tigrayans in central highlands and the north of the country between Lake Tana and Eritrea. For the Gurage and the ethnic groups of Sidama in the southern region bordering Kenya, Sudan, and Somalia, the fermented trunk and roots of *musa ensete*, or false banana, are used to make their flatbread called *kocho*, an everyday staple.[1]

This divided food culture reproduces fundamental ethnic, linguistic, and religious differences. The peoples of the north and center—Abyssinia, or the Ethiopian highland where, in pre-Christian ages, tribes from what is now Yemen first settled—speak the Semitic languages of Amharic and Tigrinya, are Christian Orthodox, and claim their origin as one of the tribes of Israel. The largest ethnic groups of the south speak Cushitic languages, such as Oromo and Omotic in the Omo River region. At the time of Italian invasion, many followed animist religions or, in the eastern regions of Harar and those bordering Somalia, Islam.[2]

The peoples of Abyssinia, with whom Italians maintained the most hostile relations, identified with the Kingdom of Axum and, since the early Christian age, exerted a dominant political role over the rest of the country and other ethnic-religious groups of the south, east, and west. The Abyssinian dominance of the south, east, and west critically accelerated in the 1880s, a few years after Italy's political unification, when, under King Menelik II, Amhara and Tigrayans moved out of the central highlands of Shewa, spread their agricultural and land tenure patterns, and imposed their foodways in new lands, selectively incorporating Oromo, Gurage, and other people's foods. They formed modern Ethiopia in the process, with Addis Ababa as the political and gastronomic capital. In a typical gastrofascist discursive ploy, Italians tried to define Ethiopian food as the cuisine of the colonized and Italian food the cuisine of the colonizer, but the opposite was historically true.

Also contravening fascist hierarchies of taste, Italian and Ethiopian foodways were not structurally foreign to one another. The premodern Italian diet was based on plants like wheat, barley, grape, and olive tree, which had reached the peninsula early via the Mediterranean, later augmented with many other foods, including durum-wheat pasta, rice, sugar cane, and vegetables such as eggplants and zucchini, introduced by Arabs from Central Asia, India, and China. Dairy and cured meat products from Germanic traditions were brought across the Alps by the nomadic invaders the Romans called barbarians.[3]

Similarly, the Ethiopian food repertoire included native cereals and grains like sorghum (durra), millet, and teff, other native delicacies like honey and coffee, and foods brought in by Arab traders through the Red Sea and the Indian Ocean, bananas and spices among them. After 1500, both Italian and Ethiopian diets were enriched and changed by new plants arriving from the Americas through the Columbian Exchange: tomato, corn/maize, potato, and chili pepper. Portuguese traders brought these new foods to Gondar and northern Abyssinia; Italy's source was its trading position as part of the Spanish Empire.[4]

Italian and Ethiopian cuisines diverged more on the political level. Widely using Columbian Exchange products first grown and eaten by poor farmers as "hunger-killing foods," in the late nineteenth century, an Italian national cuisine began to take its recognizable shape by bringing products from the New World into a strikingly diversified landscape of regional "specialty foods," such as local cheeses and cured meats, that reflected a politically fragmented nation built on an assemblage of mini-states each with their own foodways. A new food nationalism soon embodied a romantic discourse that celebrated liberation from foreign rule. France, Italy's ally in the wars against Austria-Hungary in the 1850s, became the gastronationalist point of reference for the newly unified country.[5]

Not so for Ethiopia, which, unlike most of Africa, did not endure European colonial domination. In the kingdom, food was key to the making of a nation out of a multiethnic empire through the Amhara conquest under Menelik II of lands beyond their original Abyssinian home. Ethiopian cuisine was complex and highly stratified along ethnic, religious, gender, and class lines and deemed the most sophisticated in Africa.[6] Because of its role in symbolically affirming imperial power and national identity, cuisine was deeply and widely valued by Ethiopians facing the Italian aggressors.

In Italy, a cookbook had come to define cuisine as a similar force in nation-building after the political unification of 1861–70. Pellegrino Artusi's (1820–1911) *La scienza in cucina e l'arte di mangiar bene* (The Science in the Kitchen and the Art of Eating Well, first edition 1891) is widely regarded as the foundational manual of modern Italian cuisine, praised especially for bringing together recipes from many cities and regions into rigorous, comprehensive canon of national taste. Artusi's cookbook, aimed at the emerging middle class and their values of thrift, hygiene, and respectability, was a modern product of mobility (of people, foods, and ideas) and cooperative sociability. A banker but also a gourmet, Artusi traveled the country gathering information on what he ate. At home in Florence, he collected those recipes sent to him by women across the nation. Piero Camporesi (1926–1997) famously commented that Artusi did more to make an Italian nation than Giuseppe Garibaldi (1807–1882), and more to establish a national language than any work of literature, notably Alessandro Manzoni's (1785–1873) *I promessi sposi* (The Betrothed, first edition 1827), which in that era required reading by every Italian schoolchild.[7]

Queen Taytu's Banquet and Ethiopian National Cuisine

Similarly, Empress Taytu Betul (1851–1918, ruled 1889–1913), a hero of Ethiopian nationalism who successfully led 5,000 troops against Italian invaders in the Battle of Adwa (March 1, 1896), is also widely recognized as the godmother of Ethiopian national cuisine. The feast thrown by Queen Taytu in 1887, in Addis Ababa's new Entoto Maryam Church in the royal compound, did for Ethiopian cuisine what Artusi's *The Science in the Kitchen* had done for Italian cuisine. Yet, unlike Artusi's collection that acknowledged the value of a wide range of local, regional, and class-based foods, Taytu's feast produced a national cuisine from the epicenter of an emerging imperial power. The magnificent five-day banquet involved the killing, butchering, and serving of "over five thousand oxen, cows, sheep, and goats" and the making of "rivers of *tej* (mead, honey wine)." In its setting of national standards of taste, public hospitality, and conviviality, the feast also served to proclaim the political power of her husband, Menelik II, as he set out to complete the expansion of his Shewa Kingdom and create a modern empire-state.

The feast also confirmed the new settlement of Addis Ababa (1886) as Ethiopia's capital, not only as the seat of state power but also as its largest, politically and culturally dominant city. The proscribed role of women as cooks in Ethiopian culture meant that the queen could always reassert her strong influence on Menelik II's court.[8] Fully responsible for the feast's planning and organization, Taytu oversaw the succession of the courses that were served to each group of guests according to their social standing, as commensality reproduced social stratification.[9] A noblewoman of cosmopolitan upbringing—from prominent Coptic Christian and Muslim families in the old imperial city of Gondar and the regions of Tigray, Semien, and Yejju—Taytu was familiar with the cultural power of cookery in representing ethnic and local identities. And in fact, the message of power and authority articulated in the feast was based more on its embrace of a diverse ethnic geography than on religious devotion or the politics of conspicuous consumption.

At the feast, the variety of preparations reflected the culinary diversity of Abyssinia's provinces and beyond, a gathering of foods from regions under royal control and those soon to be brought under Menelik's growing dominion. Taytu's gastronomic curation brought the products and styles of different provinces into a broad national cuisine, a compendium of Ethiopian foodways.[10] Taytu's banquet also showcased the practices by which foods were processed and preserved (drying, fermenting, pickling, and smoking), transformed and prepared (cutting, grinding, and mixing), and cooked (sautéing, stewing, boiling, roasting, broiling, and frying). The feast established that in Ethiopian culture "cooking is generally accomplished slowly and carefully, and preparation time may be substantial especially when using various imported ingredients and recipes emanating from oriental and European sources."[11]

One section of the extensive tent complex that served as the ceremonial banquet hall was dedicated to the baking of flatbread *injera* (*əngära*). Five hundred finely decorated baskets from the Muslim province of Harar were used to pass around the round bread to notable guests (Figure 5). Made from fermented teff, *injera* serves both as the starchy base of the meal and as its plate and eating utensil. It also serves as a utensil to scoop up its varied toppings such as meat stews, green legume purees, pulses,

Figure 5 Two Ethiopian women carrying a *mesob*, the Harari basket used for storing *injera*, April–May 1936. Courtesy of Archivio Luce.

condiments, and spices. At Taytu's feast, *injera* was the foundation of Abyssinian—and, by royal extension, Ethiopian—gastronomy. Without *injera* a meal would not be a proper meal, but could be a sign of poverty. Inferior versions of *injera* included "travel" or "war breads," such as *burkutta*, made from unfermented grain or a homemade barley or wheat bread (*qiṭṭa*), which was considered basic to daily life in rural areas. In Taytu's banquet, *injera*'s ritual value as the national staple was reinforced by its central place in the Ethiopian Christian Orthodox liturgy, as the bread represented the body of Christ; its companion, the honey wine (*tej*), was served in great amounts at the feast and signified Christ's blood. *Injera* was the most direct expression of the cereal-farming system and human geography of the Ethiopian highlands with Shewa at its center (Figure 6). It also articulated its class stratification: the white, all-teff *injera* served at Taytu's feast was the domain of well-off households, while the vast lots of poorer farmers ate darker *injera* made with a mix of white and red teff (*sergegna*) or a blend with millet or lesser-value grains and legumes.[12]

Other sections of the royal kitchen were dedicated to the making of *wat* (stew) and the butchering of beef and mutton. *Wat* (also spelled wot and wet; Amharic: *wət'*) was, with *injera*, the other essential of Abyssinian—and, later on, Ethiopian—cuisine. Since the nineteenth century, travel accounts noted that the combination of *injera* and *wat* signaled security, respectability, and pleasure, ensuring a "proper meal." *Wat* can be made with beef, mutton, goat, or chicken, reflecting the emphasis on pastoralism

Figure 6 Two village women make dough seated on a mat, northern Ethiopia, April–May 1936. Courtesy of Archivio Luce.

and livestock farming everywhere in Ethiopia. *Doro wat*, a chicken stew, is made by sautéing onions or shallots and then adding clarified butter (*nit'r qebeh*) for fat and color. Next, the spice mix *berbere* (*bärbärré*) is added for hotness and flavor. The use of the universally popular *niter kibbeh* and *berbere* helped make *doro wat* the Ethiopian national dish. Sometimes hard-boiled eggs are also added to *wat*. Rarely eaten alone, eggs made the dish complete within the cultural framework identifying meat as the ideal gastronomic component of Ethiopian cookery, among both pastoralist and agriculturalist peoples. The most popular traditional foods in Ethiopia, *doro wat* and *sega* (beef) *wat* (Eritrean *zighini, zig'ni*), are eaten by a group sharing a bowl of stew and a basket of *injera*, which is stripped into pieces and eaten with the right hand. The proportion of stew to *injera* reflected the social position of the household—more meat signified higher social standing.[13]

Eating communally—sitting on the floor rather than at table—and using hands to bring food to the mouth were not a strange or offensive practice to most Italians in the late 1930s. Italy prided itself on being the inventor of the fork, which, according to an apocryphal story, Catherine de Medici (1519–1589), the noble Florentine and queen consort of Henry II (1519–1559), first introduced to her French court. However, although by the late nineteenth century the fork had become a common utensil in many Italian households, the urban poor and especially peasants were excluded from its "culture," it being an unaffordable luxury item. Rural workers would eat their lunches in the fields, tearing away chunks of bread to accompany their tomato, cheese, or salami, bringing them to the mouth by knife or using a wooden spoon to scoop their polenta or soup. Well into the twentieth century, the families of farmers and sharecroppers had their meals in large groups extending beyond the nuclear family, the men sitting at the table, women standing and having their food from a bowl while serving, and children grabbing food to eat on the stoop or in a corner of the room.[14] For many Italians, their socialization into the middle-class culture of the fork came to them as settlers in East Africa, where it was meant to distinguish them from "savage" Ethiopians and acculturate them into middle-class domesticity and modern consumerism.

Conspicuously consumed by the notables at Taytu's banquet, beef (*səga*) was highly valued in the Ethiopian diet. More prized than mutton, goat, or chicken, beef held an important ritual place in holidays, initiation rites, and hospitality and helped celebrate the victorious return of troops from battle or religious holidays. To protect the productive and reproductive worth of the herd, an ox or a bull was butchered only when it was old or had died unexpectedly. Beef was economically valuable, and the animal's owner would sell the meat within the community rather than eat it. It was butchered into parts designed for different class strata, with the head, the offal, and hooves destined for servants or slaves.[15] The prevalent method of preservation was drying. Wealthier Ethiopians consumed beef both cooked and raw, as *tere sega* (*ṭəré səga*), and eating raw meat fresh from slaughter, sometimes still pulsating, signified status and masculine prowess. Knifing away pieces of raw flesh, called *brundo* (*brundō*), was prized among the ruling highland classes and struck turn-of-the-twentieth-century European travelers, and later Italians, as exotic and primitive.[16] Minced raw beef was marinated in *niter kibbeh* and *berbere* to make *kitfo* (*kətfo*), still one of the most popular Ethiopian dishes today, routinely served with *injera*. Originally a Gurage dish from southwestern Ethiopia, *kifto* was brought by many Gurage migrant laborers and domestic workers to Addis Ababa where they added it to a national cuisine in the making.[17]

Finally, at Teytu's feast, servers would patrol the big tent carrying clay pots and jars full of *berbere*, *niter kibbeh*, and honey for the queen's guests.[18] *Berbere*, *niter kibbeh*, and honey were the most distinctive flavors of Ethiopian cuisine and the ones that most strongly struck Italians' imagination at the moment of encounter. *Berbere* indicates hot chili pepper (*Capsicum frutescens* or *Capsicum annum*), but also means a blend of chili and spices (cardamom, cumin, coriander, turmeric, pepper, fenugreek, nutmeg, cloves, allspice, rue, garlic, and onion), used to give a zesty, hot taste to *wats* and many other dishes. The variety of spices in *berbere* attests to the incorporation in Ethiopian cuisine of spices and condiments from India and the Persian Gulf, as well as the American chili pepper introduced by Portuguese traders.[19] Adaptable to many cooking styles in its many iterations, *berbere* was so embedded in Abyssinian culture that it entered into the oral traditions of different northern and central Ethiopian ethnic groups.[20]

Just as essential to Ethiopian cuisine was *niter kibbeh*. A clarified butter infused with herbs and spices, including indigenous ones like *besobela* and *kosseret*, *niter kibbeh* was the most dominant of Ethiopian cuisine. Basic to the national dish *doro wat*, it also adds flavor, color, and fat thickening to other stews, sauces, and pulses—such as *shiro wat* (*širò*), an Oromo dish that became the everyday meal of most Ethiopians, made of roasted chickpea, pea, lentil, or bean flours, *berbere*, and water, and eaten with warm *injera*.[21] *Niter kibbeh* symbolized "fat" as abundance and, as an animal product, the fat or feasting days in the Christian Orthodox calendar. On fasting days, *niter kibbeh* was replaced with vegetable oils, such as nug, sesame, or safflower (*suf*).[22]

Dozens of honeys from different regions were served at Taytu's feast, some coming from as far as Jimma in the southwest. Although sweetness is generally considered marginal in Abyssinian and Ethiopian cuisine, honey was widely consumed by elites, sometimes redistributed to peasants on special occasions and holidays. Honey was typically eaten directly from the comb.

By far the most widespread use of honey, though, was to make a strong mead called *tej* (*tägg̃*; Tigrinya: *myes*), which was consumed in colossal proportions at the queen's feast. Fermenting *tej* could be made by both men and women. A good homemade *tej* would have one unit of honey and six units of water; in commercial use, the proportions were one unit of honey to seven to ten units of water. *Tej* was fermented with *gesho* (*Rhamnus prinoides*) and other herbs, added to the mixture in the same proportion as honey. The clearer the *tej* the longer its life and the higher its value. In general, only the elites regularly drank proper *tej*, as a vital part of the banquet ceremony or the ritual of hospitality, while watered-down *tej* was occasionally consumed by everyday people. Muslims made and consumed a nonalcoholic drink made of unfermented honey and water (*berzi*).

Another popular lower-social-status beverage was beer, or *tella* (*ṭallä*; Tigrinya: *siwa* [*səwa*]).[23] Freshly made *tella*, like *tej*, was both an integral part of the everyday diet and a source of intoxication. In Tigrinya, women prepared *siwa* in every household by fermenting a toasted flatbread made of barley, sorghum, finger millet, or maize, beer yeast (*Saccharomyces cerevisiae*), and dried leaves of *gesho*, also used in the fermentation of *tej*.[24]

As shown in Taytu's feast, *berbere*, *niter kibbeh*, and honey, which together defined the Ethiopian taste, were recognized as such by the Italians, for whom these three basic ingredients (in addition to coffee) represented their "taste of Africa." For Italians, moreover, *berbere* was the quintessential expression of inherent hotness and spiciness of Ethiopian food and its most distinctive, and ubiquitous, taste.[25] Likewise, *niter kibbeh*, widely used also as a cosmetic, especially by Ethiopian women to style their hair, represented for Italians the strong and, for many, overwhelming "smell of Africa"— the smell of African bodies and African urban spaces.[26] Honey, sometimes offered to Italians as a gesture of hospitality and friendliness, became nature's dessert of Africa, a ready-to-grab delicacy of the newly conquered empire. Italians also enjoyed honey fermented into *tej*, which they shared with Ethiopians on occasions of conviviality.[27]

Despite the efforts of Queen Taytu and the imperial powers in Addis Ababa to establish a national cuisine that incorporated ingredients and practices from all regions—and, later, Emperor Haile Selassie I's programs for integrating national agriculture—in the late 1930s Italian occupiers came upon a still largely diversified foodscape, characterized by numerous ethnic, cultural, and religious differences. Religion and ethnicity most powerfully regulated commensality, social distinction, and the boundaries between purity and pollution in food, such as the taboos against eating the meat of certain animals. For example, Ethiopians of the north-central highlands would consider the Wäyṭo people's practice of consuming hippo meat disgusting, even unimaginable. Eating donkeys and wild boars was similarly off limits throughout the northern and central regions. Mensa people avoided camel meat and any meat slaughtered by Muslims. The Afar of northern Ethiopia considered animal products, including meat, milk, and dairy, to be taboo for pregnant women because these would make the fetus too large.[28]

Christian, Muslim, and Jewish Ethiopians would slaughter animals according to their own rituals, and public markets had separate sections for each. As a critical difference from Catholic Italians, who processed and enjoyed pig meat in many forms and shapes, particularly cured and encased to make prosciutto, salami, and mortadella, Muslim, Jewish, and Christian Ethiopians too avoided pork, a consequence of the relative isolation of the Ethiopian Orthodox Church (in Ahmaric: Yäityop'ya Ortodoks Täwahedo Bétäkrestyan) from other forms of Western Christianity. Ethiopia's Orthodox Church prohibited "eating animals with uncloven hoofs and that do not chew their own cud." A tradition shared by Islam and Judaism, abstinence from pork was therefore the country's most widely and rigorously observed practice that distinguished all Ethiopians from Roman Catholic Italian invaders. Throughout Ethiopia, refusal of or withdrawing from commensality on the grounds of serving taboo food was the ultimate indicator of exclusion and prejudice against the ethnic and religious other.[29]

The centralizing Ethiopian food system was also complicated by persistent local differences that went beyond those of the dominant Amharic and Tigray regions. Just as the marinated minced raw beef (*kitfo*) was a Gurage contribution, the buttered chickpea and peaflour (*shiro*) was an Oromo addition to the national table. The most notable agricultural and culinary feature of the subequatorial south inhabited by the Gurage and the Oromo, however, was the *ensete* (*Ensete ventricosum*, or false banana). A tall herbaceous plant in the banana family Musaceae, *ensete* was cultivated in its domesticated form only in southern Ethiopia. In the southwestern strip of land from Kaffa to Jimma, Gurage and Oromo farmers used it to make flour and bread (*kocho* or *qocho*, ḳōčō). When the plant was four or five years old, the leaves were cut and buried to ferment for six months, when the fermented pulp would be removed and made into a dough. With the addition of water, the dough was shaped into big loaves to be baked in clay pans. *Kocho*, the *ensete* flatbread, was for southern Ethiopians what teff *injera* was for Abyssinians—their everyday staple and their defining food.[30]

War hero and "Lioness of Judah" Queen Taytu linked her name to the Ethiopian anti-colonialist identity not only by leading the fight against the Italians at Adwa but also by successfully shaping an Ethiopian national cuisine. Although Ethiopian society was highly stratified and still marked by diverse diets and styles of conviviality, its culinary structure was substantially consistent across income levels. At the same time, however, dietary differences shaped by religion, ethnicity, geography, and class persisted through the mid-1930s. The Italian occupation of 1935–41 further changed and complicated Ethiopian agriculture and foodways. As the subsequent chapters will show, the occupation generated a colonial culinary and political exchange that gave new meaning to notions of imperial domination and anti-colonial resistance.

2

Fascist Bioimperialism in East Africa: Mass Colonization as Transplantation of Seeds, Breeds, and Farming Hands

As one historian put it,

> After the occupation of Addis Ababa, on May 5, 1936, the most pressing problem which Italian authorities had to face was food production. Ethiopia had excellent agricultural resources and was to meet its needs and those of the new Italian population. There [was] no doubt that Ethiopia's greatest contributions to Italy's requirements were in the field of agriculture and in providing land for Italian farmers.[1]

On May 19, 1937, the Minister of Italian Africa and prominent fascist leader Alessandro Lessona (1891–1991), in a speech at the Chamber of Deputies in Rome, spelled out the interests of Italian colonialism in Ethiopia: "We aim decidedly at the following objectives: meat, milk, coffee, oil seeds, grains. In the Empire, we will find these and other raw materials, or the opportunity to produce them massively."[2] In his memoirs, Lessona later acknowledged the extensive preparatory work Italian scientists had done to achieve those goals while bemoaning that the Empire of Food had eventually turned out to be a major missed opportunity:

> Few know, even among the Italians, what enormous wealth [Italian] Ethiopia contained. Suffice to say that Merino sheep had already been imported from neighboring Kenya and from South Africa and had already acquainted in the vast western prairies, where we could have farmed enough to satisfy the national needs as well as exports; that the ideal lands for the cultivation of oil seeds had already been identified; that coffee, tea, cinchona (to cite just the principal vegetable products) and cattle were up to prodigious developments. In all the immense highlands wheat grew tall: in the Harar region even the grape and the olive tree.[3]

Planning the Empire of Food: Fascist Biopolitical Projects for the Colonization of Ethiopia

Indeed, fascist Italy invested an enormous amount of money and intellectual energies in the project of rural colonization of Ethiopia, at an unprecedented degree compared to any other example of European colonialism to Africa before. With the conquest and the proclamation of the empire, fascist experts and scientists were assigned the formidable work of assessing the agricultural opportunities the Ethiopian land had to offer and what had to be done to turn Italian East Africa into the Empire of Food, within the ideological frameworks of demographic settler colonization and food autarchy.

Even before the invasion, and systematically during the occupation, dozens of Italian scholars were in fact at work mapping the Ethiopian landscape and classifying its food resources, plants and animals, in an expansive taxonomy of imperial culinary provision. Between 1935 and 1940, the work of Italian scientists and scholars on the "valorization" of the new East African Empire produced an unprecedented number of academic as well as quasi-scholarly publications—reports, journal articles, and books—commissioned by and in turn fueling fascist political discourse.[4] A pivotal institution in this effort was Istituto Agronomico per l'Africa Italiana (Agriculture Institute for Italian Africa) in Florence. The institute mobilized chemists, botanists, zootechnicians, and rural technologists around the development of Eastern African tropical landscapes, plants, and animals and the transfer to Ethiopia of modern agrotechnologies such as high-yield wheat seeds, vaccination for cattle, and selected livestock semen.[5]

Under the direction of the agronomist in charge of the earlier colonization of Cirenaica, Armando Maugini, the institute trained technical personnel who studied and promoted agriculture in Italian Africa.[6] In 1938 and 1939 alone, the institute developed and transported to Ethiopia "over 300 specimen of cereal seeds, including whole and durum wheat, corn, sorghum, beer and common barley, rice, oat, and rye; over 100 specimen of leguminous plants, including beans, peas, chickpeas, fava beans, etc.; about one hundred between potato and manioc seeds and seedlings and sugary plants like sugar cane and red beets, greens, and fruits; another one hundred of oil plants like peanut, flax, soy, sesame, sunflower, etc."—a carefully structured movement in biological imperialism.[7]

The institute's journal, *Agricoltura Coloniale*, was just one in a plethora of academic, scientific, sometimes scholarly sounding journals disseminating knowledge about the Ethiopian physical and human environment and the ways to extract maximum value from its foodstuffs. As an example, the trade journal of the Regia Azienda Monopolio Banane (RAMB— Royal Agency of the Banana Monopoly), *Autarchia Alimentare*, in addition to focusing on such technical issues as processing, transportation, and industrial refrigeration, regularly explored broadly the political aspects of agriculture in Italian East Africa. Politics and science systematically merged in publications like *Africa Italiana*, the monthly journal of the Fascist Institute for Italian Africa.

In such settler colonialist plans, local labor and Ethiopians, in general, were assigned a marginal space as a source of cheap, unskilled manpower for technologically advanced Italian rulers and a people destined to eventually disappear from the new colonial landscape. Justified by the scientific racism its scholars and their institutions created, fascist policies aimed at minimizing colonizers' contacts with "colonial subjects" and, in the long run, replacing the latter with the former.[8] For the most part, Italians studied Ethiopians' rural relational structures, exchange practices, tastes, and culinary ways to build a case *against* the Ethiopians rather than to involve them in rural development.[9]

The most important discovery of Italian agroeconomic expeditions was that there was no free land in Ethiopia: land for Italian settlers belonged to the emperor and the local potentates who, loyal to him after the 1935–6 war, were given land in the tenure distribution system called *gult*.[10] Those lands would have to be expropriated while other parcels were forcibly acquired under false claims that they were free for the taking or, rarely, traded for. In the beginning, however, Italian colonization planners refrained as much as possible from dealing with the complex *gäbbar* system of tenancies and small tenures that originated in central highland Abyssinia that in the early twentieth century helped build the Ethiopian Empire. Projects for reforming occupied land were never considered by Italian authorities, who contented themselves with collecting the duties farmers had been paying to local landlords before their arrival.[11] Sahlu Berhane, an Oromo peasant who lived under the occupation of Ada'a in northern Ethiopia, recalled that

> the Italians never interfered in the possession of the landowners. They did not even collect the tithe for two years. Later on, the Italian government began exacting four quintals of teff per *gasha* of land. This applied to all kinds of grain. With the payment of the tax the landowners' possession rights were guaranteed.[12]

Italians implemented their agrarian plans on confiscated imperial land, and not on Ethiopian-owned plots. Ethiopians were to provide labor, but the modern agrarian technologies brought from Italy had to remain in Italian hands, as were overall management and the decisions about what to grow, how, when, and where:

> There was a large tract of land that was the property of Empress Manan [Manan Janterar Asfaw (1891–1962)] around Qaliti. This was farmed with tractors, and there were large grazing lands as well all around the valley. The Italians were good farmers and the harvest was immense during that time. They used tractors to farm large areas of land. The whole forest area was changed into farmlands. They used to sow seeds with machines. They did use fertilizer, but they never gave it to the local people. Yes, the fertilizer was extremely effective; even marshy areas were changed into agricultural lands. They had machines designed for the purpose of drainage and irrigation. There was a special Italian wheat that gave a good yield. They brought fallow and virgin lands into cultivation.[13]

In this complicated geopolitical imagination, the Horn of Africa was seen as, "at once a part or extension of the nation and a place of otherness and difference, a place where the colonizing people claim to take possession but which is already occupied by indigenous inhabitants who greatly outnumber them."[14] The fantasy of the frontier, where barbarism and wilderness promised sexual conquest, had to be balanced against the ideal of Ethiopia as a natural extension of a civilized Italian peninsula. Constructing an Italian East Africa as just another region of Greater Italy demanded a language that described Ethiopia as an empty but fertile space ready for domestication.[15] Italian farmers could be lured into settling the empire with the promise of familiar environments and familiar crops.[16]

In his detailed travel account, journalist Ciro Poggiali described a site selected for settlement, in what had been Haile Selassie I's estate, that evoked the landscape of the Italian region of Umbria:

The *Negus*' villa has become a magnificent farm that from the top of the hill dominates, as far as the eye can see, an immense checkerboard of fields, where wheat, sorghum, millet, chickpeas, fava beans, peas grow marvelously. Potatoes are sown every three months and harvested every three months: four crops a year. The colony extends for more than eight miles on a soil rich in humus and water, yet sparsely cultivated, on to Addis Alem, on top of a hill like there are many between Perugia and Assisi.[17]

Targeting impoverished Italian farmers, landless peasants, and the urban unemployed as well as potential investors, Poggiali voiced the official narrative insisting Ethiopian soil could produce crops that were much alike those grown in Italy. They could be obtained more easily because of the greater availability of fertile land:

Everywhere (except of course the arid, sandy, malarial lowlands) we sowed, we planted, we irrigated; and we got results much superior than those that we would have gotten with the same toil in Italian fields. There is everywhere more rapid vegetation, a faster blossoming, a cycle of rooting and ripening which easily allows for double annual harvest. It is in gardens, though, that the fertility of this land becomes evident even to the eye of the inexpert; anywhere there is water, even at high altitudes, it is possible to grow luxuriant greens like those of Campania [the region surrounding Naples].[18]

These enticing narratives were apparently successful in convincing Italian *contadini* that the new farmlands in Ethiopia could easily be extensions of familiar Italian fields and rolling hills. In the *Corriere della Sera*, Curzio Malaparte (1898–1957) reported:

[While waiting to board the ship to East Africa], I hear all around me [the other passengers, farmers,] conversing about the oxen of the plains of Cobbo, of Selale, of Harar like they were still talking about their Emilian, Tuscan, or Apulian oxen. They talk about vines, pasture lands, wild olive trees, crossbreeding, grafts: a farmer from Cesena says that at the [model settlement, provincial colonization agency] Ente Romagna d'Etiopia [which will be discussed later in this chapter], in Wedecha, they are already planting Romagna grapes. "Soon we'll drink Albana

[wine]," he says. Another man, a baker, already discourses of durra and teff, and yet another man chats about the coffee from Zege, on Lake Tana. They already know everything about Ethiopia.[19]

The narrative matching Ethiopian highlands to the hillsides of Italy drew on contemporary scientific discourse that merged human and botanical growth, assimilating the adaptation of vegetable species to new environments to the "transplant" of human organisms, notably White man's bodies in tropical regions he was due to colonize. As one of the many Italian physicians in the new field of colonial hygiene argued, "The comparison is often made between the White man who emigrated to the tropics and a plant transported out of its country of origin. It is definitively an applicable association."[20]

Fascist leaders envisioned a smooth transfer to Ethiopia of the development techniques applied in the early 1930s in the Pontine Marshes between Rome and Naples, summoning their "miracles worked there and here."[21] Poggiali conveyed the biotechnological enthusiasm that permeated the "dawn of the Empire":

> Around Addis Ababa, in a most rational farm a French ex-army officer started, excellent strawberries, smelling like wild ones, are grown all year round, without interruptions. It is proved, in fact, that all tropical and subtropical plants on both sides of the equator and from the five continents adapt and grow well on Abyssinian soil. The question is just one of the right choices of specimen and irrigation. In the last quarter century, the great agronomic institutes have come to offer modern agriculture highly improved plant breeds and even brand-new breeds (*razze* (races), in Italian). Through cross-fertilization, cross-pollination, selection, and stimulation crops have been made two or three times more productive. There is a variety of corn whose vegetation period is as short as sixty days. Science is too advanced for us to let the farmer or the gardener surrender in front of a plant's whims when science can dominate the plant and bend it to Man's needs.[22]

Mussolini despised British-style plantation and trade colonialisms for generating great wealth for a few but no benefit for the masses. For him, corporatist demographic colonialism—populating the empire with settlers who would feed themselves and the nation—was not only by far the most important variety of colonialism but also a strategy of total "valorization" of the East African Empire under the direction of the state.[23] It was also, however, the most archaic and the costliest form of imperialism.

Fascist Settler Colonialism: Settlement Types for Mass Colonization in the Empire of Food

Following Mussolini's vision of large-scale settler colonialism, the Ministry of Italian Africa, with the support of the Agricultural Institute for Italian Africa, envisioned three types of settlements: settlements of the Opera Nazionale Combattenti (ONC—National Veteran Association), which had already been tried in the Pontine Marshes and Libya; settlements of Enti Regionali di Colonizzazione (Provincial Colonization

Figure 7 Children of Bari d'Etiopia being served spaghetti for lunch. Collection of the Author.

The families of Ente Regionale di Colonizzazione Puglia (Apulia Provincial Colonization Agency) settled in Wacho, Chercher, Harar Governorate. The plan for the transplantation of peasants from their community in Italy to a similar farming landscape in Ethiopia was the most ideologically charged part of the fascist plan for mass settler colonialism in East Africa. The women in the photo wear the Fascist Party uniform.

Figure 8 A tractor pulls ahead in a field, Ethiopian peasants plow on the side in an Italian settlement, Harar region, 1937. Courtesy of Archivio Luce.

Agencies) under the control of the Fascist Party; and capitalist agroindustrial plantations, which were granted land and operating concessions from the state to utilize mostly indigenous labor.[24]

The ONC settlements attempted to embody the ideal of the ancient Roman farmer-soldier, who in between fighting for the empire returned to the land to plow the soil and harvest crops. Mussolini reclaimed this heroic heritage as his model of colonization, while Italian troops were still advancing in Ethiopian territory: "At my first signal, our soldiers in East Africa will willfully exchange their rifle with the hoe. They do not ask for anything else but working to support their families, to whom they are already sending, with a marvelous spirit of thrift, their modest earnings."[25] The ONC settlements were also practical because they could employ demobilized soldiers as paramilitary settlers, offering them small plots (25 acres) while creating the conditions for more Italian farmers to join them in the new colony.

On October 22, 1936, Lessona sent a cable from Addis Ababa to Araldo di Crollalanza (1892–1986), president of the ONC, informing him that the sites of Holetta and Bishoftu (west and south of Addis Ababa), formerly Haile Selassie's farms, had been expropriated for settlement. The locations were conveniently located on the Addis Ababa–Jimma road and along the Addis Ababa–Djibouti railroad, close to the capital market for distribution of crops, and unlike the many areas the Italian military never managed to fully pacify during the occupation.[26] Holetta and Bishoftu were the first experiments in settler colonization. Still, even though they were on already developed sites and had received significant state investment, the cost of National Veteran Association colonization was prohibitive: a budget of 50,000,000 lire was thought necessary for the initial settlement of only a thousand families.

In April 1937, plowing of the first 250 acres was completed in Bishoftu with thirty pairs of oxen complemented by two tractors, "found there and fixed." In May, twenty German Hanomag tractors were delivered to the settlement, but the enormous number of roots and weeds made as many as three plowings necessary. In Bishoftu, it became increasingly clear that both planners and workers were unprepared for the challenges of tropical agriculture. Thanks to delayed shipments of seeds, farmers had to work double shifts until midnight under the headlights of tractors, to finish sowing before the start of the rainy season. In that first year, Bishoftu settlers did eventually plant 2,900 acres, 1,700 in wheat (with a mix of seeds from Italy, Kenya, and any possible local sources), 620 in chickpeas, and 340 in teff.[27]

In late 1937, journalist Alfio Berretta (1897–1977) enthusiastically reported on happy settler families in Holetta in their traditional local costumes dancing to an accordion under the sun. He praised the settlement's agricultural production:

> about 6,000 quintals of wheat, 1,000 of barley and oat, 2,500 of peas, beans, chickpeas, and fava beans, 1,000 of teff. The livestock currently amounts to 1,400 bovines and 400 sheep, the latter subjected to cross-fertilization with fine wool breeds. The 82 settler families make up for a total population of 400. The National Veteran Association built the colonial houses, fully furnished with furniture made in the colony's sawmill. The value of the products is credited, and the expenses debited, to each family's account. The fact that many families have made a profit witnesses how much fertile and valuable the land is.[28]

Returning to Holetta and Bishoftu in January 1939, di Crollalanza encountered a far gloomier reality. He reported confidentially to Mussolini that half of the 120 former soldiers of the Sabaudia Division in charge of building the settlement's infrastructure had left, even though they were offered high salaries, free meals, and the prospect of becoming landowners there in a few years. Only 3,000 of the 10,000 projected acres were ready for sowing, and Ethiopian farmers were reluctant to trade their plots with Italians. The poorly built housing was already so decrepit and unhealthy that many settlers suffered from severe diseases ranging from conjunctivitis to scabies. By the eve of World War II, the ONC settlements in the Shewa Governorate (the Addis Ababa region) appeared to be in a state of irreversible crisis. They were a far cry from supplying the Addis Ababa market with the wheat and other foodstuffs the city's Italians needed, let alone exporting any to the Motherland.[29] By 1941, the Italian population of Holetta and Bishoftu was a mere 93 and 105, respectively.[30]

The settlements of Enti Regionali di Colonizzazione (Provincial Colonization Agencies) were supposed to represent the ideal realization of Mussolini's plans. Lessona, with the support of Maugini's Agricultural Institute for Italian Africa, crafted the original plan. His idea was to transfer entire communities of farmers from selected areas of Italy to comparable settings in Ethiopia, sustaining them with state capital and technology and helping settlers become landowners. Certain "racial" types of Italians (from Romagna, Apulia, Veneto, and Sicily) were deemed the likeliest candidates for transplantation: they were thought to acclimate easily to rural Ethiopia and adapt their ways of farming.[31] Romagna, Apulia, Veneto, and Sicily were also heavily populated by jobless peasants, and a local Fascist Party was charged, like it had done for the domestic Integral Reclamation campaigns a few years earlier, with identifying prospective colonists who "owned the proper moral virtues, such as thriftiness, temperance, spirit of sacrifice, and, preferably, a family ready to migrate together, as well as a proved fascist faith."[32] Even if Enti Regionali mostly succeeded in keeping antifascists from becoming settlers, they also failed to attract the small landowners and sharecroppers who were the regime's target categories of migrant settlers. They were left to recruit mostly landless rural laborers.

Created in December 1937, Enti Regionali were assigned land in what were thought to be prime areas for agricultural development. Ente Romagna d'Etiopia received lands in the Wegera (Woggerat) region (Amhara Governorate). Ente Puglia d'Etiopia received lands in the Chercher province (Harar Governorate). Ente Veneto d'Etiopia was supposed to operate in the Jimma region (Galla and Sidama Governorate) but never did, having wasted 1 million lire in planning costs. Ente Sicilia d'Etiopia remained an operation strictly on paper.

The settlers chosen for Ente Romagna and Ente Puglia were peasants with large families and young enough (between twenty-five and forty) to procreate. The heads of each family had to travel to Ethiopia first and work the land communally, until the day they were joined by their spouses and children (welcomed by ceremonies the Fascist Party organized). The reunited families were then assigned individual plots. Single men settlers would first work for the Ente Regionale for a salary; then, after the land started producing, they would become sharecroppers, ceding half of the harvest to the Ente; and, finally, when they had fully repaid the Ente Regionale their original payments, they could take possession of their land. The entire process would take years.[33]

All along, the Ente Regionale aggressively promoted the ease of moving to a new landscape that looked much like just another corner of Italy. "'Here we are in Romagna,' says one of the two lads who are showing me the area," reported Curzio Malaparte to the readers of Corriere della Sera after visiting the settlement of Romagna d'Etiopia in Woggerat. "I look around and the land, the plants, the hills seem familiar. What are those two gigantic papal mitres there in the distance? Beehives full of honey and wax? No, they are haystacks with that wide shape that distinguishes those in Romagna from the ones in Tuscany." Malaparte went on:

> The setting sun beats down on the haystacks with gentle violence, drawing out golden sparks. On the main road (let's call it that, as one does in Italy), this wide road leading to Gondar, protected and flanked by dusty hawthorn bushes (the same bushes one sees around Forlì, Cesena, Bagnocavallo, and Ravenna), a cart made of dark wood, pulled by two enormous horses with wide backs and breasts packed tight with muscles, full of hay, comes towards us.[34]

The Chercher highlands were selected for the settlement of Ente Puglia because of the climate, a sparse, mostly pacified local population, access to the Addis Ababa–Harar road and the Addis Ababa–Djibouti railroad, and an abundance of "wheat, barley, oats, maize, teff, durra, chickpeas, beans, peas, lentils, peppers, pumpkins, onions, garlic and tomatoes, as well as coffee and bananas" that indicated fertile soil. The settlement was supposed to attract farmers from all provinces of Puglia, so much that the Wacho area—the plain where the colony's buildings such as the church, school, and Fascist Party headquarters were built—was renamed Bari of Ethiopia (Bari is the capital city of Puglia). A group of 105 settlers left the Apulian seaport of Brindisi on January 17, 1938, amid a crowd waving Italian flags and with imperial anthems blaring. The first settlers built small farmhouses using only local stone and lime, boasting individual ovens in place of the standard communal ones. The Apulians were considered more individualistic than their counterparts from Romagna, so the collectivization stage was jumped. They also opted "against any cooperation with Ethiopians." On January 23, 1939, fourteen women and seventy-five children left Italy to join their husbands and fathers in the Bari of Ethiopia (Figure 7). By then, Ente Puglia had been able to obtain 20,000 acres, of which about 2,700 were plowed, but only 1,500 of those ended up being given to the Apulian families from Puglia (the original plan was for each family to receive 25 acres of land instead of the 50 given to Ente Romagna). Bari of Ethiopia received a total of fifteen tractors.[35]

The transplantation of seeds, agricultural expertise, and farmers was applied so forcefully that even the fascist governor of Harar, Enrico Cerulli (1898–1988), decried it as problematic.

> The regional organization of the Enti di Colonizzazione is, in principle, a good idea, as it maintains the solidarity and sense of community among the Italians transplanted to Africa, who can rely on strong and well-established relations, and reduce change in social environment at a most delicate moment in the economic life of the peasant. However, the Italian out of Italy wants to forget a little about his [sic] community of origin, and when he sees around him the same families of his own native village he feels constricted. He would like to act, dare, adopt new initiatives and new ideas, but he is psychologically held back by the same conditions and the same environment he knew from the Motherland. The colonization of Africa is a tough battle. Nobody would forget about his family while is fighting in battle, but few would like to have them there with him on the warfront. The officers of the Enti Regionali must solve this dilemma with great patience and tact.[36]

In his 1938 visit, the Inspector of the Fascist Party to East Africa, Davide Fossa (1902–1976), asserted that in Chercher "it feels like living on the Murgia [the fertile, wheat growing highlands of Puglia]." Praising the climate, the rich fauna, and the fact that malaria did not affect White settlers as long as they avoided contacts with Ethiopians, Fossa noted

> a valley extending as far as the eye can see, where livestock roams and banana trees and coffee bushes beautify with their charm and lusciousness. Today, here in these

Figure 9 Italian soldiers have lunch in an army camp during the offensive in northern Ethiopia, February–March 1936. Courtesy of Archivio Luce.

Notwithstanding the organized efforts at maintaining supply lines suitable for a highly mobile mechanized army along an extensive front, Italian invasion troops often suffered from food shortages.

fertile and gorgeous fields of life and human works, Italian colonization is in full swing. Driven by Man, the tractor, which arrived here with the first pioneers, takes off the ground and becomes almost independent, as an ineffable, indescribable force propelled it. The shining and powerful machine cuts the earth, folds it, turns it.

The spectacle of modernity was as much a display of power as an edifying tale for Ethiopians: "In the eyes of the Ethiopians that follow the tractor, the traditional individualism of the hand that plows the land gives up to the harmony of the engine that evens out all forces. All around silence reigns. The crowd of Ethiopians trail behind in the furrow drawn on the plain"[37] (Figure 8).

Once again, however, reality was much less epic than fascist propaganda claimed it to be. Overall, the total acres sown in Chercher declined from 1,700 in 1938 to 1,200 in 1939 to 640 in 1940, and the quality of yield itself suffered. In 1939, settlers managed to grow mostly "minor" cereals such as durra and maize (2,500 and 700 quintals, respectively), but much smaller quantities of wheat, barley, teff, potatoes, coffee, peanuts, and sunflowers. There was barely a trace of the production that the transfer of high-yield wheat varieties and rural mechanization had promised. Of the 105 original settlers, 42 were forcibly repatriated in the first two years for behavioral misdemeanors or "ineptitude." In a letter to his family in Italy intercepted and blocked by censorship, one farmer lamented:

Figure 10 "Here's the Somali Banana! A Delicious and Nutritious Fruit." Ad for Società Anonima Banane Italiane (SABI—Italian Bananas Company), artist unknown, 1934. Courtesy of Collezione Salce, Catalogo generale dei Beni Culturali.

> I have moved my family to Bari of Ethiopia for fifteen months now and still not a single agricultural tool nor the cattle, mules, cows they promised they would have given to us have been provided. Nothing. To give some milk to our children we have to buy canned condensed milk at the local store. On a farm, this is the ultimate shame. The colonial houses are a disaster; in the rainy season it rained inside, it's so humid and everyone suffers from rheumatic diseases. Authorities know but they don't help us; they let us suffer and make us want to repatriate. We are treated like slaves in the very place where our beloved *Duce* ended slavery [Ethiopia].[38]

The failure of mass colonization in Bari of Ethiopia was seen in its numbers: by 1940, the area had attracted only ninety-two Italian farmers.[39]

Commercial colonial agriculture operated by capitalist farmers and agroindustrial ventures was marginally more successful than mass state agricultural colonization, and more so in the older and poorer colony of Somalia than in Ethiopia. Capitalist farming, operating with concessions from the state on lands made available through different forms of land-grabbing, was considered strategic in an early stage of colonization for providing food supplies (in reality, as Chapter 3 will show, overwhelmingly imported from Italy for the entire occupation of Ethiopia) to the new empire while the settlements were organizing and becoming productive. The last prong of the colonial food system, native Ethiopian agriculture, was deemed to be unreliable and not an asset, as it was assumed that even with Italian technical and educational support, it could have taken decades for independent Ethiopian farmers to produce cash crops and reorient their agriculture to the market.

Italian commercial farming in Ethiopia came in very different shapes, sizes, and capitalizations, but largely fell into one of three categories:

(1) Micro-farms between 1 and 150 acres (in Italian these were called *orti*, or market gardens, operated by war veterans, unemployed workers, and others with little or no farming background and their families. These small truck farms were developed with modest capital and were typically located at the outskirts of urban centers or near garrisons, which represented their markets. After British troops invaded Italian East Africa from Kenya and Sudan, these plots were turned into war gardens and became the most reliable source of food security for settlers during the war.
(2) Small capitalist farms, with plots between 150 and 350 acres, which Italian farmers would purchase with their own assets and whatever public and private funding they could secure; these farms were developed with aid from agronomists and other experts and run by native labors.
(3) State-subsidized and backed firms operating large agroindustrial plantations (between 1,250 and 7,500 acres), mostly growing selected industrial crops, cultivated by African laborers under Italian surveillance.

These different operations all depended on state subsidies and, to different degrees, African labor, both of which made them dependent and fragile ventures. Dependence on local labor especially proved to be a significant problem, as Ethiopian peasants mostly refused proletarianization and, taking advantage of the large investments Italy pumped into East Africa between 1935 and 1938, regularly chose almost any occupation other than agriculture.[40]

For the Ministry of Italian Africa, large agroindustrial plantations were the most efficient solutions until the industrious Italian farmers that fascism praised made their settlements and smaller farms productive—and the new road and railroad infrastructure for food transportation and distribution was in place. Some of these plantations, in operation before the 1935-6 war on Ethiopia, had already met the challenges of tropical agriculture through trial-and-error experimentation and became models for new ventures.

Two industrial plantations in the older colony of Somalia were often cited as examples of productivity: Villaggio Duca degli Abruzzi (today's Jowhar) and Janale (Genale in Italian). In 1920, a member of the Italian Royal House—navy admiral and explorer Luigi Amedeo of Savoy, duke of Abruzzi (1873-1933)—founded an experimental model farm in the Shebelle River valley in Italian Somaliland. The duke incorporated the farm into the Società Agricola Italo-Somala (SAIS), which attracted financial capitals, utilized intensive technical research, and, by end of the decade, developed into an efficient agroindustrial farm producing cotton, cane sugar, bananas, and seed oils. Unlike most other Italian colonial enterprises, SAIS did not receive land from the Italian state or colonial authorities but purchased it from local tribesmen. It also acquired local labor through direct negotiations with the same tribes. SAIS took an innovative, more cooperative approach to the traditional problem of securing native labor by promising its workers access to land ownership after a few years at the village. After several false starts and setbacks (workers leaving for their villages before the rainy season never to return, bubonic plague epidemics), the proclamation of the Italian Empire in East Africa found Villaggio Duca degli Abruzzi working at full steam.[41]

The eventual success of SAIS inspired the Governor of Somalia, Cesare Maria De Vecchi (1884–1959), to replicate an industrial farm in Janale, in the Shebelle's lower valley, where in 1912 Italians had opened a pioneering agricultural research station for growing tropical crops such as bananas and rice. The new operation at Janale launched a vast irrigation system and a program for draining malarial lands. It also sought to offer local tribesmen sharecropping and small land ownership contracts. When these efforts proved unsuccessful, the company resorted to forced enlistment, establishing itself as the paradigmatic example of coercion for all Italian East Africa. In October 1926, De Vecchi clashed with Merca's sheik Ali Mohamed Nur, who, according to De Vecchi, was organizing the resistance to his armed pacification and unification of Somalia. In response, the fascist leader urged the Italian tenant farmers of Janale (early members of the Fascist Party De Vecchi had brought with him) to descend on Merca and slaughter the "rebels." "I gave you the canals to irrigate your banana plantations and sugar cane fields," wrote De Vecchi. "I created from nothing, one-hundred miles from Mogadishu, the Janale district, which represents your future wealth. Now give me your guns. Do not forget you were the victorious soldiers of the Great War!"[42] De Vecchi got what he wanted: between October 28 and November 7, his Italian farmers killed more than two hundred Somalis. Those who had resisted by barricading themselves in the mosque were killed as they surrendered.

The repression De Vecchi ordered was meant to be a warning of the brutal force of the Italians. With the fascist takeover of government in Somalia, the attack also politically motivated violence, meant to convince Somalis to submit to forced labor in the plantations of Janale. In Somalia, in fact, Italian tenant farmers continued to discipline African laborers with extreme, systemic violence, even after De Vecchi's departure in 1928.[43] Ironically, Janale was more successful in hiring local pastoralists, who despised farming but were more inclined than local farmers to work for a wage.[44] Like Villaggio Duca degli Abruzzi, Janale was fully functioning at the time of the conquest in the mid-1930s, running on forced labor and brutal punishments until the liberation of the colony by British troops in 1941.

With access through the Shebelle River to the port of Mogadishu and the Indian Ocean, both Villaggio Duca degli Abruzzi and Janale were integrated in the general plan to make Italian East Africa the central source of food for the empire. Both plantations were developed for the mass production of crops such as cane sugar, coffee, and especially bananas. The establishment of RAMB in 1935 created an artificial, protected

Figure 11 "The Somali Banana: The Fruit of Health." Ad for Società Anonima Banane Italiane (SABI—Italian Bananas Company), Alfredo Cavadini, 1934. Courtesy of Collezione Salce, Catalogo generale dei Beni Culturali.

Italian domestic market for Somalia's Jubba (*Giuba* in Italian) bananas, which were sold at a state-subsidized price to curtail the import of the cheaper and larger Central American Gros Michel varietals, formerly (before the emergence to prominence of the Cavendish in the 1950s) the most widely traded in the global market. Villaggio Duca degli Abruzzi and Janale were considered successes in the imperial food system. But their bananas went directly to the state monopoly; communications and economic integration with the rest of Italian colonies in East Africa were poor; and these models of agricultural efficiency in the end did little or nothing to feed the settlers they originally meant to serve.[45]

For the new capitalist farms that started up after 1935, the experiences of Villaggio Duca degli Abruzzi and Janale provided proof that viability would depend on the efficient transfer of agricultural technologies, machineries, and skilled personnel from Italy, continuing state support, and especially the "ability to tap and exploit cheap indigenous labor."[46] The experience of Confederazione Fascista degli Agricoltori (CFA— Fascist Farmers' Union), the largest consortium of independent Italian farmers starting operations in Ethiopia after the war of occupation, confirmed the value of

Figure 12 Ad for Azienda Monopolio Banane (AMB—Banana Monopoly Agency), Gianni Li Muli, 1950. Courtesy of Collezione Salce, Catalogo generale dei Beni Culturali.

these three factors. By the end of 1936, the Ministry of Italian Africa (still under its original name, the Ministry of Italian Colonies) encouraged some of its agrarian technicians and entrepreneurs to identify Ethiopian lands suited for rapid agricultural development, with an emphasis on the production of wheat—the most valuable crop in fascist colonization plans, economically, politically, and symbolically. One year later, 30 commercial farmers and 114 agrarian technicians and staff arrived in Addis Ababa. The group was armed with fifty-three high-powered tractors and sowing, harvesting, and threshing machines, and forty trucks, vans, and motor cars. Intendenza Militare (Military Office Administration), an army agency charged with promoting wheat production in Ethiopia, was to give each of the farmers an initial supply of at least 1,250 acres of expropriated or otherwise procured land and modern agricultural machinery.

Farmers were divided in four groups, each assigned to different areas in central and northern Abyssinia: Addis Alem (the settlement Poggiali would describe in his travel accounts), Ambo, and Wanji in the Shewa Governorate and Dessie in the Amhara Governorate. Most farmers immediately confronted the challenge of acquiring continuously connected plots, as opposed to a patchwork of scattered holdings whose rights of use were unclear. The plan was for Italian military and colonial officers to help the CFA farmers and local chiefs negotiate a special kind of *compartecipazione* (sharecropping contract) in which, regardless of Ethiopian or Italian land ownership, Ethiopians would provide all the labor while Italians would provide capital, expertise, management, seeds, fertilizers, and modern equipment. Ethiopian workers and chiefs, not surprisingly, were completely excluded from any decisions about or control over farming and production.

Fueled by Italian racism, the operation was crippled by hostility from the very start. By the beginning of 1938, CFA farmers had raised only 3,307 US tons of grains from the 20,000 acres they had sown. Following that first harvest, a variety of Ethiopian claimants—chiefs, priests of the Coptic Orthodox Church, self-declared landowners, tenants, or holders of tithes—argued to be entitled to a part of it. The ignorance of Italians about the *gäbbar* system, which allowed for different and sometimes overlapping rights to land and its products, ultimately caused the system to break down.[47] The retaliation of CFA farmers exacted on Ethiopians by their securing contracts by sheer force was so severely abusive that even the brutal first viceroy of Italian East Africa, General Rodolfo Graziani, protested that "farmers often behaved towards the Ethiopians in a thoughtless or bullying manner."[48]

Because the production of grain for the settler market was so important, the state had no choice but to attempt to rescue the CFA operation with a comprehensive plan of relief and subsidies. As a result, "payment for seeds due at the end of 1937 was frozen; fuel repayment was suspended up to February 1940 and amortization of the agricultural machinery, originally expected to be over by the end of 1939, was made to start by early 1940."[49] More critically, the Ministry of Italian Africa set an unnaturally high fixed price for CFA wheat and guaranteed the purchase of the entire production. Born as profit-seeking, capitalist suppliers of essential resources for the ongoing project of mass colonization, CFA farms ended up surviving only through the injection of public money. They proved to be massive disappointments, despite everything. At the sunset of CFA commercial farming in 1940, the Boidi Brothers' farm in Addis Alem, notable for its successful partnering with Ethiopian farmers and landowners and for its more cooperative approach, was also the one with the most tractors—eleven for a concession area of 2,200 acres—while all others had a number between two and five for concession areas between 700 and 3,700 acres.[50]

Reasons for the Failure of Demographic Colonization and Colonial Agricultural Development

By the fall of the empire in 1941, there were 224 Italian farming concessions in Ethiopia.[51] The total of operating farms (of any kind, including mass colonization settlements) in all of Italian East Africa was a mere 833 farms, employing as few as 4,255 workers by the end of 1939.[52] In his speech at the House of Representatives of April 27, 1940, the Minister of Italian Africa Attilio Teruzzi (1882–1950)—who succeeded at the helm of the Ministry of Italian Africa to Lessona, and Mussolini's one-year interim ministry, at the end of 1938—stated that on that date, on a surface of almost 280,000 acres of farmlands in all of Italian East Africa, there were 3,550 rural settler families with a total of 31,000 people by the most generous estimates.[53] After five years of empire and enormous investments by the regime, Italy had been able to attract to Ethiopia only 3,200 farmers and 40 capitalist agricultural companies.[54] These numbers were a far cry from the millions expected to settle in Ethiopia alone.

Mass colonization had obviously failed, and with it the Empire of Food. At the beginning of 1939, the Italian Consul in the Ethiopian city of Gondar, Raffaele Di Lauro, expressed his impatience with agrarian research and planning when echoing Mussolini's mandate that by 1938, Italian East Africa had to achieve food autonomy:

> From personal experience, I can assure that potatoes, tomatoes, and in general every horticultural products grow perhaps better in Ethiopia than in Italy; that in the midlands (between 5,000 and 6,500 feet) citrus, grape, apricot and all other fruit trees prosper. Should we wait for the publication of all studies and rural surveys to start our fruit orchard plantations we would be hopeless! We must move on, advance; because the Empire must very soon become self-sufficient, *at least in its food provisions* [original emphasis].[55]

Why had the Empire of Food collapsed? Why—despite unprecedented state support: scientific, technical, strategic, and financial—did the fascist plans fail to provide both food exports to the motherland and crops and products to feed the projected millions of settlers?

Six basic reasons for the failure can be identified, of which the sixth, which will be the subject of Chapter 3, was perhaps the most decisive. First, and clearly in retrospect, the fascist biopolitical project was simply too ambitious. Despite early propaganda to the contrary, Ethiopia proved to be an extraordinarily challenging environment for European agriculture, in a country three times the size of Italy and marked with widely diverse ecologies. Even the considerable transfer of rural technologies (in 1941, across Italian East Africa there were four agricultural experimentation district offices in nineteen provincial branches, ten farming support centers, twenty nurseries, two zootechnical stations and livestock insemination stations) did not succeed in transforming Ethiopian soil into productive farmland for European crops. The last wheat harvest by Italian farmers in Ethiopia, in 1940, was in fact the most disastrous: an invasion of grasshoppers and the rust induced by the fungus *Puccinia graminis* destroyed much of it. In addition, the transferred technologies were often still at an experimental stage and sometimes unsuited for the region. Transplanting the hybrid "elite" wheat varieties that were the pride of Italian applied genetics, such as *Mentana* and *Quaderna*, produced disappointing results, while mechanization was implemented far too slowly for the magnitude of the task. By 1940 there were fewer than four hundred tractors in all of Ethiopia.[56]

The second reason for failure was the rural colonization policy itself. The hardships caused by poor planning and shortages of essential resources created low morale and a loss of confidence among settlers as well as among the Ethiopian farmers who were supposed to appreciate the superiority of modern farming techniques and help the invaders implement them. Another shortcoming in the plan for securing land was a fatal lack of understanding the dynamics of Ethiopian society that shaped its rural life and agricultural systems. Despite extensive preliminary studies, Italians remained deeply ill-informed and thus unable to build cooperative relationships with rural Ethiopians, much to their own disadvantage. Although class differences were marked in Ethiopian society before the arrival of the Italians, farmers generally enjoyed a relationship with the land that provided them with food security. They saw no reason to cooperate with the Italians by providing their labor to imperialist mass production. Italian farmers often lamented the difficulty of securing native labor. Ethiopian farmers did work for Italians, but only when forced to do so by personal obligations and contracts they were agreed to in their own community. Many had little use for wages paid in Italian lire, a paper currency they did not trust, as compared to the Maria Theresa silver thalers they were familiar with.[57] Overall, Italy's chaotic colonization program, with different plans supported by different state agencies often representing the conflicting interests of individual fascist leaders, did little or nothing to realize the goal of food self-sufficiency for Italian East Africa, let alone for Italy and its empire.

The third reason for failure was the imperialist war of aggression and its racist, exploitative, and repressive approach that inevitably sparked Ethiopian armed resistance—most notably in northern and central Ethiopia, Italy's Amhara and Shewa Governorates—which made life in remote settlements even more dangerous for Italian farmers. In reality, Ethiopia was never even remotely pacified, and Italian insecurity led to such reactions as the ferocious retaliation for an attempted assassination of Viceroy Graziani in Addis Ababa. On February 19, 1937 (Yekatit 12 in the Amharic Ge'ez calendar), the city's Blackshirts massacred thousands of Ethiopian civilians. The fascist day of killing, Yekatit 12, is still commemorated in Ethiopia. In most of the country, Italians managed to control towns and main roads by patrolling settlements and truck convoys, but just a few miles from these relatively safe havens, they were constantly under threat from guerrilla warfare. As a consequence, farmhouses had to be "built close together in military strategic positions, with surrounding walls and defensive works."[58] Fear and uncertainty dominated the experience of everyday life of Italian settlers.

Fourth, in Italy, potential settlers were faced with a major disincentive to migration: the lack of any clear pathway to land ownership and eventual economic independence. As an old colonial officer confessed to a colleague who recently arrived from Italy,

> If I were the power-that-be, I would have helped settlers in any possible way, to persuade them to work. These people come from Italy prepared to work hard, that is true, but they also look forward to making some money quickly; but with the system we are adopting, there is no quick money to make here. The newly arrived settler receives a small brickhouse, three rooms and a bathroom, and in the bathroom that, almost invariably, has no running water, he puts vases with sage and basil: because, have you ever heard of a rural house with a bathroom in Italy? The settler gets fifty or sixty acres of land to plough and the essential tools. In exchange, he enters into an obligation to grow certain crops like wheat, corn, teff, and pay an annual fee in kind to the Ente or the concession-holder.

The Ente, after all, acts just a middleman that thrives on the labor of the settlers, is unproductive; but it is imposed by the State and the settler who belongs to it must live. The fee is paid as a mortgage. After twenty-five years, if everything goes well, if all installments are paid, the small farmhouse and the land will become the settler's property. The latter, therefore, who came to Africa because he was starving at home, who was disoriented, confused by a foreign environment, lacking the needed skills to cultivate the land profitably and deal with the Ethiopians, realizes that he faces years and years of hard work and scarcity; the land is hard to plow, it has not been plowed for centuries, in some places it was never plowed. At the same time, he sees other Italians getting rich with a little shop, a small business of any kind, with little effort. The consequence is that he is demoralized, unhappy; at the first opportunity to get another job he leaves. The Enti di Colonizzazione, Romagna d'Etiopia and Puglia d'Etiopia, build the house and provide the tools, that is true: but the Ente gets its funds from the State, as subsidies, you know? It is the Italian taxpayer who pays them! And the land costs nothing, it belonged to the *Negus*, so now it belongs to the State; or, if it belonged to someone, the Ente purchased it at the cost of a wristwatch for twenty-five acres.[59]

Prospects were also gloomy for younger male settlers who wanted to start a family on their colonial farm, especially because, at any time during the occupation, Italian women were never more than 10 percent of the Italian population. There was, in the end, hardly any incentive for Italian migrants to become farmers in Ethiopia.

A fifth reason for the failure of mass colonization was its enormous financial costs. Both the Ethiopian War and the subsequent economic development ("valorization") of the new East African Empire were funded with deficit spending that had a dangerous impact on Italy's public debt. The state capital invested in imperial agriculture has been estimated at a total of 850 million lire—400 million lire in Ethiopia alone—for the five years of occupation. The investment was almost entirely unproductive.[60] The large influx of state funds for development operations in Ethiopia and the high salaries paid to workers there, Italian and native, in the construction, industrial, and transportation trade in the early years of the empire produced skyrocketing inflation that dramatically increased the prices of everything, including food. Monetary policies such as the substitution of the traditional Maria Theresa thaler by the lira as Ethiopia's official currency, and consequent speculation on the lira, made things worse. Yet the most direct consequence of inflation and high prices was the crushing effect on food exports, which, to the embarrassment of the Italian government, declined to levels much below what they had been under the Negus's administration. The most notable failed case was that of coffee, normally Ethiopia's most valuable export crop. Problems with exports matched problems with imports, as the slow and difficult development of settler agriculture forced colonists to import the overwhelming majority of their food from Italy, in particular wheat to make bread and pasta. The trade balance between Italy and Italian East Africa, and Ethiopia in particular, contrary to plan, always disproportionately favored Italian exports to the colony (in 1938, valued at 1,816,643 lire, versus 135,995 lire in colonial exports to Italy), with food representing by far the most important article.[61]

Finally, while many factors played a part in the failure of fascist mass rural colonization plans in Ethiopia, the most serious mistake Italian decision-makers made was to launch settlements before building an effective infrastructure for food chains—transportation, processing, storage, and distribution. Priorities were fatally reversed by fascist political ideology and propaganda. Paradoxically, the building of roads, communication systems, and public works ended up at war, with the efforts at rural colonization and mass settlement they were supposed to serve almost killing them in the cradle even before World War II terminated Mussolini's "place in the sun."

3

Establishing the Fascist Food System in East Africa: The Imperial Mobility of Italian Food and the Ethiopian Struggle for Food Sovereignty

As the fascist plan for demographic colonization in every province of Ethiopia, and the valorization of Ethiopian farmlands, could have not advanced without the building of a road infrastructure allowing to transport migrants to their settlements and crops and goods to the ports on the Red Sea and the Gulf of Aden, most intense early efforts were put into imperial mobility. The building of a diffuse mobility infrastructure was also indispensable for making East Africa a consistent part of fascist Greater Italy and proclaiming it as such to the rest of the world; opening up the whole of the Ethiopian territory to the Italian army to patrol and control it; and connecting the Fascist Sea, the Mediterranean, to the Indian Ocean, imagined as the new frontier for the expansive empire in its search for geopolitical power, commerce, and economic wealth (Figure 13).¹ Poggiali reminded his readers,

> Life is on the roads. This is the motto the fascist regime adopted as its emblem in the work of reconstruction and renovation of Italy, and that is guiding the arduous construction and valorization of the Empire as well. Benito Mussolini put the problem of road infrastructure before any else; he wanted our modern roads to cut through the Ethiopian territory because that was the only way to know the country and bend it to the necessities of civilization and economic exploitation.²

The Empire of Food's Transport Infrastructure

Directly conceived by Mussolini and promoted as the making of "the backbone of the Empire," the construction of roads, bridges, and overpasses across Ethiopia required the involvement of hundreds of building and transport firms, dozens of civil engineers, and thousands of workers. A mixed-capital company, Compagnia Italiana Trasporti Africa Orientale (CITAO— Italian Transport Company of East Africa), was created to manage the investment and coordinate the construction works. Looking at the overall Ethiopian communication system, paving the way to Italian cars and trucks was strategic to circumvent the critical problem that the only viable railroad that gave access to the sea to Ethiopian exports—the Addis Ababa–Djibouti railroad—ended in a French territory and port, and goods were subjected to French customs.

> Until our Ethiopian highway system won't be completed between our sea [the seaports of Massawa in Eritrea and Mogadishu in Somalia] and the inland, the fastest and most economical way to transport commodities is that leading to Djibouti. It is through this way, therefore, that the Motherland sends any kind of goods and materials that [Ethiopia] requires for its valorization and the food that our settlers need before the Empire achieves its food self-sufficiency [autarchy].

Poggiali noted,

> When we conquered Ethiopia we found this situation, which had lasted since the [Addis Ababa–Djibouti] railroad had been built: tariffs so high that a load of wheat or coffee costed for the transport from Addis Ababa to the sea between twenty and thirty times more than what the same transport costed from the American places of production to the seaports of Santos, Buenos Aires, and New Orleans.[3]

Italian roads and highways did realize an unprecedented integration and unification of Ethiopia, efficiently connecting it to the other Italian colonies in the Horn of Africa. However, their construction absorbed a disproportionate share of financial and labor resources, diverting badly needed investments—and Ethiopian and Italian workers—from agriculture. In its encyclopedic general report for the years 1938–9, the Guardia di Finanza (Italian Financial and Customs Police) forwent the Ethiopian resistance's guerrilla warfare that relentlessly intimidated Italian settlers, to focus on another "bottleneck" delaying the economic valorization of Ethiopia: the road and transportation system. Not only was the impressive program of road infrastructure on the vast and impervious Ethiopian terrain taking years to complete, but it had stimulated the proliferation of the truck transport micro-business (at the expenses of off-road vehicles that would be vital to rural development), skyrocketing prices of all goods and services and thriving workers' salaries—two, three, or more times higher than the equivalent wage paid in Italy.[4] As a consequence, in the early years of the empire, inflation was rampant and the Italian state budget verged dangerously on bankruptcy. Early in 1937, the author of a comprehensive fieldwork analysis on the economic development of Italian East Africa, Giuseppe Tassinari (1891–1944), implored Mussolini to stop constructing paved highways and roads and remain content with building simple dirt trails, which would have been more apt to the conditions of the terrain and climate, more useful to the rural and commercial development of the area, and especially much cheaper.[5]

Migrant construction workers to Ethiopia typically articulated their satisfaction with the job opportunity the empire had landed to them in terms of food, emphasizing the new dietary security their occupation in mobility offered, in exchange for their sometimes-excruciating labor. A young unskilled laborer from Romagna recalled,

The first time I went to Africa, they sent us to work on the Massawa-Asmara road, in Dongollo. It was so hot that we just couldn't stand it. We would send an Eritrean boy to fill our flasks in a valley a mile away where there was a small spring of fresh water which we did not understand where it could possibly come from, as all around it was desert. Yet we ate so well. There was rice, cheese, pasta, and fruits of any kind that they brought us down from the highland. At noon, we would cook eggs by letting them on the sand under the sun. In fact, it was 132°F in the shade and 161°F in the sun.[6]

The truck drivers that indefatigably traveled along the new highways and roads of Ethiopia carrying food and construction materials to Italian settlements, forts, and colonial cities were also paid wages that were many times higher than they would be paid in Italy. An adventurer to Ethiopia observed with some jealousy that "600 lire a day is a fortune if you think that an office worker, in Italy, makes 350 lire a month! And [truck drivers] don't even work hard, they take their time to load their truck and try to travel as little as they can."[7] Truck drivers also experienced the changes in their diet that migration to Africa had brought as a tangible sign of an unthinkable social mobility. The abrupt access to more and better food that migrant truck drivers enjoyed attracted the attention of fascist authorities as potentially revolutionary "forbidden pleasures that were suddenly available" in the colony. An anonymous source for Opera Volontaria di Repressione Antifascista (OVRA—Fascist Secret Police and Political Intelligence) denounced truck drivers' changing lifestyle by reporting that "here we have seen teamsters that in the Fatherland would drink a glass of wine costing forty cents drinking champagne for hundreds lire a bottle."[8] In April 1937, with an executive order, Viceroy Graziani cut by 50 percent the salary of truck drivers, but not even that damaged the reputation of the trade as one of the best occupation working-class Italian migrants could get in Ethiopia.[9]

The payment of high salaries to Italian workers forced CITAO to resort more and more to Ethiopian and other African workers, and in fact the number of Italian workers declined steeply from 146,681 in 1936 to 75,688 a year later, 49,161 in 1938, and only 23,801 in 1939. Parallelly, by 1940 the number of African workers employed in the sectors of road and public works construction, agriculture, and the colonial army exceeded 750,000, for the effect of wages "four times higher than what salaries had been under the *Negus*' regime" and, as a consequence, "the much higher standard of living of the indigenous populations, with a dramatically increased domestic consumption of food products, most notably coffee."[10] Hiring Ethiopian laborers was problematic, though, as Abyssinian men culturally shunned wage work. The most attractive occupation Italians had to offer Ethiopian men was to enlist them in the Italian army or the so-called *bande* (posses), native colonial troops at the order of an Italian officer, which was more attuned to many Abyssinian men's warlike attitude and social ideals of masculinity. The reluctance of Ethiopians to proletarianize and the resulting limited availability made the contractual power and salaries of native workers in the road construction trade to rise significantly. Compared to work in agriculture, therefore, employment in road construction had the advantage of not only appearing somehow more modern, industrial, and different from mere slavery, but also being lucrative.[11]

In short, the higher wages and better labor conditions the building of road infrastructure—which Mussolini had named as his number-one priority—provided all workers, Italian and Ethiopian, turned the sector into a formidable competitor to rural colonization and farming, instead of the necessary prerequisite to rural development it was supposed to be. As Davide Fossa, Fascist Party's Inspector for the "agricultural valorization" of Italian East Africa, alerted, with reference to Ethiopian agriculture's most valuable product, coffee, which in fact crashed in terms of both production and value from the levels preceding Italian occupation: "After the end of the [Second Italo-Ethiopian] War [in 1936]," it was

> very hard to take back indigenous labor to their original work [in coffee plantations], and this was true not only in the field of coffee production but for any other kind of farming. All this was a consequence of the nearly total absorption of such labor by road construction companies, which, because of the urgent priorities of the moment, paid Black workers very high wages, especially if compared to previous [pre-Italian occupation] conditions.[12]

In Italian East Africa, the aggressive strive for automobility crippled exactly what it was supposed to serve—White colonist settlement, the formation of a native wage labor force, rural development, and international export crop trade.

The Travels of Food Imported from Italy and the Imperial Diet of Settlers in Ethiopia

However, Mussolini's highways proved to be indispensable for moving around the food imported from Italy, entering Ethiopia from Port Said, the Suez Canal, the Red Sea, Massawa, and Eritrea—as well as the little Italian farms eventually managed to produce on the land—to serve the Italian occupation army, Italian migrant workers, and the Italian settler market. Italian settlers, in turn, showed a great propensity to invest in food much of what they were earning in higher salaries and from their businesses in the colony, creating their new colonial lifestyle—whether in cities and towns, where most of them ended up living, or in rural and military settlements—around their distinctive foodways. Contrary to Mussolini's expectations of creating in the empire a new breed of Italians, thrifty, tireless, and proud of their racial identity, Ethiopia's Italians became instead (being much grateful to Mussolini for this) above all new consumers, enthusiastic about individualism, capitalism, and the high standard of living achieved by embracing a new entrepreneurial spirit of the frontier.

As in other imperial experiences—but especially so because of the largely proletarian nature of Italian mass colonialism to Ethiopia—food imported from Italy achieved a high social status and became a signifier of social mobility, affluence, and modernity for Italians in Ethiopia.[13] Rather than representing a persistence of premigration food habits, canned, packaged, and bottled Italian food imported to Ethiopia constituted, in fact, a novelty for many colonial migrants, which, as farmers and rural housewives and workers, had rarely access to industrial processed food, or food commodities overall for that matter. Imported food remained for the time of the occupation of Ethiopia an important article in the transnational food system Italians established in East Africa and on which they created much of their sense of "home" in Africa.

Enormous amounts of food, from seeds to cans and bottles, were mobilized via oceans, roads, and railroads as part of the fascist project of making Ethiopia and East Africa just a consistent part of Greater Italy and feeding Italians there with food they could call their own. For fascist Italy and its ideological imperialism and propaganda, the implementation of a modern, technologically advanced, and mobility-based food system in East Africa was important to deny Ethiopian modernity, describing Ethiopians and Ethiopian agriculture as primitive and irrational, and to reclaim Italian Whiteness in the face of Ethiopian Blackness.

That came at a high cost, for geopolitical reasons. Since the establishment of the empire, Italian ships to and from Italian East Africa came to represent a full 20 percent of the total tonnage passing through the Suez Canal, paying 25 percent of the canal's total revenues to Great Britain. Duties Italians paid for customs represented a very large share of the proceeds of French Djibouti, where the only railroad to Addis Ababa started and ended. And the slow and difficult development of farming and other extractive industries in Ethiopia reflected in the enormously unbalanced trade between Italy and Italian East Africa. The value of Italian East Africa exports to Italy (mostly bananas and pineapples from Somalia, accounting in 1936 and 1938 to a whopping 50 percent of the total exports, plus coffee, cotton, and raw hides) grew from 61 million lire in 1934 to 246 in 1937 to go down again to 137 in 1938, amounting to a meager 1.5 percent of total Italian imports. At the same time, exports from Italy to Italian East Africa rose from 71 million lire in 1934 to more than 2,100 million in 1937—more than 20 percent of total Italian exports. Like imports, most of these exports were food: wheat flour and semolina, pasta, salt, sugar, cheese, cured meats, canned vegetables and meat, olive oil, dried and candied fruit, wine, spirits, and mineral water.[14] The most important articles were those grains and grain products that fascism had declared as the staple of life of the new Italian nation and empire, and that Italians regarded as the foundations of their diet. In 1937 alone, Italian East Africa imported from Italy 127,003 US tons of wheat flour and semolina and 14,122 US tons of durum wheat pasta.[15]

Lessona, two days before his removal from the Ministry of the Colonies on April 8, 1937, telegraphed Viceroy Graziani:

> I bring to the attention of His Excellency the need to extensively develop all those production activities that will give not only to the indigenous population, but to the White population as well, the opportunity of living off the resources of the country [Ethiopia]. I can't help but notice that an amazing quantity of canned food, meat, milk, and vegetables is imported into Italian East Africa every day. In some areas, the fodder for animals and fresh vegetables are imported even from abroad! All this must stop and cease as soon as possible![16]

Poggiali expressed the disappointment for the inefficiencies of the imperial food system that the gravely negative trade balance revealed while, at the same time, offering as usual the regime's vision of what the heroic labor and ingenuity of Italians would have created as the process of mass colonization of Ethiopia proceeded:

> For two years [1936 and 1937], in the months before the rainy season, the city of Addis Ababa had to import for the fantastic sum of ten million lire foods that had all more or less the taste of paradox. Canned beef and condensed milk in a country that owns animal husbandry assets far exceeding the needs of the Ethiopians; semolina pasta in a land where the most excellent durum wheats are grown; fresh and dried fruits where one can find the most extensive wild fruit orchards; olive oil in a place that very soon will satisfy the whole Italian need of every kind of vegetable oils; ... sweets and cakes where the confectionery industry will find tomorrow a dozen of cereal varieties to make the most refined flours, heavenly smelling honey, and an unlimited amount of eggs.[17]

The sweet taste of the empire was a fascist dream yet to materialize.

As, differently from what the regime had planned, a disproportionate number of settlers ended up living not on farms but in cities, most of them in Addis Ababa, one of the most important functions of "the backbone of the Empire" was to supply Italians in Ethiopia with the food they were familiar with, they could now afford with the higher wages imperial jobs or trafficking provided, and they deemed safe. The jewel in the imperial crown was always difficult for Italian invaders to govern and exploit, but they always considered controlling the mobility of food across the land one of the prime ways to actually "win" Ethiopia.

The *Corriere della Sera* reporter Orio Vergani (1898–1960), widely considered the first Italian photojournalist, described the excitement and the confusion of the frantic and seemingly casual circulation of food in Italian East Africa—with all its flavors, tastes, shapes, colors, names, and denominations of origin. The empire functioned as the centrifuge thrusting food to every corner of Ethiopia, including unexpected and unwanted places, assuming different meanings for different people at every node of the network.

> The miracle of commerce began. Food provision was occasional and unbalanced, bizarre as the times of the conquest [of Ethiopia] commanded, or just because a truck had fallen down a ravine. One was waiting for prosciutto and a thousand pairs of shoes arrived. The residents of the new Addis Ababa ingeniously tried to get provisions to make up for late deliveries, and those who had managed to hide a hundred soaps under their bed exchanged them with those who had a suitcase full of canned tomatoes. In a way or the other, Addis Ababa ate, drank, smoked, had its coffees, and, albeit dimly, lit the city's nights. There was a dearth of buttons, of toothpicks, of aperitifs; and then came, as falling from the sky, the chocolate with almonds, and—to please the regional nostalgias of the palate—the brown panforte [a specialty dessert with candied fruits and nuts from Siena in Tuscany], panettone with its little eyes of raisins and candied fruits, torrone nougat, liquors

Figure 13 Ad for Lloyd Triestino, Gino Boccasile, 1937. Courtesy of Collezione Salce, Catalogo generale dei Beni Culturali.

The construction of a mobility infrastructure connecting the Mediterranean Sea to the Indian Ocean for the transportation of foods and other colonial goods was at the center of the geopolitical and bioeconomic project of fascist Italy and its empire. In this ad for the logistics company Lloyd Triestino, the bodies of colonized bare-breasted women are both presented as promise of sexual conquest for Italian men and incorporated in the system as a means of transportation of the bountiful food that came with the conquest of Ethiopia. AOI is the acronym of Africa Orientale Italiana (Italian East Africa).

from Abruzzi and marzipan from Palermo. Sweet tooth? In a city where women were so few, men became boys again, and panettone soothed the sobs for the distant fiancée.[18]

Mobile food across Ethiopia sketched transnational geographies of remembering, identities, and politics of taste and power.

Whatever its shortcomings and inefficiencies, fascist politics of taste and consent guided the implementation of an imperial system of food logistics and distribution by focusing on the quality (cultural appropriateness) of the food to be delivered to Italian soldiers, workers, and settlers even more than on quantity. Not only did Italian migrant workers occupied in construction work and other industries receive much higher

Figure 14 Ad for L'Acqua dell'Impero (Mineral Drinking Water of the Empire). *Etiopia* Vol. 3, No. 1 (1939).

Contradicting the fascist-mandated strive for autarchy (food self-sufficiency) of the empire, bottled mineral water imported from Italy was immensely popular among Italian settlers to Ethiopia. Acqua dell'Impero was an effort at producing mineral water from local springs in Eritrea for distribution across Italian East Africa.

salaries in Ethiopia than those paid in Italy, but in their workplace, they were supposed to get plentiful rations of food made with ingredients and preparations they loved and reflecting consumer styles that in Italy would have been defined as middle class. The corporatist authority of the Fascist Party in charge of overseeing labor conditions and labor relations in Italian East Africa, Ispettorato Fascista della Produzione e del Lavoro e per l'Africa Orientale Italiana (Fascist Authority for Production and Labor in Italian East Africa), had among its tasks to monitor the food provision Italian workers received in construction and other worksites. Italian workers in Ethiopia were to be provided a full 6,500 calories a day, the Ispettorato imposed, broken down in 2 pounds of bread, 10 ounces of rice, 10 ounces of pasta, 9 ounces of meat, 7 ounces of potatoes, 3.5 ounces of beans, 1.75 ounces of Parmesan cheese, 1.75 ounces of olive oil, 1.75 ounces of sugar, 0.8 ounce of coffee, and half a quart of wine (canned tomato products strike for their absence here, and that could have had something to do with the imagined prevalence among the workers of northern Italians, which were much less heavy consumers of tomato sauce than their southern coworkers). This was a much bigger and more varied fare than most urban or rural workers, skilled or unskilled, could hope to consume on the workplace at home.

The Ispettorato considered wine, in particular, less a working-class vice, consumed for the purpose of intoxication and reducing labor efficiency, than a drink workers were entitled to as an important provider of caloric content in their diet, a popular medium of sociability and conviviality, and a pleasure that met their taste and style of commensality. The physicians of Ispettorato conclusively argued,

> All our workers are used to drinking wine on a daily basis, and here [in Ethiopia], because of the heat and the harder work they perform, they need it even more. The provision of such nutriment [wine] is included in their contract and the worker has the right to request it at will. We think, though, that wine definitely needs to be part of the daily rations, because it has been proved that, while it represents a toxic substance for those who are forced to conduct a sedentary life, for manual workers it is just a complete food, generating energy and strength for the body.[19]

Migrant Italian soldiers and settlers, in fact, expected to drink wine in Ethiopia, starting from the time of the crossing, on the ship that took them to Africa:

Sailors told us: "If you don't want to get seasick, eat vertically and lay horizontally." We obeyed that [laughs]. We would eat, but no liquids, eh, although many many gallons of wine got drunk by pretty much everybody; I'm not, personally, a great wine drinker, I would eat some bread ... I didn't get seasick.[20]

The Bolognese truck driver Guerino, traveling on the ship *Biancamano*, confirmed, "Honestly, I have been eating so well, we're 8 at each table, and the tablecloths are spotlessly clean; 3 dishes, one for pasta or soup, then steaks with many sides, fruit, coffee, dessert and wine galore. Tonight, by eleven, we will be in Suez."[21] The consumption of wine was so taken for granted among soldiers and workers that the occasional lack of it elicited protests: "One Easter we've got just a spoonful of wine to drink!" lamented a Venetian soldier. Italian women too seem to have developed a taste for wine and hard liquor in the colony. In her diary, Alba Ferter Sartori noted that "eating a lot of substantial food, drinking a lot of alcohol, that's the cure for any tropical disease," and when the car she was in broke overnight in the middle of nowhere, "we found refuge on the driver's seat to try and get some sleep; but first a good drink of cognac."[22] As a result, wine ended up being one of the most widely imported products from Italy and being ubiquitous in the geographies of consumption that Italian settlers crafted across Ethiopia, producing often inebriated settlers, workers, and soldiers. The abuse of wine or, in the original language, the "alcoholic excesses" was one of the most frequent causes of mental health issues classified under the diagnosis of "tropical neurasthenia" among the settlers who were repatriated from Italian East Africa on hospital ships and treated as psychiatric patients at the asylum of Naples between 1936 and 1941.[23]

The large consumption of alcohol among Italian regular and colonial troops, military police, and fascist Blackshirts certainly fueled and encouraged the atrocities—from mass rape to indiscriminate massacres, mutilations, and executions of captured prisoners—that Italians committed during the Italo-Ethiopian War and the guerilla warfare they engaged with Ethiopian partisans in its aftermath.[24] An Italian colonial administration officer reported,

> The flask of Brolio or Antinori [Chianti wine] is on every table, red, white, ice-cold: it gives a transient sensation of refreshment. Wine never stops flowing, and Ethiopians learned to love it, a lot, too. Our national winemaking industry will easily find a very large market in the Empire, and solve all its problems, even if wine, at these temperatures, hazes the brains already dazed by the heat, stimulates transpiration.[25]

The consumer culture of alcohol for inebriation purposes permeated colonial life as an everyday presence few were exempt from. Poggiali annotated in his private diary:

> December 12, 1936, Saturday. Lunch at Hospital n. 558, lovely. I met Doctor Izzo from the University of Naples, a young and bright lieutenant who conducts most interesting biological and pathological studies on the indigenous race. He is also a wonderful maker of Vov [a hard liquor containing egg yolk, similar to eggnog but alcoholic] with locally purchased eggs and the pure alcohol that should be used in the hospital and he serves that to us liberally. While we were eating, a *Sciumbasci* [the highest rank of the Eritrean, Libyan, and Abyssinian *Askaris* serving in the Italian Army, reporting to the Lieutenant (a rank colonial troops could not attain) and superior to the *Bulucbasci*; a necessary requisite to ensign to the rank was the knowledge of the Italian language] came to alert the officers that an *Askari* was missing—they get drunk, and during the night they wander around, harassing people in their tukuls and shooting.[26]

Differently from the ideal of thriftiness and sobriety the fascist regime aggressively promoted at home, the colonial food system under construction in Ethiopia was designed to serve Italian settlers and soldiers' food habits and their working and killing bodies rather than reshape them.[27]

Archeologist of the contemporary past, Alfredo González-Ruibal, was amazed at the quantity and variety of bottles and tin cans he found even in smallest and most remote garrisons in his expeditions to the remnants of Italian military sites in Ethiopia. But what he was especially quizzed about was the reasons behind the

> enormous logistical effort [that] had to be made to bring supplies to this isolated outpost: The Eritrean ports were situated well over a thousand miles away and were only communicated by roads, most of them dirt tracks. What surprises most is not the logistical effort as its pointlessness from a practical point of view. Only a handful of Italians lived in Gubba and Afodo. The colonial presence was overwhelmingly represented by Ethiopian and Eritrean [soldiers enlisted in the Italian colonial army]. They would have been very glad to keep on with their customary eating and drinking habits. Yet they were provided with European foods and drinks at an enormous cost.[28]

González-Ruibal speculated that the only possible rationale behind Italians' apparently misguided investment in food mobility was to "civilize" the native people. Having Ethiopians eating the food of the masters, cooked and served in lilywhite European dinnerware (González-Ruibal also recovered a great quantity of plates and cups in Italian military sites) was a way for Italians to display the racial and technological superiority of their foodways, from the advanced system of provision that brought food from thousand miles away on the Ethiopian highlands to the taste of the food itself—about which Italians could be proud to the point of arrogance—to the modern norms of hygiene and table manners. Bringing Italian food up there from long distances and at an exorbitant cost was definitely a way for Italian imperialists to show their power at taming Ethiopian nature and people. It probably also worked as "a strategy to underpin the difference between colonial troops and the rest of the population, to foster the dependence of colonial servants from the colonizers, and to create a esprit de corps among the alienated indigenous soldiers," as González-Ruibal suggested.[29] In that sense, it was a peripheral reflection of the apartheid that fascism declared in Italian East Africa in 1937, barring opportunities for the sharing of food between Ethiopians and Italians in public places like bars and restaurants, as well as at the domestic table, altogether. It was a way to reaffirm once again Italian modernity and Ethiopian barbarism and sub-humanity, Italian Whiteness, and Ethiopian Blackness.

Yet, the seemingly incomprehensible degree of effort put in the construction of a supply chain that delivered Italian canned food and wine to Italian soldiers on the imperial frontier had also inner-looking reasons that had less to do with the othering and remodeling of Ethiopians. Achieving food sovereignty for the Italian nation at home and in the empire was simply what fascist imperialism was all about; it was the central purpose and ideological justification of the entire demographic imperial project, with all its modern technological equipment, and only delivering on that—even, or so much more so, on the outposts of the empire—could bound Italian citizen-eaters, with their bodies and minds, to the project. González-Ruibal's valuable archeological research does not tell us anything about the Ethiopian reception of Italian food from faraway, and it is also too extreme to argue that, as the archaeologist did, Italian soldiers and settlers in remote quarters in the Ethiopian heartland would "not eat Ethiopian food except in case of starvation."[30] As we will see further, Italians did taste Ethiopian food other than the fermented teff *injera* they replaced their cherished wheat bread with when they were under siege by Ethiopian patriots and British colonial troops and desperately hungry. Italian racism and Ethiopian resentment and will for revenge did create quite a degree of impermeability between the respective foodways, but those borders were crossed many times in liminal spaces and situations, such as Gubba and Afodo military settlements, sometimes with disgust, sometimes with curiosity and even pleasure. The foodscape Ethiopians and Italians created together, albeit largely for attrition and in conflict with one another, was much larger than the sum of two utterly independent culinary universes. In the would-be Empire of Food, the bureaucratic system of the Fascist Party, the Italian Army, and the colonial administration prioritized Italian food sovereignty as the strategic weapon to effectively make Ethiopia Italian, and that included whatever product of the Italian Ethiopian food cultural intersections it made sense to include.

Within this strategy, truck drivers, some of the most vital imperial institutions and dramatic characters, were both the essential carriers of the food of the empire and participants in the developing colonial food system and food culture. Contributing significantly to the out-of-control proliferation of microbusinesses in the early years of the empire (1935–7), many truck drivers started as employees for big transportation companies, saved on their comparatively hefty monthly wages (1,500 lire for a driver; 1,700 for a driver-mechanic), purchased a vehicle such as the popular Fiat 34, and became self-employed (*padroncini*). Benefiting from the criticality of road transport in the imperial mobility system—the demand was so high that the rental of a heavy truck could cost as much as 1,300 lire a day—they were popularly known among settlers as being remarkably successful and enjoying luxuries like a nomadic lifestyle and regular sex with African women.[31] Because of the emphasis on mobility of the fascist empire in East Africa, particularly for the distribution of food, the truck itself became a status symbol, functional for work or individual, independent, and leisure mobility, and the male-dominated trade of truck-driving came to define a specific hegemonic masculinity in Italian Ethiopia. By the end of 1939 there were about 3,400 Italian drivers in Ethiopia, slightly more than the total number of farmers countrywide! If often economically gratifying, as other settlers jealously thought, the occupation was nevertheless quite risky because of the high chance of failure when a truckload got lost or the vehicle got wrecked, physically demanding, and—because of the activity of Ethiopian resistance over much of the land, regularly ambushing Italian trucks—dangerous.[32]

An Italian truck driver, a Guerrino from Bologna, wrote to his wife in Italy over two years documenting his crisscrossing the physical and mental map of Ethiopia with his truckloads of food: "Yesterday evening I picked another load in Dekemhare and today I leave for Addis Ababa with a load of condensed milk, and, if all goes well, as I hope, I'll be back by the 10th."[33] In such transnational conversations, references to food made the narrative meaningful and familiar: "As you see, we are in Massawa, and, as we have begun to work, we are going to load about fifty quintals of eggs to take to Dekemhare.

I'm so sorry that I don't have time to write for longer." "This is to let you know that tomorrow we're going to leave for Addis Ababa with about 1,500 pounds of salt."³⁴

Truck drivers' experience of mobility overlapped with the movement of food across landscapes and changing seasons and climates, conflating time and space in a topography of emotions and the senses:

> Now we are in Dessie and the trip continues well, except for some flat tires. But the rainy season has started, and I'd rather be very cautious, even if it's going to take some more days, as I want to return to Dekemhare safely. I hope to arrive to Addis Ababa on Saturday night, if all goes well. Last night I slept in Dessie. Before leaving I bought a crate of wine bottles, a crate of beers and many cans of meat, milk, fruit jams, and a crate of mineral water bottles, because here [on the Ethiopian highlands] food, and especially drink, are very expensive, a flask of wine costing twenty lire. Dear Lucia, don't worry because I've got food, good food, and my stomach isn't hurting. I bought milk of magnesia, laxatives, quinine, etc. but as for now I didn't use any of it.³⁵

The trucker's constipation (bowels' immobility caused by an unusual rich diet) and malaria, which was rampant in the scorching hot lowlands he drove through on his way to Ethiopia's capital, were diseases of mobility, and mobile food was the cure to keep his working body healthy and productive.

Food indeed appeared to be in motion everywhere across Ethiopia and on different, mechanical as well as animal, means of transportation.

> Caravans of trucks come through bumping on the road, wreaking havoc to the scared herds of cows. The columns of colonial troops come along, snaking around not to step on cultivated plots, picturesque processions of people, of animals, of things, of mules that disappear under the heterogeneous loads of weapons, ammunitions, bunches of chickens, pans, pots, and shields, and their following of bleating goats, and jars of beer, and jars of mead, and jars of tea.³⁶

The mobility of food could be felt in the senses in Italian Ethiopia. The look, the sound, and the smell of mobile food gave it a particular taste—of sweat, of dirt, of diesel: "The organization was a mess, believe me," an Italian soldier remembered. "The trucks loaded with flour came down from Asmara and along the way the Abyssinians would attack them. Then, when they stopped to fill up, some of the gas would overflow and soaked the flour. When you ate that bread, you would taste the flavor of gas [laughs]."³⁷

Among the most widely imported Italian goods, besides the predictable bread flour and pasta, was the bottled mineral water the teamster Guerrino stuffed his truck with. Since 1935, an amazing supply of bottled mineral water imported from Italy passed through Massawa and Asmara in Eritrea to be distributed even in the remotest part of Ethiopia: "crates after crates of wine flasks, liquors, and bottled mineral water, which seemed to be the goods that Italian Ethiopia desired most ardently," Poggiali noted, describing the arrival of Italian foods from the Red Sea as an imperial cargo spectacle.³⁸

A rarity in Italy, consumed on occasion by the sick, babies, and elderly people in middle-class urban families, more as part of a special diet than as an everyday drink, in Ethiopia bottled mineral water became almost an Italian settler's necessity—a modern and portable protective antidote to the perils of African food, deemed to be polluted and unsafe by definition, and a prized item in the nostalgia foodways that settlers shaped for themselves (Figure 14). Even working men bent on saving as much as they could from their African migration experience delighted in the consumption of the mobile mineral water bottle. As a migrant peasant turned into construction worker in Ethiopia remembered—with the insistence on money to measure time, space, and decisions so typical of migrant correspondence, diaries, and recollections—drinking imported mineral water was for him a thoughtful consumer sacrifice: "A bottle of mineral water could cost up to two lire. As I had intestinal pains, sometimes I needed to eat out at a restaurant if I wanted to have something decent. For a soup or pasta dish and a bottle of mineral water I could spend up to six lire."[39]

Poggiali, voicing the concerns of the regime and the colonial middle class, surreptitiously reprimanded the enjoyment of such import luxury on the part of rural migrants while praising the advancing fascist modernization of Ethiopia that would have solved the drinking water problem and opened even new possibilities for exploitation:

> The most particular and expensive article in [Italian exports to Ethiopia] was mineral water. The bottles of the humblest remedy to thirstiness that Italy sent to Ethiopia from the start of war operations to a full year after the conquest can be counted in the hundreds of millions. Indispensable in the beginning, the importing soon looked frivolous, then even paradoxical, when it was ascertained that three quarters of Abyssinia had water—in need, of course, of rational aqueducts funneling it to the places of consumption; and also many natural spas, which can compete favorably with Italy's most celebrated hydrothermal springs.[40]

Bottled mineral water remained for the duration of the Italian occupation of Ethiopia a protective drink from the poisonings of Africa, like gastroenteritis—a high-status product that the colonial experience had turned into a more widely accessible necessity and a sign of the modern advancing of Italian food in the empire.

The captured Ethiopian patriots deported to Italian concentration camps in East Africa had to confront most painfully the hegemonic modernity of Italian bottled mineral water, as in the camps Italians used awfully insufficient rations and contaminated water as a weapon of prisoners' coercion and extermination. When interrogated by the Ethiopian Court on War Crimes, Michael Tessema described his experience in the concentration camp of Danane, Somalia—where he was interned between September 1937 and December 1940—as one of programmed starvation:

> At first, the food was four hard biscuits (*galletta*) [in Italian in the text] in a day. As we used to drink sea water the daily death rate was between six and thirty persons, who died from dysentery. Up to the end the Italian authorities never provided potable water for prisoners at Danane. From 6,500 persons, who were at Danane,

3,175 died. The reason why not all of them perished was because the prisoners used to receive some money from their relatives and bought *acqua minerale* [mineral water, in Italian in the text] which was brought from Italy in sealed bottles.

Ethiopian prisoners fully understood how the mineral water imported from Italy conveyed the capitalist transformation of a natural resource into a commodity, as their own life as colonized subjects depended on acquiring it in exchange for money:

> All the prisoners were tormented by lack of drinking water. I myself told an Italian sergeant to buy me water for 500 liras from the money which I kept in secret, but the sergeant felt pity for me and brought me a bottle of water without accepting the money. When he did this, he was wriggling on his stomach, to avoid being seen by the Carabinieri [Italian military police].[41]

To the Italian settlers in East Africa, however, sparkling mineral water was an acquired taste of modernity and social mobility, and with its portable living contents originating from a spring somewhere in Italy, bottled mineral water was also one of the most characteristic forms of nostalgic consumption, sharing this property with canned food in general.

Canned foods of the kind the Bolognese teamster hoarded in his truck suggested, more than anything else, the global dimensions of the circulatory food mobilities that crisscrossed East Africa at the time of the Italian occupation of Ethiopia—canned food's Italianness had for the most part to be constructed in the empire. Tin cans from Italy, Europe, and elsewhere entered East Africa through Massawa and Assab in Italian Eritrea or Djibouti in French Somaliland and traveled the Ethiopian heartland by truck or train. "Among the many ironies of Italian East Africa is the provisioning of our soldiers and settlers with canned milk and butter from Holland," Poggiali protested.[42] A young colonial administration officer from Rome deployed to a remote settlement in Gidole (Gardulla) in southwestern Ethiopia wrote to his father, "Dear dad, I have never felt better in my whole life: I managed to buy, paying its weight in gold, a whole box of Swiss sterilized milk; 30 half-a-quart cans, exquisite."[43]

In Italy, mass industrial production of canned vegetables started in the 1860s with the Piedmontese Francesco Cirio (1835–1900) and his "method" of preservation and brand of the same name. Canned beef was not commercialized until the turn of the century. The principal developer, the Milanese Pietro Sada (1855–1935), gave way to another popular brand name, *carne* Simmenthal (named after a valley in Switzerland where the best beef was supposed to come from). As late as the 1930s, though, canned food remained expensive, a modern novelty enjoyed by the urban middle class as part of their conspicuous consumption practices and because of the portability, but foreign to lower-class consumers, which watched it with suspect (and reasonably so, as the materials and technology of preservation made it indeed sometime unsafe) and found its taste unappealing. Most of the national production was actually exported abroad. Cirio shipped much of its products to northern Europe, finding strategic new markets for the Italian agricultural surplus of "Mediterranean" greens and legumes there. Most of the canned tomato paste—and, later, San Marzano whole-peeled tomatoes—made in small factories around Naples or Parma found its markets in Great Britain and especially in the swelling Italian immigrant urban communities of New York, Chicago, São Paulo, and Buenos Aires.[44]

Most young Italian rural men were first exposed to canned food on the warfront in World War I, as food from cans was used to cook their rations. During World War I and under fascism, especially after the invasion of Ethiopia and the sanctions the League of Nations declared against Italy, home economics classes and political propaganda encouraged Italian working-class and peasant women to preserve food at home as their patriotic contribution to the war effort and national mission of achieving food self-sufficiency. However, different from their urban middle-class counterparts, they had little use of industrial-brand canned or packaged food for its much-advertised convenience, rationality, and time-saving properties. Working-class women in cities, who had to resort to shopping on a daily basis for their food, continued to buy all their groceries and produce in bulk, whether at open markets or in grocery shops.[45] It was only in 1929 that Colonel Ettore Chiarizia (1871–1938) patented canned meals of beef *spezzatino*, minestrone soup, and pasta and chickpeas for the Italian army. Although the taste of *chiarizia*, as the ration was called after the name of the inventor, was disputable at best, the food was ready to warm up and eat, and the cans were lighter and easier to open, making them fit for modern, highly mobile, armed forces such as the mechanized and airborne Italian troops that invaded Ethiopia in 1935.[46]

It was just in the Second Italo-Ethiopian War of 1935–6 and in the process of settlement to Ethiopia that the modern Italian mass consumer of canned foods was invented. Italian soldiers and settlers in Ethiopia familiarized with, and actually learned to crave, imported canned food products within the framework of a transnational politics of food security, taste, and nostalgia: as a consequence, they created a new market and, along with the demand of the million consumers in the global Italian diaspora, gave a tremendous boost to the domestic food industry, then still mostly made of small family businesses that were less capital-intensive and technologically rudimentary.[47] The tremendous consumption of imported canned foods among Italian settlers responded to their conservative idiosyncrasy toward Ethiopian food, their presumption that African food was at least potentially unsafe, and their subscribing to a notion of food sovereignty that extended from the motherland to the colonies: "We, soldiers and civilians, eat [canned beef] every day, also because in a country that we found being absolutely deprived of any vegetables that met our taste (hence the fantastic magnitude of our imports of canned vegetables) it has turned out to be the most nutritious and inexpensive food."[48]

However, as has been noted for other migrant groups, canned food in the diaspora also assumed immaterial values they did not own at home and that transcended the meanings of modernity, rationality, industrial processing, and consumer's alienation from production place and time often associated with it. To migrant cooks and eaters, the cans and their labels told stories and described landscapes of the imaginary, enticed memories and reproduced familiar gastronomies, articulated transnational feelings of belonging, and fed into a transnational market of nostalgia.[49] A quintessentially impersonal commodity the food industry delivered on a mass scale in innumerable identical exemplars, in Ethiopia canned food reverted to the status of a good, with use value, exchange value, and emotional value; it could be bartered, or exchanged as a gift, thus embodying the subjectivity of the holder and the giver. More than fifty years after the events, the Italian soldier Francesco Bolongaro remembered a particular can of soup as the catalyzer of a web of relationships and bonds across space and time:

> I had a friend, now he's dead, he was a truck driver, and while our battalion was marching on to the Amba Aradam, he drove by and saw our platoon [named after the place in Italy where they both came from]: "That's the Intra Batallion, there must be Bolongaro among them, he's my age, got drafted with me." Somebody heard that someone was looking for me, it went to the grapevine, we found each other, we hugged. He gave me a can of *chiarizia*, the canned soup of the military. So, I had this can in my backpack, always, I carried it with me for miles and miles, everywhere. I thought: "This, this can, I'm going to eat it when I'm really starving, and I can't stand it any more." At some point I was indeed starving, then, I was with four or five friends, I said: "Come on, let's open it." We opened it. It was a half-a-pound can, we mixed it with water in the mess tin, we heated it and with the biscuit … The biscuit swelled as it soaked inside the soup, right, and we had our meal together, happily.[50]

For this soldier and his comrades in arms, cooking was the cultural work that revived the peripatetic canned soup to the state of a meaningful food making taste and commensality.

The scale and nostalgic significance of imported canned foods embedded them in the colonial experience of both Italians and Ethiopians. The circulating tin can object became a vital element of the material culture the Empire of Food produced, even when it had been emptied of its nutritious contents. Tin cans were so sturdy and yet so light, standard-sized, and easy to stock and transport, often beautified by gorgeous images and logos—from smiling young peasant women and landscapes to coat of arms and flowers—that in their second or third lives they became widely used as construction material, containers, and decorative stuff. Italian settlers' vernacular architecture routinely utilized empty imported food cans and wine barrels as building material. Vergani noted: "[At the intersection in Dekemhare] where the architects hadn't taken over yet, and the early buildings were built with the wood from Chianti wine or pasta boxes, pride of the carpenters, new constructions now arise, modernist, rationalist to the extreme."[51] "After a while we got some real iron furniture, but in the early times all our furniture consisted of two chairs, a folding table, and two small beds supported by tomato cans in place of their legs," recalled a colonial civil officer who had settled in Gondar with his wife.[52] An Italian woman living in a small settlement in southwestern Oromia near Jimma described her sense of displacement and disorientation by referring, and anchoring, to the image of a popular brand of canned food: "The little Oromo boy, dirty and tattered, walks through the garden-backyard, whispering a song, a never-ending dirge, on his way to the well to get water with a shining, flashing Cirio vegetable can."[53]

Italians sometimes claimed that they were able to trade empty tin cans, along with other "worthless" objects, with some of the populations of southwestern Ethiopia where contacts with Europeans had been minimal, but the meaning of the empty food can that did most profoundly stick in Ethiopian memory is as a symbol of fascist oppression of racism. So many of the elder Ethiopians oral historian Alessandro Volterra interviewed remembered being left outside the bars and restaurants they weren't allowed to patronize after the introduction of the apartheid laws in 1937 and being served their drink or food in empty, sometimes rusty, food cans, instead of the cups, glasses, and plates reserved to Italians and other "Whites." Dicodimos Tesfamikel, who had served with Italians in the colonial army, remembered, "Even if at work we ran elbows with the Italians, we weren't allowed to get in public spaces like bars or restaurants. They served us from a little window on the side, in a tomato can."[54] These witnesses, just like others whose memories have been collected by Irma Taddia, were teenagers or in their early twenties at the time. Another man, identified as T.T., echoed, "When we'd go to a bar they [Italians] wouldn't give us to drink in glasses, but in old, dirty cans that used to be food cans."[55] The recollection of this dehumanizing practice of consumption, aimed at creating and instructing the colonized (and the colonizer) about sharp racial borders, is repeated so routinely in the interviews with witnesses from different cities and walks of life to represent a national discourse, revealing the deep emotional and psychological distress this exercise in colonial power caused to Ethiopians. When emptied of its original food contents, the food can became a tool for Italians to perform diverse colonial activities, including inscribing Ethiopians in the realm of the sub-human, the nonhuman, the animal, as per the fascist racist project of domination.

In fact, empty tin cans found their way even to some of the war atrocities that Italians performed on Ethiopian bodies. On September 24, 1937, in a photo series the army photographer Angelo Dolfo immortalized a group of Italian soldiers in the act of extracting the severed head of Abyssinian *Degiac* (chief officer of the imperial guard, rank equivalent to colonel general; when used as a title to indicate the status of a leader, just inferior to *Ras* and superior to *Fitawrari*) Hailu Chebbede from a Lazzaroni brand cookies metal box (Figure 15). Later, Hailu Chebbede's head was mounted on steel wires and hung on a pole. In the photographs, the Italian soldier holding the cookie can is smiling while showing the detached head to two officers; the officers have serious facial expressions as they examine the head in the box for identification check.[56]

Apparently, the contrast cannot be any more violent between the memory of delicious cookies made by a fancy and expensive brand like Lazzaroni, redolent of family holiday dinners and celebrations, and the consumption of the ferocious mutilation of the body of a feared enemy as just another reason to celebrate. But the imperial life of canned food allowed for such seeming contradictions. It adds to the irony that *lazzaroni* in Italian means "petty street criminals," or "evil persons," its etymology deriving from the Spanish word for "lepers" that the foreign rulers of Naples used in the seventeenth century to disparagingly call, for extension, all the plebeians of the city. In Ethiopia, the imperialist hegemony of violence endorsed the "bad guys" to act just as their cruel self and butcher the native people. In the colonial consumer code of the Empire of Food, canned food produced and articulated a variety of uses and meanings for different subjects in different contexts of exchange.[57] Even the memory of Italian occupation and colonization of Ethiopia sometimes survived and arrived to us in empty tin cans of cookies, chocolate powder, or panettone containing family photographs, letters, memoirs.

Figure 15 The severed head of Hailu Chebbede in a cookie box, Kerem, northern Ethiopia, September 24, 1937. Photo by Angelo Dolfo.

Italian soldiers present to their officers the severed head of the captured Ethiopian Resistance leader Hailu Chebbede in a box of imported Lazzaroni cookies.

Along with bottled drinks and canned foods, wheat bread and pasta were most representative of the hypermodern mobilization of food that the attempted mass colonization of Italian East Africa invited.[58] With the Battle for Wheat, fascism had elevated wheat bread and pasta not only to the rank of undisputable foundations of the national diet but also as key symbols of *Italianità*, representing the Mediterranean landscape and imperial aspirations and the Latin agrarian tradition of manly integrity and power. However, as late as the 1930s, these two foods were more frequently idealized and desired than actually consumed in Italy. *Contadini* (peasants) had to regularly resort to black bread made with whatever coarse flour was available—or, in the north, cornmeal polenta—not to go hungry. Durum wheat pasta, which requires an industrial process to manufacture, was on sale in the market, which made it out of reach for most rural Italians except on special occasions. The chance of eating white bread and pasta every day was one of the most convincing promises that Italian East Africa—and especially Ethiopia, which fascist propaganda described as the world's ancestral cradle of grain cultivation—had to offer to prospective migrant settlers.

This consumer dream was made true the moment settlers and soldiers boarded their ship to Africa. For many of them it was a double initiation, as they were seeing

Figure 16 Ethiopian troops and an allied Australian officer pose with their rifles as two soldiers cook a meal at an unspecified location in Ethiopia, February 18, 1941. Courtesy of Getty Images.

The guerrilla warfare between Ethiopian patriots and the Italian troops policing the occupied territory was often a struggle for food, as the belligerents tried to secure food supplies and starve the enemy. Understanding that the imperial food system that Italians were painstakingly creating was at the foundation of their presence in Africa, the Ethiopian Resistance focused on attacking the infrastructure of food provision to colonial settlements and cities as the most effective way to bring Italian rule to collapse. Finally, for Ethiopian patriots, persisting in cooking and eating traditional and decolonized food was a strategy of participation in the anti-imperialist fight for freedom.

the sea for the first time in their life and the patriotic idea of Italy as a nation seemed finally making sense to them:

> The trip was very nice. Some people smoked, I didn't smoke, I had some beers. And there were those white bread rolls that were so good … I can't help but remember that bread after so many years. On the ship, they would make those white bread rolls … Then, there was always pasta, which wouldn't make you seasick and throw up. At night we could take a last glimpse of the seafront of Catania [Sicily]. Ciao Italia. And then we arrived at Suez.[59]

Testimony that the regime saw these quintessential "Mediterranean foods" as a necessity for the imperial food system in the making and which Italians in Ethiopia could not do without, the volume of imports of wheat flour and pasta from Italy between 1935 and 1941 dwarfed any other article and contributed more than anything else to the catastrophic trade deficit of Italian East Africa.

Every battalion of the Italian Army in Ethiopia had its portable bakery and special squad in charge of baking bread daily. Soldier Pierino Bertinotti recalled:

> I was in the sapper army. Among us there was a squad that would go chopping the wood to bake bread. As there were tuff quarries all around, they dug ovens into the tuff, any size of ovens, three feet, four feet, five feet. They would cut into the tuff and make the oven. The bread was baked to perfection there, it was delicious. And then, you know, every day we would send two or three men to chop wood, they would come back and always bring some bags full of bread loaves. The rest of the soldiers got rolls, like this, small. There was a guy from Gattinara [a neighboring town from where Bertinotti was from] and he'd say: "I have no bread." "Come with me, I've got bread." "How can you have all this bread?" "Never mind." You know, in the army, you've got to be a little smart, otherwise you go hungry. So, I gave him five or six loaves.[60]

The deployment of transport technology to maintain Italian soldiers and settlers in Ethiopia into food sovereignty was particularly intense as regards wheat bread and pasta: "After the Battle of Amba Aradam, we got less and less food, until we went hungry," remembered a soldier. "So, they'd send us flour with airplanes, you can imagine that flour dropped from above, from the airplane, what those bags looked like."[61] "Sometimes there was nothing to eat," reaffirmed another one. "I remember that come Easter we hadn't eaten anything for days. Then there came an airplane that dropped two big bags of flour and us, with our bare hands, we scooped the flour from the rocks, so we could eat."[62]

For many soldiers and settlers to Ethiopia "to eat" was synonymous with having had bread and/or pasta for meals. Bread and pasta were universally intended to be the basics in the diet of Italian settlers, and the provision of such foodstuffs was a priority for the state: the suggested daily ration of bread for Italian workers in Ethiopia was a full 2 pounds.[63] Each head of family in the colonial settlement of the Opera Nazionale Combattenti (ONC— National Veteran Association) in Holetta and Bishoftu was, at least in principle, entitled to a starting package of seeds, agricultural tools, and a generous supply of wheat flour and pasta.[64] Bakeries were among the most popular food stores everywhere Italians settled; in early 1937 there were twenty-seven of them in Shewa and fifteen in Harar.[65] In Jimma, the capital of the Galla and Sidama Governorate, in March 1938, bakeries were ten out of a total of hundred independent stores, the majority of them food retail businesses (twenty-one general grocery stores, selling pasta; eighteen cafes, wine shops, and dairy stores; six butcher and delicatessen stores; four restaurants, with and without bars).[66]

Because of demographic colonization's failure to supply the grains the settler market required, and the going underground of preexisting Ethiopian agriculture (which anyway had always privileged teff, durra, and barley over wheat), large imports and long-distance motor transportation of wheat flour and pasta continued unabashed for the duration of the Italian occupation of Ethiopia. In 1939, the quantity of wheat imported from Italy into Ethiopia passed the 100,000-ton mark.[67] Durum wheat spaghetti and macaroni, in particular, were just the perfect product for the purpose of feeding settlers even in the remotest corners of Ethiopia; transportable, preservable, durable, almost indestructible, and ready to transform, with the addition of water—which costed nothing and was made safe by the boiling process—into a nutritious food that most Italians loved regardless of regional origin and was so versatile to be good to sauce with pretty much everything according to taste and availability of ingredients.[68]

In 1935, when the aggression to Ethiopia began, Tommaso Marinetti (1876–1944) had already published his culinary manifesto, *Il manifesto della cucina futurista* (The Futurist Cookbook, 1932), and attacked pasta as the quintessential "pacifist food" that quenched any energetic, dynamic, belligerent masculinity in Italians: the gendered virtues essential to the violent conquest of the empire. The futurist attack on pasta was an artistic and rhetorical call to fascism to return to the revolutionary, uncompromising origins that it had abandoned for the political alliance with the Catholic Church and the national bourgeoisie.[69] The colonial civil officer Francesco Pierotti echoed Marinetti's preoccupation in his observation of the anthropology that the massive everyday consumption of pasta had purportedly created among the Italians of Ethiopia:

> The sun perches the tukuls [traditional thatched-roofed circular homes] of the Ethiopians and make streams of sweat run beneath the shirts of the nationals [Italian settlers], who, oblivious of the Ethiopian climate, every day burden their stomach with heavy pastas; woe betide if they don't have their pasta, they would die without pasta. Perhaps, many of our troubles stem exactly from their pastas, that is, from wrong food habits. Sweat drips from craniums covered by cork helmets, down on foreheads, down on ungroomed beards, it broadens in grayish stains under the armpits, releases nasty acidic smells.[70]

Informed by middle-class disdain for working-class lifestyle and body maintenance, Pierotti's multisensorial perception of Italian Ethiopia reflected the central space that pasta occupied in Italian settlers' diet and everyday life. Recollections after recollections confirm that Italians in Ethiopia enjoyed to the fullest the opportunity to regularly consume pasta that the imperial system of food import and distribution offered them. It was for fear of social envy back in his hometown that teamster Guerrino was shy to write to his wife that pasta had become an everyday pleasure for him:

> Dear Lucia, I'd like to stay with you some more, but I have to go eat the pasta we made here with Zini. As per the food, I'm doing very well here in Dire Dawa, even if I spend a little more than when I was at the construction site, but I want to eat what I like, sometimes I have tagliatelle, sometimes I have tortellini, but these only on Sunday. For sleeping, I sleep in the truck. But dear Lucia, please don't tell what I have just said to anybody.[71]

In Ethiopia, pasta was undoubtedly the comfort food of choice for working-class Italians; as the most Italian (and non-Ethiopian) food of all, its regular consumption away from their diasporic home was one of their most significant Ethiopian conquests.

Ethiopian Resistance and the Anti-colonial Attack on the Imperial Food System

The enormous prize that Italians put on the establishment and maintenance of a colonial food system they saw as a vital instrument for making Ethiopia Italian did not go unnoticed by the Ethiopian armed resistance that relentlessly tantalized Italian settlements and colonization projects from the end of the Second Italo-Ethiopian War in 1936 until the liberation of the country in 1941. Damaging and ultimately dismantling the colonial food system that the Italians were painstakingly implementing was one of the Ethiopian resistance's primary guerrilla objectives. In oral histories recorded after World War II, leaders of the Ethiopian resistance noted that until 1937, they engaged the Italian colonial army in open battle, suffering heavy casualties. After that, they adopted more effective tactics, targeting trains, convoys, and isolated trucks carrying food with the specific goal of shattering Italian supply lines.[72] As Angelo Del Boca observed, "The production of goods in Italian East Africa, and therefore exports, was significantly constrained by the Ethiopian guerrilla, which disrupted transportation and trade and destroyed products. But these figures rarely appeared in official documents."[73]

However, numerous anecdotal accounts suggest that Ethiopian patriots, through their guerrilla actions, disrupted food transportation and delivery for the Italians. One Italian truck driver, a O.G. from Ravenna, recollected his experience as a transporter of the food of the empire as one of constant awe and terror. To prove his point, he alluded to the Gondrand massacre (February 13, 1936), a famous episode in the anti-Italian Ethiopian warfare in which partisans assaulted the logistics company camp near the town of Rama (Mai Lala) in Tigray, killed eighty workers, and castrated some of the corpses:

> I applied to work as a truck driver for the sapper army. They sent me to Abyssinia, at Maychew, on the road to Gondar. My job was to bring food provisions to the men building bridges on the Mareb River. But it was so dangerous to drive in that area, there were many rebels. They had attacked the Gondrand camp, killing more than one-hundred people; we were all scared to death.[74]

An A.F. from Forlì, deployed to the Lake Tana area, remembered accordingly, "We built forts, we were armed, but we could not move around for fear of the Ethiopian guerrilla, which cut our supply lines. Then we had to be supplied wheat flour and the other essential food items from the airplanes, without parachutes, so much of the food got lost."[75]

The Italian soldiers involved in colonial police operations and retaliation against the Ethiopian guerrilla fighters had a clear perception that the main objective of the resistance was indeed the disruption of the colonial food system, hitting Italians, that is, in the showpiece of and what was dearest to them in the whole imperial construction. Soldier Luigi Pilosio ironically reported about the course of the battle he participated in on Christmas 1937:

> Christmas what a beautiful day, what a joyful celebration in our families without any news about us, unaware of our whereabouts (We hope they received the letters we mailed twelve days ago), with no food, except a cracker and half a can of beef,

and tomorrow there won't be any, absolutely no water, under this scorching sun, our throats burning from thirstiness, we beg for a drop of the liquid, not wine, not liquors, just water, and more than that, this morning the [Ethiopian] rebels made fun of us from their positions, yelling, in good Italian, come here, we'll give you water, accompanying those words with rounds of dum dum expanding bullets.[76]

In his private diary, where he annotated comments and references to people and situations that would have never passed through the screen of political censorship, Poggiali mentioned many episodes of anti-colonial guerrilla attacks to the imperial food system, with the goal of cutting on the supply lines of food imported from Italy and, as a consequence, to terrorize, depress, and lower the morale of Italian settlers. After several Ethiopian partisans' assaults on the Djibouti–Addis Ababa train, on Sunday, July 19, 1936, Poggiali noted, "The accidents of the railroad [Ethiopian partisans had uprooted the tracks] stopped the food provisions for Italians. There is no wine to drink. We eat tough meat and bad bread, that's all."[77] And again, on Friday, March 5, 1937: "Permanent state of alert. Our airplanes fly westward. Cases of violent attacks, some massacres, and an attempt to poison the aqueduct of Addis Ababa on the part of the *shifta* ['bandits' in Amharic, was the way Italians called Ethiopian resistance fighters] were reported."[78] Notwithstanding the enormous investments in it, the Italian East African system of food distribution and logistics was not only complex but frail, its fragility a consequence of the effectiveness of the Ethiopian resistance at incapacitating Italians to end war economy and warrant security to settlers.

On their part, Italians tightly linked their military might, ability to patrol the land, and capacity to repress the warfare operations of the "rebels" to the strength of their food stockpiles and supply lines, especially as regards to wheat. The colonial government was wary about a possible siege of Addis Ababa, the capital of Italian East Africa where most Italians lived. In April 1937 it was alarmingly noted that the city had supplies of pasta for thirty-six days only, and, in preparation of an Ethiopian partisans' massive attack, a special effort was made to increase pasta stockpiles to last for 175 days by the end of the year. Viceroy General Graziani formed a Defense Commission to overview the accumulation of a stockpile that made the military securely supplied with food and ordered military camps and schools to grow their own food (again with an emphasis on wheat) in emergency gardens.[79]

Pressed by the prospect of military vulnerability caused by scarce provisions, between 1937 and 1938 Italians finally began to look at Ethiopian agriculture to increase their food security. The colonial administration encouraged the stipulation of share-cropping contracts between Italian and Ethiopian farmers and created administrative units in charge of "native agriculture," which were supposed to promote the production of wheat in Ethiopian farms with supplies of seeds and tools, or just acquire wheat crops from Ethiopians.[80] But it was a case of too little too late. However progressive the efforts at reaching out to Ethiopian farmers and well-disposed local lords were, in many instances Italians' dishonesty and racism, land-grabbing practices, and forced requisitions floundered any long-term collaboration, only producing more passive resistance and more supporters to the partisans.[81] The official sources presented at the negotiations for peace treaties after World War II spoke of a total 5 million heads of livestock, 7 million goats and sheep, 1 million horses and mules, and 700,000 camels slaughtered or confiscated by the Italians for all the duration of the occupation, for an Ethiopian request in war debts of 185 million British Pounds.[82] The theft of food, grains, and cattle by the fascists was so widespread that it became a recurring theme in Ethiopian literature from the 1940s to the 1970s.[83]

The raids and requisitions of cattle the Italian troops perpetrated in their policing operations in Ethiopian villages were so damaging to the prospects of pacification that the new Viceroy Amedeo of Savoy, duke of Aosta (1898-1942), who replaced the brutal Graziani at the end of 1937, early in 1940 issued an order "prohibiting all regular, colonial, and irregular troops everywhere operating to confiscate or otherwise take cattle, four-legged animals, and things in general from the native populations under any circumstance."[84] The Italian workers occupied in construction sites and public works were well aware that the theft of cattle and food the Blackshirts and the army perpetrated in Ethiopian villages was the most important reason behind the mobilization of "rebels" of the armed resistance, who turned their life—already made difficult by the acclimatization to a foreign and hostile place—into a nightmare of terror and insecurity. In 1937, a group of construction workers, many of whom had fought in the war of occupation of 1935-6, wrote a letter to the secretary of the Fascist Party, Achille Starace (1889-1945), to denounce the "real conditions" in which they lived and worked. The workers confessed to living in constant fear of a guerrilla attack, so much that they kept their gun always with them, even when sleeping, mentioning an episode when the army officers commanding the labor camp asked them to procure some fresh meat: "

> Of course our officers decided to take it from the Abyssinians, who don't want to sell their cattle, because they wanted to speculate and being corrupt in this circumstance too. The Abyssinians of course did not want to sell because the price offered was ridiculous; the officers wanted to give them thirty lire for every big animal. Sometimes they don't even want to give the Abyssinians the thirty lire and just steal the cattle. Have we come to Africa to colonize and bring civilization or to loot? Are we liberators or pillagers?

After receiving the order to take the cattle from the Ethiopians by force, the workers had to suffer the retaliation attack of "some two hundred of those Black devils" on their camp. The workers resisted, but spent the whole night in terror, waiting for another assault of the Ethiopian resistance who would come to "set their livestock free":

> Our sleep is constantly interrupted by the alarms: is it right to risk our lives in this stupid way when we pay for that garbage they call rations? Sir, we beg you to put this disgrace to an end. We work hard all day, at night we are tired and we want to sleep quietly, dreaming of our faraway families and children. We don't want to have awful dreams. Some of us already cry in their sleep; if things don't change, our life in Africa will be just a nightmare.[85]

While the armed Ethiopian resistance unrelentingly focused on dismantling the colonial food system Italians had created with its guerrilla assaults on Italian trains, convoys, and settlements, Ethiopian peasants fought the same struggle with the means of passive resistance, in particular refusing to be paid in lire, a paper currency they distrusted, in exchange of their foodstuffs.[86] Ethiopian farmers were so resilient to the forced introduction of the Italian lira, refusing to sell Italians any kind of food—as well as other products like heating wood—with that money, that the European invaders had to yield and pay in the silver Maria Theresa thalers.[87] As a consequence, between 1937 and 1938 the mint of the Bank of Rome had to coin some 500,000 thalers, the majority of them utilized for the purchase of coffee—which, as we have seen, represented the most important item in the less-than-modest Italian imports from Ethiopia—from the southwestern parts of Ethiopia for Italian domestic consumption.[88]

Particularly untimely was Mussolini's decree ordering that by July 1, 1938, Ethiopia had to be self-sufficient in wheat, while the *Duce* privately knew that it would have been a resounding success for Ethiopia to produce just one-third of the grain needed to satisfy the Italian army and settlers' demand for bread and pasta.[89] According to the historian of Addis Ababa's urban food system, Tekalign Wolde-Mariam, just like the Italians, Ethiopian "patriots were well aware of the connection between wheat production and Italian military security." The oral history Wolde-Mariam conducted in 1990 among the farmers in southwestern Shewa suggests that the Ethiopian resistance mobilized farmers against collaborating with the Italians in the cultivation of wheat by convincing them that the high-yield, pest-resistant wheat varieties Italians supplied them with "would bring about impotence in men and sterility in women." Given the history of massive use of biological weapons on the part of the Italians, as well as their strategy of biological imperialism aimed at replacing local agriculture with genetically developed European crops, the story was actually highly plausible: Wolde-Mariam's sources argued that the Ethiopian partisans' propaganda succeeded in preventing the expansion of wheat farming the Italians encouraged in the area to the south and west of Addis Ababa.[90] According to Italian intelligence, in April 1937 Ethiopian patriots also spread rumors among rural communities around the capital about an alleged program about to be introduced by the new colonial government: "Ethiopian population, another enemy [the Ethiopian resistance] is coming, he is not only ours but also yours," went the text. "Get armed and defend yourself. Give to the Italian government all of your belongings—if you have three children, one is for you and two for us—in regard to cattle it is enough that any farmer has two oxen and a cow, the rest will be consigned to the government."[91] The history of Italian theft and violence on Ethiopian farmers made these stories credible and fed distrust in any possible form of cooperation.

The participation of Ethiopian women in anti-Italian warfare activities was also remarkable, and not limited, as important as that was, to securing, transporting, and supplying food and drinks to the groups of combatants they were part of: women carried utensils and pots, fetched water, chopped wood, foraged for wild plants, grinded grains, and prepared teff *injera*, *doro wat*, *tej*, and *tella* to feed partisans. After the war, General Guglielmo Nasi (1879–1971) cited among the distinctive military customs of Ethiopians, "women's (followed by children's) participation in warlike operations, with the function of pack animals for ammunition, food, water, tents, transportation and with the function of effective fighters in ammunition supply and firearms loading on the firing line and participation in fighting."[92] According to the historian of the Ethiopian anti-colonial struggle Aregawi Berhe, "In the countryside, not only did women prepare *quanta* (dried meat), *qollo* (roasted cereals), *besso* (instant cereal powder) and various foodstuffs that may be compared to 'dry rations' in modern military jargon, but also sharpened swords and shuttled between the zones of operation and their houses."[93] During their exile in London, the Ethiopian Women's Association organized fundraising campaigns aimed at providing the combatants of the Ethiopian resistance with food and weapons and raising the awareness of the international public opinion about the antifascist struggle taking place in Ethiopia.[94] Some Ethiopian women, like Lekyelesh Beyan, Kebedech Seyoum, Shewareged Gedle, and Qeleme Worq Tiruneh, participated in the resistance as fighting soldiers, but many did in information services, some of which aimed at starving the Italian enemy.

In this sense, a legendary precedent and inspiring memory were set for partisan women by Empress Taytu Betul leading Ethiopian forces at Adwa (March 1, 1896), the first major battle a non-European army ever won against European invaders, which left six thousand Italians dead and brought national shame and trauma on Italy. Taytu's superior savviness was demonstrated in the earlier battle of Imba Alaje, when defeated Italian brigades had regrouped in the fort of Makalle: instead of ordering an attack as her soldiers expected and wanted, Taytu commanded to besiege the Italians and cut off their water supply. Taytu's plan worked perfectly, as after two weeks, on January 21, 1896, Italians, suffering from extreme shortage of water, unconditionally surrendered.[95] The literature on Ethiopian women's participation in the long anti-colonial struggle against Italians emphasizes their gendered attributes, gaining victories with the use of bravery, intelligence, and elegance more than force: their activities in the resistance of 1935–41 included stealing rifles, bullets, grenades, and classified information from the Italians they socialized with; smuggling firearms in the stretchers carried at a dead's burial and in water pots they pretended fetching water with; sneaking through Italian lines and into Italian garrisons with the excuse of selling chickens, eggs, milk, and butter.[96]

Paradoxically, the Italian technological and logistical advancement in their colonial food system and attention to the quality of food the settlers of the empire enjoyed became most apparent in the darkest hour of Italian East Africa, when British colonial troops invaded Ethiopia and the Ethiopian resistance joined them to defeat Italian occupation forces in 1941 (Figure 16). While their military equipment and supply of essential resources like gas for tanks and vehicles was inferior to the British armed forces, Italians could boast much better food provisions. Pier Marcello Masotti, an Italian colonial officer deployed at Dembi Dolo, in southwestern Ethiopia, reported that

> according to British sources, Italian military warehouses at the warfront in Italian East Africa operations were fully supplied of what the British considered unnecessary luxuries, from champagne to bottled mineral water, I believe for the use of our senior officers. Dembi Dolo was not an exception. I must admit that the British, South African, and various other African colonial soldiers I met looked emaciated and seemed to have quite poorer food supplies than we did.[97]

This perception was often corroborated by the other side. The Nigerian troops that occupied Mogadishu on February 25, 1941, were shocked and excited about the booty when they found that Italians had left behind "enough food and drink to keep ten thousand men well-nourished for seven to eight months."[98]

Thus, the British colonial forces advancing from Kenya and Sudan into Italian East Africa did not only rapidly end the Italian Empire and shatter for good fascist dreams of mass settler colonialism but also left Italian settlers with a tremendous sense of loss for the vanished imperial food system upon which they had created their sense of belonging in Africa and utopia of an Italian Ethiopia. Masotti recalled that, when the Italian contingent in Dembi Dolo was eventually evacuated and marched to Addis Ababa,

> Our impression [of the capital] was strange. We realized that the last months in Dembi Dolo had not been as plentiful as before and the eighteen days of marching had made us even thinner. The other Italians we met in the city looked fat and well-fed. In the stores there were all sorts of good things, from wine to Parmesan cheese to pasta, albeit the latter made in Addis Ababa. All delicacies that—we realized—we had forgotten about. And we were mad about our own [army's] naivetés at not defending a city fully stocked with all sorts of good foods.[99]

The Ethiopian resistance enjoyed its ultimate victory in disarraying the colonial food system and killing the morale of the enemy.

Ironically, because of the disruption of international trade and communications with Italy, autarchy (national self-sufficiency with food)—which had been the primary ideological reason for Italy to invade Ethiopia but was never by far realized in East Africa—became a necessity for Italians in Ethiopia at the fall of the empire. In Italian Ethiopia, rationing began with the start of World War II in Europe, actually even before Italy entered the war. As early as September 1939, the butcher shops in Addis Ababa were closed on Tuesdays and Fridays, and restaurants could not serve meat on the same days, "for the protection of the animal populations."[100] During the fateful summer of 1940, in Addis Ababa, food stamps were introduced and all essential goods were rationed; since June 13 olive oil and sugar, since July 1 bread, pasta, wheat flour, and rice.[101] The more the war progressed, the more the settlers of the Empire of Food, for whom a tremendous system of food importing and distribution had been implemented, felt like they were let down and disappointed, as their letters that the censorship seized conveyed: "In Harar you can't find anything to eat, you can buy only with food stamps and life is hard"; "I'm sick of this life, I don't understand, they charge you four lire for a glass of wine, food is bad, and a construction worker who works every day still cannot make enough to eat"; "if it goes on like this we will starve. There's no wine, no butter, I don't remember anymore what cheese is. These are the sacrifices of Africa."[102] The collapse of the imperial infrastructure of food distribution made scarcity, all of a sudden, the dominating tone of everyday life in Italian Ethiopia, giving the settlers' sense of loss a concrete material dimension.

Italian women, who had organized most of their colonial life around cooking dinners to entertain and socialize with their local community, even in remote outposts, experienced the stoppage of food communications as a crushing blow to their project of creating "home" in Ethiopia. When in 1941 British colonial troops occupied her village and cut off Italian supply lines, the diehard fascist middle-class woman Jolanda Rapaccini made her resilient effort at making Italian dinners symbolic of Italian settlers' will to hold on to the mass colonization dream in pursuit of which they had come to Africa. For Rapaccini, to keep on making Italian food at the sunset of Italian Ethiopia—regardless of all the challenges in finding the ingredients, and so on—was an outcry against history for having unjustly stolen from them that dream (or nightmare, for the Ethiopians who toiled as her servants). In Rapaccini's remembrance, pasta appeared as usual as the ultimate comfort food in times of defeat and sorrow:

> [The men in the Italian settlement, civil engineers and army officers,] asked me if I could make some pasta for everybody. They hadn't had any pasta for a long time. God knows for how long they wouldn't eat it again. So, I promised and today I invited everybody to a pasta dinner. Very early in the morning I sent [Ethiopian servants, all young men] to look for eggs, greens, and meat. I sent Uorcù [her favorite servant boy] with a note to all my friends explaining to them what I needed to do and asking them for anything they could share to stretch my dishes. I want to make [the men] a surprise. They won't get only pasta, but a whole meal, a real meal, the best that can be made in these times. I will do anything to make the dinner perfect. The return of my messengers was successful. My friends heard my request. Some sent a can of olive oil, some a can of canned fruit, some—what a wonder—three packages of spaghetti. With the three I own I will be able to make a big pasta dinner. One of the servants did a good job and brought chickens and eggs. What I miss is the greens (*verdura*). I take courage and I go to a farmyard (*orto*) nearby. I go, I call, I look around; there's nobody here. Nobody in the house, nobody in the farmyard. I have no time, so—sometimes the end justifies the means and God forbids me—I take off my apron and steal zucchini, fennels, eggplants. When I see that I have what I need I run away with the stolen goods. At noon I set the table. The finest tablecloths, all neat, shining. I filled some vases with flowers and in the middle of the table I placed a green-white-and-red ribbon. If it wasn't for the grief we have in our hearts, it would be a feast. I dressed my darling [baby girl] with a white dress and now she stood out on her highchair. Even Simonetta is invited. She will have her food with the officers. At the last minute come the bread loaves that [officer] Vireni (in the know about the secret dinner) managed to get from the sapper army and two bottles of liquor. We also have dessert. Me and [my friend] Luisa get dressed, make ourselves beautiful, and go to the construction site. The officers are grouped together and talk among themselves. Maybe they know something? They are all shaved, well-groomed, almost elegant in their old and faded uniforms that were in the battlefield for months. We invite them. When they enter the dining room and see the preparation, they're speechless, they're confused, while we stand up happy and proud. They say that for a moment each of them believed to see their home table and praise our goodwill. They enjoy everything. At the end of the dinner we raised our glasses to the glories of the Fatherland and in the name of Italy we offered our sacrifices, our sorrows, because victory soon crowned all the efforts and the struggles of our soldiers.[103]

The excitement about making an Italian meal on African land; the exhilaration at finding the needed familiar ingredients; the ingenuity in appropriating and turning what was unfamiliar into an ingredient for "Italian" cooking; the joy of conversing with other cooks and with guests about the quality of the food, thus creating a nation of taste; the fondness for the memories of dear ones, communities, and national landscapes the food excited; the recognition of the value of packaged and canned food as mass-produced mobile means of nostalgia and identity; the paternalistic racism in the exploitation of the labor of Ethiopians constructed as inferior, uncivilized, and childish, as reaffirmed in the contrast of the tidy baby girl in a white dress who is invited to the table from which African servants are obviously excluded; the endorsement of the role fascism had prescribed for Italian women in Ethiopia as heralders of motherhood and civilization; the conflation of nation and empire into the dinner table: so many of the ideological motives that made the mobile colonial food system strategic in the making of Italian Ethiopia emerge from Rapaccini's recollection.

Empire is not just a political organization of ruling over diverse populations and lands and a system of images and meanings, but a network of conduits that connects distant places to each other, whether by ports and roads or through the circulation of material cultures. In its biopolitical frenzy, fascist imperialism in East Africa aimed at creating a colonial space of circulation of bodies, crops, agricultural and genetics technologies, foods, and culinary practices, ultimately intended to support demographic expansion. The fascist model of mass colonization between 1935 and 1941 centered on the transplantation of life from the Motherland to the new colony of Ethiopia and the realization of demographic settler colonialism so as to make the imperial farmland space homogeneous and continuous and Ethiopia just another part of Greater Italy. Within this plan, fascists regarded Ethiopians, Ethiopian agriculture, and Ethiopian human landscapes as inherently inferior and deemed to ultimately disappear under Italian civilization. Actually, the most noted legacy of the hypermodern and technologically advanced Italian aggression and occupation of Ethiopia is the construction of a detailed road infrastructure, which was vital for establishing a system of food transport and distribution aimed at guaranteeing total food sovereignty to Italian settlers. As a consequence, Italian settlers in Ethiopia participated in a modern consumer society and levels of private consumption and social mobility that many other Italians would have experienced only well after World War II, in the years of the Italian "economic boom." Ironically, this ambitious project of logistics and mobility development absorbed so many resources to flounder the overall plan of mass colonization of Ethiopia it was supposed to serve and being a strategic element of. The Ethiopian resistance grasped the vital importance of the mobile colonial food system Italians were completing for the fascist scheme of oppression and domination and made the destruction of it—whether through nonviolent passive resistance or guerrilla warfare—the core of their anti-colonial struggle to repossess their land and own food sovereignty. The fascist project for mass colonization, imperialist technology transfer, and destruction of Ethiopian biodiversity and cultural diversity unchained the anti-imperialist forces that brought to its demise.

Part II

Colonial Gastronomies: Food Apartheid, Intercultural Practices of Taste, and the Senses

4

Forbidden Commensality in a Supremacist Society: Food and Racial Segregation in Italian Ethiopia

Besides demographic colonialism and advanced-technology bioimperialism, the third defining factor shaping the dynamics of food in Italian East Africa was organized state racism. Unlike the politics of race in the British colonies of sub-Saharan Africa, the Caribbean, and Southeast Asia, where a small number of Europeans exploited a much larger local population and where racism was a product of colonialism itself, Italian racism was legally, politically, and culturally programmed in advance. Racist practices were imposed by the fascist regime as a founding requisite meant to be rigorously enacted by Italian settlers in everyday interaction with local populations—or to force them to abstain from any interaction.

As they were in the programming of colonial agriculture, scientists and pseudoscientists were called to advance fascist imperialism. The goal was to legitimize Mussolini's proclamation of the superiority of an unquestionably White Italian race—and, from the late 1930s on, an "Aryan" one—which was to be defended, improved, and promoted in a Foucauldian political-scientific discourse of power/knowledge.[1] The *Manifesto of Race* was originally published in the *Giornale d'Italia* on July 14, 1938, under the title *Il fascismo e i problemi della razza* (Fascism and the Problem of Race). Widely attributed to ten racist scientists—among them the physiologist Sabato Visco, one of the principal scholars of East African foodways at the time—the ideas elaborated in the *Manifesto* had largely been the work of Mussolini himself.[2]

As developed in the *Manifesto* and journals such as *La stirpe* (Ancestry) (1937), *La difesa della razza* (1938), and *Razza e civiltà* (Race and Civilization) (1940), fascist scientific-political racism was particularly concerned with "racial purity" and ways to prevent miscegenation in the colonies. In the oldest colony of Eritrea, concubinage and intermarriage between indigenous women and Italian men had been widespread. Marriages were celebrated according to local rituals, but were not recognized by the Italian law, and it was not binding on Italian men, sometimes already married in Italy, to support native women and the children born of the "marriage." So common were these arrangements that a term was coined to describe them: *madamismo* or *madamato*, from *madama*, which identified the African woman involved in a marriage-like relationship with an Italian man, while *sciarmutta*—the Italianization of the Arabic *sharmāta*—identified the prostitute. Each type of union produced many children to whom Italy granted citizenship if their fathers had legally recognized them, or, if they were illegitimate, their phenotypic looks showed the court that their biological father was Italian.[3]

With the occupation of Ethiopia, the colonial authorities' obsession about preventing the production of biracial bodies prompted the planned migration of Italian women to Ethiopia (later on, only married men and families could migrate), the opening of racially segregated brothels, and the prohibiting of interracial cohabitation and sexual promiscuity.[4] Just three months after Italian troops entered Addis Ababa, the Italian Minister of Colonies Alessandro Lessona telegraphed Viceroy Graziani the orders for the organization of the empire, including the section *Rapporti tra nazionali e indigeni* (Relationships between Nationals and Indigenous People):

> The conquest of the Empire imposes on us obligations of moral and political nature. In Italian East Africa, Italians must conduct absolutely distinct lives from indigenous people. This colonial government will hence enforce that, a) the quarters of nationals are separated from those of indigenous people; b) any familiarity between the two races is prohibited; c) public premises and facilities [such as restaurants, bars, food stores, and markets] patronized by White people cannot be patronized by indigenous people.

> The regulations

> 1) Oblige every married male settler to bring their family to the colony as soon as circumstances allow for it. Superiors must lead by example. While before they would say that colonies were for singles, in fascist times we will say that the colony is for the married. In the second phase this will be a prerequisite to move to Africa. 2) Limit to the maximum extent, through police enforcement, any contact between national [men] and indigenous women. Those—especially public officials or officers—who practice the intimate life characteristic of marriages with indigenous women must be immediately repatriated. 3) As long as local conditions impose the stay in East Africa of masses of soldiers and workers who, for different difficulties of life, cannot bring with them their families, set up whorehouses, even itinerant, with White women, strictly forbidding the access to Ethiopians.[5]

Food, Sex, and Intimacy: The Racial Segregation of Eating in Domestic Spaces

As Ann Laura Stoler has theorized, the political-legal control of interracial sexuality was the cornerstone of control of social relations in European colonies in Africa, Asia, and Latin America.[6] A 1937 law (Regio Decreto Legge 19 aprile 1937, n. 880, Sanzioni per il rapporto d'indole coniugale fra cittadini e sudditi (Sanctions against Intimate Relationships between Citizens and Colonial Subjects)) punished Italian men with one to five years in prison if they were caught living with indigenous women. At the same time, love and sex between Italian women and African men was considered such an aberration that no legislation was thought necessary to suppress it.[7]

Under the 1937 sanctions, prohibitions against interracial familiarity, intimacy, sex, and love were broadened to include the preparation, sharing, and consumption of food between Italians and Ethiopians in the privacy of the home. Colonial courts typically found Italian men guilty of *madamismo* if there was proof of either repeated sexual contact or the sharing of meals, both acts demonstrating "beyond any doubt" the existence of a monogamous relationship comparable to marriage. Eating the same food together at the same table, unlike the "racially correct" scenario in which a Black woman cooked for and served a White man, signaled a dangerously egalitarian relation and some level of interracial emotional involvement.[8] In the Italian colonies, the body was the preferred ground for political action and control, obsessively exercised on the primary functions of sex and eating.[9]

On January 13, 1938, the Court of Addis Ababa sentenced an Italian man, Giuseppe Puccinelli, to one year in jail for having lived for three months under the same roof with an Ethiopian woman as husband and wife, sleeping in the same bed, eating the same food at the same table, and, even worse, eating from the same plate. Ascale Zewde, the Ethiopian woman, did not receive any money either for sex or for domestic service. Having ruled out the existence of prostitution or paid domestic work, which would have exonerated him, the court's decision demonstrated vividly that sharing food proved the affective dimension of the relationship and thus Puccinelli's guilt. "If these are the evidences, everything suggests that the two suspects conducted by any means a conjugal relationship," the court concluded.[10]

Italian men suspected of *madamato* could escape legal punishment if they were able to prove in court *not* to have shared food with an African woman. In another case, the Court of Appeal of Addis Ababa acquitted one Mr. Manca from the charge of "conjugal-like interracial union" because the Ethiopian woman Manca, claimed to have been hired as his servant, "was still living in her own home and was not admitted to the table of her master."[11] Another defendant also eluded jail and deportation for the same crime because "the indigenous woman had her meals at a different time and place from the Italian."[12]

The colonial courts also condemned the fairly widespread custom of an Italian man hiring an Ethiopian woman as a domestic helper but whose role would later be expanded to that of "wife," a new status defined by her preparation of shared meals. In 1939, the Court of Gondar ruled against a defendant couple when the indigenous woman testified that she, Desta Agos,

> came to Gondar about four months ago and here she met Mr. Spano, who asked her to live with him "as his wife," and she accepted, so he fired the indigenous boy who was his live-in servant; they lived together for three months, he paid for all bills, while she did all housework and cooked all the food, which they consumed together at the same table.[13]

The fascist politics of the body directly connected the consumption of food to the consumption of sex. Interracial heterosexual conviviality was repressed, since acts of intimacy, affection, and care could lead to miscegenation, the procreation of mixed-race children, and damage to the "prestige of the race." Eating the same food threatened to create the same blood and the same flesh in White and Black bodies.

In a 1940 guilty verdict against Luigi M., the Court of Asmara sentenced him for the crime of *madamismo*. The indictment against Luigi M. for the crime under *atti lesivi del prestigio di razza* (acts harmful to Italian racial prestige) had been issued when Cagigia (likely Khadija) I., an eighteen-year-old Muslim woman, went to the colonial police station with her face covered in blood, claiming that she was attacked by Luigi M., her cohabitant. To defend himself from the accusation of concubinage that had followed from Khadija's testimony, Luigi M. told the judge that he had hired her as domestic help, paying her regularly. He confessed that he repeatedly took advantage of her sexually but with no amorous intent or involvement. However, upset that Khadija "granted her [sexual] favors [also] to others," he admitted that he often beat her and did disfigure her with a knife to teach her a lesson. Khadija's version of the facts differed substantially from that of Luigi, however. Her testimony—that she had been living in the same room with Luigi and that he treated her as "his wife," sharing meals with her daily—moved the court to sentence Luigi to eight months' imprisonment for "acts damaging the prestige of the race."[14]

Trial records are among the few available sources that illuminate the experiences of Ethiopian and Eritrean women involved with Italian men. The women were often victims of violence and rape, and the racism of colonial society, as they were despised and disavowed by their own communities. *Madamas* also faced extreme material insecurity working for Italian men, who would often abandon them for new relationships. Their own families and communities having been torn apart by the war and invasion, for these women being "fired" by the Italian man and barred from returning to their own patriarchal society left them no other choice than resorting to prostitution. In some cases, however, *madamas* were able to carve spaces of autonomy and social mobility around their relationships with Italian men, as suggested by their willingness to press charges against the abuses and restrictions they suffered. They would also find ways to transfer some economic benefits they gained from these relationships to the Ethiopian community: "Depending on the perspective of the narrative, these women led multiple lives as concubines, spies [for the anticolonial resistance], whores, and heroines."[15]

Colonial authorities constantly sought ways to repress any contact between Italian men and Ethiopian women in the private sphere. One way was to pressure settlers—single men or families—to hire African men exclusively as domestic help. In a short time, the homes of settlers, including those who in Italy could have never afforded any domestic staff—swelled with Ethiopian men, for the most part young and very young (including children), who cleaned, washed, shopped, cooked, and served meals. In many Ethiopian ethnic cultures, men and boys working as domestic labor faced the humiliation of stigma—their work was considered emasculating and infantilizing. Some, as will be discussed later, were often sexually exploited by their masters.

Even if in the vast majority of Italian homes servants were all males, and the possibility of miscegenation not a serious threat, the architecture of segregation organized domestic space to minimize interracial contacts. Civil engineer Giorgio Rigotti (1905–2000), the author of the most comprehensive study of residential architecture in Italian East Africa, noted that the design of Italian settlers' homes reproduced racial segregation, especially in response to the presence of a large number of Ethiopian men as cleaners, janitors, handymen, cooks, and waiters. In the Italian homes he visited, Rigotti found that

> in the plans we note right away a clear division between the house of the master, that of the [Ethiopian] servants and the utility buildings. The master's house is in the center of the plot as far as possible from it are the servants' quarters; near the master's house but well separated from it are the utility buildings. Surrounding the buildings, there is much open space, many trees and fields.[16]

"The plan of the villa has nothing particular to recommend it," noted Rigotti.

> It is shaped by the usual corridor that leads from the entrance to each of the rooms, an extremely banal solution. However, we find in it a clear separation between daytime areas, nighttime areas, and service areas. The door that normally divides the corridor in two is usually closed and separates the masters' area from the service area. [Only] the dining room has two doors, which respectively lead to the two domains.[17]

As the historian of Italian colonial architecture Mia Fuller has pointed out, only the consumption of meals and the "need" to consume the service work of Ethiopian boys connected two otherwise separate sections of the house. Rigotti continued:

> The servants of color thus have their own passage within the master's house. Service comes down to the simple "boy," as the other servants are hardly ever admitted into the residence. Usually the boy does not go beyond the already mentioned door. He goes to the dining area to prepare the table and remains there throughout the meal. He does not enter the other rooms unless he is called there, and he only goes there for cleaning and for service. The servants' house, on the other hand, is of the characteristic construction type of the tukul; in each room lives a servant with his or her own family. A row of plants isolates and nearly hides the building. These families have nothing to do with the masters, the entrance to the villa is forbidden to them, and they may not circulate on the grounds. The service of the European master consists of a boy, who by rights lives with his family on the master's land, a gardener, a cook, and a night guardian. The master normally gives his orders to the boy, who represents the head of the servants, and he reports orders to the other servants.[18]

For the Prestige of the Race: The Racial Segregation of Eating in Public Spaces

The segregation of domestic space was a more intimate version of the segregation of public spaces—particularly those intended for public food distribution and consumption. It was pursued by Mussolini, Lessona, and local authorities throughout

Italian East Africa, and implemented by a cadre of urban planners, architects, and civil engineers under their command. In particular, the racial floor plan of colonists' houses faithfully reproduced on a smaller scale the racial layout of the food markets in Addis Ababa, with separate paths and entrances for Black and White people aimed at minimizing any interracial contact, visual or otherwise. In Lessona's instructions to Graziani on "Relations between Nationals and Natives," fascist authorities installed racial segregation in the most complete and systematic way possible—most notably in the food exchanges between different races in food markets, shops, bars, cafes, restaurants, and hotels (Figure 28).

A vast literature has shown how racial segregation in colonial and postcolonial contexts, such as apartheid South Africa, controlled the very visible spaces connected to food. In the southern United States, from the end of Reconstruction to the civil rights movement in the mid-1960s, Jim Crow laws thoroughly segregated these same spaces. Civil rights movements from the late 1950s to the 1960s struggled to claim the right of Black customers to be served in places reserved for Whites; the most well-known of these protests was the sit-in movement at a lunch counter in downtown Greensboro, North Carolina, in 1960.[19]

A similar ideology linked the racial segregation of these spaces in the Jim Crow United States, apartheid South Africa, and Italian East Africa: the fear that desegregated restaurants, cafes, and bars would destroy White supremacy. Although in Italian East Africa there was often no separation, and usually some physical proximity, between White and Black subjects in colonial kitchen and table service work, only Whites could be served by Blacks, never vice versa.

A second fear concerned contemporary European culinary and hospitality practices, which were carefully contrasted with the incompetence, backwardness, and lack of both cleanliness and taste associated with Black eating habits. Commensality and conviviality reproduce, more than any other social activity, structures of inclusion, belonging, and group solidarity. Excluding Black people from dining alongside White people meant excluding them from the larger sphere of cuisine as a practice and tradition that affirmed European superiority, while "protecting" White diners from the spectacle of "wild" Black diners.

The third fear was related to the world of the senses and the perceived bodily distinctions created by race. The act of "lip contact with the product" (food) distinguished restaurants, cafes, and bars from other racially segregated spaces such as public transport, cinemas, and dance halls. The contact with Black lips was believed to contaminate cups, glasses, and plates with fluids that were thought to be doubly infectious—medically and socially. In places dedicated to serving and eating food, the sensory construction of the Black body, from smell to touch to sight, articulated as otherness or disgust, was charged with a special intensity.

Finally, the last fear concerned the protection of White women who frequented places designated for food consumption from exposure to Black men, considered the most dangerous threat to their sexuality and honor.[20]

Not surprisingly, the laws of Italian East Africa reflected these anxieties about interracial contacts in public places. On June 12, 1936, Minister of Colonies Lessona wired Viceroy Graziani about rumors that, in the hotels of Addis Ababa, "Italian waiters and Ethiopian servants were socializing among themselves." He ordered Graziani to put an immediate end to the practice.[21] Undersecretary of the Ministry of Italian Africa Attilio Teruzzi alerted Graziani in a 1937 telegram that some Italian shopkeepers were suspected of serving Ethiopian customers. "It is recommended that an absolute separation be maintained between Italians and Ethiopians in public places and in shops; it must always be absolutely prevented that a native is served by a White person in these places."[22]

The segregation of public spaces derived for the most part from Mussolini's idea of the "prestige of race," a fundamental value to be defended at all costs and to be internalized by all colonizers. Paradoxically, though, the most significant threat to the "prestige of race" came from the type of mass demographic, or classical-agrarian, colonization that Mussolini had chosen for Ethiopia. Italian peasants and proletarians who migrated to Ethiopia to become colonizers found that they had to pave roads or turn the soil on which they would settle, providing the unskilled labor that other Europeans such as the English and French required of their colonized people. For fascists, however, it was essential to hide the spectacle of toiling, idle, or poor Italians from the view of supposedly "inferior" Ethiopians. When they did observe the misery endured by settlers, Ethiopians regularly commented that Italians had brought with them their "White slaves," or, more typically, their "White Gurage," after the principal ethnic group performing servile work for the Amhara.[23]

Mussolini made clear the uses of segregation in a speech to the National Council of the Fascist National Party on October 25, 1938:

> The lack of racial dignity had very serious consequences in the [Governorate of] Amhara and was one of the causes of the Amhara uprising. The Amhara had no intention of rebelling against Italian rule, no interest in doing so. But when they saw Italians who were shabbier than them, living in dirty tukuls (huts), they said, "This is not a race that brings civilization." And since the Amhara are the most aristocratic race in Ethiopia, they rebelled. That is why the racial laws of the Empire will be strictly enforced and anyone who violates them will be expelled, deported, punished, or imprisoned. Because for the Empire to be preserved, the indigenous people must have a clear, strong understanding of our superiority.[24]

Following Mussolini's speech, in 1936 Lessona ordered Graziani to ensure that

> in Italian East Africa White people must lead a life clearly distinct from that of the Ethiopians. This General Government will provide, in the meantime: a) that the homes of Italians and those of Ethiopians be kept separate; b) that familiarity between the two races be avoided; c) that public places frequented by White people [such as bars] are not frequented by Ethiopians.[25]

On June 12, 1937, in Decree no. 620208, the governor of Eritrea, Admiral Vincenzo De Feo (1876–1955), forbade Italians and European foreigners from living in neighborhoods inhabited by native people and in native villages on the outskirts of cities. On July 1, 1937, with Decree no. 12723, the Governor of Somalia, General

Ruggero Santini (1870–1958), prohibited "metropolitan citizens [Italians] from frequenting public places managed by native people," threatening "severe penalties on offenders." The rules for racial segregation of public spaces were posted in Ethiopian cities and villages. "Within a few weeks, therefore, [in Ethiopia] the partitioning of public places (bars, restaurants, cinemas, hotels)" into separate White and Black spaces was completed.[26] On June 29, 1939, Law no. 1004 established the crime of "injury to the prestige of the race," sanctions throughout Italian East Africa. In addition to strengthening the prohibition against "conjugal relations" (Article 10), the focus of legislation of 1937, the law made it a crime for an Italian settler to patronize a restaurant or bar reserved for Black people, with "imprisonment for up to six months or a fine of up to 2,000 lire" (Article 12).

The effects of segregation were first felt most vividly by Eritreans, who, unlike Ethiopians, had had lived under decades of Italian colonization, from the liberal to the preimperial fascist era (1890, when the colony of Eritrea was founded, to 1922, the advent of fascism). Born in Eritrea in 1909, H.Y. recalled that

> when the Mussolini era came, things changed and strong racial discrimination began. We couldn't go [anymore] in places where the White people went, this was for White people, this for Black people, there was a distinction of race. We Eritreans could not in any case go to places reserved for Italians, if we entered they kicked us and sent us out. We were treated like dogs, like animals, not like human beings. For example, they didn't give us a glass to drink, but a can or a zinc box, we couldn't do what the Whites did.[27]

M.G., born in Eritrea in 1913 and a veteran of the Italian colonial army, illustrated the direct connection between the segregation of food spaces and the hardening of racist ideology:

> I was a soldier for the Italians; I was in Libya, on the side of Benghazi, and then also in Cyrenaica. Then, after returning from Libya, my comrades and I went to Ethiopia, we conquered Ethiopia. After the conquest, I stayed there for five or six years, in the Italian Empire in Ethiopia. There were numerous discriminations there, for example in bars, restaurants, and shops. They gave us food separately, we couldn't join the Italians, and this hurt us.[28]

The Eritreans could easily appreciate the painful effects of the segregation of food spaces in the new East African Empire; they saw clearly that the policy was the cornerstone of racist ideology and fascist colonialism: "For example, in bars, the bar was divided into two, one for the Eritreans and one for the White people, and then the Eritreans felt offended," Asfaha Chasai said in an interview.[29] "You couldn't ride in a car with Italians," remembered Paulos Tesfemariam. "Everything was divided both in bars and on the bus. We couldn't pass through the wheat market, there were the Carabinieri who would arrest you if you did. They called us *negri* [niggers, in Italian in the original]."[30]

The Racial Segregation of Eating in Roadside Grocery Stores and Restaurants

Italy's attempt to colonize Ethiopia created a varied landscape of segregated commercial establishments and public spaces for eating and drinking. The urban markets, the grocery stores selling imported products, and the roadside restaurants that sprang up along new roads fed the people of Italian East Africa, serving different types of consumers and implementing different degrees and modalities of racial segregation. They were nodes in an ambitious system for feeding the empire.

The informal roadside grocery stores or work camp/military camp stores known as *spacci alimentari* were an original colonial institution that made possible the widespread mobility of food (Figure 17). The *Guida dell'Africa Orientale Italiana* (Guide to Italian East Africa) published in 1937 by the Italian Tourist Board noted that "everywhere along the roads, near the construction sites and markets, are *spacci*, which can be said to be a typical institution of Italian East Africa; the simplest expression of the colonial warehouse, generally shacks built with makeshift wood, packaging boxes, etc., or huts that can be easily transported elsewhere according to the changing flows of traffic or construction work."[31] The *spaccio* in Adi Kuala was a simple shack next to a state-owned Agip gas station, where "the petty vendor, among mountains of caciocavallo cheese and bars of green soap, displays bunches of spaghetti tied with a green, white, and red ribbon."[32] The *spacci* were filled mostly with imported foods that could last for months: "Every one, even the smallest [among *spacci*], offers canned food, cured meats, cheeses, pasta, wine, beer, sodas, liquors, etc. More rarely, fruit and vegetables can also be found," warned the *Guida*.[33]

The grocers of the *spacci* (*spaccisti*) were generally immigrants, demobilized soldiers, truck drivers, or construction workers with an entrepreneurial spirit, a little capital, and family members or acquaintances who would work at minimal cost. These microbusinesses were by their nature fragile enterprises, subject to volatile market and political conditions, as well as the vagaries of corruption associated with obtaining licenses, supplies, and police protection. A young immigrant girl in Jimma recalled the *spaccio* her father opened in a building purchased from an Ethiopian:

> The new building is ready, it has whitewashed brick walls, a metal roof, fabric ceilings, and terracotta floors. It has two entrances: one for the house and one for the store. The store is furnished with many shelves loaded with food. On the counter, the cash register brought from Italy is on display. Its bell rings a few times; customers are scarce. Although the grocery store is located on the main avenue that leads from Jimma to Giren, it is not in the city center where the mass of White people lives. "We are in the outskirts of town," says my father, "but the land in the city center is only for the friends of the fascist higher officers and for those who came here to fight, not for those who want to start a business and do not engage in politics. Here, as in Italy, if you do not engage in politics, you do not work; it is always the same story."[34]

A note from Poggiali's secret diary confirmed how political power and the corruption it generated controlled the economic life of the *spacci* and the *spaccisti* through taxes and access to licenses. The popular notion of *spaccisti* as adventurous, independent risktakers was, in reality, mostly myth. "[Along] the Addis Ababa-Eritrea road, construction workers party with songs, shoutings, and wine drinking at the *spacci*; those *spacci* which, as they say, have been lucratively monopolized by and made the fortune of [Arrigo] Chiavegatti, [Alessandro] Melchiori, and other fascist leaders."[35]

In *La via nera* (The Black Way), a collection of travel reporting on Ethiopia from the early years of the occupation, Orio Vergani offered romantic accounts of *spacci* and *spaccisti*, including the first store he encountered in Keren on the mountain road that ran from Eritrea down into Ethiopia:

> Illuminated in that first darkness of dusk like a cave of a hundred wonders, [the *spaccio*] exhibited the glory of thousands and thousands of tomato and fruit cans, ancient candy jars, and a towering machine for slicing ham. Mr. Peppino himself, whose name appeared in capital letters three-foot high on the plaster of the house, had come to bring us a greenish liquor diluted with a little soda water.[36]

These *spaccisti*, many like Peppino migrants from elsewhere in the colony, opened their modest shops in isolated places, where their chromed salami slicers offered a glimpse of modernity. Stores could close fairly quickly as nearby roads were completed and workers moved on, but the *spaccisti* were regularly praised for their tenacious attempts to become self-employed microcapitalists. "One day the *spacci* will be just a memory," Vergani noted.

> But they bravely did their part in the war and they are bravely doing their part now, on the endless road that crosses the conquered country. I want to praise the *spaccisti* who for seven hundred miles of road always found a way to give me a bottle of mineral water or a slice of salami, alone in their tent, alone in their shack, alone for six months, for a year, who knows for how long, in the middle of a meadow, sheltered by a clump of euphorbia, leaning against a rock, young men who have their girlfriend four thousand miles away, others who have four children at home.[37]

The *spacci*'s clientele were typically the transient workers building the infrastructures of the empire. At some point, the work would be finished and the *spaccio* would be gone, its mission accomplished. Vergani again:

> First there were soldiers. Now there are workers from the construction sites who are completing the great backbone road of the Empire. The road is almost finished: every fifty, every hundred kilometers a city was born, a village of sheet metal, with an inn, trattorias, shops, warehouses full of everything, and the *spaccista* now has little left to do. The more comfortable the road, the thinner the business becomes. Who stops at the *spaccio* anymore?[38]

Figure 17 A *spaccio* (informal grocery store) in a construction camp, October 1935. Courtesy of Archivio Luce.

Racially segregated roadside grocery stores functioned as micro nodes in the extensive network of distribution of food imported from Italy across Ethiopian territory as well as sites of socialization, information exchange, and diasporic identity formation for Italians in East Africa.

Yet, despite the impermanence of the *spacci*, *spaccisti* became heroic figures in the imperial project.

> The *spaccista* with the cyclist hat is capable of driving a truck and cooking minestrone, learning Tigrinya in ten days and answering workers and soldiers in ten Italian dialects. An hour after the conquest [of Ethiopia], while the wounded were still being taken away, he was already there: "Who wants a bottle of mineral water?" "Who wants to upgrade their army ration with a good can of *antipasti*?"[39]

In the anthropology of the *spaccio* and the roles played by its toiling migrant entrepreneurs, the selling of imported food in "ethnic" shops also served larger symbolic purposes. Just as it does in the twenty-first century for Indian women in the Bay Area of San Francisco or Arab women in Edmonton, the makeshift *spacci* along the rough roads of Ethiopia were centers of diasporic identity for migrant Italian travelers, workers, and soldiers in the 1930s. Inside the *spacci*, *Italianità* was displayed in the names, colors, flavors, smells, and brands of the food and drink for sale ("the bottle of mineral water," "the can of antipasti") in a space also filled with the voices

Figure 18 Italian supermarket in Addis Ababa, October–December 1936. Courtesy of Archivio Luce.

of Italian language radio and piles of newspapers from home. Grocery stores became transnational, multisensory places of belonging, building a diasporic nationalism based on food from thousands of miles away. These simple stores enabled conversations that created a common "language" for immigrants from different regions of Italy and a haven from the "outside world" of East Africa—a human landscape polarized between Italian Whites and Ethiopian Blacks.[40]

The *spacci* held deep emotional significance for Italian settlers. "Where did they find these mysterious mineral waters that come out from under the counter with a crust of straw and mud that is, like the dust for old wine bottles, the guarantee of their authenticity?" Vergani wondered.

> And where did these Chianti, Grignolino, Bardolino wines with obscure labels come from? Mysterious ubiquity of vermouth factories, mysterious sources of iodine and iron-rich water, mysterious alchemies of *antipasti-giardiniera*. The vendor doesn't even know where he found this stuff, how many hands it has passed through, what commission scheme it has set in motion, how many typewriters have worked to send it to its destination, how many trains, ships, and trucks have worked to bring it here. Who will write the history of a salami that starts from Lombardy and arrives, intact, at kilometer 931 of the Asmara–Addis Ababa road, and waits there for a month, two, three, attached to a string, until a worker, seized

by nostalgia for a *cacciatore* salami, points to it, to go to the shade of a tree to cut off a few nice slices, pressing it with a knife on the thumb? Night falls, the stars come up, and the eyes of the jackals light up in the dark. [The grocer] does the accounts by candlelight: "Three soaps, two mineral waters, a mirror, two pencils, six envelopes, four salamis, a vermouth."[41]

The comforts of diasporic belonging on display inside the *spacci* were constructed primarily by excluding Ethiopians from spaces where Italians practiced their *Italianità* on their own. "African native subjects" were allowed access to Italian food only when serving it to the master race. An African veteran of the Italian colonial army, Asfaha Chasai, described an encounter with a *spaccista* that illuminates how food reaffirmed White power:

I was in Dessie, I walked in a bar—it was not a classy bar, it was a *spaccio*—I go to the grocer who was Italian and ask him: "Do you have any food?" "No," because he doesn't want to give me any. "And what canned food do you have?" "We only have these canned beans." "Alright, what can I do? I'm hungry, give it to me." He opens [the can] and tells me "Go, go outside, eat outside." I said "no" but went outside. I experienced this. This is the main reason, racial discrimination, that created antagonism between us and Italians.[42]

Chasai's testimony vividly demonstrates how the segregation of food helped construct a separate White society in Italian East Africa and control both colonized people and "poor Whites" (Italian proletarian immigrants).[43] The obscenity of colonial racism and racial segregation prevented any form of closeness and equality and reversed social relations, giving supreme power (over access to food and consumption spaces) to Italians even if they were socially underclass and of low status in the army. The humble grocery stores temporarily set up on the streets of Ethiopia thus became theaters where Mussolini's discourse on the "prestige of the race" and, in W. E. B. Du Bois's definition, the "wages of Whiteness" that Italian colonizers were quickly learning to appreciate were being represented.[44]

The unequal power relations at work inside the *spacci* were also manifested in another scenario, one equally criminalized by colonial law. In this case, Italians, "forced by circumstances," patronized grocery stores run by Ethiopians. In a trial at the Asmara Court, four Italian workers were charged with "acts that damaged the prestige of the race" because they shopped in a grocery store run by the "African subject" Bairu C., near an Italian construction site—rather than for the acts of violence and theft they had committed on the premises.

In September 1936, the workers went to Bairu's store around eleven p.m., after closing time, to drink and sleep with [Bairu's] indigenous servant, with whom they had spent the evening singing *Faccetta Nera*. When Bairu refused to serve them more alcohol, Vittorio S. kicked and shoved the door of the place, grabbed the man by the neck, and threatened him with a gun. Having managed to break free, Bairu ran away into the open country. Hailu A., his assistant, did the same. When

Bairu returned to the store, he noticed that eight bottles of beer and two bottles of vermouth were missing.

The four Italians were acquitted of theft, and, more significantly, their sentences were suspended provided they refrained for five years from committing acts that could damage the prestige of the race.[45]

The fact that *spacci* were contested spaces of segregation, racism, and conflict as well as essential local institutions made the stores, just like the trains and trucks that supplied them, key targets of the Ethiopian resistance. In his private diary, Poggiali reported on an assault on the train he was taking from Djibouti to Addis Ababa and the following siege carried out by Ethiopian patriots of the town of Mojo. Poggiali took refuge in a grocery store run by a Greek citizen—racially "neutral" —while guerrilla warfare between Italian troops and Abyssinian resistance fighters raged just outside town:

> Squalid breakfast in the Greek inn by the station, whose owner, still uncertain about the fate of the battle and perhaps hopeful that the rebels would be victorious, cannot decide to bring out all the food he certainly keeps hidden, because he does not want to run out of it in the event that the victorious rebels question him about his stand. With my usual practical sense, I rummage around and search in every corner of the shack and discover a salami hidden in a terracotta pot. And without much ado, I eat it. You have to understand the psychology of the innkeeper: he has been the concessionaire of the train station restaurant for decades, which has represented a bonanza for him; he understands that with the advent of the Italians, the bonanza is over and therefore hates us.[46]

Poggiali also noted massive amounts of leaflets in Amharic urging Ethiopian guerrillas to strike at Italian food supply lines, "in order to starve the capital [Addis Ababa], whose sustenance depends on the food it receives daily from Djibouti." Destroying the *spacci* would also destroy the Empire of Food.[47]

Racial segregation was as intensely cultivated in the trattorias (informal roadside restaurants) operated by settlers and settler families that served the truck drivers who traveled between Ethiopia and the other colonies of Eritrea and Somalia. Recalling tastes, memories, and "visions of the world" with the food they served, trattorias reproduced racist differences not only between Italian Whites and Ethiopian Blacks but also between Italian settlers from different regions, particularly Northerners and Southerners.

The tourist *Guide to Italian East Africa* described trattorias as functional extensions of *spacci*, advising travelers that "in smaller towns, at the main stops along the roads, there are grocery stores-restaurants, generally in makeshift huts or shacks."[48] In a report for the *Corriere della Sera*, Malaparte described stopping at a trattoria on the road between Adwa and Axum. He saw in the simple restaurant an opportunity for workers from Romagna and the Veneto to socialize and enjoy familiar foods. The trattoria was

> crowded with drivers and the smell of beer and salami. Two Venetian workers talk to each other and the words flutter like yellow paper in the thick air of sun and flies. The gardens, freshly watered around the shacks, and the girl who enters the tavern

with a large basket of salad under her arm, saying in Romagna dialect: "guys, it will rain soon!" and everyone stands at the door, looking up at a cloud of locusts from behind the Leper Mountain.[49]

The trattoria as gathering place offered an intimate "inside" of familiar smells of beer, salami, and lovingly cultivated gardens, against an "outside," Africa, whose "thick air of sun and flies" held the threat of locusts, diseases, and attacks by Ethiopian partisans. Malaparte was well aware of those African dangers, unmentioned in official propaganda, as he always traveled with colonial troops of *Askaris* fighting the local guerrillas of commander *Ras* Abebe Aregai (1903–1960).

Malaparte's reporting is filled with imperial themes: the fertility of Italian peasant women and the social production of the new Italians of Africa; bread as the staple food of the diet and identity of the colonizers; and the constant movement of foodstuffs along new road.

> In front of the tin-roofed shack, the pregnant woman calls out: "Giovanni! Giovanni!" and I look at her fat elbows, broad shoulders, and protruding hips, until a child appears in the doorway holding a huge slice of bread in both hands that hides his face up to his eyes. And suddenly in the distance, the roar of engines can be heard, a column of trucks enters the square: and immediately the square is full of a happy commotion, voices, laughter, cheerful calls, to which the clinking of glasses from inside the tavern harmonizes, as the regulars line up in great haste at the bar counter.[50]

Popular memoirs also praised the heroic work of the pioneers who built and operated trattorias on the colonial frontier. Alda Brunelli left Romagna at the age of twelve, accompanying her parents who opened a trattoria in Ginda on the Massawa–Asmara trucking route. Brunelli emphasized the courage of immigrant entrepreneurs like her parents in opening a business on a still unconquered part of the empire. She hints at how this "courage," learned in the colony, assumed the need for violence and the subjugation of Ethiopians for their labor:

> My father obtained permission to build a restaurant on the road that connected Massawa to Asmara. It was a completely deserted location, a few miles from Ginda, where there was a railway station, a general store, the Vice Intendent's office, telegraph, and telephone. Masons and carpenters, both indigenous and Italian, arrived, and for a few months the construction site resounded with songs that accompanied the work of the native people, but were overwhelmed by the exhortations of the White people, almost always in the Romagnolo dialect, which urged them to work harder.[51]

> My father and mother were on the site from the beginning of the work, and, until a house could be built to accommodate them, their home was a truck container, covered with a tarpaulin, where two cots had been arranged, divided by a crate that served as a small table and a kerosene lamp as the only lighting. Above one cot hung my father's hunting rifle, which my mother had also learned to use in

case of any eventuality. For cooking meals, a rustic brick stove, which ran on wood, provided the necessary food for about twenty people. On the slope of the hill above the restaurant, two huge concrete tanks were rising that would be the reservoirs for the water necessary for the "village," a cluster of buildings that included the bakery, the warehouse, the workshop with the generator that provided electricity to the entire complex, and further back, the barracks for Eritrean workers and their toilet facilities. Further back, there were vegetable gardens and a chicken coop with a noisy colony of guinea fowls. To the right of the restaurant, there was a large sycamore tree that shaded a platform where you could dine and sometimes even dance. Just a little higher up, a small house, overlooking one of the tanks, housed the Italian employees; the cooks, drivers, and baker. Behind the restaurant, a slightly sloping hill led to two pretty villas, framed by papaya trees: one was our home, the other could accommodate a friend or relative who had come to visit us.[52]

Brunelli's memoir reveals much about cuisine as a source of diasporic identities. In this as in other documents, tagliatelle (long egg noodles) emerges as the most distinctive and widespread food in the restaurants of Italian East Africa. Easy to prepare, tagliatelle required inexpensive all-purpose wheat flour, the staple most imported from Italy; local eggs; and water, which, once boiled, lost its threatening "Ethiopianness." Tagliatelle was profitable and more than any other food tasted of "home," of comforting Sunday family dinners. They were made with the "good" ingredients of Italian culinary civilization, gifts of the earth (golden, nourishing wheat) and the timeless rural cycle of birth and resurrection (eggs, with their life-giving proteins and ability to turn flour into food). For these reasons, throughout Italy egg noodles were reserved for holidays and expressed a sense of family festivity. Unlike commercial dried pasta, which had to be made from more expensive durum wheat, homemade egg noodles embodied the loving work of a homemaker, a substitute "mom" for the many single men who worked as truck drivers, road builders, and government employees. Tagliatelle also held the affections of the most represented group of settlers, especially road workers and truck drivers, through a shared origin in Mussolini's birthplace: the region of Romagna.

So deep was the identification of tagliatelle with Italy and with Romagnolo culinary traditions that it could withstand the touch of the Ethiopians who worked in the trattorias they were not allowed to patronize as clients. And so solid was its identity that Brunelli's trattoria "didn't even need doors" to mark a border between the threatening African outside and the safe Italian inside:

> The name of the restaurant [Tagliatelle] came from its main feature: at any time of the day or night, one could enjoy this dish, cooked on the spot, and seasoned with the fragrant Romagna meat sauce. In fact, the place never closed, it couldn't even if it wanted to, because there were no doors. The kitchen was the undisputed kingdom of my father, who learned the art of gastronomy from various cooks here, and became so good that he later surpassed his masters. There was also a room where pasta was made for tagliatelle, by hand, with pounds and pounds of flour and baskets of eggs, and a hand-operated machine to thin it out. Here tagliatelle was born, and sometimes, on special occasions, the unmistakable smell of *piadina*

(Romagna's flatbread) would spread, awakening memories and nostalgia for the distant home village and loved ones. Every morning, at dawn, the smell of warm bread crept in from the adjacent room, where there was a wood-fired oven, and where E., called Pasticcio for his pastry-making skills, baked baskets of crunchy rolls. The customers were mainly truck drivers traveling from Massawa to Asmara. Dongollo was the first relatively cool place for those coming from Massawa through the scorching Saberguma plain. A plentiful plate of tagliatelle and a glass of good Sangiovese or Chianti wine made them leave for Asmara more tempered. But there was also a clientele of motorists, merchants, and professionals who stopped gladly to enjoy good cuisine. Especially on Saturdays and Sundays, whole families came, attracted by the temperate climate and the certainty of spending a peaceful day, eating well and breathing good air.[53]

Trattorias like Brunelli's performed a variety of supplementary functions for the mobile Italian workers and settlers. First and foremost, they were a meeting place where key information was exchanged (about the job market and employment opportunities, housing options, healthcare issues, etc.), more valuable than ever in a transient society where support from family and neighbors was absent. E.M., a construction worker who arrived in 1936 from Alfonsine, Ravenna, testified to this:

> From Massawa they sent me to Dessie, where a large airport was being built. I worked for the Cappelli company from Turin and was paid 30 lire a day, which was a lot compared to Italy. When I arrived, I went to a trattoria to eat something and there I found my brother who was also working in Africa but whom I knew nothing about. Since he knew all the truck drivers who went to Asmara, he had one of them take me to the Regina Elena hospital where I stayed for a month.[54]

Like *spacci*, trattorias played a similarly practical role in the lives of migrant proletarians in Africa. Among these was the Bolognese truck driver Guerrino, who wrote to his wife Derna in Italy,

> I am writing this from a café where there is a radio and sometimes I hear news from Italy, but don't think it's like the Modernissimo Café in Bologna, for heaven's sake, and please don't think I go to cafes every evening to have fun or play cards, I beg you. My only concerns are your health, mine, taking good care of the truck so that it is always in good condition, working, and achieving my goal [to earn, save, and return to Italy with a capital that would allow him to emancipate himself from his social condition].[55]

The trattorias employed many migrants without jobs or opportunities but with an immediate need for money. As F.M., an immigrant from Villanova di Bagnocavallo, Romagna, recalled:

> They sent me to work on the road that went from Gondar to Asmar. Near the construction site, there was a Sicilian woman who had opened an inn because her husband had died and she was looking for a man to make bread. I went to work

there. I stayed there for about six months, then the construction site moved, there was not much work left, and the woman closed the inn. At the trattoria, I made ten lire a day, plus room and board. Much less than at the construction site, where I usually earned thirty lire.[56]

As Guerrino the truck driver pointed out in a letter to his wife, trattorias sometimes offered drivers and travelers hospitality, even for long periods. They served as informal lodging for migrants from the same Italian village or region, especially when the trattoria was run by women settlers or could rely on unpaid female labor.

Here in Aba [a neighborhood of Addis Ababa], it's like a boarding house, and I pay about twenty lire a day. Now that [the truck] is gone, I sleep in a cot with other friends, including my sister Maria's brother-in-law. Since it's about two miles from the center of Addis Ababa, we only come here in the evening, after dinner we play a game of cards and then go to bed.[57]

Finally, trattorias hosted group events, such as the 1936 Christmas dinner organized by the Ethiopian Fascist Party for construction and transportation workers who "sat at the same tables, eating the same food," or the Easter lunch in 1937 the Tuttobene construction company gave for all its Italian employees.[58]

The racial segregation of the trattorias differed in practice from that of the *spacci*. As highlighted in Alda Brunelli's memoir, Ethiopians, although excluded as customers, worked in kitchens and dining rooms performing menial tasks, such as peeling potatoes, washing dishes, cleaning floors, and serving tables. Without their labor, trattorias, unlike *spacci*, could not have functioned. As Orio Vergani noted,

Korem was now only a half-hour's walk away. In the shack of the *Impero* trattoria the boy who served us was a Moor with a pretty silver ring in his earlobe. Tables were like those in war zones, with nails that ripped holes in the tablecloths. Clientele from the construction site. Arms and chests full of sun and hair. Two-pound sandwiches. The boy offered us tagliatelle and asked if we wanted wine. We asked what wine there was. He interrogated the air with his enamel eye, made the ring in his ear dance, and syllabized, almost as a child, the new, difficult, and rare names—Bar-do-li-no … Gri-gno-li-no … .[59]

Vergani's portrayal of the waiter as a laughably effeminate caricature managed to spotlight the infantilization and emasculation that racial segregation produced. The Black waiter's failed attempt to master Italian wine served to reinforce the sophistication of Italian cuisine. Preventing Ethiopians from enjoying Italian food culture, even in an informal trattoria, was a powerful way to have these new imperial subjects accept their new state of inferiority.

Vergani described another trattoria in Dessie.

From the hill come rows of [Abyssinian] women with their beige tunics sweeping the grass and mud, and the baby bundle on their backs. They find the path blocked by this house that was not there last week when they came down to the market. They look through the windows and see what they have never seen before: large rooms with rows of tables, white tablecloths, glasses, bottles. There is also electric light, polished wooden floors, flower pots, and a counter with serving dishes, mayonnaise fish, galantine, veal with tuna sauce. Up and down the rooms move agile young men in white jackets yelling strange words. With the zeal of neophytes—they are new to the job and until yesterday, perhaps, they were masons and carpenters—the waiters shout, "*Una milanese! Una doppia Bologna!! Una fiorentina!!!*" The whole group—women, children peeping out from their sacks, animals, and the mysterious powerful native— enjoys the spectacle, as if, framed in that window, they were seeing cinema for the first time.[60]

In these roadside trattorias, Italian cuisine, with all its material apparatus ("white tablecloths, glasses, bottles") and the choreography of Italian masons-turned-chefs-and-waiters was a performance of modernity and superiority, observed by African spectators through closed windows. Abyssinian cooks "faithful to the cuisine of pure *burkutta*" (travel bread cooked on coals) were expected to be impressed by such middle-class dishes as Milanese cutlets or Florentine-style steak, or *vitello tonnato*, the Piemontese specialty of cold boiled veal in tuna sauce which, ironically, the majority of Italian colonizers were only now experiencing for the first time.

Here, a similar regime of taste and distinction, not entirely free from racist intent, could also articulate the differences between northern and southern Italians, *settentrionali* and *meridionali*. One goal of state racism in East Africa was, in fact, to overcome the divisive regionalisms in Italy by focusing on Whiteness to unite settlers from different areas of origin around colonial racism and, in particular, to end the discrimination by northern Italians of all social classes against southern Italians. The widespread anti-southern prejudice that arose immediately after political unification was "scientifically" corroborated by a Lombrosian anthropology that explained among Italians as racial in origin: the difference between an Alpine-Celtic North and a Latin-Mediterranean South—the latter a "degenerate" race soiled by interactions with African and Levantine peoples.[61]

Against this background, the choice to proceed with regionally based colonization agencies appeared contradictory. According to data from Nicola Labanca, about two-thirds of the immigrants to East Africa came from the North, in particular from Romagna and the Veneto, while southern immigrants, mainly from Puglia and Sicily, preferred the colony of Libya in the same proportion.[62] Bourgeois settlers in Ethiopia often privately attributed the disappointing results of colonization and development in Italian East Africa to the poor racial quality of settlers; in other words, to the overly large presence of Southerners. In letters to her family, Pia Maria Pezzoli (1905–1995), wife of the official Giovanni Battista Ellero (1910–1942), referred to southern settlers as "Arab-Sicilians," emphasizing how their in-between identity needlessly complicated the clear racist architecture under construction.[63]

In segregated, supremacist colonial society, southern Italians were especially disliked and even feared because of their presumed indifference to the color line. For example, Vittorio Natali-Morosow (1927–), son of the superintendent of the residences of Viceroy Duke Amedeo d'Aosta in Addis Ababa, insisted that

> in Ethiopia, a new presence had emerged: the "Cicilians," the plebeians of the South, immigrants or demobilized soldiers, who had set up fruit and vegetable stores, butcher shops, etc. They worked side by side with their Black employees and their children played in the street together. If the conquest had lasted a little longer, [southern Italians] would have happily intermixed [with Ethiopians].[64]

In his private diary, Poggiali lamented that

> it is painful to say, but in Ethiopia we sent too many Southerners. They are too backward to have authority, to impose European civilization. Some of them are perfectly at ease in the filth of the tukul, because in their Puglia or Calabria they never had anything better. It's laughable to talk about the prestige of the race. If you take away the color of the face, what difference is there between some of our shabby compatriots, true human wrecks, sent here who knows why, and the Ethiopian peasants who, on the other hand, are beautiful in form and appearance?[65]

Italian cuisine was used to articulate these internal ethnic prejudices by delineating the boundaries of regional identity. Trattorias often offered separate dining areas and menus to clients from different regional backgrounds. A.P., a worker from the province of Ravenna, recalled that

> they sent us to Gura, a village of tukuls near the city airport. I didn't actually work on the road but collected wood with three others, one from Mantua, one from Bergamo, and the other from Modena. By often going to the kitchen, I managed to get something extra, especially when Southern workers arrived and two kitchens were made: one for the Northerners and one for them. The first was run by Romagnoli that I knew, so we got along very well.[66]

Whether selected for settlements by the Regional Colonization Agencies or recruited by construction, road building, or transportation companies, the existence of large communities of workers from the same region encouraged the persistence of regional foodways, however transformed they might be in new settings. The Bolognese truck driver Guerrino wrote to his wife that

> tonight I ate, like many other times, at the Continental restaurant. The owner is Greek. I had the *primo* [pasta], the *secondo* [meat], fruit, and coffee [for] ten lire plus two lire for a quarter liter of wine. I also go to eat in a trattoria outside Dire Dawa, where there are people from Modena, and I eat tortellini and tagliatelle alla bolognese, but certainly not like the delicious ones you make for me.[67]

Colonial kitchens serving familiar, localized dishes were central to the diet of immigrant settlers, reflecting the insularity of their regional communities and the wide gap between northern and southern Italians. However, as the widespread popularity of one regional specialty, tagliatelle, has shown, a creolized Italian-Ethiopian cuisine would likely have taken hold over the long term has the colony succeeded. The new cuisine would have included formerly regional dishes like tagliatelle that became beloved expressions of colonial life and identity, hybridized with "Ethiopian" foodways that managed to find their way through the filters of racist exclusion. By the end of the 1930s, this process was already underway in some trattorias, which were becoming laboratories for the development a distinctive Italian-Ethiopian cuisine.

As R.G., a worker from Romagna turned restaurateur commented:

> In Italy, I worked for Mr. Ragazzini, the owner of the Hotel S. Marco in Lugo, and it was precisely for this reason that I went to Africa. He decided to open a restaurant in [Ethiopia] and we moved there, me, Ragazzini, two waiters and a cook. The restaurant was in Dekemhare. It was a meeting point for truck drivers who were traveling from Asmara to Addis Ababa, and not far away there was the Sassari Brigade camp. We worked from morning till night and didn't have time to go anywhere. It was a hellish life, even though we made a lot of money. The truck drivers left very good tips. I sent a lot of money home to my wife. I worked there under Ragazzini for about a year, and when he decided to open a large hotel-restaurant in Asmara, me and three other partners took over his business .... Business was good until 1938, then there was a significant decline. The state no longer financed us as generously as before, and traffic had decreased. In the restaurant, I had two Eritrean employees who had learned the trade and the Italian language perfectly. In fact, one of them spoke to the truck drivers in their own dialect depending on where they were from.[68]

The Racial Segregation of Eating in the City: Cafes, Restaurants, and Hotels

The power of roadside grocery stores and restaurants to enforce a comprehensive pattern of segregation was necessarily limited by their small numbers, isolated locations, and by the transience of the Italians they served. In cities, on the other hand, segregation could be applied more easily and systematically, and it was to dramatic effect in urban bars, restaurants, and stores where relations between large, dense concentrations of settlers and Ethiopians could be closely monitored. The design of new cities, moreover, always included segregated commercial spaces for colonizers and colonized peoples, from markets and shops to cafes and restaurants (Figure 18).

The comprehensive racial segregation of urban life was also made possible by the presence of the military, which kept the threat of guerrilla actions by Ethiopian patriots at bay and was ready to control the Ethiopian population as needed. In the cities, the socialization of Italians into a modern, middle-class colonial lifestyle began with the separation from Blacks and Black culture, except, of course, when Ethiopians were servants or unskilled workers, always without citizenship rights.

As it was for Eritreans, for Ethiopians the experience of discrimination and exclusion from public spaces for food consumption constituted one of the most common and painful memories of the occupation. Especially painful are the stories of Ethiopians who, as workers or soldiers in the Italian army, developed relationships with Italians. "Even though we worked with the Italians, we were not allowed to enter public places like bars. We were served through a window," recounted Dicodimos Tesfamikel.[69] And Berhane Ghebregherghis recalled that "during the Italian presence, you could feel that society was separate. They drank with a glass and let us drink with a rusty metal container."[70] What's more, "If we went to the bar, they gave us to drink not in glasses, but in dirty tanks, or in old boxes. Here in the Empire they treated you like in South Africa, I know how it is there, even though I have never been, I know it's something like that."[71]

The Ethiopians' response to dehumanization could only be anti-colonial violence, even if imagined and fantasized, as in the memory of Ghebremicael Feseha (although there is no confirmation of the event):

> One day we went to a bar at the Gondar station, it was called Bar Dopolavoro, they gave us wine from the window in a broken bottle, there was a colonel with me who went into the bar and I stood outside holding his bag and his raincoa. He turned to see if I was coming but they didn't want to let me in. I was with a *Bulucbasci* called Bezaabeh who fought in [Libya] and was an Amhara who said to me: "I will kill an Italian, I am a person who has served for twenty-five years in Tripoli, and now being an Amhara I am fighting against my flag, you see that the Italians give us wine with a broken bottle, I am not an animal, so you run away I shoot," and he dropped many Italian soldiers. He then fled and went to the *shifta* [Ethiopian partisans]. He killed many soldiers and two young waiters there.[72]

The *Askari* Berachi Menghescia Hailu echoed the necessity of anti-colonial violence, real or imagined.

> In Ethiopia, where we were, there was a place with some shops, and when I went to buy bread I heard a voice saying, "Niggers, niggers." I turned and saw a Sicilian who kept saying "Nigger, nigger." I asked what he was saying, and he told me I couldn't enter his shop because I was Black. I replied that I had come to buy bread, but he didn't want to let me in, and with the handkerchief I had in my hand, I put it around his neck and started pulling, then I beat him up. The Carabinieri arrived, who were Italians and Eritreans, and I told them that he had called me nigger, and the Italian continued to call me nigger. At the police station the commissioner told me that Ethiopia was for the Italians and was no longer for the Ethiopians.[73]

Not all of the regime's plans for building racially segregated public spaces in cities and settlements were fully realized, however, due to the priority given to constructing long-distance roads, bureaucratic and political bottlenecks, and, of course, the defeat of the empire itself in 1941. It is more accurate to say that the overall design for urban and architectural segregation proceeded at different speeds in different contexts.[74] As in other racist spheres such as the prevention of the "plague of miscegenation," urban segregation demanded a physical presence: effective racial control required its coercive architecture.

In many ways, both colonial jurisprudence and the built environment were designed to instruct Italian settlers in the culture and practice of racism. In one of his reports, Poggiali called for a pedagogy to create genuinely racist colonists. He referred, as usual, to the dangerous appeal although they were excluded as customers, of interracial commensality:

> Workers, without any prejudice, landed in the Empire armed with an innocent curiosity. They took a position of confident friendship with Black people, learning about their customs, and their methods of love, and giving them an importance that the Ethiopians themselves could not understand, convinced that White people knew and could do everything. Often sharing their housing and often their food.[75]

Abandoning the idea of building from the ground up grand "imperial cities" to display Italian colonial power, fascist urban planners employed the principle of "zoning, the modern urban planning tool that would be used to achieve perfect racial segregation."[76] Four regulatory plans, including one donated by Le Corbusier (1887–1965) to the Italian ambassador in Paris, needed to be in place before construction could start on the building of a new capital of Addis Ababa in January 1939 under the direction of architects Cesare Valle (1902–2000) and Ignazio Guidi (1904–1978). The Italian population of the city had by the start of 1937 grown from a few thousand individuals and just 150 families, to 40,000 at the beginning of 1940, of whom 33,059 were male, 6,998 females, with about 4,000 were family units. From 1937 to 1940, the Ethiopian population of the capital doubled, but still amounted to only 12,000 people.[77]

Creating segregated urban spaces for commerce and food consumption was an essential part of the colonial plan, as the pulsating heart of Italian modernity in East Africa and true strategic nodes of daily life—unlike the "native markets" where Ethiopians sold and drank *tej* and *tella*. Food stores (grocery stores, bakeries, butcher shops, and delicatessens), bars, cafes, restaurants, and pizzerias quickly and predictably constituted the bulk of Italian commercial activities in Ethiopian cities. In 1938, the Fascist Party's inspector for economic activities in Italian East Africa, Davide Fossa, noted that among the businesses in the Governorate of Shewa, which included Addis Ababa, 174 were grocery stores; 161 were bars, cafes, and restaurants; 17, pastry shops; 28, butcher shops; 25, fruit and vegetable stores; 27, bakeries; and 7 vendors and distributors of mineral water and sodas. In Gondar and Dessie, the two main cities of the Governorate of Amhara, independent food and catering businesses were similarly overrepresented. In Gondar, out of a total of 151 commercial establishments, 41 were grocery stores; 16 were food import and export businesses; and 12 were restaurants and hotels. In Dessie, of 158 commercial establishments 43 were grocery stores; 17, food import and export businesses; and 19, restaurants and hotels.[78] In Jimma, capital of the Governorate of Galla and Sidama, in there were twenty-one grocery stores; eighteen dairy shops, coffee houses, and wine and liquor stores; sixteen general stores and wholesalers of various goods; ten bakeries, pasta shops, and pastry shops; six butcher shops and delicatessens; and four restaurants.[79]

In every city, hotels were bastions of segregation. The tourist *Guide to East Africa* listed hotels, everyone strictly segregated, newly built or renovated by the Concessione Italiana Alberghi Africa Orientale (CIAAO—Italian East Africa Hotel National Agency), and managed by another agency, the Società Gestione Alberghi Africa Orientale (SGAAO—Italian East Africa Hotel Management National Agency). By 1938, there were CIAAO hotels open in twenty-one cities, all "equipped with running water, baths, showers, sometimes a pastry shop, and always a restaurant; restaurants, generally supplied with all Italian foodstuffs, are numerous in the main cities."[80] Travelers were reassured of uninterrupted access to Italian food imports and spared of any encounter with African food. Far from being an "exotic" attraction, Ethiopian food was represented as a threat to taste and health.

Indeed, the rapid emergence of so many food retail shops, cafes, bars, and all sorts of restaurants was an indication that the imperial food system was aimed primarily at providing colonizers with a degree of food security and sovereignty they had never experienced in their homeland. The easy availability of imported food and drink was an important incentive for immigration to the new colony, offering a taste of modernity and access to high levels of private consumption in an Ethiopia they were asked to imagine as part of a Greater Italy. The *Guide* described "shops in the Ethiopian cities being well stocked with Italian food; even the wine, whose alcoholic content is useful to withstand long travels, is all imported from Italy and generally of good quality; the beer is of the export type with higher alcohol content, and is excellently preserved. Italian sodas are available everywhere."[81]

In Addis Ababa the segregated foodscape was the most visible sign of Italian imperialism. There, colonial authorities vigorously supported the opening of bars, cafes, and restaurants as an essential step in the construction of a properly imperial, segregated capital city. Its newspapers, *Corriere dell'Impero* and *Il Giornale di Addis Abeba*, prominently covered every new opening as proof of the progress of Italianization. "The inauguration of Zio Carlo's bar," a 1938 article noted, "was attended by the Governor and the Federal Secretary of the Party. After their speeches, refreshments were served, including homemade ice cream."[82]

The *Corriere dell'Impero* described how the pastry shop-confectionery Sabaudia had expanded in just one year of business to include a dining room, a "serene and discreet place that gives the developing city a new elegant meeting place where it will be delightful to spend leisure time."[83] Its appeal derived first and foremost from the absence of Ethiopians. Similarly, the settler-painter Giuseppe Serra testified to the enthusiasm surrounding the opening of a large number of segregated bars and restaurants as early as 1936: "The city is already very developed both urbanistically and commercially. Luxurious public buildings and elegant restaurants with pools and tennis courts have sprung up. Even bars and hotels are better than those one finds in Italy. European women who stroll along Mussolini Avenue and Littorio Square in the evening emanate so much elegance."[84] Shortly after occupation, Italian settlers, former truck drivers, demobilized soldiers, and some Armenian and Greek merchants opened place like

Caffè Romano, Ristorante Cucina Bolognese, and the pizzeria Bella Napoli.[85] Former legionnaires Mancini and Dell'Osso opened the Bar Aragnino on Corso Vittorio in 1937; Colonial Militia veteran Mario Summa owned the restaurant La Gazzella; while former cavalry officer Renato Guli, aiming at a classier clientele, "launched Cavallino Bianco, a tea room popular for its evening dances and refreshments, enjoyed by 'the most distinguished public of Addis Ababa.'"[86]

The *Corriere dell'Impero* noted that "as of December 15, 1936, the Shewa Governorate had granted 397 operating licenses to 374 Italian new merchants, bar-owners, and restaurateurs, including 299 ex-soldiers and officers and 98 former truck drivers. One hundred and twenty more applications were denied due to insufficient capital. Two weeks later, the number of licenses had risen to 437."[87] By excluding Africans and African food and by serving only imported Italian food cooked "in the Italian style," these establishments enjoyed an unbeatable advantage over small Ethiopian shops and the places of Greek and Armenian restaurateurs, who had long controlled the city's "European" restaurant market. These competitors were pushed out with the political help of a discriminatory licensing policy that strengthened Italian restaurants in their pursuit of gastronomic "purity."[88]

The Racial Segregation of Eating in the City: Open Markets

Urban outdoor markets were seen as a key site of exchange, taste-making, and sensory encounters with the food of the Other, and as such prime targets in the making of the racially colonized city. Transforming these markets into racially appropriate spaces, however, would require costly investments in planning and redevelopment, including projects such as sanitization and even deodorization. And because of their fluid, mobile, and easily crossable boundaries, urban markets would also prove to be the most controversial and complicated undertaking in the race to create fully segregated spaces.

In their ambitious plan to segregate Addis Ababa's food system, authorities constructed two new food markets, one reserved for Italians, and the other reserved for Ethiopians in the northwestern "indigenous" part of the city. According to Gian Luca Podestà, "the markets—the Ethiopian one in [Piazza] Tekle Haymanot [Ketema] and the one for Europeans—were the heart of the city." In these markets, "over 75,000 heads of cattle were slaughtered, and thousands of tons of foodstuffs were sold over the course of a single year [1938]."[89]

Addis Ababa's Ethiopian market had to be clearly separated from the Italian city and the two main roads where the Imperial Palace, City Hall, and the three squares of the Imperial Theater and Cathedral were being built. The *podestà* (mayor) of Addis Ababa, Carlo Boidi (1900–1966), energetically promoted the segregation of markets. Likewise, in the other main centers of Italian Ethiopia (Gondar, Jimma, Dessie, and Harar), the "native" neighborhoods and markets were always placed on the city outskirts, while a monumentalized European quarter of government, residential, and commercial areas occupied the center.

The construction of a separate "indigenous market" began immediately after the occupation of Addis Ababa with the relocation of the original city's main market from the historic center of Arada to the peripheral district of Addis Ketema (Figure 19). This new market, Merkato Ketema, was opened in the "native city" in northwest Addis Ababa, separated from the Italian city by a river and forest (Figure 20). Its single entrance was guarded by police to limit any contact between Italians and Ethiopians. The entrance was also a "sanitary checkpoint," where Ethiopians had to undergo forced disinfection to enter the city of their colonizers.

As noted by Mia Fuller, planners paid special attention to areas of potential interracial contact and traffic between districts. Gherardo Bosio (1903–1941), architect of the master plans for Gondar, Jimma, and Dessie, made clear that

> an important problem is the canalization of caravan traffic [transporting food by donkeys, with cattle and sheep in tow] so as to keep it separate from national [Italian] traffic: caravans and native traffic ending up in the indigenous quarter must reach the market and the native quarter without crossing [the Italian part of] the city. The national market will be completely separate from the native one, although there may frequently be trade with the latter.[90]

To allow essential flows within the constraints of segregation, Ethiopian access to the Italian markets had to be carefully regulated. Ethiopians were not allowed to live in the same area as the Italian market or stay there longer than strictly necessary. Separate roads were built for White residents and tourists to visit the Ethiopian market. Blacks and Whites were to have no opportunities for contact that were not essential, or at least useful to White people.[91] The head of the municipal technical offices of Addis Ababa, engineer Contardo Bonicelli (1901–1973) limited the number of roads and access points between the Italian to the Ethiopian sections to a maximum of three. The plan was to control the movements of Ethiopians in the name of "the adoption of hygiene measures" at "cleansing stations" through which the dangerous bodies of Ethiopians had to pass: "in a perfect colonial city the destruction of parasites and the disinfection of clothing [of Ethiopians] must be exercised to a total extent."[92]

Addis Ababa's Merkato, today the largest marketplace in all of Africa, is a legacy of segregation. The colonial government placed the new Italian market downtown where the old Arada market had been, renamed it Piazza, and surrounded it with modern European-style stores that displayed Italian imports in their windows (Figure 18).[93] The new marketplace displaced westward many Arab and foreign merchants, creating a clear color line across the city, and from atop its hill dominated the native Merkato Ketema down below. The contrasting positions of the Merkato and Piazza visibly reaffirmed the fascist control of strategic spaces and the food systems they made possible.[94]

The Italian administration of Addis Ababa further strengthened the segregation of Merkato with the decree of September 21, 1938, which prohibited Italians and foreigners from entering the "native quarter" entirely. Issued formally for public health reasons, the measure aimed at "minimizing contacts between Italian citizens and Ethiopians." While Article I prohibited "all Italians from entering the homes of [Ethiopians]," Article II explicitly prohibited Italians from entering the "new market" of Ketema, with the

Figure 19 The Addis Ababa market in the central Arada neighborhood, close to Saint George's Cathedral, c.1934. Courtesy of Getty Images.

Italians displaced the market, replacing it with "Piazza," a white-only shopping area with stores, cafes, and restaurants.

sole exception of those who went there to work. Article III required Ethiopian workers entering the white city to obtain a police pass in advance and undergo disinfection at a checkpoint each time. The decree was published in the *Corriere dell'Impero* and accompanied by an editorial warning that it was "indecently imprudent for 'nationals' to make any kind of purchase in the native market, even through the mediation of a servant or another native."[95] Still, segregating the Merkato faced significant problems. For one thing, the fact that the city officials deemed it necessary to segregate Merkato revealed how many Italians were visiting it despite being strongly discouraged to do so. The need for legal prohibition in Addis Ababa and even more so in other urban centers of Italian Ethiopia laid bare the real-world obstacles racist planning encountered in trying to restructure the daily life of food marketplaces.

There were a number of tensions inherent in the vision of "indigenous food markets." The first tension concerned the perception of Ethiopian markets as seductive occasions for the sensory and economic consumption of the Other. At the same time, markets were where all the dangers of the colony were concentrated. In contrast to the propaganda representing Italians as welcome liberators of enslaved Ethiopians, the "dangerous" Ethiopian market was seen as a hostile, inscrutable place of disease and contagion. And where Europeans "got lost," literally and figuratively, in an alien world.

Figure 20 The "rationalized" Merkato Ketema, which Italians opened in the "native city" in northwest Addis Ababa, early 1937. Courtesy of Archivio Luce.

Separated from the Italian city by a stream and a forest, Merkato was racially segregated, supposed to be patronized only by Ethiopians. Today it is the largest marketplace in Africa.

A Luce Institute newsreel of October 14, 1936, entitled *Il mercato di Addis Ababa* (The Market of Addis Ababa), offered Italian cinema audiences the excitement of virtual tourism colored with virtual danger. The newsreel opened with the narrator announcing: "Chronicles of indigenous life in the capital of the Empire. The characteristic appearance of the market, which, despite the rainy season, is experiencing an unprecedented prosperity, an animation of negotiations, and an influx of livestock, grains, and spices." With its fast-paced, rhythmic editing and a score punctuated with Arabic accents, in less than a minute and a half the newsreel presented a frenzy of images:

> [a] crowd of Black men in the market square in Addis Ababa; a street full of people walking; corners of the market with people walking or sitting on the floor with their merchandise in front of them; a flock of sheep surrounded by Black men; donkeys with hay bales on their backs; a pile of eggs on a cloth in front of the vendor with other men of color; women of color on the floor in front of objects; Italians in uniform examining the merchandise of a stall.[96]

In ninety whirlwind seconds, the newsreel conveyed the liveliness of the market, the primitive authenticity of its transactions taking place in a setting of extraordinary diversity. Virtual tourists were proudly shown the "flourishing" market and the quantity and quality of goods exchanged; from meat and eggs to exotic spices that promised aphrodisiac properties. On the other hand, the images also could not avoid conveying the anxiety from seeing disorderly crowds of Africans with enigmatic expressions; the closeness of humans and animals that suggested the dangers of infection, odors, and the shared bestiality of both species; and such practices as placing food in the dust that illustrated a racism of the senses that associated dark skin with filth.[97]

"The Market of Addis Ababa" newsreel turned both the appeal and the danger of the market into a spectacle consumable from a safe distance. In this sense, it brought to the new Italian imperial audience a taste of urban voyeurism similar to the practice of "slumming" that had been emerging in major metropolises after World War I when urban tourists from the new middle classes would pay to be led in walking tours of the "ethnic neighborhoods" of capitals like London, Paris, and New York and to gaze upon the growing numbers of immigrants, people of color, and the working underclass. In the 1920s, with their display of strange but exciting "exotic" foods, the street markets of the Little Italies, Chinatowns, and Jewish ghettos of big American cities were one of the main attractions of urban tourism.[98]

The cinematic journey through Merkato Ketema offered a rare opportunity to experience the "authentic" cultural diversity of the Other, even in its frightening aspects, while at "home" in Italy. But the newsreel also managed to betray the contradictions of segregation by showing glimpses of Italian soldiers and settlers in the off-limits market space. Despite official prohibitions, there were in fact innumerable "participant" tourist-anthropological descriptions by Italians from inside the Merkato and "indigenous markets" of other Ethiopian cities. Expressing both attraction and fear, settler Manlio La Sorsa observed the segregated Eritrean market of Adi Ugri (now Mendefera):

> At Adi Ugri the indigenous town is separated from the Italian or Europeanized quarter. On the way to the African neighborhood, many vendors are scattered along the street, with a little bit of everything: wheat, cereals, herbs, coffee, tea, red peppers, onions, etc. From the street, you can see some trees here and there, and the countryside around is richer in vegetation than any other place I have seen so far.[99]

In 1937, rural development expert Enrico Bartolozzi was sent to Ethiopia by the Italian Colonial Agricultural Institute to study local material cultures. For two years, Bartolozzi focused his investigation on food markets (including the Merkato) in Addis Ababa. "In Ethiopia," Bartolozzi argued,

> among populations still relegated to most backward stages of development, the market is socially very important, as it represents the only means for food producers to exchange, albeit within a small radius, that part of their production that they think they can spare from self-consumption, in order to obtain, through barters and sales, those goods that cannot be obtained from the land.[100]

However, as La Sorsa suggested, a large variety of food was available in Ethiopian markets, especially after Italians constructed a viable road network. Bartolozzi categorized the food Ethiopian farmers offered as "a) locally-grown agricultural products, which gave rise during a market day, to infinite small exchanges [bartering]; b) the main cereal productions of the area, coffee, livestock, etc., which are exchanged for metallic currency in larger quantities."[101]

For Bartolozzi, the dark side of Ethiopian food markets was the sight of miserable sellers and buyers, victims of inferior agricultural and trade systems:

> Vendors and customers are generally squatting on the ground, facing each other in two rows, and presenting their foods spread out on the ground in containers or bags or, more often, on small mats, pieces of cloth, crushed sheets of metal or, in the absence of anything else, on a corner of their filthy shawl. Between these two rows, which multiply in the largest markets, circulates a mass of men and women, sellers or buyers, and numerous curious onlookers examining and comparing the various foods, discussing prices, making small exchanges, procuring the goods to offer in exchange. The spectacle of the people, dressed in identical fashion and engaged in identical negotiations, would be totally uniform, if not for a cacophony of languages coming from the swarming white-clad crowds.[102]

As major gathering places crowded with inscrutable, seemingly interchangeable people, food markets were obvious targets for strict racial segregation while presenting the highest potential for anti-colonial and anti-racist conflict and revolt. As the February 1937 assassination attempt on Viceroy Graziani demonstrated, anti-imperialist fighters, including women who acted as spies or secretly carried weapons in butter jars and egg sacks, could easily blend into the crowds on market days.[103] Colonists were forever fearful of markets as hotbeds of insurgency. In her diary of July 1936, Red Cross volunteer nurse Maria Landi wrote, "For a two-mile radius around the city [Addis Ababa], the rebels are constantly attacking; gunshots are heard every night. It is feared that the Abyssinians may try to attack en masse, or infiltrate the city on a market day."[104]

The segregation of Ethiopian food markets, whatever the benefits of security or racial separation it offered, created a serious problem: it proved harmful to economic growth. The food markets that fascists wanted to wall off and contain the Ethiopian community prevented Italians from visiting, purchasing food, and tasting the cuisine. The policy closed vital points of access to Ethiopian agricultural production that could have been connected to the trade networks of the colony as a whole. Racist policies ended up weakening the entire colonial economic system.

Ironically, the marginalizing of Ethiopian markets also undermined the grand investment in expensive roads and infrastructure that was supposed to move food and people easily, integrate different areas of the country, and create new levels of capital and consumption. Until the mid-1930s, even the Arada market in Addis Ababa had been quite small. The flow of foodstuffs to the capital was limited both by the lack of paved roads and the inadequate number of trucks for transporting large quantities of commodities. The scarcity of trucks and the fact that only one railroad connected

Addis Ababa to the port of Djibouti made transportation so costly that road and rail were almost exclusively reserved for shipping coffee and other higher-value export goods. Foods for sale in Arada were delivered on foot or by mule from the peasant communities just outside Addis Ababa: they included teff, sorghum, barley, wheat, and corn; cattle, goats, sheep, and chickens; butter, eggs, greens, legumes, fruits, and spices. This process reflected the organization of Ethiopian semi-feudal agricultural communities, with access to land governed by highly personalized systems of ownership, tenancy, and production. The royal family, clergy, and landed gentry administered food distribution in the countryside and the city, creating a noncommercial, largely subsistence agriculture in which most food was exchanged by payment in kind or barter.[105]

Poggiali regularly commented on the backwardness of Addis Ababa's food market before Italians "transformed" it.

> In Addis Ababa the predominant transport system was made of mules or donkeys loaded to the brim; but since the *Negus* and his aristocracy made contact with Europe and replaced the shawl with dress uniforms they were gifted with automobiles that roared and trembled on the rough and steep roads; until even here, among the alleys, paths, and dirt roads, climbing through the bushes and makeshift buildings, some asphalted tracks appeared and became a problem for the bare feet of the multitude, which were literally burned when the equatorial sun hit and melted the tar. Between those two extremes of means of transportation, there was no middle ground. Gurages, working men of a race that their Abyssinian masters considered little better than donkeys, continued to be mercilessly loaded with foodstuffs on their shoulders. Even the bicycle, which had conquered the world, could not conquer Addis Ababa; first of all, because people who walk with their own legs are not in a hurry, and then because the deficiency of oxygen of the Abyssinian plateau that makes motor engines pant, much less allows too much effort from human engines.[106]

Notwithstanding its paradoxical role as competitor of the colonization project it was intended to serve, the building more than 4,000 miles of paved roads all converging in Addis Ababa connected the city's markets to the most fertile rural areas of Abyssinia—Dessie to the east, Jimma to the south, Addis Alem to the west, and Wuchale to the north and expanded the role of Merkato Ketema in elaborating an Ethiopian national cuisine.[107] The longstanding tradition of the market as a place where women sold dishes from family recipes helped catalyze the fusion of different foodways. During market days, small, informal restaurants along the nearby streets where vendors sold regional varieties of breads, spiced meat stews, boiled eggs, and other foods. The culinary diffusion enabled by the exchanges and encounters of the market helped create a popular national cuisine.

Despite the benefits brought by expanding the range of supplies and integrating local markets in a new road network, the impact of Italian occupation on the traditional *gäbbar* system of allocating and redistributing agricultural resources was devastating. Plundering Italians, with their frequent theft of livestock and grain, forced local *Ras* (landlords) to maintain their own militias in resistance; those fighters went on to form the bulk of the armed opposition to the occupation. The occupation forced peasants to continue their loyalty to the old landowners and pushed Ethiopian agriculture inward, back to safer traditional subsistence farming. As a result, despite a greater variety of food available at the Addis Ababa market, the narrowing of supply lines forced recurrent shortages of fresh local food—grains, meat, butter, greens, legumes, and fruit—and made the settlers' dependence on canned, packaged, and bottled food even stronger. Market prices for local food were generally high, and availability unpredictable. "Meat is expensive—a sheep costs 150 lire, when before it cost just two dollars—vegetables are very difficult to find, and fruit is completely nonexistent," wrote A. D. Bethell, the representative of Britain's Arabian Trading Company in Addis Ababa in 1936.[108] Traveling through Ethiopia, the English writer Evelyn Waugh (1903–1966) echoed Bethell, stating that "prices are abnormally high in the city; most foods cost three, four times, sometimes ten times more than usual; eggs, milk, butter, and vegetables are almost impossible to find."[109]

Finally, the unrewarding economy of segregated food markets helped drive Ethiopian labor from agriculture to salaried work in road construction. More robust supply lines were needed to feed the cities that faced starvation under sieges by partisan guerrillas. During one siege in the summer of 1936, "every connection between the capital and the outside world was simply cut off; the only thing to eat people could find was dried cod, and at a high price," recalled the Hungarian antifascist doctor Sáska László (1890–1978), an important witness to the brutalities Italians carried out in retaliation for the attempt on the life of Graziani.[110]

Throughout 1936 and 1937 and after the outbreak of World War II, Ethiopian patriots frequently isolated Addis Ababa and its markets from the surrounding agricultural areas. Italian police operations were specifically aimed at regaining control of those territories to ensure the city's supply. And when, in 1937, after the attempt on the life of Graziani and the massacres that followed it, Ethiopian peasants gradually withdrew from the Merkato in fear of new reprisals, Italians interpreted the move as deliberate support for the resistance in its attempt to starve the city and colonial troops. In a vicious circle, this led to heightened repression against Abyssinian peasants and to many episodes of violence, theft, and confiscation. Only with the arrival on October 21, 1937, of the new Viceroy Amedeo of Savoy, Duke of Aosta, did Italians undertake a more diplomatic approach with rural communities.[111]

Throughout the occupation, colonial authorities attempted to reconcile the demands of racial segregation with the development of food markets reserved for Ethiopians by modernizing food exchanges. Once again, the goal was both to exploit Ethiopian material and human resources more efficiently and to inculcate Ethiopians as well as Italian settlers in the system of racial superiority. As Poggiali reported in the *Corriere della Sera*,

> The problem of separating the indigenous element from Italian settlers was immediately addressed [upon the occupation]. By mid-1937, more than 10,000 Ethiopians, roughly one-tenth of the colored population, were transferred to the district created for them. Ninety-five percent of the tukuls in Addis Ababa were in

conditions of terrifying decrepitude. The new [Merkato Ketema] district has all the necessary facilities to improve indigenous life: shops, stables, a covered market.[112]

In the open space of the Merkato, the free circulation of vendors, buyers, and visitors had once reflected "the ancient tradition of the Ethiopian market; the relationship of trust between customer and seller; and the Ethiopian culture of gathering, characterized by interaction between people."[113] Segregation replaced those open spaces with a tight grid of parallel rows of fixed, identical stalls, individually assigned to vendors and covered for protection from the sun and weather.[114] Similarly,

> In Dessie the new market was made up of a large two-story square building with a large courtyard, looking somehow like an Oriental cloister, with large porticos on the outside of both the ground floor and the upper floor, where there were the warehouses reserved for the merchants and companies that were co-owners of the entire building. These were merchants of Amhara or Tigrayan race, or Muslims from Harar, or sometimes Arabs, Yemenites, or Eritreans, who until then had their warehouses in the old open food market, down in the ancient quarter among the eucalyptus trees.[115]

The rationalization of "indigenous markets" was intended to ensure the economic viability of a racially separate food system based on hierarchies of colonizer and colonized. But the success of marketplaces lay precisely in the regular encounter of different foods and different people, the interactions across race and ethnic group that are the very basis of commerce. Because of this reality, open markets throughout Italian East Africa posed a critical obstacle to the segregationist and supremacist policies that fascism had planned for its Empire of Food.[116]

Food markets displayed the varied abundance of Ethiopian resources, supposedly the main reason why Italians had launched a bloodthirsty war for mass colonization. Poggiali himself seemed to wonder how it was possible to segregate such a showcase of wealth: "The Abyssinian markets, moreover, offered proof that the Abyssinian land gave countless varieties of cereals, grains, and aromatic plants; a sort of complete sample of the known and even the unknown flora. These markets, in short, gave the feeling of a potential wealth that offered itself as a splendid promise to our abilities and will to make it real."[117]

The steady circulation of people and food between Black and White markets was a significant problem. Italian markets could not exist without Ethiopian labor and the informal flow of Ethiopian agricultural products they sold. Vergani noted:

> The Italian vendor directs the Black man in the construction of a stall made of boards from a crate branded with the name of a famous Chianti wine, and with some eucalyptus beams sawn an hour before a few steps away in the forest. The stall is not yet ready, the nails have fallen to the ground, a gust of wind threatens to carry away all the newspapers, and already, from all sides, people gather and form a group. The tangerines stand there, wrapped in tricolored thin paper, they have made a very long journey, they are perhaps a little battered and musty. But

everyone has a sudden irresistible craving for tangerines. For two months they have only eaten apples. Welcome tangerines! Who could have imagined that they would be so popular? The truck drivers with their dusty and oily jackets stop, the respectable fifty-year-old gentlemen with their gold badges on their khaki hats stop, and the driver of some colonial authority gets off the car to do some shopping. Tangerines, what a nice surprise![118]

The tangerines mentioned by Vergani had indeed "made a long journey," but not from Italy as the author seems to believe, but most likely from the Dire Dawa area, east of Addis Ababa, grown by Ethiopian farmers. According to Baron Ferdinando Quaranta, appointed by the Ministry of Italian Africa to study Ethiopia's resources, "the only native [Abyssinian] concession to be seen in Ethiopia growing fresh fruit is to be found at Errer-Lya, near Dire Dawa, where tangerines of exquisite flavor grow almost to the size of Sicilian oranges."[119]

The plans for modernizing "indigenous markets" were in effect acknowledgments that the forced separation of the food trade along the color line was anything but rational or efficient. Lino Calabrò, a civil officer in the provincial government of Seka recalled that

> the influx and quantity of foods brought to the markets were the measure of the pacification of a territory and the Ethiopians' trust in the Italian government's authority. The market was an important and festive meeting place where chatting and exchanging news were as valuable as the goods for sale. Especially in the inland regions, the marketplace was a vital center of information and a sure index of the region's situation. Those who participated, mostly peasants, wanted to barter the scarce goods they owned with others they needed more than they wanted to sell. Alongside these people, who represented the masses, there were also—when Ethiopians trusted us to keep the market in an orderly and safe manner—real merchants who offered textiles, clothing, everyday objects, hides, honey, wax, civet, and cattle, horses, and sheep. In Seka, this activity had long since disappeared due to fear of bandit raids and the abuses of some Black soldiers [in the colonial army], so that the market was almost nonexistent. To revive it, it was essential to recreate the atmosphere of security. I summoned the leaders and notables, explained my point of view, and, with their collaboration, drafted a notice that assured full freedom of trade and guaranteed that any dispute would be resolved in an unappealable manner by the market chief. After surrounding the marketplace area with a sturdy fence, I had a pen built for the livestock and stalls for the more valuable goods. I also established a guard service that, alongside the market chief, ensured respect for the law. The market began to function regularly and without incidents, and after a few weeks, it returned to being what the elders remembered it to be in the past.[120]

The "rationalization" of segregated markets posed additional economic problems. One roadblock to development was replacing traditional practices of exchange by bartering or payments in kind into impersonal monetary transaction that could integrate the markets into the imperial food system and its international trade. Calabrò, defending the newly imposed transaction protocol, described typical methods of exchange:

> Gore [a village in Oromia] was also the headquarters of an Italian commercial company interested in purchasing Ethiopian coffee and selling cotton, canned foods, and salt, all highly sought-after in local markets. Salt was highly in demand among the Ethiopians, especially the bar salt, each weighing about a kilogram, used not only for cooking but also as currency, each bar corresponding to a Maria Theresa thaler, or about ten Italian lire. It was a rare and expensive commodity. Before our occupation, the risks arising from frequent brigand attacks and tolls that merchants, mostly Arabs, had to pay during their caravan journey also contributed to its value.[121]

In usual supremacist language, Poggiali confirmed the difficulty but also the necessity of incorporating Ethiopian market systems.

> Conquering Italian troops did manage to gain a practical understanding of the political economy of Ethiopia. An Amhara or Oromo peasant willingly traded a large zebu [a subspecies of domesticated cattle also known as humped or indicine cattle] for a torn jacket, a battered helmet, or a pair of worn-out shoes—objects that could excite his [Ethiopian] vanity—but he would never consent, willingly, to use banknotes. In one market, Ethiopians wanted nickel but rejected copper, in another, they wanted copper but rejected nickel; in one place they accepted 10-lira silver coins, but not 5-lira coins. In an agricultural area in Guder [an Oromo village], brand new copper coins worth one or two *soldi* continued to circulate for a while. One of them could purchase a pumpkin or a *gombo* [a large terracotta jar] full of excellent fresh beer, which for some reason could not be obtained with a two or five-lira coin.[122]

Italians learned that market transactions were made mostly through noncapitalist means, and that the Italian lira was still accepted only with great difficulty. Commercial integration in the colony was already problematic. Segregation made the problem worse.

Market rationalization also included modest attempts to control prices, which were constantly rising between 1936 and 1937 due to growing Italian consumer demand, despite the racist restrictions on Ethiopian marketplaces. Rising prices were also greatly affected by the agrarian crisis created by the occupation: after Italians confiscated Ethiopian farmland for colonial settlers, rural society began to disintegrate and furious guerrilla warfare against colonial troops began in earnest. The increase in food prices in the segregated markets went hand in hand with enormous inflation caused by the massive influx of state capital for the construction of roads and other public works, an investment that caused the salaries of Italian immigrant workers to skyrocket. Poggiali blamed the price increases on Ethiopian sellers:

After the occupation, in 1936, prices rose vertiginously. It was the Ethiopians who did it, responding to events with immeasurable capriciousness. Early settlers, accustomed to living in Addis Ababa with minimal expenditure, saw the few products of the land that Italians liked—vegetables, fruit, eggs, poultry—being offered on the market at ten or twenty times the previous prices. A ragged peasant woman who came from her village to the capital with a handful of carrots or tomatoes or potatoes shamelessly asked, for a small pile of those vegetables weighing a few hundred grams, a *carta* (ten lire worth), which had in the monetary chaos, become the accepted currency. And the worst part was that Italians bought the food because they had been forced to fasting for many months, had made a lot of money, and were seized by an irresistible shopping mania.[123]

In reality, the rampant inflation of 1936-7 affected Ethiopians' food security much more so than Italians'. The prices of the main ingredients of the Ethiopian diet, all locally produced—teff for *injera*, sorghum, chickpeas, peas, eggs, chickens, to name a few—increased sharply. Prices for packaged and preserved food imported from Italy, which most colonists consumed—pasta, canned tomatoes and vegetables, cured meats, Parmigiano and other aged cheeses, wine, and mineral water—increased less. In any case, as Poggiali suggested, the high salaries of Italian workers generally kept pace with prices. The efforts of a series of colonial governments to control the prices of some food items in Addis Ababa and Jimma between 1936 and 1940 reflect the way price trends in fresh local food differed from those in food from Italy. The price of local butter was usually two to almost four times higher than that of imported olive oil or Parmigiano.[124] The differential impact of the increased food prices in the two parallel markets—harder on Ethiopian than on Italian consumers—largely explains why the colonial government made tepid efforts to control prices in Ethiopian marketplaces, continuing to import large quantities of cereals and other foods.[125] Regardless of its concern about the ups and downs of Ethiopian agriculture and markets and the pressure from Mussolini to make Ethiopia immediately self-sufficient, not until 1938 did the Italian government systematically regulate the prices of food products. The deflationary effects of price regulation and the consequent slowing down of the economy affected both the Italian and Ethiopian markets.[126]

The story of Ethiopian food markets during Italian occupation demonstrates above all that the racial segregation of public places for food trade and consumption was not only ideologically repugnant but also economically destructive, politically disadvantageous, and in almost all ways ineffective. As shown by observers like Poggiali, despite the high prices they had to pay for fresh foods produced and sold by Ethiopians, Italian settlers habitually used indigenous markets, breaking the law of segregation, or more often circumventing it by sending an Ethiopian servant to do their shopping. Despite racist policies and propaganda, Ethiopian foods regularly filled the homes of Italian settlers and sparked new culinary practices. These unanticipated gastronomic developments were more prevalent outside Addis Ababa: "I was sent to work in the Gura'i plain, a large valley where an airport had to be built," recalled the Modenese worker A.L. "We had to level the roads and bulldoze a small mountain in the center of the runway. I had little contact with the local population because we lived in the camp. We met the Ethiopians mainly at the marketplace, where we bought their goods, especially food."[127]

The market still remained, directly or indirectly, a lively interactive node for Italians and Ethiopians. Violations of the law on market segregation typically occurred out of economic necessity, another indication that the fascist food system was not working. As the following chapter will show, the Italians' frequent, easy patronizing of Ethiopian markets was just one of the ways in which the barriers imposed by the government were regularly transgressed.[128]

The unlawful crossing of racial boundaries did not, by any means, suggest an underlying culture of tolerance, sympathy, or benign attraction toward the Other. In other contexts, crossing racial boundaries often led to exploitation and violence against the colonized. Most Italian men, for instance, interacted with colonized women to obtain sex and sometimes establish affectionate domestic relationships, all prohibited by law. These relationships did not signal an absence of racial prejudice or suggest that Italian men did not see Ethiopian women as inferior beings who owed them deference and pleasure.[129]

Ethiopians understood that racial segregation in coffee shops, restaurants, and markets was designed to reinforce hierarchies of race, gender, and class. They saw that this practice not only affected them—the colonized—as primary victims, but also affected secondary victims, those nonracist Italian settlers whose security and prosperity were constantly at risk. It was precisely in markets, coffee shops, and restaurants that fascist restrictions on service and hospitality dissolved into intercultural sociability, revealing the absurdity of racist practices in plain sight. Y.H., an Ethiopian Orthodox priest interviewed by Irma Taddia in Addis Ababa in 1990, recalled:

> We were in Dekemhare, in the most important year of fascism [1938], when everyone exalted Mussolini and his empire. I went to the Bologna restaurant. Dekemhare was an important town in the empire, twenty thousand Italians lived there, and I walked into the restaurant. The restaurant owner said, "Listen, Father, there's a place for you over there in the corner in the very back. If they see you sitting here, it's not good. You must excuse me." So, I got out and went to the colonial authority, Santucci. I said, "I am a friend of Italy, I have been to Italy, with all this, I wanted to eat at the Bologna restaurant paying my check, they kicked me out." But the restaurant owner later invited me as a guest to his home, he told his wife in advance, and I had a great lunch; he felt humiliated, offended, but in public he couldn't do anything. They put me at the head of the table that day, and we ate Italian delicacies. Then he asked me where I was going, and I told him I had to go to Segeneiti that day. And he called a cab to take me there. That's how our relationships were then, in public and in private.[130]

Italian settlers regularly violated the norms of racial segregation in public food places, whether because they considered it harmful to their business or as a way to steal from Ethiopians without being punished (despite a law officially protecting "indigenous subjects" from abuses by Italians). In one of many cases, in 1936 the Governor of Eritrea, General Alfredo Guzzoni (1877–1965), learned that an Italian and an Eritrean were running a café together in Adi Keyh. The Eritrean partner had provided the initial capital. Guzzoni ordered the local colonial authorities to "immediately cease this partnership between a national and a native for obvious reasons of protecting the prestige of the White race, and also to avoid the realization of illegal profits to the detriment of the colonial subject."[131] In another case of an Italian settler breaking the laws of segregation to exploit colonized subjects, Achille B. was a cook in a restaurant in Axum, where he had a relationship with an Ethiopian dishwasher. Achille B. had appointed himself administrator of the woman's savings, and when the colonial police investigated the case for suspected "madamism," they discovered that he had already stolen more than 1,000 lire from her. Another case was that of S., who worked as a bricklayer in Senafe, where, according to the Carabinieri "he frequented the bars of the Ethiopians, where he ate and drank, and where he had contracted several debts with Eritreans; S. is known for hiring young African boys, whom he promises high wages but pays them less than the minimum wage required by law for native workers."[132]

There were many occasions when the food borders imposed by racial segregation were crossed, in different ways and in both directions. The next chapter will explore how, along the edges and in the corners of a closed racist system, entirely unsuspected food encounters and gastronomic exchanges lead to the formation of an Ethiopian-Italian/Italian-Ethiopian cuisine in the Empire of Food.

5

Liminal Colonial Gastronomies: Ethiopian-Italian Food Encounters in the Interstices of Segregation

In a colonial society that segregated public food spaces from fears of interracial intimacy and conviviality, culinary exchanges between Ethiopians and Italians took place at the frayed margins between the communities of colonizers and colonized, where cultural, political, racial, gender, and class differentials collided.

In addition to the food marketplaces discussed in Chapter 4, these interstitial spaces included (1) military life, where metropolitan and colonial troops mingled in camp kitchens, as well as in the procurement of food from Ethiopian villages by Italian soldiers; (2) the work of cooks, waiters, and maids that a number of Ethiopians, mostly men, performed in colonial homes for Italian masters, including serving nearly all adult Italian women and their children; (3) the sex work that Ethiopian women and some Ethiopian men performed for Italian men, which often included a food dimension; (4) the banquets that served as diplomatic occasions for Ethiopians and Italians to sit together, either as an act of benevolence or as a way to forge political agreements; (5) the role of the settlers called *insabbiati*—the equivalent of British and French colonial "poor Whites"—who, dropping out of White society, embarked on new lives with an interracial family in an Ethiopian community; (6) the growth of travel and transport through Ethiopia, which led to the mutual discovery of different gastronomic worlds; and, finally, (7) the wartime imprisonment of Italian soldiers in British camps in Kenya and Sudan as well as the concentration camps Italians established in Ethiopia and Somalia for captured Ethiopian patriots.

All of these varied spaces encouraged food exchanges across racial lines, but also produced a new repertoire of perceptions, tastes, techniques, rituals, and memories. These borders also enabled the emergence of a new Ethiopian-Italian/Italian-Ethiopian cuisine. With its own identity, a composite of delights and disgusts, the new hybrid cuisine clearly reflected diverse cultural worlds meeting at the margins, precisely where the confrontation of differences was most intense and respective nationalisms were continuously strengthened and redrawn.[1]

Gastroborderland 1: The Army

Despite the massive logistical effort to ensure food supplies for the invading troops along a large, geographically complex, and fast-moving warfront, Italian and colonial soldiers in Ethiopia often found themselves short of provisions, sometimes to the edge of starvation.

Regulations stipulated that an Italian soldier in the occupation army receive a daily ration of 700 grams of bread (later increased to 750), 300 grams of meat, 200 grams of pasta, 60 grams of vegetables, 20 grams of coffee, 25 grams of sugar, 15 grams of salt, and fruit three times a week (Figure 9). The rations of native colonial soldiers from Eritrea, Ethiopia, and other parts of Africa who fought with the Italians were in every way inferior. Rationing food of lesser quantity and quality served many purposes: reinforcing for national and colonial soldiers the rule of White superiority; discursively constructing Ethiopians, Eritreans, and Africans in general as subjects of lesser value and with lesser needs, who needed only enough food for survival; and differentiating Italian and Abyssinian diets: the former, varied and balanced, and the latter, monotonous and primal. An African soldier's ration amounted to 600 grams of flour, 20 grams of tea, 20 grams of salt, 40 grams of sugar, and 500 grams of meat, the latter delivered only twice a week.[2] Even allowing for the nutritional inequalities imposed by racism, both the African and Italian peasants who filled the ranks of the occupation army often enjoyed a comparatively rich diet, realizing the promise made to them that serving in the Ethiopian campaign would provide good food, as well as easy sex.

However, many accounts suggest that this promise was just as often broken. Oral histories and other personal sources describe instead the difficulties of getting supplies through, the poor quality of canned goods and rations in general, and the inability of the network of *spacci*—frequently accused of charging prohibitive prices—to adequately supply soldiers with food in exchange of money. While boasting most modern supply lines, the highly mechanized Italian invasion army, operating across a wide combat area, was regularly forced to rely on "indigenous food." First during the 1935–6 invasion, in the operations against the Ethiopian resistance between 1937 and 1939, and finally in the war against the British between 1940 and 1941 when supply lines with Italy were completely cut off, the army of the Empire of Food often turned into a hungry and voracious body that could spend more time hunting down food in corners of the Ethiopian backcountry than it did fighting its enemy.

"We built forts, we were armed, but were mostly inactive for fear of guerrillas. We always lacked food and we were supplied with flour and the other basic necessities by planes, without parachutes, so many things were lost. The Italian army was always short of provisions, and it had happened to us even before we were resupplied," confessed the soldier A.F. from Forlì, deployed in the Lake Tana area.[3] The reality of supply logistics in the ultramodern war on Ethiopia was quite different from its official image: "The troop is tired, since the beginning of the war we haven't stopped yet; since February 10 [1936] the soldiers haven't even changed their shirts, for twenty days they have been tighten their belts with tin cans and *chiarizia*, often reduced to half rations, they no longer remember what wine tastes like."[4] Soldiers complained that ration food was both scarce and of very poor quality:

Thanks to those black, greasy, pots that at various times were so necessary for us to cook that leather-like meat or pigwash soup with "tubes" of prehistoric pasta …; which we left without regret to other recruits. Thanks to the inseparable backpack that was our faithful companion as a soft pillow and wardrobe for all our gear—loaves of bread and moldy biscuits, tin cans of buffalo meat and condensed milk that often spills out sticking everything together—and a torment to our shoulders during the transfer marches.[5]

Even when the army managed to deliver imported foods, quality remained substandard. "The entire Division is constantly busy taking advantage of the few hours of good weather to work on making the road serviceable again all the way to Addi Arkay," recalled private Sergio Botta.

Thus operating, in the first days of August the first trucks began to trudge forward to our positions. First came the transportable ovens … as well as the distribution of the ration of meat and broth and soup with the usual cracked pasta. After so many days of dry hardtack biscuits, the first loaves of bread distributed are greeted with lively satisfaction. Those hard biscuits with nests of maggots inside gave little relief to our hungry stomach, and [we] welcomed the advent of the fresh and soft loaf. Unfortunately, however, from the earliest bites, the welcome daily bread is disgusting, due to the long pilgrimage that the flours must take. Bagged in jute sacks, from Italy they landed in Massawa and were piled on the dock for several days before being sorted to be sent to the troops in the most advanced battle zones. Before arrival at destination after several transfers and hundreds of miles, these sacks are reduced to a pitiful state. These dear loaves give you the surprise of concealing several quite thriving worms; some in small groups twisted together and others solitary. Some worms surface and float in the soup, but others remain hidden in the soaked bread so they are ingested along with the bread as a filling cooked to perfection and … of high nutritional value; competing on a par with the use they make of them in oriental cuisines![6]

Italian soldiers were thus challenged to seek "fresh" food locally—typically milk, butter, eggs, chickens, zebu, sheep or goat meat, vegetables, herbs, spices, honey, and grains, all bought or raided in Abyssinian villages, in addition to animals that could be hunted or fished, even if it meant crossing cultural and racial boundaries and ingesting the food of the savage Other.

The way in which the rations were consumed by enlisted men (officers ate in their own canteens, enjoying the best available provisions) was, moreover, just as bad and "primitive." Another soldier, charged with escorting Italian reporters, remarked:

I was struck by the confusion in the barracks, the filth, the disrespectful treatment of the poor soldier torn away from his family, his comrades, his factory, while such genteel treatment was reserved for the officers. The difference in food, except in rare cases, was nothing short of shameful. To that poor little soldier, in Africa, with hobnailed boots unsuitable for sand and heat, they gave a quart of water a day, a biscuit, and a can of meat. Given the blazing sun, they ate their poor meal with their heads under the trucks, while the officers boiled the water for their pasta on their Primus [camp stove] in their tents; all this began to make me reflect and doubt about my trust in the [fascist] regime.[7]

Under these conditions, there was little choice but to seek nourishment in the foods of Africa, overcoming barriers of taste and disgust, learning how to procure it, process it, and eat it. In the popular language of the soldiers, this was "belt-tightening" and mastering the art of making do. "Sublime word, that of 'making do.' A word we had learned to know in [World War I], but which so many thousands of miles from the homeland becomes an everyday experience, becomes the only way to eat, to drink, to save one's life from beasts and men."[8] For Poggiali, "food scouting" by Italian troops recalled the glorious ancient Roman legions also formed by farmers who had left the plow to create another empire. Poggiali wrote of "the first valiant soldiers who crossed the Mareb River [in Eritrea] and began the conquest of Ethiopia. The majority of the soldiers, as in all wars, were peasants, people of the land; and while they marched on the hard path of conquest, their experienced eyes did not neglect to scrutinize what was being conquered."[9]

The ways in which hungry Italian colonial soldiers sought to find African food were far more prosaic than Poggiali's romanticized portrayal. From hunting animals in highlands and forests or eating animals dead from combat or fatigue, to stealing food from the corpses of slain enemies, the struggle to find food testified once again to the brutality of the war in Ethiopia, where the boundaries between man-hunting and food-hunting, between the fear of the enemy and the terror of hunger, were erased: "Meanwhile, my hunger continued to be undaunted, to the point of going so far as to eat certain kinds of grass that we didn't even know," remembered soldier Luigi Marini.

> Once we anxiously witnessed the slow death of a horse, ready with a bayonet to cut it to pieces. In a few minutes, only the skeleton remained there. We somehow adapted to cook it on a fire we had previously lit: it was a real feast for us! But in the meantime, hunger was setting in again, and we had no provisions. I and a friend from Arezzo, G.D., then decided to leave the camp momentarily in search of something to eat. On our way we encountered only dead people with birds on them slowly devouring them, until we spotted an abandoned village. As soon as we arrived, we entered the first tukul we came across, but even there instead of food there were only dead people. Fortunately, among the corpses we spotted earthenware jars with grains; unconcerned about the situation we picked them up, filled our pockets with grain and set off.[10]

The most common tactic used by hungry Italian soldiers to find food was to locate a nearby Ethiopian village and inspect it under the (well-founded) suspicion that its inhabitants were hiding as much food as possible. Italian soldiers not only took whatever food they could find, but also wrote detailed observations of how this food was to be prepared and consumed. "Being stationed closer to the village, and having to supply ourselves the best we can, we attempt begging the Ethiopians for some of their 'food,'" soldier Botta recalled, describing the preparation of *injera*:

> The main meal favored by them is the traditional *injera*, which they prepare with a mixture of water, salt, and durra [sorghum] flour; which is the most sown cereal in these regions. This mixture is then spread in thin layers on a special sheet and put to cook over a brazier that burns between a shelter of stones, and after a short time, without the use of any seasoning, they take out a fried dish that has the taste of scorched flour. Heading to the village with the desire to find something to put between our teeth, we set out at once on a quest to get a few handfuls of that precious flour.[11]

Botta noted that

> this all-natural mixture is sold to us at a high price but, to quell the urges of hunger that grip our stomachs, we are ready to make any sacrifice. Putting aside all perplexity, we adapt ourselves to the same "food" of these Negroes ... in order to make ourselves some of that "delicious *injera*"; the local gastronomic specialty! A few days later, we discover another food source that these Abyssinians, who have quickly learned how to take advantage of us, offer us. It is a certain quality of honey that they find in tree trunks or hollowed-out stumps or who knows where. Inside their primitive containers made from emptied gourds, they mash together honey, honeycombs, and bees crushed to form a not-so-edible mass. Drawing it with their hands, they fill your gavel many times over for many liras each time. [It] is then enjoyed with slices of *injera*. It's almost the end of the month and the food situation is getting worse and worse every day.[12]

For soldiers, hunger constituted a sufficient, and legitimate, reason for crossing officially sealed cultural boundaries, and even for breaking food taboos such as consuming the meat of "disgusting" animals considered not worthy of a "civilized" European diet. Behind the veil of disgust, the testimony by soldier Giuseppe Morettini betrays the morbid fascination with the transformation of one's self into "a savage" through the consumption of camel meat. Morettini remembered its forbidden taste:

> It was Easter Day 1936. Around ten o'clock, having had nothing to eat, we got to the ground under a blazing sun that one could hardly see the sky from the weakness. We said to our officers, "We want to eat! We want to eat!" And they would reply, "What should we give you that we have nothing? There, there is a camel. Do you want that? Kill it and eat it!" For me, not even if I starved, but someone jumped on this camel and killed it. They took all the lean parts and then lit a fire. We had no salt or oil. They would put this lean meat over the coals, roast it a little bit, they would make little pieces, without chewing they would swallow. It was kind of sweet.[13]

The war between Italian forces and the Ethiopian resistance was also a battle for food, aimed at starving the enemy and securing food supplies. Its victims were the peasant villagers, who, forcibly or not, sometimes fed Ethiopian patriots, sometimes Italian imperialists.

The struggle for food waged across Ethiopia. In Abyssinian villages, regular and irregular Italian units, *Askaris* of colonial troops, as well as Ethiopian anti-colonial guerrilla bands negotiated with farmers for, or simply looted, anything they could find to eat. Luigi Pilosio, an Italian soldier, remembered:

> Saturday, September 25, 1936. Two platoons moved to the Tekeze River, they had only weapons and work tools on them, we've been all day without eating. Bands of native warriors loyal to us arrive, loaded with every kind of stuff, food, meat, cattle, everything they captured from the rebels; unfortunate the one who falls into their hands, they're cruel, uncivilized, heartless people! Meskel feast [Ethiopian Orthodox religious holiday] began today, big fires, dances, prisoners brought in, and then shot on the spot. Fine weather. Monday, September 27. Work on bridge and road to Belenta and Sekota, half of the unit works on the makeshift bridge, they work in the water up to their belly, for fourteen or fifteen hours a day, eating nothing else than two hardtack biscuits; they make do with some calf they found around, or goats, scattered in the nearby mountains, butchered, cooked on embers, smoked, without salt; it is delicious any way you make it this meat, or fish that abounds in the river, but this without oil and salt is tasteless.[14]

In his diary, Pilosio recounted coming face to face with the fascist failure to create a modern food system and had to admit his reliance on Ethiopian food. "Friday, December 30. At sunrise, the entire battalion went to work, and kept working hard until 4:30 p.m., building several miles of track. Having again no provisions, today we received a little flour to make *burkutta* the way the Abyssinians make it, what have we become?"[15]

The Italian military's policing operations were, of course, meant to be temporary, ending with the "pacification" of Ethiopia and securing the success of the planned imperial food system. Instead, armed conflicts never ceased, from the Italian victory in 1936 to the declaration of war by Mussolini against Great Britain and its Allies on June 10, 1940. For Italian soldiers fighting both anti-partisan operations and later British colonial forces, "Ethiopian eating" thus became the norm in the absence of a working Italian food supply system. Ironically, by the time the Italian Empire in East Africa faded in its twilight during 1940–1, Italian soldiers and settlers had finally come to learn and master the once-marginalized Ethiopian cuisine to which they had by sheer necessity been exposed. The war against the Allies also imposed fresh constraints that forced Italians to turn even more to Ethiopian food and cooking. As the closure of the Suez Canal and other access routes at the outbreak of war severely handicapped the supply chain, Italians secured new survival resources by incorporating Ethiopian foods into their diet. An Italian in Dembi Dolo (bordering Sudan), Pier Marcello Masotti, recalled:

At that time on the banks of the river there was only one platoon from the garrison in Dembi Dolo, and I was on my way there with about sixty men. Much too little for a counteroffensive. In the evening, we had indigenous cabbage, *kocho* [the thin flatbread made with fermented *ensete* pulp], with polenta in a small tukul by the light of a flashlight, but we turn it out because it served as a point of aim for [enemy] rifles that could have sent our polenta and cabbage up in the air.[16]

"As we descended through the fields to cross the river," Masotti recalled,

we were shot at from the opposite slope: there was a group of armed men—they had been in hiding in the forest for a long time—with two White men near some tukul up high. The two White men began shooting the opposing representatives of the White race [the Italians], who did their best to respond. We quickly set off to conquer the village. The two Englishmen thought it best to flee with their armed men without waiting for us, leaving behind a nice can of pears and a can of ham. Nothing could be more welcome than these war spoils for those reduced to indigenous cabbage and mutton.[17]

By the end of 1940, the war had become a war of all for food. "The attendants of the officers went to steal potatoes from the Mission fields." Masotti wrote.

Meanwhile, the battalion of *Askaris* that had just arrived caused all sorts of trouble. They dispersed, went to shoot at the peasants, and stole as much food as they could. When these petty thieves finally left, they had done more to irritate the population than continuing raids by [Ethiopian partisans], who at least presented themselves for what they were. The Askars left, and we waited for the Belgians, who in turn waited for reinforcements while eating the potatoes from the Mission.[18]

As Masotti's words suggest, the Eritrean and Ethiopian *Askaris* who fought alongside Italian occupiers were the main sources of contact with Ethiopian food and cuisine. Serving in segregated units under the command of an Italian officer, *Askaris* often acted as valuable cultural mediators, knowledgeable about local ecology, agriculture, and foodways, helping Italian troops feed themselves with "indigenous food" when military rations were scarce or of abysmal quality (Figure 21). Italians initially viewed *Askaris* as reckless, cruel, and violent, but later came to see them as noble, courageous, and loyal Allies indispensable for their tenacity in battle and their local knowledge.[19] *Askaris* were doubly racialized: first, as militiamen who, in Eritrean, Amhara, and Tigrinya culture, met prescribed ideals of masculinity but also, as attendants procuring, preparing, and serving food to Italian soldiers, a role Ethiopian culture identified as feminine and servile. By attributing these traits to Black men, Italian soldiers used the culinary services of *Askaris* as a substitute for the unpaid domestic work that Italian women had always provided them as mothers or wives.[20] The *Askaris* usually sourced the best local food available, purchasing or stealing it, and served it to Italian officers as personal field cooks and waiters.

While the soldier Pilosio was more impressed by the brutal methods the *Askaris* used to get food for Italians, officers like Unno Bellagamba appreciated the work of *Askaris* as a welcome relief from the hardships of military life: "The wake-up call in the cold dawn, with the *Askari* preparing coffee Ethiopian style, with salt, was a liberation." Colonial officers like Masotti, stationed on the peripheries of Italian East Africa, counted *Askari* cuisine among their sweetest war memories: "The *Askari* who is with us lights a nice fire and prepares flatbreads on the coals and some tea that we consume peacefully around the fire."[21] In the town of Seka, Lino Calabrò remembered that on Christmas Day 1939,

> after Mass, under the shade of a grove near the Residence, I offered a dinner to which everyone participated. My *Sciumbasci* [the highest rank attainable by Eritrean, Ethiopian, Somali, and Libyan *Askaris* in the Italian army, equivalent to the rank of marshal] made an impressive cake with the traditional inscription "Merry Christmas." In addition to being a brave and loyal soldier, he was an excellent cook.[22]

Malaparte spent several months with colonial troops in anti-guerrilla operations.

> When a battalion of *Askaris* approaches a village, the village chief offers the customary gifts: the girls bring baskets of *injera* (a *teff* focaccia), bottles of sour milk and *tella* (beer), jars of honey, bags of *berbere* (ground chili pepper of a beautiful red-gold color). There is always a crowd of rascals following the battalion, sneaking among the *Askaris*, and so, little by little, from village to village, the battalion swells with gangs of boys from ten to fourteen years old who want to become soldiers. *Askaris* provide their little friends with food from their own ration of flour, sugar, and tea. The boys in the battalion change their name: they are no longer called boys, they are called *gurba*. Every self-respecting *Askari* has his *gurba*: a kind of valet who, when they arrive at the camp, lights the fire, goes in search of water, puts the teapot on the flame, kneads the flour for the *burkutta* (wheat focaccia), and makes red-hot the round stone around which he will wrap the pasta sheet.[23]

During combat, the wives of the *Askaris*

> bring water and bullets to the heavy machine guns, treat the wounded, transport the corpses to the edge of the battlefield, bury the dead; or, sitting around their little fires, prepare tea for their men who are fighting. When, towards sunset, the column stops and pitches its tents, it is the women who light the fire, knead the flour, heat the round stones to cook the *burkutta*, prepare the tea and the *zig'ni* (beef stew).

In the camp near Lake Tana, "there were *Askaris* everywhere drinking *tej* and *tella*. *Askaris* crouched in front of the fires cook the balls of *burkutta* in the ashes, others stir the *zig'ni* sauce in old tin cans, others eviscerate oxen and goats."[24] Malaparte added to the popular portrayal of *Askaris* as good savages, whose knowledge they shared with Italians resembled what Native Americans shared with pilgrims on the first Thanksgiving Day in North America.[25]

Askaris used their skills to hunt game. "During a stop in a village on the edge of a forest, I participated in a buffalo hunt, considered in Ethiopia, along with the rhinoceros and elephant, the most dangerous wild animal," Calabrò recalled.

> We targeted a large male specimen. I fired first, but hit the animal in a nonvital spot, which provoked its reaction. Snorting loudly, it charged in our direction, but was stopped by the infallible shots of the two *Askaris*, who fired almost simultaneously, and fell heavily to the ground. [The *Askaris*] quickly slaughtered it, skinned it, and cut it into pieces. It was a great feast for all the people of the village, who, with singing, dancing, and drumming, devoured that massive amount of meat in the night.[26]

Although he was discussing hunting as a traditionally male activity, Calabrò's representation of the *Askaris* cast them as feminine, almost maternal figures, nourishing and protecting Italian soldiers from the dangers of Africa. In a similar vein, Giuseppe Berto (1914–1978), a lieutenant in command of a battalion, recalled the role of *Askaris* in recreating aspects of middle-class formality and domestic conviviality on the battlefield. In Berto's testimony, *Askaris* provided Italian officers with two valued resources—fresh meat and coffee—that were relatively abundant in Ethiopia but which the Italian army chronically lacked. He served them in a style appropriate to the norms of colonial superiority, respectability, and decorum.

> I went out to dinner. There were a number of fires lit inside the circle of the camp, and somewhere the *Askaris* were singing, clapping their hands in time. They had already started eating. I began to eat seriously, laboriously, the rubbery meat of the freshly slaughtered animals. Under the eyes of the *Bulucbasci* [the second highest rank for *Askaris*, equivalent to sergeant major], the four *Askari* waiters, in white jackets and white gloves, went back and forth noiselessly with bare feet. There were steaks, liver, brain, and kidneys, as much as one wanted. After the meat, they brought dried fruit, almonds, and walnuts, and then the coffee in tin cups that burned the mouth and had a particular smell. There was coffee as much as one wanted, but only the first cup was sweetened because sugar was scarce. So, we sat drinking bitter coffee and chatting, always the same discussions about antipartisan police operations, political information, increases in allowances and salaries, White and Negro women.[27]

Askari fighters were also feminized in their eating habits and tastes: journalist Vittorio Gorresio (1910–1982) noted that

> these soldiers are so elegant, well-groomed, and impeccable could be quite intimidating. With the distinctive green and black vertical striped wool scarf of the battalion, they wrapped and rewrapped their waists, cinching them like a corset, with the coquetry of women. Sober, they sustained themselves with *burkutta*, which is a kind of unseasoned pizza, and with very sweet tea.[28]

In fact, the admiration Italian officers and officials felt toward the *Askaris* often developed into homoerotic feelings and behaviors, especially toward children and boys following the colonial army, such as the *"gurba"* cooks mentioned by Malaparte. An officer in charge of field hospitals, Manlio La Sorsa demonstrated affectionate feelings toward *Askari* children, suggesting that intimacy between officers and these boys was common:

> Today I witnessed the baptism of a beautiful Black boy about twelve years old. He was found wandering and was picked up by a captain. He was malnourished, hungry, ragged, and in a few days, he fattened up, cleaned up, and was dressed in military clothes of the right size; he became a handsome boy, so well-liked by all that he was elected as the battalion's mascot. He eats at the officers' mess, and sleeps in their same tent. The captain, his protector, wanted to baptize him, and this morning there was the ceremony; at the end he was given the standard: the soldiers celebrated him, the superiors kissed him.[29]

Sometimes, such relationships between colonizer and colonized resembled the quasi-conjugal but heterosexual life of physical intimacy the regime had outlawed: "My 'little pest' (that's what I call my little Black boy) clings to me more and more every day, imagine that now he eats with me at the table and how nicely he holds the spoon, and how he cleans his mouth before approaching the glass. He sleeps with me," wrote Marshal Aldo Polcri.

> Enough: I won't write anymore: if I didn't have music and my little Black boy—the little chocolate, as General Marchi calls him—I wouldn't feel like going on. In the moments when I am most overwhelmed by nostalgia for Italy, I let those two little black arms embrace me, I put that beautiful black face next to mine and I feel all tender and good.[30]

The nickname "little chocolate" referred to the fruits of the invasion and creation of the Italian empire: in Italian popular culture, chocolate was the archetypal colonial food along with coffee and bananas. The "loving" nickname given the *Askari* child referred to the consumption of the colonized body in an affective-sexual relationship. It also exposed the reality of intimate food exchanges under racism—in this case, the introduction of European table manners to the Ethiopian child by the Italian officer.

These food encounters went in two directions: *Askaris* introduced Italian soldiers to Ethiopian food, while Italian soldiers introduced *Askaris* to Italian food. Despite the discrimination they suffered, *Askaris* were remembered in Eritrean memory as those who ate best, much better than peasants and salaried workers. The wives of *Askaris*, who regularly followed them on campaigns, recalled the time their husbands served in the Italian army as the one of the most satisfying of their whole life. To be a colonial soldier was to be well-fed, and on a coveted path to social mobility. In *Askari* villages, where a large part of the male population had enlisted in the colonial army, families tended larger herds of animals and could afford to buy modern packaged, canned, and bottled food imported from Italy (Figure 24).[31]

Gastroborderland 2: Domestic Work

The dynamics of food exchange between *Askaris* and Italian soldiers characterized the domestic work performed by Ethiopians in the homes of Italian settlers. Here too, Ethiopian cooks and servers occupied a similarly complicated space as culinary mediators between colonizers and colonized. Like the *Askaris*, they were racialized as primitive, dirty, ignorant, incompetent, unreliable, unfaithful, and treacherous, as well as docile, loyal, faithful, generous, and as affectionate as children. These domestic spaces were points of contact for Ethiopian food and cuisine, which in a segregated marketplace included the mostly fresh foods—milk, butter, eggs, poultry, red meat, vegetables, fruit, spices, flour, mead, and beer—that only Ethiopians were allowed to procure (Figure 23). Italian settlers instructed their servants about preparing food to satisfy their European needs and preferences. These instructions, on cooking and cleanliness, introduced the colonized to the protocols of modernity, with the ultimate goal of accepting as natural the superiority of White society, culture, and technology.[32]

Affirming European culinary superiority was a daily routine in the kitchens and dining rooms of Italian homes. The practice also linked modernity, race, dominance, and subalternity. Italian cuisine was thus prescribed as the only one to adequately nourish Italian colonial bodies. Many Italian settlers themselves were sometimes at odds with this ideology, whenever they were curious about or simply compelled by circumstances to taste the "inferior" food of the colonized, served by the colonized, in the privacy of their "European" homes. And while many popular publications instructed Italian women on how to manage their African homes and take care of their children with the help of their Ethiopian servants, there is, strangely, not a single cookbook, published or unpublished, on the Ethiopian-Italian/Italian-Ethiopian cuisine emerging from these encounters.

The fascist regime assigned great importance to the role Italian women would play in East Africa after 1935. Fascist planners looked forward to a future in which only heterosexual family units would be allowed to immigrate and form the basis of the new colonial society. The "mission" of Italian women in Africa went beyond reproducing a pure Italian race. They were entrusted with the broadest of civilizing missions: enabling the transition from military occupation to a stable and orderly human partnership; bringing decorum to the social lives of Italian men; and disciplining the Ethiopian servants under their command, in the homes where future generations would be born and raised. The propaganda literature on this "mission" of Italian women mixed ideology with practical information about the life they would face in the colony, from "spiritual preparation" to rules of hygiene during childbirth and breastfeeding, from purifying water, tending backyard gardens, and defending themselves from snakes and scorpions to conducting proper "relations with native people."[33]

To prepare women for life in the colony, the Istituto Fascista dell'Africa Italiana (Fascist Institute of Italian Africa), in collaboration with the Fasci Femminili del Partito Fascista (Women's Groups of the Fascist Party), organized courses in hygiene, childcare, and home economics in camps in major cities and provinces.[34] Participants had to take an exam and receive a diploma, patriotically "delivered every year on the solemnity of May 9, anniversary of the foundation of the Empire, Colonial Day." In a

1940 special issue of *Africa Italiana* entitled "Women and the Empire," an illustrated article featured the activities of the camps, including an experimental truck garden, "rational" poultry and rabbit farms, and the "homemade" preparation of butter and bread in a professional kitchen.[35] Other articles provided useful information about creating a modern home in Africa, with an emphasis on cleanliness and hygiene, clothing, and food. In his article, the director of the Tropical Diseases Clinic at the University of Modena, Giuseppe Acanfora, stressed the importance of nutrition for the health of White bodies in subtropical Africa. Acanfora recommended a "predominantly vegetarian diet: vegetables and especially fruit"—vegetables to be eaten cooked to avoid gastrointestinal diseases, especially those vegetables grown "fertilized with human excrement," and fruits eaten raw for their vitamin content. He then invited women, assumed to be responsible for family nutrition, to make "a more moderate use of starchy substances (pasta, bread, potatoes, legumes) than in a temperate climate [i.e., in Italy], while equal use can be made of meats as in the homeland." "Chickens and eggs," likewise, "are excellent food, provided that the chickens are well raised; indeed, it would be advisable for each settler to have her own chicken coop."[36] Such recommendations were meant to discourage eating products imported from Italy (pasta, baking flour, canned vegetables, and fruit) and encourage more fresh local foods (vegetables, fruit, meat, poultry, eggs, milk) that Italians were supposed to be producing in Ethiopia. Acanfora warned, however, that fresh local meat

> must be well cooked, especially if coming from animals not subject to medical examination, and since it cannot be stored in the refrigerator, it must be eaten immediately even if it is somewhat tough, because trying to preserve it in a hot climate can give rise to serious intoxications. Milk is also an excellent food provided it is milked and collected with all hygienic standards (avoid getting milk from Ethiopians).[37]

In its many educational publications, the Istituto Coloniale Fascista (Fascist Colonial Institute) was even more insistent than Acanfora in urging Italian women not to eat Ethiopian food: "White people cannot adapt to the diet of the Ethiopians, and if they were to do so, they would soon fall prey to serious gastrointestinal disorders. It is therefore necessary to follow the rules of food hygiene that are the norm in Europe, with applicable modifications."[38] The Institute suggested avoiding pork (in Ethiopia, "the native, who in this regard can teach us a lesson, does not eat it") and popular cured meats like "salami, mortadella, and sausages." African meat had to be eaten in moderation and with caution due to the lack of refrigeration in a very hot climate.

> Cattle and sheep meat can be found: the former are generally small and not very fine breeds and give tough and not very good meat; instead, sheep, of which a lot is consumed everywhere [in Ethiopia], are generally good, except for their smell, which is very penetrating. Chickens are also quite common, usually very small but good, as are their eggs. Butter can be found made by Ethiopians, but it is usually very bad and therefore one must use canned butter. Oil must be brought from Europe.[39]

Figure 21 *Askaris* of the Italian colonial army on their route to enter Addis Ababa butcher a camel, April–May 1936. Courtesy of Archivio Luce.

Askaris scouted the territory for food, sourced supplies for the troops on the line of combat, and introduced Italian soldiers to the edibles available on the land and how to cook them.

Fascist experts set nutritional and dietary standards that were unattainable for colonial housewives unless they consumed local products, which racial segregation prevented:

> A mixed diet is advisable, in which a vegetarian regime should prevail for the duration of the stay in the colony. Meals should not be abundant, so as not to overload the digestive system with an extra work that, by causing more blood flow to the internal organs, would predispose it to congestions that constitute a favorable ground for infectious germs. The food should therefore be frugal and consist of fresh foods, with the abolition, as far as possible, of preserves and canned foods, which too often hide serious health hazards.[40]

Before leaving for Ethiopia, Italian women were given warnings about avoiding contact with the "natives," but also encouraged to strive for self-sufficiency by growing, processing, and preserving food themselves, and educated about the modernized role of domestic spaces. "Where the common sense and balance of our women are called upon to make a decisive contribution [to the colonial project] is in the distribution of spaces, in their form, in their size, in their furnishings," argued architect Luigi Piccinato (1899–1983).[41] Because "the dwellings of indigenous servants had to be separated from the [colonial] house,"

Figure 22 Ad for Amaro Ramazzotti, Gino Boccasile, 1937. Courtesy of Collezione Salce, Catalogo generale dei Beni Culturali.

Piccinato imagined the homes of settlers as models of middle-class taste and functionality, with "a large living room to be lived in as the true center of the house; a room in which the family gathers for meals, for rest, for hours of shared quality time."[42]

Piccinato insisted on the ideal of a single-family house surrounded by a lawn and trees and perhaps a vegetable garden. It would have either a single floor with an American-style veranda (as in a "bungalow," in English in the text), or two floors with bedrooms upstairs. Its spaces, organized by gender and generation, would protect the privacy of each member of the family. It would also help to counter the odors of a hot climate—the smells of Black bodies and wild animals. "The kitchen and the bathroom should never be in immediate contact with the living room or the bedrooms and possibly always downwind from the rest of the house, so that unpleasant odors do not spread throughout the environment."[43]

Ethiopian servants were called upon by White women to keep their deodorized spaces hygienic and efficient. At the same time, house staff was to be nearly invisible, making minimal contact with the mistress and her family, spending the least time necessary inside to perform their tasks of cleaning and cooking.[44] If, as Italian women were told, Ethiopians had little or nothing to offer in the kitchen, they nevertheless provided an untapped pool of low-cost labor for maintaining White domesticity. Thousands of Ethiopians and Eritreans, women and men, were employed as domestic servants in major cities and in the provinces, making possible an Italian domesticity that proclaimed the "prestige of the race."[45] The laws aimed at combating miscegenation and "as man and wife" relationships between Italian men and African women gradually made it illegal or at least prevented the hiring of Ethiopian women as domestic workers in the homes of single Italian men and in those of families with women and children. As a result, African servants, personal cleaners, handymen, cooks, waiters, and dishwashers in Italian homes were largely male, most of them young or very young.

Intersecting issues of gender, race, and class defined the role that these young male employees played in the development of an Ethiopian-Italian/Italian-Ethiopian cuisine. Since procuring, cooking, and serving food were defined as feminine tasks and since salaried work was associated with servitude, working in Italian homes represented a double experience of emasculation and degradation for Ethiopian men and boys.[46] In the war of 1935–6 and in the guerrilla warfare that followed, the practice of castrating the dead or living enemy, which was occasionally conducted by both sides, was the most feared aspect of the conflict. For male domestic servants, their sense of emasculation and confusion was exacerbated by having to follow the orders of a White mistress, and by showing deference while avoiding even a suggestion of a sexual nature. Vergani described how Ethiopian cooks in Italian homes learned to make pasta dough (*pasta sfoglia*) in the early years of the Italian Empire: "A thousand more Italians [arrive to Ethiopia] every month, their wives struggling to explain to the Ethiopian servant how to make pasta for lasagna."[47]

The letters sent from Ethiopia to Bologna between 1936 and 1941 by Maria Pia Pezzoli represent probably the richest collection of testimonies of Italian housewives and Ethiopian servants, illuminating everyday power relations and food exchanges.[48] Pezzoli arrived in Ethiopia with her husband Giovanni Battista Ellero, a civil servant in the colonial administration. Due to her husband's work, Pezzoli frequently moved during her five years in Africa, living in Piccinato's typical middle-class houses in towns across northern Ethiopia's Tigray region. So often on the move, Pezzoli managed a large Ethiopian or Eritrean staff always at her disposal.

Pezzoli, from an urban middle-class family, wrote about the radical novelty of having a large number of servants:

> Adigrat, August 10, 1936. Then there are the Ethiopian servants: each settler has one to clean their shoes, make the bed and sweep, and bring coffee to the bedroom in the morning. The dining room has three, one of whom is a young boy in charge of pouring wine, really cute. They speak a little Italian. Overall, they are good and kind. Some are Catholic, others Coptic, and others Muslim. The servants wear white with red sashes around their waist when serving breakfast, the Muslims wear a turban.[49]

She often addressed the relationship between servant and mistress:

> Adigrat, August 16, 1936. If you say something and ask if they understood, [the Ethiopian servants] invariably reply yes, except they bring you a chair instead of

your shoes, water instead of the kerosene lamp: with a little kindness and a little harshness, however, you can get everything you want. My servant was so terrified of serving a White woman that every time I spoke to him, he secretly crossed himself![50]

In reality, Pezzoli seemed to use much of her time in Ethiopia controlling the bodies, movements, behaviors, and thoughts of Ethiopian servants, trying to shape them to conform to her standards of European life—social time dictated segmented into work and rest, cleanliness defined by the scientific theory of germs, fashionable clothing as a sign of the respectable body, and, of course, the segregation of public and private spaces.[51] "Enda Selassie, October 14, 1937," Pezzoli wrote in another letter. "When the new kitchen is ready, I hope, with patience, to reduce these [Ethiopian servants] to a different concept of cleanliness. For now, there is nothing but laughter!"[52]

For Pezzoli, European domesticity in the colonial home began in the kitchen, thoroughly cleaned and sterilized. She needed to proclaim herself an emancipated Italian woman, ready for the adventure of an imperial frontier and for her gendered role in the construction of a new society, where installing a civilized Italian cuisine was a woman's responsibility. As Vergani noted,

> One day Addis Ababa woke up and realized that it could dress up for the evening. It became the city with the largest number of women in the Empire. Commerce found in women its greatest supporters. Alongside the men who were content with a bed and a plate of pasta, came the women who wanted a complete dining room, a china coffee cup set, a cart for appetizers. Addis Ababa was populated by more or less improvised horseback riders, tennis players, and dinner reception hosts.[53]

In Addis Ababa, as in the countryside where Pezzoli lived, the presence of African servants allowed settlers to cultivate a middle-class social life and enjoy levels of consumption largely unattainable in Italy, especially in an era of economic sanctions and autarchy.[54] After a modern, comfortable home, the most desired consumer goods included a gas stove, an icebox, quality cooking utensils, dishes, silverware, and table linens. When she entered a new house, Pezzoli first removed everything that was old, dirty, and "African" from the kitchen:

> Enda Selassie, September 26, 1937. The house ... I wouldn't know how to define it! It has all different shapes and aspects, because it was built, as they say, in pieces and chunks. Don't even mention the kitchen, which gave me shivers just by poking my nose in it: black walls, shabby furniture, few utensils, unbelievably dirty, a kitchen stove that emits smoke from all sides: in short, a complete disaster. So, it's been a week since I've been washing non-stop: under the terrified looks of the cook and the laughter of my little servants, I threw pots, coffee makers, pans and various other kitchen items down the hill.[55]

Similarly, teaching servants how to cook and serve Italian style was an attempt at replacing Ethiopian cuisine with a superior Italian cuisine and Ethiopian standards of cleanliness and health with Italian ones, just as technologically advanced fascist agriculture was to replace primitive Ethiopian farming. However, the plan for culinary replacement turned into a "gastronomic recombination, which, while relying on a strong Italian structure, absorbed local ingredients and proposed adaptations and compromises."[56] Pezzoli and her peers ironically faced an inconvenient reality. Without Ethiopian cooks, waiters, and helpers—without their work as cross-cultural mediators—colonial housewives would have needed to resort to preserved food from Italy and on their own labor to create a "home" in Africa. African servants were indeed essential during a time of rising expectations about the quality of colonial domestic life. In fact, in large cities with booming populations such as Addis Ababa and Asmara, the shortage of available African servants reduced the availability of fresh food for settlers: "Adigrat, August 19, 1936. Thank God we escaped [from Asmara] after only three days," Pezzoli wrote. "The infrastructures, housing, and food provisions can't put up with the boom of the city. Go figure that the Reviglios, who had three Black servants, have seen them all quit for other jobs because of the astonishing increase in wages. The *Signora*, fortunately assisted by the girls, now has to do everything herself, and makes do with canned goods."[57]

When her own Ethiopian cook got sick and "failed her," Pezzoli was forced to cook for herself. She noticed how much her tastes had been changed by an emerging Ethiopian-Italian/Italian-Ethiopian cuisine and in daily interactions with her kitchen staff.

Enda Selassie, October 14, 1937. Can you believe it? That sort of a cook got sick, and for about a week I've been the cook!!!!!!! In the kitchen one cannot stand the smoke, and all the pots and pans are half-broken. The recipes in the cookbook Ida sent me [from Italy] refer to ingredients unknown and unavailable here: *fiordilatte* mozzarella, ox marrow, lemons; and to non-existent objects: molds, oven, porcelain that withstands fire ... To the cry of *viva le uova* [hooray for the eggs], salads, and canned food, I go ahead anyway, and I'm making a reputation for myself with *risotto alla milanese*, the signature dish of my cooking (not to say the only one!)[58]

As months went by, Pezzoli's interest in Ethiopian food culture grew, as she joined her husband in banquets with local elites. Pezzoli learned about Ethiopian ingredients, tastes, and styles in the act of eating together. Her Ethiopian cooks, waiters, guests, and hosts became cross-cultural facilitators of Italian influences that changed Ethiopian cuisine as well. Pezzoli described what she ate and drank at the banquets, observing as well how Ethiopian food rituals were shaped by social class.

Enda Selassie, February 17, 1938. We ate *zig'ni* and drank *tej*, well hidden from the eyes of the Ethiopians by various cloth drapes attached to the *dass* [a pergola]. Indeed, it is not allowed for lower-class people to see notable people eating. I'm sure that if you were here, these people would amuse you greatly, so wise and so childish at the same time. Perhaps you would like their hygiene habits a little less: but it's just a matter of getting used to them! To a higher-class person, for example, you never offer food without first tasting it, perhaps taking it with your hands from the same plate, just as taking something out of your mouth to offer it to another diner is a sign of special affection, and it means very much when it's an inferior person doing that towards a superior. Similarly, rising from the table, you're supposed to offer the wine that remains in your glass to your attendant. But one must be careful not to show any bit of preference for one servant over the other, because jealousy is rampant. I have had two or three little incidents already, in which I have been scolded because "the Mistress' heart has changed," or "the Mistress no longer looks at her son."[59]

Pezzoli's culinary identity developed from daily conversations with the Ethiopians in her household. Although she insisted to her friends back home that she remained "Italian" and that her European culture was not dissolving in wild "Africanness," she made clear that she was adopting at least some Ethiopian foodways.

'Āddi Qa'yeh, January 20, 1937. None of the many *"porcherie"* [garbage, awful food] that I eat and drink is bad for me, and I always digest very well. It may be the climate that makes local foods totally acceptable, in fact if the Ethiopians eat like this, there must be a reason. Those in the lowlands feed almost exclusively on milk, because with the great heats *zig'ni* would not be digestible! However, when we are not invited by the Ethiopians, we do not fail to eat European-style.[60]

After five years of empire-building, Italian women settlers felt they had mostly succeeded in disciplining their Ethiopian servants and turning them into efficient kitchen helpers. At the same time, the women conceded that their diet now included many elements learned from their staff and from local food purveyors. In her usual paternalistic tone, Jolanda Rapaccini recounted how in May 1941, with the British rounding up the Italians in her village for deportation, her Ethiopian servants no longer addressed her as their mistress, but as their *"mamma."*

They [had] given me two little boys for service in my house. One is a little older, he must be about five years old, he is thin with very fine features, big eyes, a calm and dignified air; the other, younger and shorter, ugly, with a pockmarked face, I think from having had smallpox, but so quick-witted and so clever! I know that they reluctantly agreed to come working for me, because they believed that a woman did not know how to treat them and would beat them. If to receive beatings from a man could be a harsh punishment, to receive them from a woman would be an offense to their dignity, and the first few days they looked at me fearfully and suspiciously. I let them be, and little by little, teaching them the chores they had to take care of, I saw them grow fond of me. I open the door to the veranda and see beyond the gate on the street my old suppliers. I call to them: "You, Fulmine [one of the two servant-children], open the gate!" They come in and stand in front of me, I recognize one I haven't seen in a while. "Mistress, we come to say goodbye, give this to you" and they place on the ground a chicken, a bunch of bananas, a rag full of eggs, and some peaches. "I understand, but I don't want to buy it." Abdissa steps forward and says, "No mistress, don't buy, we don't want money, no, don't want. We come to give this and say always you be like a mother, be a great mistress, always buy, give money, give medicine. You gave us bread, gave us clothing."[61]

Since Italian single men, unlike women, were not expected to act as guardians of their culinary and domestic traditions, they seemed much more open to exotic gastronomic inputs from their servants. Although both men and women settlers racialized their help as incompetent, unreliable, stupid, naïve, or childish, a certain "masculinity of the imperial frontier" uniting Italian masters and Ethiopian servants created a common ground for everyday food exchanges. Italian men were confident that their teachings would fairly easily turn Ethiopian servants into excellent cooks.

As sometimes happened in the army, the rapport between male Italian masters and male Ethiopian cooks and waiters living together could develop into a homoerotic relationship, albeit one configured by the unequal dynamics of colonialism: "Having set up my tent in a coffee forest, I chose a 'boy' from among the many Ethiopians who offered their services," settler Lino Calabrò wrote of his arrival in the remote western town of Seka.

> I provided him with a plentiful supply of soap and clothed him from head to toe. His name was Zelleca Mangascia and he was a young Amhara man, intelligent, tall, sturdy and with regular features. He learned Italian quickly and from day one performed his duties with great care and absolute honesty. He remained with me, as a faithful, devoted, and irreplaceable collaborator until the last day in Ethiopia.[62]

Even proletarian settlers could for the first time afford the care provided by Ethiopian children and boys who worked for little money and food, sometimes offering sexual services. "Our *morettino* [pretty Black boy] cleans up in the barrack, fetches water to drink and wash ourselves, shine our shoes, goes to do some shopping, brings us coffee in bed, etc., etc.," Guerrino, the truck driver from Bologna, told his wife in a letter.[63]

In their earliest accounts of the helpers who cooked for them, single officials and settlers complained about their servants' backwardness, incompetence, ignorance, and superstition. Masotti recalled,

> I had returned before dawn, dodging my Balilla convertible through hyenas and bushes, and had discovered that the servants, in twenty-four hours, had celebrated the birth [of Masotti's daughter] with our liquor, leaving behind a pile of empty bottles. Unfortunately, there was no possible punishment, no matter how desirable, as they responded to reprimands with a complacent face and a deaf ear. The passion for liquor is widespread among Copts, who prefer it to beer and indigenous mead, and also among Muslims who are supposed to be teetotalers. I asked the cook Abdu, whom General Cubeddu had appointed *Basciai* [or *Pasha*, an honor granted *Askaris* for twenty years of service] for his culinary virtues, to at least exercise a little discretion when he was clandestinely drinking the General's alcohol, especially since he was a Muslim. He answered by swearing on his own son's life that he had not touched a drop of alcohol.[64]

Masotti again reported:

> We found us an attendant, a Muslim *Shanqella* [a pejorative name for "Black" or "dark-skinned" applied by Abyssinians to the non-Abyssinian peoples of western Ethiopia] from the eastern lowlands, small, with a face all tattooed and pitted by smallpox, but always cheerful and full of good will. He would shine my boots with one hand and try to boil coffee and make us breakfast in the morning with the other, with the inevitable result of serving us shoe grease-flavored coffee with sugar. I well remember the tribal marks on good Mahammud's face, his cheerful smile, as well as his tears when I reprimanded him because there was too much shoe cream in the coffee or he had spilled coffee on my boots.[65]

Another young colonial officer, Vincenzo Ambrosio, echoed Masotti's complaints but also insisted on his ability to "educate" his servants with the combination of paternalism and toughness typically portrayed as the colonial "toolbox" of Italian men. He wrote to his sister in Rome:

> Jimma, November 30, 1937. My new waiter is Momo; in white gloves, impassive, silent. He must shave every week. Of course, he is the cleanest of the waiters, plus he acts as my "cut-throat" as he specializes in catching rats. We exchange a few words a day. I: "Momo!" (brusque command in a low voice); He: "Sir?" (very correct); I: "Water to drink"; He: "There is no water"; I: "You are a fool, you know that …"; He: "Yes, Sir." And so continuing.[66]

The metanarrative of settler's letters and memoirs also reveals that, despite official racial segregation, the tastes of Italians and Ethiopians were changing. "In Bedele, a large and comfortable shack equipped with a fireplace was designated for the canteen," Calabrò recalled. "Next to it, another shack was built that functioned as a kitchen. The cook, a heathen Oromo, under the guidance of the doctor and myself learned very well how to do his job—even though, for religious reasons, he never tasted the food he cooked—succeeding, in spite of this, in preparing excellent dishes seasoned just right."[67] "We found an excellent cook, an *Askari* who had been in the employ of a general of the colonial troops, General Cubeddu, who is remembered not for his military virtues but for those of a gourmet, which he had transmitted to his [Ethiopian] cook."[68]

Ethiopian home cooks served Italian settlers in another important way, by feeding their children. Having learned Italian culinary practices, they were charged with caring for children born in Ethiopia or brought there with their families at a young age. In many ways, Ethiopian cooks, although almost entirely young and male, filled a role comparable to one played by African American women as nurturers of White children in the American South. Their role went beyond simple care giving into taste-making that—as a dimension of cultural hybridization—powerfully influenced the development of African American cuisine, the cuisine of the southern United States, and American cuisine as a whole.[69]

Largely ignoring the reality of child care in colonial homes, Italian medicine served its political purpose by warning parents against feeding their children "Ethiopian food," starting with the use of African wet nurses.[70] In the article "The Feeding of the Child in the Colony," which appeared in *La difesa della razza*, the eugenicist Giuseppe Lucidi (who had proposed a "census of blood" to determine the racial makeup of the Italian population) discussed the subject of wet nursing.[71] He identified breast milk as food and its sharing between Ethiopian women and Italian children as a moment of reciprocity and interracial proximity, which inevitably posed a challenge to the "problem" of biological contact and the interracial transmission of bodily fluids that underpinned Italian racist thought.

> An extremely important and worthy of study issue is the feeding during the first months of life of the Italian child in the Colony. If it is true what an old proverb says, "she who breastfeeds is the mother, not she who gives birth," it is neither desirable nor advisable for a White person, and even more so for an Italian child, to have an indigenous wet nurse, especially today that the laws for the defense of the Race have established in our Empire not only clear racial differences, but also racial superiority. They also prohibit indigenous mercenary [paid] wet nursing for hygienic and prophylactic reasons given the high prevalence of infectious diseases among those populations.

Above the caption "White children should not be entrusted to Black wet nurses," a prominent illustration depicted a Black woman who, with her large hands, took a White newborn from the crib to breastfeed. "It is well known, in fact, that Whites who have received the milk of a Black wet nurse (this has frequently occurred in America and rarely among us)," Lucidi argued, "have subsequently suffered not only from infectious diseases, but also from intestinal and nervous diseases that have made them physically and mentally impaired."[72]

For Lucidi, any food produced by Ethiopians was harmful and thus unsuitable for Italian children:

> The cow's milk from the Ethiopian highlands has a high percentage of fat and casein, which can cause dyspepsia, delayed gastric emptying, and severe digestive disorders in the child to whom it is fed. Like cow's milk, goat's milk, camel's milk, etc. are also not recommended for the same reasons, as well as for the ignorance of hygiene standards on the part of the indigenous people in charge of milking. They often dilute milk with dirty and infected water. Until Italian experts organize dairies that produce hygienically safe milk, [Ethiopian] milk must be avoided.

The only food suitable for Italian children was imported from Italy or otherwise "European," at least until Italian agroindustry began producing "Italian" food in the colony:

> For the vitaminization of the child, it is good to add diluted or sweetened orange or lemon juice between meals from the third month of life, or mashed banana juice according to the use introduced by Belgian doctors in the Congo. Recommended for the child are fruits, both fresh and dried, canned or in jelly. As for the problem

of drinking water, the highlands are rich in springs, but while waiting for Italian hydraulic works to proceed, the best precaution to avoid infections is boiling it or using bottled mineral water.[73]

Propaganda photographs frequently showed Italian children being nourished by imported food.[74] In most cases, however, evidence suggests that Italian children, more so than adults, were fed "Ethiopian food" grown in truck gardens, purchased at "native markets," and cooked by Ethiopian servants. "I was busy preparing breakfast and watching that Fulmine [the Ethiopian child cook-waiter] did not burn the breadcrumbs, with which I prepared the porridge [for Simonetta, the settler's newborn daughter]," Rapaccini recalled. "I want to clean up my little garden of so many weeds and sow some lettuce, some zucchini, because now it is so difficult to find vegetables [from Ethiopian vendors], I want to always have them available for Simonetta's soups."[75]

Gastroborderland 3: Sex Work

Another liminal encounter between Ethiopians and Italians was prostitution, a privilege enjoyed by almost the entire male Italian population during the years of occupation between 1935 and 1941. Of the one hundred or so male memoirs and correspondences consulted for this book only a few do not report sexual relations with African sex workers. Most of these encounters can be fairly classified as rape and sexual violence because of the very young age of the women and their lack of consent.[76] In collective male memory, African prostitutes are exoticized and celebrated at the same time as they are denigrated and feared as transmitters of diseases and especially as enchantresses who could make Italian men forfeit their identity and sense of self. Malaparte represented this dual nature of *sciarmutte* as pagan saints and deadly threats: "There is something warrior-like about them. I wouldn't be surprised if they carried a long sword hidden under their clothes."[77]

Encounters between Ethiopian women and Italian men frequently involved food. The places where prostitutes often worked were informal taverns (*tej bets*) where *tej*, *tella* and other foods were served, or their own homes, where they usually served coffee and food to clients. Sometimes the payment for sex work was in kind and often consisted at least in part of parcels of "Italian" food. As one of the few institutional opportunities for interracial contact, sex work was also an encounter across food boundaries—a multisensory repertoire of smells, tastes, and sensations on the margins of two segregated communities.

Prior to the Italian invasion, prostitution was generally accepted in rural Ethiopia since it usually involved women of a lower social class and/or without ties to a man, unmarried, widowed or divorced. The prostitution of a daughter could be a family's acceptable response to an economic crisis such as a livestock epidemic. Prostitution could also provide an escape from an oppressive family. Many Ethiopian women entered the sex trade as independent workers, having opened informal shops (*tej bets*) where sex was offered by themselves and by other women. The expansion of *tej bets* into full-scale brothels was particularly successful in Addis Ababa. From the beginning of the twentieth century to the mid-1930s, the capital city grew rapidly, mostly from migrants from rural areas and transient single men. Even in smaller cities like Jimma prostitution was already widespread by the early 1930s, linked to places serving alcohol. The king of the Gibe Kingdom of Jimma, Abbā Jafar II (1861–1932), had banned the sale of alcohol to control rampant "vice" in the city. Despite the ban, at the time of the Italian occupation in 1936 there were still many places where *tallā* and *taj* were served, managed by women (called, in Oromo, *komārits*, or distillers and brewers) who were also sex workers.[78] For urbanized rural women, the sex work they found in *tej bets* was the most widely available and profitable occupation.[79] With the arrival of the Italians, sex work grew rapidly enough to "change the morphology of the city."[80]

The arrival of Italian soldiers and settlers not only spread the practice of prostitution, but transformed it into a more organized commercial activity. There were a number of reasons for the ubiquity of sex work: the numerical imbalance between Italian men and women; the appeal of sex as a reward of the colonial experience, something off limits in Italy; laws against miscegenation that prevented Italian men from having families with Ethiopian women; the destruction of Ethiopian communities that left "single women" with few economic alternatives; and the failure of colonial authorities to bring in more than a minimal number of European sex workers.[81] The fascist state considered prostitution in Italian East Africa an issue on which the entire racist and segregationist structure of the empire was based. Colonial authorities attempted to organize sex work, regulating brothels for Black and White women—the latter obviously reserved for White men—and separating them into brothels for officers and "respectable people" on one side and soldiers and proletarians on the other. Strict medical control was also imposed on prostitutes.[82]

For Mussolini, "ideally Italian men's sexual relations with African women were to be limited to client/prostitute relations: depersonalized relationships, where the colonized only served as instruments to perform what Italian rulers conceived as a physiological function."[83] In effect, prostitution was the largest state-authorized breach in the structure of racial segregation in Italian East Africa. As a result of official encouragement, prostitution swelled throughout the colony. According to German journalist and fascist sympathizer Louise Diel (1893–1967), by 1937 there were 1,500 African sex workers in Addis Ababa alone (while White prostitutes numbered only forty-seven).[84]

For Italian clients, sexual intercourse with Ethiopian women often accompanied the sharing of food in a bonding of the senses. The settler Manlio La Sorsa wrote that

> here in Adi Ugri I found the Ethiopians to be a little more evolved and refined. We were invited to have coffee by a family consisting of a widowed mother and two daughters, one of whom was seven or eight months pregnant, and since I see that she has preserved the hairstyle of a virgin, they explain to me that she got pregnant by an Italian officer (and they say this with pride, and as if her virginity had remained intact …). The other girl is rather ugly in the face, with horribly protruding teeth, but kind and affable to deal with. The coffee is pounded in the usual rudimentary wooden pestles, while the water boils in a small container. The coffee is truly excellent and genuine, but seeing it prepared by such dirty people with

such unhygienic means is initially somewhat repugnant, which must be overcome so as not to offend the pride of these people. In this house they also prepared the Abyssinian bread or focaccia [*injera*] made of wheat flour and water, mixed in a liquid blend, and poured onto the circular surface of an oven. This is made up of a kind of countryside stove: the lower part is lit with wood, and the upper surface made of black or blackened stone is perfectly smooth and circular. The liquid dough is poured in such a way as to form a thin circular layer, and a kind of thick conical lid is placed on top. They cook it for a few minutes, then they remove the layer of bread and place it in a basket to cool. This Abyssinian bread has a yellowish white color, without crust, flattened, soft, pitted for rising, and has a strong smell of fresh wheat. Another specialty is Abyssinian wine or beer [*tej*], prepared with honey made to ferment and sour. Each bottle is sold for two lire, has the appearance of a milky liquid, similar to *orzata* [Italian sweetened almond syrup mixed with water], and has a slightly sour, not unpleasant, refreshing, slightly alcoholic taste.[85]

La Sorsa realized that in the context of sexual relations, the language of food flowed better than other attempts at communication.

While sipping the coffee they offered to me, two other girls in their twenties, friends of the family, entered the house. From the way they dressed, and from that desire to imitate Europeans, painting their nails, adorning themselves with various useless trinkets, and perfuming themselves with cologne, I understood that they were easy women. I ask if I can go home with them. They make a sign for me to follow them, and we enter a discreet little room, with two European-style beds, with mosquito nets and two rich oriental carpets as blankets. Although there are no furnishings other than a few benches and a table, there is some order and cleanliness. Even the women, relative to the others, are clean and wear washed clothes. A stupid conversation ensues: of course, it is not easy to understand each other, nor do we know what to say; we make some jokes, we squeeze some pinches in the soft parts, just for laughs, but not because we can feel the slightest desire for these women so different from ours, but above all so dirty and dangerous ... I have noticed, however, that even the prostitutes here have a certain modesty about themselves, they are jealous of their own person, even though they put it at your disposal for a couple lire, and are more bashful ... It's been a month since I left Italy.[86]

Even here, the exchange of food worked in two directions. Poggiali recalls how on Easter in 1937 in Adigrat, many Italian men went to the local brothel bringing with them leftover food from the Easter banquet as a payment in kind, and that, after "venal acts of love, an empty can that had contained tomato sauce, filled with water, was used for ablutions."[87] In Berto's account of committing a pedophilic (and Oedipal) sexual act with an Ethiopian teenage girl, the chocolate he offers the young woman is meant to "break the ice" and establish a relationship that—to his relief—bears some semblance of human connection. For Berto, the "gift" of chocolate could reaffirm his position of power and the superior taste of Italian food. It also anticipates the pleasure of consuming the undernourished Black body and, not least, paying for sexual service.

She was sitting on the ground, her head entirely covered by a very dirty white shawl. "*Ancì* [hey you]," he called her, "what is your name?" Through the fabric, he perceived the thickness of her hair, which had the usual smell of rancid butter he now [after years in Ethiopia] immediately associated with the possession of a woman. He forcefully moved the shawl from her head. The face, not very dark, was small and regular, with closed eyes and lips tightened in an expression of frightened uncertainty. She looks like a child, he thought tenderly. He searched in the chocolate box and offered her a piece, putting it right under her nose. She accepted it, holding out her two hands cupped together, but then she remained with the chocolate in her hand and her head low, and he had to explain to her with gestures that that stuff was for eating, and she, still distrustful, put a piece in her mouth, and then she even smiled, to show that she liked the stuff. He waited for her to finish eating the chocolate, then he took her by the arms and made her stand up. He told her to undress, but since she did not move, he undressed her himself after untying the belt of her dress. She had a small body, as expected, and thin, with all the ribs visible, and the small, barely pronounced breast. She was perhaps not even twelve years old, but after all, it was not her fault if a twelve-year-old girl was a prostitute, and then those were particular countries and people, it would have been ridiculous to have scruples. He fiddled with the box to take out some coins and chocolate, all the chocolate he had left. She accepted it with a bow and kept the chocolate in her hand, continuing to look at it, although she now knew that that stuff was to be eaten. He no longer knew what to do. But to welcome the child next to him in the narrow bunk, and to warm her and caress her gently, a little like he was a child in his mother's big bed, this he wanted, only this. He explained to the child, with gestures, that she had to move into the bunk. She got up, docile. She put the chocolate on the box and then looked at him, questioningly, as she prepared to take off her dress.[88]

In her study of a century of prostitution in Addis Ababa, Laketch Dirasse argued that the Italian occupation led to the decline of traditionally accepted sex work that formerly took place in small establishments serving mead, beer, and food, and run for regular clients by the women themselves. According to Dirasse, prostitution became a purely monetary, capitalist enterprise with the arrival of European invaders and their state control of brothels and segregation of public spaces for food consumption.[89] In July 1937 colonial authorities closed, in Addis Ababa alone, "about seventy *tej bets*, harmless and simple places where native people found enjoyment with so little."[90] However, the liminal areas for prostitution continued to support a significant interactive food dimension until the end of the empire.

Gastroborderland 4: Culinary Diplomacy

An emerging focus of food studies is gastrodiplomacy, or culinary diplomacy—the use of food as a diplomatic instrument in international relations. In its broadest sense, culinary diplomacy includes such practices as official dinners during meetings or international conferences; the use of food and cuisine for branding identities and soft power initiatives to promote cities, regions, and nations; and food aid as solidarity for communities affected by wars, natural disasters, and famines.[91]

For both Ethiopians and Italians, gastrodiplomacy was commonplace. The banquets offered by one group to another were held for various reasons, but always constituted a vital exception to food segregation. They permitted the two communities to represent themselves publicly to one another, to communicate who they were and who they wanted to become. Such boundary-crossing hospitality was reserved at formal banquets and dinners for Italian army officers, administrators, and middle-class settlers, and, on the Ethiopian side, the *Ras*, higher Christian Orthodox or Muslim clergy, and other potentates and lords. At lower social levels, such occasions of commensality were for the most part possible only when Italian men entered into Ethiopian society, voluntarily or not. These were the men called *insabbiati*, who will be discussed later.

Within all the variant forms of culinary diplomacy, social class differences were always in play: the photographs in the book *Colonialismo e fotografia: Il caso italiano* edited by Luigi Goglia illustrate the very different foods, dinnerware, and tableware used in a banquet for Ethiopian and Italian notables compared to the lunches Italian authorities offered Muslim villagers, the poor of Addis Ababa, or Ethiopian students in segregated colonial schools.[92]

For Pezzoli, the luncheons to which she and her husband were regularly invited were a rare opportunity to meet Ethiopians outside the racial hierarchies of her domestic life. They dined mostly with village chiefs, some of whom gifted her with food. These gifts were not acts of submission but rather gestures of hospitality and relationship-building. "For the table, we joined the Colonel commander of the garrison and ate divinely well," Pezzoli wrote in a letter. "Legume soufflés, rice and semolina puddings, pureed soups, and custards à la Portuguese. Fresh fruit also appears in the form of bananas brought to us by the [Ethiopian] district chiefs of the lowlands."[93] The interaction with local chiefs occurred almost exclusively through food: "'Äddi Qa'yeh, December 16, 1936. The chiefs and notables have started to arrive with gifts: the village chief, *Fitawrari* (Commander of the Vanguard, a high Ethiopian military title) Ghebresghi, has given us a kid (baby goat), apologizing for not being able to give us a cow today!"[94]

In preparing banquets for Italian guests, Ethiopian notables instructed their chefs to consider the identity of the guests and make concessions to their taste, so that menus were typically hybrid creations. Diplomat Luigi Pignatelli Della Leonessa recalled a dinner given by a *Ras*:

> The table was set, white and bright in the dim light of that honorable cave. One of the *Degiac*'s servants had been a waiter at an officer's table, and another, also an ex-*Askari*, had been the cook and knew how to cook Italian dishes as well as prepare local dishes like the celebrated *zig'ni*, made of pieces of chicken or lamb drowned in the sauce of fiery red peppers. Resting on the floor was the large, finely woven and colored basket of *injera*, full of soft gray discs that for the majority of Ethiopians replace bread. Soon the servant appeared, carrying, instead of the soup

tureen, an enameled iron basin in which a small mountain of macaroni in tomato sauce was smoking.⁹⁵

Culinary diplomacy was often practiced by Italian authorities in Muslim communities in Harar and other regions. The Italian policy toward Muslims was generally benevolent, in an attempt to isolate them from the Abyssinian Christian Orthodox communities with whom Italians faced constant struggles—the victims of Italian brutality were largely ethnic Amhara and Tigray people of Coptic Orthodox faith. As Poggiali demonstrates, culinary diplomacy could bypass Islamic law to accommodate the supposed preferences of Italian guests:

> July 26, 1936, Sunday. At 5 pm, tea at the home of a Muslim leader. It is a villa in the middle of the swamp, with a dirty veranda, and a sumptuously set table. There is no tea, but there is chicken, roast beef with garlic, anchovy fillets, salmon, goat butter and cheese, jam, cookies, and whiskey. I feast. The attestation of Muslims' loyalty to Italy is solemnized.⁹⁶

Ethiopian hosts sought to please their Italian guests while demonstrating their personal power by serving not only Ethiopian cuisine but also prestigious Italian import, such as spaghetti, wine, and vermouth, and setting a European table. For Ethiopian notables, culinary diplomacy helped them redefine their identities. Internalizing imperial hierarchies and participating in the construction of a racially inferior self was, as Fanon famously theorized, the deepest legacy of colonialism.⁹⁷ Culinary diplomacy was, however, a tactic Ethiopian leaders deployed to negotiate with Europeans, obtaining the greatest advantages possible within unequal power relations and asserting their own cultural hegemony as colonized elites.⁹⁸ These dynamics—produced by what Fanon called the "total project" of colonialism—were on display in the lunch that an Abyssinian nobleman offered his Italian guests in Ambo, a town in western Shewa in November 1936: "*Ras* Hailu Tekle Haymanot was the chief of royal blood who, at the head of eighteen hundred men, was roaming across the plain to cleanse it of bandits and insurgents," remembered Poggiali. "He received us in the main room of the ramshackle dwelling, reclining on a wicker armchair with a semicircle of stools carved from the trunk and a table set with many glasses for vermouth, which he offered liberally, perhaps in homage to memories of his pleasant stay in Turin."⁹⁹

Similar strategies shaped a lunch party that the *Ras* of Dessie hosted for Italian guests. The menu included *doro wat* (chicken with red pepper) followed by spaghetti, a sequence in reverse of the classic Italian first and second course order.

> Upon arrival in the morning, in addition to the necessary ceremonies, mutual flattery, praise for the great Italian Government, congratulations to the District Chief for his impeccable honesty and integrity, lunch was served. The rulers of the Dessie region knew how to live in the world, even if their villages were two days' march from the city, and they wanted to demonstrate it. So, lunch with a large glass of cognac as an aperitif, chicken with red pepper, massive quantities of spaghetti after the chicken, and Chianti wine for dessert. After lunch, the government official

began the work of studying the situation, examining some rulings by the District Chief, visiting some village chiefs, always trying not to offend the sensitivity of the *Ras*, and not to diminish, but rather to increase, the deference of their subjects toward them.[100]

Italian functionaries faced similar protocol issues in preparing banquets for Ethiopian guests invited to improve alliances and strengthen group relations. These issues concerned the appropriate rules, customs, and techniques of consumption and commensality. In bourgeois European culture, the use of a fork represented civilization; the use of hands was a mark of inferiority.[101] In Ethiopia's convivial culture, a sophisticated behavioral code signaled the social, familial, and generational status of the diners. The hands, as well as the rest of the body, were the instruments of good manners and sociability, expressing respect for each diner. The right hand alone could be used to take food from serving platters and bring it to the mouth. The use of a common serving tray or platter and the woven wicker basket containing *injera*, the *agelgel* or *mäsob* from which diners took food and placed it on the *injera* in their individual plate required careful movements. The act of dipping pieces of *injera* in the spicy meat stew of wat or in the stew of legumes and spices of *shiro* had to be done only once: to avoid contamination, the guest had to finish eating the entire bite in his plate before ripping another piece of *injera*. Diners had to respect a system of getting their food in turn. Burping was a sign of approval of the quality of the food. The gesture of a lower status diner feeding a superior by hand, or a host feeding a guest in the same fashion, expressed a highly stratified and personalized dining code.[102]

In turn, Italian culinary diplomats had to please their Ethiopian guests of importance, even as they insisted on the superiority of European culinary practices. Masotti ironically reflected that a "picnic" (in English in the text) may have been a compromise made between the table, foreign to African traditions, and the lowly carpet, where Abyssinians dined, crouching: "As for the local leaders of Dembi Dolo, one could have a picnic on the grass with them, but making them sit at the table was a torture for both the guest and the host."[103] Masotti also wondered about another Ethiopian practice that Italians felt compelled to incorporate into culinary diplomacy, the custom that people of higher lineage could not be looked at while eating by individuals of a lower social class or an inferior ethnic group.

> Another tradition is that when the chief eats, and a quick meal along the road was normal, must be kept away from the public eye; therefore, four *Askaris* spread out just a few inches from the Intendent's nose and his Italian companions four not-so-clean shawls. While any Ethiopian beggar who has received a little *injera*—their unleavened bread—turns his back on the next person to eat it, dining leaders to maintain their status had to be hidden from indiscreet eyes.[104]

Even these carefully orchestrated interracial banquets and dinners could not completely conceal deeply seated differences in identities and mentalities. The ingrained values, behaviors, and tastes each group learned in their stratified societies—what

Pierre Bourdieu called *habitus*—were ultimately revealed for all to see across well-set tables.[105] Pezzoli provided an example:

> Om Hager, December 12, 1939. We will have dinner in Teseney with His Honor Gasparini, who is the president of the cotton company. He cares a lot about elegance and appearance: imagine that every evening, even when he is alone, he dines in a tuxedo! Then we will have visits and dinners with the British authorities in Kassala, and so we will have the opportunity to prove our taste and stylishness.[106]

In Adigrat on August 19, 1936, Pezzoli met leaders who collaborated with Italians:

> I went by the office (which is a shack about a hundred yards from our "house") to enjoy the spectacle of the procession and songs of the Eritrean Coptic and Catholic Easter. We had *Ras* Seyoum Mengesha [1887–1960] over for breakfast. He is a beautiful type, very polite, but, however, towards the end of breakfast he could just not resist the temptation and started eating with his hands![107]

Malaparte, experienced in culinary diplomacy, concluded that the table manners of an Ethiopian leader were proof that he was a "crook, enemy of Italy": "I read in a French newspaper that I found on a coffee table in Addis Ababa a profile of Abebe Aregai [1903–1960], the infamous rebel, the larger-than-life hero. Abebe Aregai is just a bandit like many others, He eats with his hands."[108]

Another type of culinary diplomacy was practiced mainly by Italians, who distributed food in order to win popular sympathies and counter their all-too-accurate image as brutal invaders. Colonial authorities offered banquets to communities in the regions of Ethiopia (Oromia) that had had fewer contacts with Europeans, to Muslim communities considered more "friendly," and occasionally to the needy in cities like Addis Ababa. Stationed in Seka in the Jimma district, the official Calabrò frequently used culinary diplomacy to achieve—as Fanon would have said—"the normalization of relations between colonizer and colonized," including the cooptation of Ethiopian leaders.

> The receptions I received [from the Oromo] and their declarations of loyalty and friendship were certainly sincere, but there was no doubt that the inhabitants of those villages were also obliged to have contacts with the bands hostile to us [the Ethiopian resistance partisans] to whom they had to provide food, livestock and sometimes shelter, under penalty of brutal reprisals. I therefore intensified my visits, going to the various districts at the head of *Askari* units stationed in Seka. During these trips, I always carried abundant supplies of food with me, not only to ensure the food for my men, but also to be able to distribute it most generously to the neediest people everywhere. I was able to assess the local leaders who enjoyed the most prestige. Among these, I chose as my trusted collaborators the *Cagnasmacc* [a title indicating a status inferior to *Ras*, *Degiac*, and *Fitawrari*, as a "commander of the right wing"] Sada Beyan, the head of the Coptic clergy Aleca Makonnen, and a Muslim holy man, Ali Mohammed. I charged them with

Figure 23 Italian soldiers peruse fruits at the Harar "indigenous" market, May 8, 1935. Courtesy of Archivio Luce.

Notwithstanding the racial segregation of markets and all public spaces of food consumption, Italians heavily depended on Ethiopian purveyors for fresh local food, such as all kinds of produce, dairy, and poultry.

Figure 24 An Italian soldier offers canned food to a group of Ethiopians, April 26–May 5, 1936. Courtesy of Archivio Luce.

Contradicting the notion that occupied Ethiopia should have immediately been self-reliant on its food supplies while contributing to Italy the quality calories in grains and meat it needed, at the same time as Ethiopian exports to Italy were minimal, enormous quantities of canned and packaged food were imported from Italy to Ethiopia to feed Italian settlers in the colony. Ethiopians selectively incorporated Italian industrially processed food into their cuisine.

the task of pacification, assuring them that all members of guerrilla bands who presented themselves to me voluntarily would be able to return undisturbed to their villages.[109]

The ongoing warfare between Ethiopian partisans and Italian troops was mostly about food. Guerrillas constantly attempted to destroy the infrastructure of the imperial food system while Italians conducted a scorched earth policy to isolate and starve areas around the "insurgents." In this larger context, culinary diplomacy was one strategy for winning consent. Traditionally, food was distributed through a feudal regime as a customary bond of loyalty between peasants and lords. The building of consensus through food distribution by local powers represented the Ethiopian version of what E. P. Thompson identified as the "moral economy of food, hunger, and protest" of the Ancien Régime, when peasant masses expected that elites would save them from starvation in times of famine or war, but responded with bloody revolts when their expectations were betrayed.[110] Calabrò recalled:

To help the Oromo villagers whose crops had been destroyed, I bought thirty-five tons of corn and half a ton of salt using market tax revenues, and had them distributed among the population by the committee of elders. It was the first time in the history of the region, and I believe of Ethiopia, that the government authority was concerned with helping populations affected by a calamity. The measure was therefore greeted with great joy and aroused a wave of gratitude that moved me and made me reflect on the importance that a basic gesture of humanity like the distribution of food to the hungry could have among those simple people.[111]

For Calabrò, as for many other Italian officials, these diplomatic ventures were also opportunities for exploring Ethiopian foodways, sometimes with pleasant surprises:

During visits to various districts, I was, according to tradition, a guest of local leaders. The food was served on a large wicker tray covered with *injera* (an unleavened and unsalted flatbread made with teff, a cereal similar to millet) and a series of dishes: chicken, lamb, hard-boiled eggs, and an extremely spicy sauce called *berbere*, made from butter mixed with red chili powder. When they first presented it to me, convinced by the red color that it was tomato sauce, I tasted a teaspoon of it, with the result that I remained unable to breathe for several minutes. Sometimes, traditional foods were accompanied by roasted gazelle and antelope meat, always seasoned with the same sauce. The drinks served during these meals were *tej*, or mead, and *tella*, beer obtained from the fermentation of barley. Both of these drinks, when produced with the necessary hygienic precautions, were not at all unpleasant and served very well to mitigate the spicy taste of the various dishes.[112]

Calabrò described the customs of Ethiopian conviviality that had impressed him most:

During these meals, I learned that a chief had to eat alone and away from the sight of strangers. The only person who could approach him, in order to direct the service, was the host who was also required to taste the food and drinks offered first, to guarantee their good and safe quality. Initially, this custom made me feel embarrassed, but later I got used to it because it was practiced towards the local chiefs themselves and by them towards chiefs or higher-ranking notables. Its application was so strict that, during caravan stops, the distinguished guest was shielded from the gaze and curiosity of others by placing sheets around him. These rules had ancient origins and were part of the feudal system that regulated the political-administrative organization of Ethiopia.[113]

Culinary diplomacy could also yield valuable strategic intelligence, as Calabrò demonstrated in a report from yet another banquet. "I asked [*Ras* Lij Abate] where the rebels [Ethiopian patriots] obtained their food, while they were forced to live in the bush in rugged and mountainous areas, and he replied frankly that they purchased all the food they needed from various villages or markets. The *Ras* specified that unlike bandits (*shifta*), who stole, they paid everything at current prices. In this way, he wanted to highlight the political character of the revolt of which he was a leader. The conversation, which had begun at ten in the morning, lasted until one in the afternoon, and at that point Lij Abate invited me to stay for lunch. I replied that I accepted with pleasure and that I wanted my two companions, Sada Beyan and Aleca Makonnen, to sit at the table with us. My request was granted, and after a few minutes the servants brought several wicker trays filled with the usual dishes of Ethiopian cuisine. I was always served first, but all the courses were, according to tradition, first tasted by Lij Abate. For the other diners, about twenty people, a steer was slaughtered and skinned. On this occasion, I had the opportunity to witness for the first time a banquet based on raw, still warm, meat from a freshly slaughtered animal. The diners, each armed with a sharp knife, removed large pieces of meat from the carcass hanging from a tree branch, divided them into strips, and bit off a piece that was eaten after being dipped in the usual spicy red pepper sauce. I was amazed at the speed with which this operation took place without the knife injuring the faces and, in particular, the noses of the diners, as well as the amount of meat that each one managed to devour. The only disturbance that resulted from it—I later learned—was the tapeworm, which, transmitted by raw meat, had to be periodically eliminated by means of a special mixture of medicinal herbs called 'kosso.' Since the men in the entourage had to consume the meat of the entire steer, the meal would have lasted until four in the afternoon and would have continued if I had not given the signal to leave, concerned about the abundant libations to which everyone had indulged. Lij Abate replied that he was very satisfied with the meeting and the conversation he had with me, promised me that he would consult with other notables, and inform me of any news. He also assured me that no Italian would be attacked as long as he remained in the area. He then accompanied me with his following for a couple miles, bidding me farewell with the hope of meeting me again soon."[114]

The encounters between Ethiopians and Italians that took place in regions far from the central and northern Abyssinian highlands, in the Oromo regions of the south and west and the predominantly Islamic regions of the east, encompassed a wide range of gastronomic exchanges. Poggiali noted in his diary:

> December 8, 1936, Wednesday. Restful day by a stream in Chelba, near Abaya Lake. An old chief governs a village of about twenty tukuls. Festive welcomes; they offer us tea, beer, sugar cane, and zebu milk. It is the time of the teff harvest. We are greeted by an old woman naked from the waist up, with breasts that look like saggy pears. A slave (needless to say, the old customs haven't changed here) is pounding fragrant cabbage seeds; with that she makes an oily flour, similar to mustard, to season dishes.[115]

Because Ethiopia was a heavily multi-confessional nation, Italians invited to banquets were exposed to many different religious dietary principles. "December 4, 1936, Friday," annotated Poggiali.

> At Ambo, *Ras* Hailu gives a zebu to our band, which for now consists only of about fifteen Oromo. Frenzied joy, but the animal is not killed because it is Friday and Ethiopians do not eat meat on Fridays. We do; in fact, for breakfast, we delight in a big piece of boiled zebu's hump. It is the most delicious part of that animal.[116]

Italians were guests in festivities where ritual foods were prominent. In 'Āddi Qa'yeh on February 22, 1937, Pezzoli attended a wedding party:

> Given the importance of the family, the wedding procession was composed of two hundred armed men, most of whom were wrapped in lion skin (which is actually embroidered fabric cut like leather), complete with shields, spears, and rifles. The bride is in a car with her bridesmaids and her "guarantors." She is completely veiled. The entire procession performs a dance for a few minutes, gunfire, flutes, and drums, then the bride is led into the house with the other women. We make a triumphant entrance under the *dass* where the table is prepared for us, under a canopy adorned with carpets, mats, cushions, *Askari* bands, and flags: everyone stands up, and, except for the chiefs and notables, kisses the ground as we pass. Incredible things, for us Europeans![117]

Masotti was invited by the Oromo to a religious ritual for the consecration of the harvest:

> An interesting ceremony that I witnessed with all the chiefs and notables was the invocation to God to bless the harvest. It took place far from the city, in the middle of the fields. All the chiefs and important people were present, but not the representatives of the Coptic and Muslim religions. In reality, it was an animist ceremony that had been passed down from generation to generation. It was not really about asking for divine blessing, but about asking for the blessing of the Sun God, which was considered the same thing. The Chief of Chiefs stood with his arms raised and open towards the sun, and at the end he knelt with his forehead to the ground. There was a certain mystical atmosphere. A bull was killed and everyone cut and ate a piece of the warm meat of the sacrificial animal. I found the ceremony moving, simple, and deeply felt by people for whom a good harvest was a condition and a prerequisite for a happy life.[118]

Italians often expressed feelings of empathy, curiosity, and respect for Ethiopians in their celebrations. In many other encounters, however, Italians felt alienation, danger, and the fear of poisoning by exotic food. "August 4, 1936, Tuesday. I go to interview Seyoum Mengesha, of royal blood, in his *ghebbi* near the French consulate," Poggiali wrote.

> He came to Addis Ababa to renew the solemn act of submission to Italy. Great hugs and bows; the poor of the city kiss the ground around him. In a corner, silent, very attentive, there is an old Ethiopian man, with salt and pepper hair and beard, who listens without speaking. Suddenly [*Ras* Seyoum] offers us champagne. Exchange of "smart" glances between me and Bernasconi, and also some loud remarks: "This big shot won't try to poison us, will he?" The old Ethiopian man remains impassive. But at the farewell, he comes forward and we learn that he speaks Italian very well.[119]

Political tension and mutual resentment often marked the tone of these diplomatic banquets. "June 20, 1937, Addis Ababa. In the afternoon, I attend the great dinner offered under a tent at *Ras* Hailu's house to all the Coptic clergy to celebrate the reconsecration of the Church of St. George," Poggiali noted again.

> People squatting on the ground in front of low tables made of corrugated iron sheets, very dirty and covered with dark *injera*, on which the servants arrange sauces, pieces of a roasted baby goat, and then shreds of raw meat. Great consumption of mead. They offer me *tej* in a dirty bottle. The behavior of the clergy is rather reserved. It is said that the situation in Addis Ababa is not good and there is fear of some new terrorist act.[120]

Finally, while the banquets were most frequently gatherings of Ethiopians or Italians of some political, social, or religious stature, some might include a lower-class Italian settler invited by an Ethiopian potentate. The Calabrese Giuseppe Serra arrived in Addis Ababa in 1939 hoping to find work as a painter. The opportunity was given to him by the young "*Ras* Lij Desta, nephew of the *Negus*," who—wrote Serra in his diary—

> asks me to execute his portrait, which I do with pleasure and pride. He comes to pose in my studio several times. When I finish the work, I ask him if I can bring the painting to his residence. As soon as I arrive at the prince's residence, he and his "favorite" woman come to meet me: I am introduced into the house where the family members are waiting. Oriental rugs and mats cover the entire area of the house's floor. We all sit on the rugs cross-legged in the large room. Tea and *injera* is served. In the center of the carpet is a large basket with *injera* slices and a large plate decorated with oriental designs filled with spicy sauce. I am sitting between the *Ras* and his "first woman." I am young and being in the presence of such grace is a summer dream. I see that the women are busy preparing Turkish tea. I am worried because I am not used to eating those concoctions. I follow all the preparation carefully. The service begins. One of the women bringing the large porcelain tray with the tea, another with a tray in which transparent Japanese cups with "geisha" figures stand out, and a third woman with another tray containing *injera* slices, begin the ceremony. The first cup is filled with tea. The host makes everyone taste it, one by one, and finally takes the cup and passes it to me. At first, I am confused and disoriented, but then I drink the remaining tea in the cup. I understand. The tea in my cup has not been drunk, but only touched with the lips in the act of tasting it. The *Ras* points out to me that the act is the Abyssinian way of showing the guest that the drink is not poisoned as well as a demonstration of respect and friendship. At this moment, I would have preferred less respect and fewer passes from mouth to mouth! The woman sitting next to me takes a piece of *injera* from the tray, dips it in the spice sauce, signals me to open my mouth, and feeds me with her hands. My stomach and my self-control are really put to the test. I'm about to puke. When it's all over, I feel like I've been acquitted from a sentence.[121]

Having dinner with the *Ras* was a decisive moment for Serra. The meal helped forge interracial relationships that provided him with work as well as with an understanding of Ethiopian culture. A few days later the *Ras* visited him:

> November 15, 1939. Around 5 pm, *Ras* Lij Desta came to my studio accompanied by two Black men, bringing gifts. Once the gifts were delivered, he told the two young men of color to wait outside. He thanked me again for the beautiful portrait, and I thanked him for the splendid gifts. He promised me that he would often come back to show me his own paintings to get my opinion. We said goodbye as good friends.[122]

Gastroborderland 5: Insabbiati (Italians Living with/as Ethiopians)

Much more common than the contacts such as Serra's between working-class settlers and Ethiopian elites was the culinary connection between poor Ethiopians and poor Italians. It was poverty that caused Italian settlers, voluntarily or not, to abandon their White communities and cross the borders of segregation to live among Ethiopians.

These Italian men were popularly called *insabbiati* (or lost, stuck, or swallowed in the sand, *sabbia*), to signify that they had betrayed their European identity to embrace an African one. The label of *insabbiati* applied to different classes of Italian men "dispersed in Africa": workers in Italian companies who had been fired or lost their jobs but decided to stay in Africa; settlers in trouble with the law who resisted orders of repatriation; and settlers living "on the margins" of White society, conducting informal and illicit business with Ethiopians. In this last category were Italians who exploited Ethiopian prostitutes or sold food and alcohol in partnership with Ethiopians. The rulings of colonial courts say much about these cases: an Antonio Z., who, fallen into poverty, lived on the meals Eritrean prostitutes offered him, sometimes willingly, sometimes under the threat of violence. Antonio C., a demobilized and unemployed soldier who remained in Ethiopia after the war, working sporadically for an African washerwoman who supported him.[123] The colonial economy could also cause a settler to flee poverty for the relative security of an Ethiopian community. Some *spaccisti*, the roadside grocers who served military campaigns and construction workers' camps, started to roam Ethiopia in their vans to sell their foodstuffs to "the natives," often being paid in kind after soldiers were demobilized and settlers went back to Italy.[124]

When Italian settlers socialized with Ethiopians, feelings of sympathy and attraction could be present alongside occasions of exploitation and plunder. Indeed, the relations between poor *insabbiati* immigrants and the Ethiopians they lived among, sometimes as peddlers, were daily challenges to the racial policies of the fascist regime and a constant source of embarrassment and subversion. Expelled from the colonizers' society, they offered Ethiopians the spectacle of themselves as "White outcasts." Their numbers moved many Ethiopians to believe that subordination was not entirely based on race, but was also on status. This realization struck a hard blow against the idea of the "prestige of the race" that Mussolini wanted to make the ideological and practical foundation of his empire. By crossing the color line and forming interracial families to produce a new class of "mulatto" children, the *insabbiati* were blatant violators of perhaps the most sacred of the racial laws of 1937. In the eyes of the fascist state, *insabbiamento* was the worst form of (food-based) desegregation, "ugly to see" and politically dangerous. To fascist observers, in fact, *insabbiamento* referred to the effects of eating Ethiopian food: ingesting the colonized Other and thus assuming their identity. Crossing the culinary line of color paved the way to Africanization, race betrayal, abandonment of the homeland, and degradation. "The reasons for creating a discourse against indigenization are fundamental," declared the fascist writer Franco Ciarlantini (1885–1940).

> When an Italian loses the taste for traditional foods of his [sic] country and turns to nasty African food, when he trades the genuine Italian wines of his region for [Ethiopian] beer or worse, it's all over, it's the end; he will lose his language, his memory of the landscape of the homeland, his way of thinking, suffering, and even loving.[125]

Confirming the fascists' worst predictions, it was in the homes of *insabbiati*— some of whom were still married in Italy but now living in bigamy with an African woman among Africans—that the closest thing to a coherent Ethiopian-Italian/Italian-Ethiopian cuisine developed. According to Ethiopian and Eritrean religious customs, the children of a mixed couple of different confessions (in this case, Ethiopian Orthodox and Roman Catholic) had to be raised in the religion of the father, even if the father was absent or dead. Ethiopian and Eritrean Christian Orthodox mothers raised children born from marriages with *insabbiati* in the Roman Catholic tradition of the father, most notably in the commitment to Italian foodways. However, as devout Christian Orthodox Christians, they did not give up their foods or renounce the dietary rituals of the Ethiopian religious calendar, which included periods of fasting and abstinence from animal products. Nor did they violate dietary taboos, such as those related to pork and rabbit, which Italians ate and the Ethiopian Orthodox church prohibited. One of the Eritrean women interviewed by Giulia Barrera recalled having frequent arguments with her *insabbiato* husband because he bought meat from a Muslim butcher. She had chosen to raise their son with "Italian" food.[126] Zegereda, who had lived with an *insabbiato* for almost twenty years, revealed that in her family they always celebrated two "Christmases." "For the 'Italian' Christmas, she prepared home-made pasta or gnocchi, panettone, they drank wine, and so on. For the 'Eritrean' Christmas, instead, they had *zig'ni* and *dulet* [a stew of spiced minced tripe, liver, and beef], drank *siwa* [homemade beer made with toasted barley, yeast, and *gesho* leaves], and so on."[127] The result was a hybrid cuisine during the weekdays, and two different cuisines served on festive and public occasions, a culinary calendar that accommodated the religious dictates and dietary habits of the father alongside the mother's faith, beliefs, and personal practices.

In the early 1980s, the historian Fabienne Le Houérou conducted an extensive ethnographic study of the *insabbiati* who were still living in former Italian East Africa.[128] According to Le Houérou, "The *insabbiati* cultural modification was mainly confined to their personal and intimate life. It concerned their way of living, cooking, eating, and their family integration as individuals. They borrowed traits from Ethiopian culture. They used to drink coffee in the traditional and ritual style of the Ethiopians and eat *injera* bread."[129] Across the diaspora, Italian immigrants, in particular in the United States, have tended to behave as "Americans" in public life and as "Italians" in the domestic sphere, investing in Italian food as an anchor of a rich family life and as a powerful tool for sustaining a collective identity.[130] In a reversal of this strategy, Italian *insabbiati* in Ethiopia used visible forms of distinction in public—dressing in "Italian" fashion, in particular wearing the Borsalino fedora hat—while "their domestic life was completely Ethiopian," except for pictures of Rome, the Pope, or other obviously Italian scenes decorating the walls. However, the gendered division of labor involved in preparing family meals (from planning and shopping to preparing and serving food according to a precise protocol) showcased most vividly the unequal power relations between colonized women and colonizing men. Those relations could be violent. As Barrera found in her interviews, Le Houérou's participant observation of family meals illuminated "the series of humiliations to which [Ethiopian] women" had been subjected in *insabbiati* households. Although food consumed in the house was identified as Ethiopian,

> The [Italian] men ate alone at the table and the [Ethiopian] women served them. One of these women explained to me that thirty years ago [during the empire], "Whites were better than us because of [the color of] their skin." Practically all Ethiopian women had assimilated the racist theories of their Italian husbands. The woman married to this *insabbiato* owned a restaurant outside Addis Ababa: she was cooking and working very hard in the kitchen when her husband was playing cards with his friends. She confessed that she was dreaming to be White and she was really proud to have very light-skinned children, *quasi bianchi* (almost White) [in Italian in the text].[131]

Nonetheless, some adult women in the interracial families of *insabbiati* held significant decision-making power within racist and sexist domestic domains (while showing absolute deference in public). "The house of Oreste"—ruled by a settler from Naples, a serial rapist whom Le Houérou, using Hannah Arendt's categories, defined as an "ordinary monster"—"was full of women and children of all ages and he justified that he did not know who was and who was not his own children."[132] Oreste functioned as the *abat* (father-master) of everyone. "He identified all the women in the house with the global term *servitù* (servants) [in Italian in the text], and it was understood that this vague notion embraced a various series of relations including ex-girlfriends, daughters, servants, adopted daughters; a very heterogeneous social group more or less alike a *harem* or a tribal unit." Some of the women had tangible power, Le Houérou argued.

> All decisions were taken by the older woman, the first Ethiopian lover of Oreste. She was the organizer of the household and everything relied on her: cooking, shopping, and cleaning. She had a pivotal position in the household agency. When we mention the subaltern position of the women of the house we should not caricature the complex relations inside a family.[133]

Gastroborderland 6: Travel

Ethiopians and Italians met each other and each other's food in their travels, off the beaten paths of racial segregation. European travel in the colonies was richly documented, in novels and stories or as popular memories in diaries, letters, other private writings, and in oral transmissions. Taken together, these accounts were influential in the construction of the empire for settlers, Italians of the diaspora, and especially Italians in Italy.

In *Imperial Eyes: Travel Writing and Transculturation*, Marie Louise Pratt argued that European travel narratives typically presented an image of the rest of the world as available for White control and open to European global dominance and "created the imperial order for Europeans 'at home' and gave them their place in it."[134] The accounts of travelers in the "colonial contact zone" of Italian East Africa particularly emphasized experiences with food to give readers—of newspapers, memoirs, or letters sent home—a sense of the Ethiopian world that Italians had come to dominate.

The young colonial official Vincenzo Ambrosio wrote to his family in Italy:

Dancia (towards Baco), March 4, 1938. Dearest Dad, [I'm writing] after three days of marching and a day of rest at the Weito River, a tropical landscape with cotton, grain, and tobacco. The Gamo chiefs offer honey, eggs, and baby goats. Tonight, like this morning, a delicious fried fish, caught by me and the *dubats* [soldiers from Italian Somaliland employed in the colonial army]. I will be in Baco, so will God, around two o'clock on March seventh.[135]

As Pratt suggested, travel stories from the empire exposed Italians at home to realities they would have never imagined or experienced without colonialism. These narratives also gave them the knowledge to understand and control a foreign culture, and the many culinary discoveries and multisensory descriptions of the imperial territory were popular chapters in Italian travel literature.

The "journey," during which Italians and Ethiopians were in close contact for days, wrapped in the same climate and landscape and crossing lands unfamiliar to Europeans, was a topos of imperial travel writing. This subgenre offered evocative descriptions of cooking and eating in the camps under the night sky, of colonizers and colonized coming together to share meals, of the meeting of culture and nature. In a letter to his mother, Giovanni Battista Ellero, the colonial official and husband of Maria Pia Pezzoli, wrote:

Enda Selassie, April 12, 1938. We have recently returned from a pleasant caravan trip. Gorgeous panoramas, unforgettable rides, equally memorable indigestions of local foods and drinks: but above all, a fond memory of the indescribable confusion of the indigenous escort personnel, excited by the novelty, by the honor of accompanying the master, by the abundant libations, I believe above all for the temporary plunge into their original nomadic life.[136]

If the feasts inspired Ellero, they filled Calabrò with a multisensory understanding of "Africa."

> Without the caravans, I would never have truly encountered Africa, its solitudes, its spaces, its silences, its nights illuminated by a dazzling moon, or black as a velvet cloak dotted with countless stars; I would not have been able to admire the rapid twilights and the radiant spots animated by the singing of countless birds and the screams of monkeys; I would not have known the sun that shines on the savannah of motionless afternoons, the torrential rains, the ancient forests, the slow and solemn rivers and the roaring and foaming torrents, the many animal species subject only to the eternal laws of nature.
>
> The caravans gave me the best of what Africa had to offer. The long and arduous rides on rough and steep terrain, the endless marches, the loyalty, dedication, and affection of my *Askari*, the rest in a comfortable tent quickly set up or the leaden sleep, in the cold, wrapped in a field blanket, the joy of bivouac bonfires and the chatter of the escort, the comfort of a lordly table set up in the shade of a sycamore or the elemental satisfaction of a healthy appetite, in a brief stop, with a can of meat, and some biscuits, drinking the water of any stream. They allowed me to live like a soldier, like a leader, like a poet, like a gypsy, always far from mediocre life, in a return to instinct and its immeasurable resources. For all this, they constitute one of the most vivid and rich heritages of my existence.[137]

Despite Ellero and Calabrò's idealization, much of the "indigenous" local food that Ethiopian and Italian travelers exchanged was in fact "food on the move" that had come miles, sometimes thousands of miles. Foods in travel literature often reflected the look, smell, and sound of mobility: from *burkutta*, the travel breads shaped into spheres or flattened into focaccia and cooked until crackling on stones heated by campfires, to the diesel fumes that permeated even the canned food brought in by truck from the ports of Djibouti and Massawa. "In the midst of this panorama of improvisation, smelling of gasoline, sounding of ten dialects, colored by hundreds of signs—'tavern,' 'tire depot,' 'soda factory,' 'carpentry shop,' '24-hour tagliatelle (noodles) restaurant,' 'Bella Napoli' and 'Bella Romagna,' 'Alla Vera Pavia' and 'Al Ritrovo del Friuli'—the road, road number 1, the road of the Empire, the Road with a capital R, made its way, gray, solid, shiny, compact," wrote Vergani. "To Addis Ababa: 677 miles."[138]

The truck drivers delivering food embodied the mobility of all ethnicities delivering food and people on the new roads through Italian East Africa. Truckers like Guerrino transported and ate the food of the empire on their daily routes. "So, I spent Christmas Day, St. Stephen's Day, and Christmas Eve 125 miles from Addis Ababa in a small village made up exclusively of tukuls," the driver wrote to his wife in Bologna.

> Since there are no restaurants in Gedo, on the evening of the 24th we made our own dinner. On Christmas Day we were invited to eat at the mess of the noncommissioned officers of the Gedo fort, as well as the evening itself and on St. Stephen's Day. In those two days I bought three chickens to bring to the mess,

paying only about three lire each and twenty eggs at thirty cents each. Dear Uciona, this is how I spent Christmas.[139]

Travel stories about food encounters were marked with feelings of nostalgia for familiar tastes and smells and awareness of new landscapes and newly captivating African flavors. "So I look at Addis Ababa from this crossroads, peeling these mandarins that send their fragrance so far away in this air that is too dry, still dense with the smell of roasted chili pepper, flour, indigenous butchery, sweaty armpits and dusty feet, mixed with a smell of gasoline and diesel, cement and lime," Vergani remembered.[140] "We left the next morning, still in the rain, to climb to the three thousand three hundred meters of the Debarq highland, from where the road then begins its descent towards Gondar," wrote Masotti.

> Our car was stopped at a certain point by a skirmish between a company of *Askaris* and a group of rebels. We had all the time to observe the operation, sitting in the car, while the commander of the zone offered us a breakfast of bread, salami, and red wine, which I still remember as one of the most pleasant things of the trip.[141]

These descriptions of meals taken on the road, in the company of Ethiopians, seemed to communicate to metropolitan Italian readers the feel of the empire that Mussolini wanted all Italians to sense.[142] "During the stops, at noon rest, meals were prepared by the cook in the *Askari* troop who took care of me and who sometimes was also a helper cook at home. His name was Chicchi," wrote Masotti. "As a cook, the knowledge of the brave Chicchi was not very extensive, but you could always count on two eggs, a steak of any animal, or on the common roast chicken."[143]

After Italy's surrender, the last journey through Ethiopia for many Italian soldiers and settlers ended in deportation or imprisonment in British prisoner-of-war (POW) camps. Rapaccini remembered being rounded up by British soldiers and transferred from Addis Ababa to the concentration camp for Italian civilians in the Somali region of eastern Ethiopia as he was looking for food for his six-month-old daughter:

> We've been traveling for two hours. On the hard iron seat, I've spread a blanket, so I'm almost comfortable. The Ethiopian landscape unfolds along the road. We'll travel all day and spend the night in Jijiga. We've been supplied in the morning for the whole day. We have a bag with bread, meat, and some bananas, a bottle of water and one of milk. In Harar, we can buy oranges and lemons for disinfecting water. There are seven other women and twelve children with me, but almost all of them are grown up. There are only three as small as mine.[144]

Gastroborderland 7: POW Camps

POW and concentration camps were one final ground of culinary interaction between Africans and Italians. The prisoners and detainees included Italian soldiers captured by Ethiopians during the 1935–6 war and, in some rare instances, in the anti-colonial liberation war that followed; Italians, both military and civilian, deported to British camps in Africa in 1941; and victims of the cruelest conditions of all, Ethiopians held in Italian concentration camps, many of whom were starved to death by their captors.

The feeding of prisoners of the Second Italo-Ethiopian War was the subject of international controversy and mutual accusations between Italy and Ethiopia.[145] Ethiopia's nonmembership in the Geneva Convention for the Amelioration of the Condition of the Wounded and Sick in Armies in the Field (July 27, 1929) and the fact that war was never officially declared by Italy meant there were no clear agreements about minimum rations for POWs. However, Italian "national" soldiers who fell into Ethiopian hands seemed to be treated decently enough, likely due to the value they held in prisoner exchanges. British sources reported that

> on February 20, 1936, two Italian soldiers, Silvio Meloni and Domenico Palazzo, were captured during a reconnaissance patrol carried out with their *Askaris* on the western high plateau of Tigray. The two feared first that they would be killed but soon found out that this was not the intention. Instead they were very well treated. In the days after their capture, they received food, milk, eggs and even *tej*, Ethiopian honey mead.[146]

Even though Italians often executed captured Ethiopian fighters, including those who had surrendered, toward the end of the 1935–6 war camp officials created regulations for the distribution of food to Ethiopian prisoners. A few weeks before the occupation of Addis Ababa, Vice-Governor of Eritrea General Guzzoni decreed that each captured Abyssinian be given a daily ration of 1 pound of flour and 15 grams each of tea, sugar, and salt, and a weekly ration of half a pound of meat, two lemons, 60 grams of oil, and 5 grams of chili pepper. The Italian High Command opposed Guzzoni's proposal, arguing that POWs should receive the same treatment as political prisoners, and limited the ration to only 1 pound of flour and 16 grams of salt per day.[147] The conflicting policies were ultimately resolved, however, with the entry of General Badoglio's troops into Addis Ababa on May 5, 1936, the end of the state of war, and the subsequent release in July of most of the Ethiopian prisoners. The release was celebrated with great fanfare in a public ceremony documented by a Luce Institute newsreel that emphasized the exceptionally humane treatment Abyssinians had received in Italian POW camps.[148]

Many memoirs testify to the food experience of Italian male soldiers and settlers in British POW camps in Africa, as well as those of interned women and children repatriated by British authorities after the Italian defeat in 1941. The memoirs recall how shocked Italian inmates were by the scarcity and poor quality of camp food. In Ethiopia, settlers had come to benefit from the regime's massive transnational food system, enjoying a diet better than that of their counterparts in Italy. Eating well was a tangible sign of the social mobility they had enjoyed because of their move to Africa. For Italian POWs, then, the collapse of the empire was a traumatic change from a life of plenty. The memoirs also note the absence of any widespread resentment toward Mussolini and fascism for the suffering prisoners had endured after the defeat, including widespread hunger. The prevalent feelings among Italian POWs were of fatalism and resignation, although some interned settlers still believed that the defeat represented a mere pause in the imperial project and that Italians would soon "return." Memories of the food security and abundance that most settlers enjoyed in Ethiopia played a fundamental role in those desires. Finally, some memoirs revealed an ironic aspect of the internments: in British camps, many former settlers became small farmers, gardeners, and vegetable growers, successfully cultivating their favorite greens and fruits in ingenious mini-plots surrounded by barbed wire. On a miniscule scale, these plantings transformed the African landscape into an "Italian" one, just as the planners of demographic colonization had dreamed. Only now, as captives of a despised enemy, did they manage to achieve the self-sufficiency and food sovereignty promised by fascist project for Ethiopia could never fully deliver.

According to a 1947 parliamentary report, the number of Italian POWs and internees during World War II amounted to 1,350,000. Their experiences differed widely, depending on whether they were captured on the Russian front, surrendered to the Allies in North Africa, or deported to Germany after the armistice of September 8, 1943. Recent studies have shed light on the fate of soldiers and settlers in Italian East Africa, including conditions in Allied POW camps.[149] Between May 19, 1941 (the surrender of Viceroy Amedeo d'Aosta at Imba Alaje) and November 28, 1941 (the surrender of General Guglielmo Nasi in Gondar), the British held Italian military prisoners in provisional camps before sending them to different camps depending on where they were captured. Those captured in Tigray and Eritrea were sent to Sudan and then, for the most part, to India. Those captured on the central and southern Ethiopian and Somali fronts were interned in Kenya. The British had other plans for captured civilians. In the established colonies of Eritrea and Somalia, only able-bodied Italian residents were interned, sent to Kenya, Sudan, and Rhodesia, while Italian civilians in Ethiopia—where Italians had committed the greatest atrocities—were all sent to POW camps. Men in this group were shipped to Kenya and South Africa, while women and children were deported to camps in eastern Ethiopia and in Kenya before being repatriated in 1942–3 on *navi bianche*, four former transatlantic liners that the Italian government confiscated and repainted white in missions of mercy.[150]

Italian internees in British camps in Kenya quickly felt the effects of losing the high-quality diet they had enjoyed in Ethiopia. Prisoner Masotti recalled,

> I must admit, after many years, that the British did their best to treat us humanely, but in 1942–3 we had difficult times in Kenya, especially in terms of food. My waistline shrank again—not that it needed to—as camel meat and certain dried vegetables that were the staples of the diet were not always sufficient. I don't mean that that was all the food that arrived at the camp, but that was what they served us.[151]

Upon arrival, Italians typically suffered from thirst, heat, and dysentery. "On the morning of April 9, 1941, the British brought us water to drink in our own [captured] trucks, outside the barbed-wire fence," recalled sailor Mario Cassisa, taken prisoner in the fall of Massawa on April 8, 1941.

Our soldiers and other veterans of the War of 1936 removed the lids from some empty gasoline barrels that were inside the airport where we were prisoners, and the British filled the barrels from across the barbed wire using the hoses on their trucks, and all the hell broke loose. All the prisoners, thirsty, crowded together in great confusion, filling buckets, bowls, and tin pails. There was truly an animalistic struggle, everyone wanted the water before anyone else. I watched that terrible brawl from a distance, as I was so weak, and did not want to get involved in that avalanche of thirsty men. By now, the many barrels were almost empty, there was very little water left at the bottom with a lot of sand. I sank my bowl in the barrel and collected water and sand and waited for the sand to settle. I returned to my place and sat on the deck, having a sip every now and then. The British limited themselves to giving us water to drink, but from outside, as if we were wild beasts inside a cage.[152]

Italian POWs were somewhat able to cope with their conditions because of their familiarity with "Ethiopian" and "African" food. Calabrò recalled the early days of roundups and internment in makeshift camps:

Around ten in the morning, we were each given a slice of meat that we cooked as best we could. An Ethiopian servant of the district chief secretly brought me some *injera* and a chicken, which I shared with those around me. About ten days after my capture I began visiting the wounded entrusted to the care of Dr. Natale Mistretta, who not only performed the duties of a doctor but also those of a nurse and a quartermaster. To procure food, he cared for the armed Ethiopian partisans who repaid him in kind. With the help of a convalescent soldier, he cooked and distributed the food he obtained to the patients, reserving only some for himself. I also contributed eggs and some chickens often brought to me by the locals. Among the most generous was Zelleca. Noticing my embarrassment at accepting his gifts, having realized the difficulties he encountered in procuring them, he said to me, "you have done so much for me that today you should not be reluctant to accept the little that I bring you."[153]

As important as it was for simple survival, food built solidarity among prisoners through sharing, exchange, and communication. "The ration is not bad, and animated by the liveliness of the boys in the camp, we improvise a table from a cot," recalled Rapaccini, held in Jijiga.

Here comes Carletto, holding a beautiful bowl of warm milk. "Ma'am, give me your bowl, I saw that there is a fine, fine soup for the little children, you know, that small, tiny pasta. I'll go get it for your baby, I saw it and it looks very good." "Yes, dear, if you want to go, but you've taken so many trips, if you're tired, no, don't go." "No, ma'am, give it to me, I'm happy to go, I'm not tired." And he happily sets off. I also thank Carletto's mother, who is proud of her eldest [son]. The face of a soldier appears in the tent opening, politely asking us if we need anything. He is one of our Carabinieri, I recognize him by his insignia. He informs us that they have made mozzarella and ricotta because there is a lot of milk in the region and they have prepared this surprise for us. Mozzarella and ricotta! Just thinking about it is a delight, and I joyfully say to bring it. Shortly thereafter, here comes Carletto. He was right, the soup is good, and Simonetta eats it happily while we celebrate the unexpected lunch. The children, tired, fall asleep early, and even Simonetta falls asleep in my arms. I rock her and look at her with so much tenderness.[154]

Rapaccini's memory of mozzarella and ricotta suggests that a distinctive feature of Italian prisoners' experience in British camps was their production of food, drawing on their own farming and culinary skills, and improved through contacts with Ethiopians. The food they grew provided familiar tastes under difficult conditions, far from loved ones, and facing uncertainty about the future.

Felice Benuzzi, a former settler but a prisoner in Kenya in 1946, provided one of the many testimonies about the importance of food sovereignty for his fellow POWs.

The British authorities allowed us to cultivate certain small plots of land between barracks and outside the camp in a space monitored by sentinels and commonly called *gli orti* (the gardens). We planted tomatoes, lettuce, turnips, peas, bell peppers, celery, parsley, and so on. There were flower beds kept with extreme care, bordered by canes, protected from the heat by sackcloth, watered in the evening and morning, and fertilized with coffee grounds and ash. In addition to being a useful activity, the garden or *shamba*, as the "old Somalis" called it, gave us the illusion of ownership and creation. It is always a moving spectacle to follow the growth of sprouts from good soil.[155]

The cooks and servers in the Kenya camps were for the most part Italian prisoners.[156]

The experience with food was dramatically different for the thousands of Ethiopians who were interned in Italian concentration camps. Ethiopian patriots and political dissidents were imprisoned in different waves: immediately after the end of the Second Italo-Ethiopian War, when Italy arrested and deported the political leaders of the Ethiopian Empire and all those suspected of being supporters of the *Negus* in exile; later in 1936, when, fearing a Resistance attack on Addis Ababa and other major cities, religious leaders, intellectuals, and other "uncooperative subjects" were rounded up; and finally in 1937, after the assassination attempt on Viceroy Graziani in Addis Ababa, in the massive wave of arrests of Ethiopians following the revenge massacres by Italian residents in the capital.[157] For Ethiopians imprisoned in Dire Dawa in Ethiopia, Danane in Somalia, and elsewhere, it was not just a matter of enduring suffering—from hunger, thirst, heat, illness, and isolation—many times more intense than that faced by Italians in British camps in Kenya. They also faced the prospect of engineered death when Italian authorities implemented a feeding system evidently aimed at exterminating prisoners through starvation.

The testimonies of Ethiopian prisoners who survived the concentration camps of Dire Dawa and Danane, published in newspapers or collected by Ethiopian war crimes investigation commissions, illustrate the deadly effects of the food system imposed by the Italians. In fascist camps, food brought from Italy became their only source of nourishment. When they did manage to obtain it, they had to survive on small, scientifically designed rations that were meant to kill.

The Danane camp in Somalia was most infamous for its horrific conditions and high mortality rate. Out of 6,200 internees during the five years of the camp's operation, only 3,000 survived.[158] At the end of the Second Italo-Ethiopian War in 1936, the camp had only 191 detainees, but after the assassination attempt on Graziani, 1,500 men, women, and children were transferred there from Addis Ababa. By the end of 1937, Danane was filled to its capacity of 2,500 people. According to Italian authorities, in the three weeks between June 22 and July 18 of that year, twenty-eight prisoners died, almost all of them officially from "heart problems," suggesting strong evidence of severe malnutrition.[159]

Official testimonies give a sense of the role food restrictions played in the deaths of internees in Danane.[160] Michael Blatta Bekele Hapte was a judge of the Ethiopian High Court when he was arrested in July 1936 as a suspected participant in attempt by Resistance leaders to recapture Addis Ababa. After passing through Italian camps at Dire Dawa, Harar, and Mogadishu, Blatta Bekele Hapte finally arrived at Danane, where he stayed until British troops liberated the camp in 1941. In 1946, he testified to the Ethiopian War Crimes Commission.

> The food which the Italians gave us was very bad for our health. The food was rotten biscuits with many worms in them and we also got tea and coffee alternately. We all became sick. When we were imprisoned in the criminal jail, the commander was Brigadier [Leopoldo] Baroni. We repeatedly complained to him about the food, but he said he could not do anything about it, because it was ordered by his superiors. Even if we possessed a small amount of money, we were forbidden to buy any kind of food from the neighborhood.[161]

After the assassination attempt on Graziani, "The food conditions were even worse than before. Because of the lack of sufficient latrines, the filthy conditions and the lack of suitable food, many got sick, and the death rate was four to five persons daily."[162]

Imru Zelleke was twelve years old when he was arrested in Addis Ababa with his entire family in early 1937 and deported to Danane, where he stayed until the fall of 1938. Zelleke remembered how

> the first few months were terrible. Food consisted of boiled vegetables and *galletta* [hardtack biscuits, in Italian in the text] that were already rotten and full of worms. Drinking water was drawn from wells dug in the vicinity of the sea, which made it salty. In the beginning there was no medical treatment, although later they assigned a doctor to the camp. People got sick with malaria, dysentery, scurvy, typhus, tropical sores and all sorts of diseases caused by extreme malnutrition. Several hundred died during the first few months. I think that more than one third of prisoners that were taken to Danane died there. Conditions in the main prisons were terrible because of the high walls surrounding them, there was not enough air circulation. The hot climate of the area made it suffocating and very unhealthy. There were only eight or ten holes in the latrines, you can imagine what it was like with hundreds of people suffering from diarrhea.[163]

Since the camps were designed for the ultimate extermination of prisoners, access to safe and uncontaminated food—namely the "Italian" food of the colonizers, who were now guards and executioners—marked the difference between survival and death. Michael Tessema, an employee of the Ethiopian Ministry of Justice accused of collusion with the Resistance, was interned first in Dire Dawa and then in Danane, where remained until December 1940. In Dire Dawa,

> prisoners were fed on dry biscuits (*galletta*) [in Italian in the text] every thirty-six hours. There were many elderly people who used to cry from hunger, because they did not possess teeth with which to eat dry *galletta*. They were all tormented by the lack of drinking water. I myself told a sergeant to buy me water for 500 liras from the money which I kept in secret, but the sergeant felt pity for me and brought me a bottle of water without accepting the money.

In Danane,

> as we used to drink sea water the daily death rate was between six and thirty persons, who died from dysentery. A total of 3,175 persons died. I was able to know this, because I was given a job as a medical assistant, and so kept records of the sick persons and obituary notes. Up to the end the Italian authorities never provided potable water. Of 6,500 persons at Danane, 3,175 died. Not all of them perished because the prisoners used to receive some money from their relatives and bought *acqua minerale* [mineral water, in Italian in the text] brought from Italy in sealed bottles, and churned milk from Somalis.[164]

Whether in the field kitchens of an invading army, the dining rooms of settlers' homes, the tukuls of sex workers, the tents and palaces where Ethiopian potentates held lavish banquets, the homes of *insabbiati* interracial families, the caravans traveling across highlands and deserts, or in POW camps, countless food exchanges took place in the empire's racial borderlands. In these liminal zones, Ethiopians and Italians created an embryonic Ethiopian-Italian/Italian-Ethiopian cuisine, and through it, redefined their shared identity in the inextricably mutual relationships in which colonialism had entangled them.

6

The Empire of the Senses: Food Tastes, Disgusts, and Identities in Italian Ethiopia

The European empires of the eighteenth and nineteenth centuries were simultaneously many things: not only political, military, and economic structures but also cultural, anthropological, and mental ones. The modern empire was a geopolitical achievement; a form of military and administrative control; an infrastructure of transportation and communication; an instrument for the economic exploitation; a system of scientific, technological, moral, and artistic production; and a mechanism for creating colonial subjects. Like any other human activity, empires were shaped by the five senses: colonizers and colonized built relationships with each other through the use of all five senses. Mussolini asked Italians to see, smell, feel, taste, and touch the "sense" of empire in order to understand its complexity and meaning, to engage with its distant bodies, animals, landscapes, spaces, places, architectures, objects, and, finally, foods and cuisines.[1]

The senses, tools for understanding reality, are also "historical formations" shaped by a culture, place, and era.[2] Marshall McLuhan famously argued that sight became preeminent with the introduction of mechanical printing and the mass circulation of written words.[3] For Alain Corbin, the war against smell in cities and domestic spaces was critical to modern European bourgeois culture.[4] In Italian East Africa, the multisensory experience of food was an essential component of a broad ideology shaped by gastrofascism: the myth of food as a vital expression of rural traditions and cultures; the patriarchal family, its liturgies and its memory; a xenophobic national identity, under threat from foreign powers; distinctive agriculture and consumer styles; demographic, racial, and sexual policies based on food self-sufficiency; and, ultimately, Italy's place in the world.

When Italian colonizers said that injera reminded them of tripe and Ethiopian women thought that spaghetti resembled worms, both parties made statements about the appeal or repulsiveness of the other's foods—in appearance, taste, and smell—the sense Immanuel Kant defined as "taste at a distance."[5] By tasting, observing, smelling, tasting, and touching the food of the empire, its subjects—both colonizers and colonized—constructed an Empire of the Senses. Their experiences with food shed light on how, in the cultures of Italian East Africa, (1) combinations of taste, texture, and flavor complicated received categories of salty, sweet, sour, and bitter; (2) the sensory qualities of food-embodied forms of social distinction; and (3) taste was an essential gateway tool for exploring and interpreting another's way of life.[6]

The Disgust of the Empire

The sensory landscape of the empire was marked by reciprocal tastes and dislikes, pleasures, and aversions. The word "taste" (Italian *gusto*, French *goût*) has two distinct but interconnected meanings when referring to food. The first refers to its objective qualities: flavor, smell, texture, composition, nutritional value in terms of carbohydrates, fiber, fats, proteins, and vitamins, and the general effects on the human body. In the case of coffee, for example, its bitter taste, absence of calories, and stimulating effect on the nervous system all significantly determined its social history.[7] The second meaning of "taste" refers to a culture's "food preferences and culinary principles" that create distinctive individual and collective identities of social class, gender, race, ethnicity, and nation.[8]

For the Empire of Food, taste, in its intertwined material and symbolic uses, was a way to discipline Black and White colonial bodies and help distinguish colonial subjects by race and color, but also by class and gender. The taste of a food reflected, and was perceived to reflect, the distinctive behaviors, styles, clothing, and body nutrition of two groups, Ethiopians and Italians, facing each other. For both groups, the perception of each other's food was deeply embedded in the value of each other's bodies.[9]

The massive circulation of images of Ethiopians—photographs, postcards, and illustrations broadcast to Italians about to depart for Africa—had strong ideological connotations: Ethiopian bodies appeared savage and primitive, just like their agriculture and cuisine, and unsuitable for an Italian diet. Conquest would be followed by the installation of a modern, rational, and hygienic food system. The role of Ethiopian women in this forced replacement was also clear. Since the second half of the nineteenth century in Italy, Ethiopian women were represented as nude "barbarians" for the male gaze. After the vaunted military conquest, they were to serve as occasional objects of easy sexual consumption—for the "physiological" needs of Italian soldiers and settlers—not as producing subjects (of food), even though Ethiopian women were entirely responsible for feeding their nation. They were the exact opposite of Italian family women, whose sexuality was jealously protected and who, as cooks, were the nurturers of Italian men. European invaders believed that the bodies of the colonized determined their (Ethiopian) food, and that the food of the colonized shaped their (Ethiopian) bodies. As a consequence, eating Ethiopian food meant eating an extension, or "piece," of Ethiopian bodies and the fluids they contained, with serious consequences for the blood, flesh, body, and identity of the colonizer.

"Only women are skilled millers, who, bent over a specially made millstone on a donkey's back, pour these grains little by little and rub them back and forth with another smaller stone until it becomes a kind of flour," noted Private Botta.

> This grinding is very slow over time and must also be tiring, seeing these women struggling with that heavy stone that serves as a mill. To alleviate the heat of the

effort, they work with their torsos bare, and in doing so, they give free rein to the sweat that sprays from every pore. And even more, it creates a certain sense of disgust to observe some rivulets of this sweat, coming from the thick hair all braids and greasy [from cosmetic butter], mixing with ointment and flowing down along the bell-shaped hanging breasts, down to the two knee-catching nipples.[10]

Botta's words are almost identical to those used two decades earlier by the first Civil Governor of Eritrea and then Minister of Colonies Ferdinando Martini to describe the same culinary process: "I believe that nothing has disgusted me as much as certain Abyssinian women, still young, whom I saw kneeling to grind the durra. This nudity is more effective than any exorcism to drive away [any erotic] temptations."[11]

The sensory disgust that the "repulsive" foods and bodies of Ethiopians provoked in Italian men resulted from an underlying tension of gendered politics. The Italian found himself in the presence of a productive dimension (of food) that in Ethiopian culture was completely socialized as feminine in contrast to the equally gendered domestic regimen to which he had been socialized. For their part, Ethiopian women working in teff mills sought to resist the occupation of their land and the "rationalization" of their agriculture and cuisine by preserving their senses, their tastes, and their gastronomy—and with them the social role in which much of their capacity for anti-colonial action resided.

The same sensory disgust transmitted notions of impurity, contamination, danger, threat, or extreme estrangement from familiar tastes. For newly arrived Italian settlers the backwardness of Ethiopians was first signaled by the scrawny and malodorous appearance of their livestock: "Unselected stuff: mangy cows, scabby sheep, goats for the slaughterhouse, donkeys for the dead."[12] In Poggiali's five senses, the inferiority of Ethiopians was a cause and consequence of the ways in which they did (not) cultivate the fruits of their land: "Even the fruit grows all over the highland, but it has nothing to do with the excellence of our products. The lack of selection, grafting, and pruning, brings about an uninterrupted flow of efflorescence, fruit rooting, and jumbled ripening, hence a qualitatively deficient product."[13] In the markets, there was a promiscuous mixture of human bodies, animals, and contaminated food.

> Market of Adigrat, August 10, 1936. I won't tell you the smells and sights! A horde of people, wrapped in dirty rags, sitting on the ground around baskets full of wheat, millet, teff, or piles of goat skins. A deafening roar, but it seems like few deals are actually completed! A spectacle of a kind, worthy of being seen, in its own mess, even if that requires defying the smell of rancid butter, and the countless little animals [parasites].[14]

Eating foods from a such a primitive agriculture caused Ethiopian bodies to emit a "tremendous odor of black putrefaction."[15] The smell was aggravated by a total lack of personal care and hygiene: "The Abyssinians never washed."[16] The preparation of food, exclusively by women, took place in "primitive mud and hay houses," "dwellings—the cylindrical tukul with thatched roofs, and the *hudmo*, huts either rectangular or square—worthier of the name of dens," from which "the characteristic indigenous stench that immediately assaults your throat" emanated.[17]

The local soundscape only heightened the disgust: "The monkeys would have been horrified to hear the tearing chorus of dissonances that the ignorant congregation of savages instead listened to with supreme dignity and delight."[18] Finally, particularly offensive to Italian colonists—even those from poor rural areas or working-class neighborhoods—was the physical proximity of spaces for consumption and defecation.[19] Science historian Warwick Anderson called the presence in settlers' houses of an indoor toilet "excremental colonialism": a novelty for many, it marked a clear boundary between Italians and Ethiopians.[20]

Disgust provoked by food was often triggered in periods of tension, insecurity, conflict, and fear. Ethiopian guerrillas, for example, often used food—tainting or withholding it—as a weapon against the invading army. One of the most pervasive signs of the food of the empire was the blinding heat of the ubiquitous spice mixture, *berbere*. "We would go inspecting the coffee plantation, entrusted to an old Fitawrari [an Abyssinian Commander of the Vanguard corresponding to the rank of Brigadier General], a good farmer and an old fox," Masotti recalled.

> Once we went for breakfast, and the Fitawrari offered us the usual chicken with a very strong berbere sauce and hard-boiled eggs. I'm not sure if he did it on purpose, for the pleasure of playing a nasty trick on us rather than offering us a delicious local dish. The fact is that we all remained open-mouthed with our throats on fire. After the initial shock, we gave some sauce to a stray dog that had come looking for something to eat, and he enjoyed it very much without any signs of disturbance.[21]

The Fitawrari turned out to be a member of the Ethiopian resistance.

There were other sources of unease about local foodways. At the beginning of World War II, when the colonies were isolated and only African food was available, Masotti worried about finding sterilized food for his infant daughter.

> In Dembi Dolo we began to have difficulties of supply, we were rationed, flour and pasta too often tasted like oil, the Greek and Armenian grocers had hidden their provisions waiting for better times. The problem was to get milk. The scarcity of livestock and the insufficient nourishment of tropical pastures resulted in a very low milk production. We managed to have enough for the baby, with the addition of powdered milk from Jimma or Addis Ababa. We also found butter because we became customers of a friendly Oromo petty breeder who sold us his butter when we asked for it and when he didn't sell it all to the local beauties who used it as a kind of hair gel. But our butter had a strange taste and was full of black dots. For a while, we tolerated it, thinking it was some kind of local specialty, then my wife decided to boil and filter it and discovered that the black dots were ants, which she diligently put aside. The strange taste remained, and only later did we discover that it was due to the dried cow dung containers used by our supplier. At that point, we gave up.[22]

Of all the sensory experiences that Ethiopians and Italians shared on first contact, the most likely was nausea. Defined as a sickness at the stomach, especially when accompanied by a loathing for food and an involuntary impulse to vomit, nausea can be induced by emotional factors and increased stressors and stimuli.[23] At the end of the 1935–6 war and the beginning of the empire, the disgust provoked by deprivation, fear, and mutual resentment caused widespread nausea among colonizers and colonized.

In interviews conducted by Irma Taddia, Ethiopians and Eritreans who were young boys at the time of the Italian invasion expressed their frustration with the shattering of their communities and lifestyles in physical symptoms of nausea.[24] Similarly, constant feelings of nausea accompanied Italian settlers in their moves throughout a confusing space and time: "[In the scorching heat of Massawa,] we reached the railroad station for Asmara gasping for air," Masotti recalled about his arrival in East Africa, feeling of faint (dyspnea) from a mysterious "odor of red pepper, which is characteristic of the local population's cooking." "Envying the light canvas outfits of those who served in Massawa," he bought a ticket to the capital of Eritrea:

> The little train that climbed about 55 miles from Massawa to Asmara and 8,200 feet in altitude in about three hours quickly took us to the first cool zone, Ginda, a town at about 3,300 feet. We immediately suffered the first effects of the highland climate and were unable to swallow any food. In Gondar, we finally had our own cafeteria for us state employees. That cafeteria would be responsible for our stomach problems for many months to come.[25]

For the many who never fully acclimatized themselves to the climate or foods of empire, nausea was so strong and so chronic that it forced them to repatriate, as it did to the construction worker from Ravenna building the road between Asmara and Addis Ababa: "We were unhappy. We ate poorly, very poorly. Sometimes there were worms in the soup, and for this reason I had intestinal diseases. Partly because I was not well, partly because they did not give us the promised money, and it was very hot in the plain, I applied to go home."[26] Despite systematic preparation and instruction, Italian women experienced Ethiopia as an impenetrable place, especially in its rural corners: "You wander in the African noon," recalled a settler,

> and you see the red earth of the path between the velvety green of the teff moving in the wind; you hear the arid crackling of dry grass under your feet, you see the brown mass of distant mountains, the immense plain over there, towards Jimma. You don't move, yet you are everywhere: you drink the sun and the distances of this new and ancient land, gorgeous and dirty, virgin and ancient. You are not "at home," you are in Africa, you feel like you were born here, like you have to die here.[27]

One food was a major source of nausea for settlers: *niter kibbeh*, the clarified butter used almost everywhere as a basic ingredient and as a women's hair cosmetic. Feelings about *niter kibbeh* could be said to encapsulate the Italian experience in building its Empire of Food. Ethiopian women styled their hair with a substance that tended to melt in the sun, dripping and spreading on their skin, and sharply scenting the air. In many ways, *niter kibbeh* was by far the most characteristic odor perceived daily by Italians. The smell of *niter kibbeh* on Ethiopian women identified them as colonized and sexually available subjects; the smell would stick to the bodies of women and men after sexual intercourse. It would be impossible to avoid or ignore. The pervasive smell of *niter kibbeh* hovered problematically over sexual encounters between Ethiopian women and Italian men. In her colonial novel *Voci sull'altipiano* (Voices on the Ethiopian Highland), Maria Luisa Astaldi, reporting on a conversation among Italian men about "making love to colored females," wrote: "First of all, I will tell you that [Ethiopian women] emanate a nauseating odor from the rancid butter with which they smear their hair."[28] The ubiquitous smell of *niter kibbeh* in so many private and public spaces with the idea of "Ethiopia" or "Africa" branded every occasion of intimacy as "Ethiopian" or "African."[29]

The nausea that *niter kibbeh* caused in Italian soldiers and settlers had origins that were more social than physiological. For the Italians involved in building an imperial state that could feed the "Italian race" and strengthen fascist power, the sexual consumption of colonized female bodies was a significant source of tension. On the one hand, the possibility of having an unlimited number of legalized sexual relations was an irresistible attraction for Italian young men, and they took advantage of prostitution on such a scale that their presence created a mass ethnic war defined by rape. On the other hand, the law prohibited and punished any affectionate relationship with an Ethiopian woman. The regime building the empire considered any offspring from such unions an abomination that would undermine the purity and prestige of the Italian "race." Sexual intercourse with an infibulated Ethiopian woman incapable of feeling any pleasure, often obtained through violence or performed on young girls, lacked any authentic eroticism. Even for the perpetrator, it was a sordid exercise in satisfying base instincts with subjects made to participate in terribly unequal relations of power. Floating through Italian Ethiopia, the omnipresent smell of *niter kibbeh* evoked all these tensions.[30]

The reception of the most popular song of the fascist era and symbol of the war in Ethiopia, *Faccetta Nera*, reveals the tensions provoked by the smell of *niter kibbeh*. The story of *Faccetta Nera* is in itself a story of national embarrassment. The text of the song addresses an imaginary Abyssinian slave who awaits the young, virile bodies of Italians who will "set her free." Yet it is clear to every listener that the intended recipients of the song were the Italian young men about to depart for Africa. The beautiful Abyssinian was nothing more than a willing sexual prey, in a classic representation of voluptuous African women ready to satisfy the fantasies of the White/Italian colonizer (Figure 25).[31]

For the regime, inculcating thousands of future colonizers in the doctrine of White supremacy and protecting the "prestige of the race" against the "plagues" of *madamato* and miscegenation, the immense popularity of the song represented a serious problem. Its appealing message of interracial sexuality forced the regime to instruct its writers, journalists, and political cartoon artists to dismantle any interest in *Faccetta Nera*.[32] In response, the media began to attack *Faccetta Nera* with a negative counter-imaginary of Abyssinian women, representing them no longer as attractive virgins, lascivious and exotic, but as deformed, ugly, dirty, sick, and smelling badly, often from *niter kibbeh*: "In

Figure 25 Ad for Caramella San Giacomo, Luciano Bonacini, 1936. Courtesy of Collezione Salce, Catalogo generale dei Beni Culturali.

Faccetta Nera (Pretty Blackface, 1935) was the most popular imperial war song and is to this day the most popular fascist song of all. The lyrics describe an attractive young Ethiopian woman waiting for Italian soldiers to set her free from slavery, with obvious sexual overtones, which this ad for a candy brand endorses and emphasizes.

the Negro races, the mental inferiority of the woman often borders actual mental retardation," argued the racist anthropologist Lidio Cipriani. "Indeed, in Africa, some female behaviors lose their human traits, to resemble very closely those of animals."[33] In his editorial in *Gazzetta del Popolo*, "Moglie e buoi dei paesi tuoi" (Wife and Oxen of Your Countries—an untranslatable proverb meaning that it is best to be suspicious of the foreign and stick to one's own), Paolo Monelli (1891–1984) described Ethiopian women as

> always fetid with rancid butter that drips in droplets on the neck; worn out at twenty; made frigid and inert in the arms of a man by centuries of sexual servitude. For everyone beautiful, with a noble and handsome face, there are one hundred with elusive eyes, hard and masculine features, and buttery skin. The lyrics of *Faccetta Nera* are worse than idiotic.[34]

Figure 26 Three Oromo and two Italians capture a crocodile in southeastern Ethiopia near the Somali border, April–May 1936. Courtesy of Archivio Luce.

Hunting was an activity of food procurement and leisure that Ethiopians and Italians often performed together.

Monelli's article was followed by a cartoon entitled "Words … and Facts (with Rancid Butter)," published in the humor magazine *Il 420* on July 5, 1936. In the cartoon, two African women with exaggerated lips, breasts, hips, and thighs chatter about the traditional hairstyle made with *niter kibbeh*: "Who is that white man who passed by us and ran away covering his nose?" "He is the author of the lyrics of *Faccetta Nera*."[35] Cipriani added a photograph of an Abyssinian woman with her hair styled with *niter kibbeh* in his article "Rites and Superstitions" in *La difesa della razza* to argue the congenital subhumanity of Africans. The caption read: "It looks like a fashionable hat, but it is a hairstyle obtained with rancid butter and dung."[36]

The senses were a fundamental tool for testing the potability of water, often contaminated by germs, animal and human excreta and possible poisoning by resistance fighters of the Addis Ababa aqueduct, an attack on which could kill all the city's inhabitants. In 1935–6, the invading Italian army had actually used the same terrorist tactic, bombing rivers, streams, and other watercourses with poison gas. As an Italian soldier recalled, "The water, for the gas, could not be drunk, but those poor people, who did not know, ran to the river to quench their thirst and died instantly. There were thousands of dead at the stream."[37]

In its educational materials, the *Fasci Femminili* and the Fascist Institute for Italian Africa emphasized how in East Africa, "to compensate for the water losses that the body suffers in the hot climate due to sweating, it is necessary to drink more," while it warned of the danger that African water could pose. Colonists, travelers, and tourists were advised to "always carry a water bottle drawn from safe centers or sources on their travels to avoid drinking well or stream water. Filters, which became very popular after the war, are recommended. An effective and practical method of purification is sodium hypochlorite or a few drops of iodine tincture."[38]

Italians attributed the quality of the water not to natural circumstances, but to the poor hygiene of the Ethiopians (and in particular, of the troublesome Abyssinians). Masotti recalled,

> Since Dembi Dolo was more of a village than a real city, municipal services were greatly simplified. Naturally, there were no sewers, there was no running water, and since the village spread over three hills and the water flowed down to the valley where there was also a vast swamp, and a lifting pump would have been needed to bring water up. Since the pump was not there, other means had to be used. The first was to dig artesian wells. The problem was that the specialists dug cylindrical wells in the clay soil. But once finished, they had never thought of building a protective wall around them. Accidents, almost always fatal, were therefore not rare.[39]

Bringing clean water to settlers along sterile aqueducts was a priority. "It was an Italian engineer who, in association with Ras Desta Damtew first provided Addis Ababa with an aqueduct and public fountains about ten years ago. Today [after the occupation], that infrastructure has naturally been improved and increased, provided with a more copious water flow," Poggiali noted. "If the ex-slave [Ethiopian woman] tasked with bringing home the terracotta jar filled with water several times a day encounters a dirty puddle along the way, you can be sure that she draws water from that puddle, being certain that her masters won't complain."[40]

In their vast epistolary literature, settlers tried to reassure their loved ones in Italy that they had taken precautions against the danger of contaminated water.

> Addis Ababa, three o'clock in the afternoon on Sunday, January 9, 1938. Dearest Papa, the journey will be long. I think, from Gardula to Baco, fifteen days. Supplies: lots of Buitoni pasta in tin boxes, six cans of butter (6 pounds), four cans of olive oil (4 pounds), ten cans of peeled tomatoes (brand "*Mamma*," 8 pounds), sugar, army's hardtack biscuits in abundance. Steridol for disinfecting water, a little Iodosan (at my expense), iodine tincture (free), mosquito net; in short, I'm doing the best I can [to be safe].[41]

The fear of local water and the corresponding clamor for bottled water from Italy was a response to the waterborne intestinal disease amebiasis (*Entamoeba histolytica*), which caused chronic diarrhea. For settlers, amebiasis was a constant metaphor for the infiltration of uncivilized Africa into their Italian bodies. "The British transferred us to Sudan. We stayed for five months in Zeidab, on the outskirts of Khartoum," recalled an Italian prisoner of war. "Here I fell ill with amoebiasis because we always drank water from the Nile, without being able to filter it. The place was very hot, there was no other water to drink and we had no choice."[42] Amebiasis could become a critical condition. "Particular precautions" were taken, for example, "for the return to Italy of the 75th Infantry Regiment of the army from Somalia, composed of national troops heavily affected by the epidemic of amoebiasis that spread to Kismayo early in 1936, and was still ongoing in August, when the contingent landed in the port of Syracuse."[43] When it came to potable drinking water, Italians never remotely achieved food safety, as Ambrosio remembered. "Baco, March 1938. Dearest [brother] Michele, I like Baco more and more. We have the most delicious bananas here that mom could dream of buying and plenty of honey to make *tej*. However, water can only be drunk after boiling, otherwise you will get infectious jaundice. But I only drink *tej*."[44] "I will return [to Italy] in August, it is the most beautiful season for the water and grapes will be close to be ripe," wrote settler Edoardo Costantini (1903–1987). "In two years, I did not taste any grapes, milk, or a glass of our pure water."[45]

Just as Poggiali identified the "taste" for polluted water as an Ethiopian trait, the use of alcohol distinguished both colonizers and colonized.[46] The *Guide to Italian East Africa* warned White travelers that "alcohol is one of the worst enemies of health in the hot climates of the lowlands; the use of liquors must be avoided and the consumption of wine and beer limited as well."[47] In a typically class-bound directive, colonial powers were urged to be tolerant of the high consumption of wine, beer, and liquors among migrant Italian soldiers, manual workers, and farmers. Except for cases of blatant, "deviant" alcoholism, punishable by repatriation, the mostly middle-class authorities considered beer and wine a positive part of settlers' lifestyle: they increased aggressiveness in battle and resistance to fatigue and pain, and were fundamental to sociability and relaxation. Thanks to their traditional use of alcohol, proletarian settlers were also thought to be entirely capable of managing its effects on their own.

The "taste" of Italian settlers for alcohol was at odds with the "taste" of Ethiopians, whose apparent inability to handle alcoholic beverages was a problem that needed to be repressed. The solution was to shut down the many "native" places where Ethiopians gathered to consume *tej* and *tella*, which were also seen as incubators of "vice" and rebellion. Masotti noted:

> Alcohol was a plague in the cities of Ethiopia: it was the first and main vice that Ethiopians had taken from Europeans, just as Europeans got many nice venereal diseases as a reward for their love for local women. The legal sale of alcohol and wine was limited to very few shops, both Italian and Ethiopian, in the hope that this could reduce inebriating tendencies, with a doubly negative result. On the one hand, those who wanted to drink managed to get the desired alcohol one way or another. On the other hand, the few who had the license to sell alcohol made a fortune.[48]

Ethiopians' taste for alcohol was shaped, ironically, through their regular exposure to "Italian" drinking practices as part of their socialization as imperial subjects. "The remains of two wine bottles were located during the survey in Guba and dozens in Afodo," noted archaeologist Gonzales-Ruibal about the fieldwork he conducted at the remains of Italian military sites in western Ethiopia. "Here, besides wine, a large variety of bottles, belonging to different liquors and alcoholic beverages, appeared. The consumption pattern implied by the bottles is similar to the European and very different from the collective drinking parties, using large communal vessels, prevalent in [Ethiopian culture]." Consuming drinks in bottles and presumably from glasses, distinguished Italian and Ethiopian patterns, "also contributing," Gonzales-Ruibal concluded, "to mark off the Askaris [collaborators of the Italians, with whom, as seen, they sometimes shared meals] in a 'third space,' which was neither that of the locals nor the colonizers."[49]

The archaeologist went on to consider that

> the use of white ware [cups and plates] attested in Guba and Afodo, was also part of the production of differences, since it reinforced the civility of the foreigners who used clean individual dishes instead of filthy communal pots. At the same time, the use of [cups and plates] reassured the colonizers psychologically [about their own superiority].[50]

Civilizing Ethiopians to accept the food of the empire was a complicated task: the colonized had to be made to perform their subordinate roles well, but there needed to be a clear separation between two contrasting sensory universes.

The most common strategy for giving Africans a feeling for the food of the empire involved the role of the Italian housewife-settler—the regime's principal delegate for civilizing domestic and public realms—and her young male Ethiopian servants. The housewife-colonist Rapaccini fully identified with her role as the *maîtresse* of conviviality, perfecting the sensibilities of both Italian and Ethiopian men. She remembered a dinner at the start of World War II, when the colony began to suffer from significant food shortages:

> The table, our cheerful table, gradually disappeared; we were reduced to five; us and three other colonial employees. We couldn't run the regular routine of meals; the cook had gone. The indigenous cook was busy keeping the kitchen for the workers' canteen going. I decided that with the help of an Ethiopian servant, I would try and host a nice dinner for us and the employees with the little food we had. I started by asking Fulmine [an Ethiopian servant, a boy] if he wanted to cook with me. He looked at me astonished, and I insisted: "Do you want to work in the kitchen with me? You already know something, you have been working with a white cook for many years, I will teach you what you don't know." "Madam, I will come right away, I will be very good, I will work with you, right away." And now he is my helper, attentive, clean. The idea of him cooking our dinners makes him proud and makes him full of good will. He goes shopping and tries to get the best pieces of meat. Fulmine becomes more and more valuable by the day; with his advice, we tend the garden. Soon we will have zucchini, chard, parsley, cabbage, green beans. And our table, although reduced to few people, continues

peacefully. In the evening, we wait for the radio program and in silence, with our hearts suspended in anxiety, we listen to the voice of the Homeland and the daily war report.[51]

In the same way, Ethiopians were needed for the important work of deodorization, or at least the elimination of the worst stenches, such as those of animal and human carcasses. "Wood for cooking was everywhere abundant and excellent," Masotti recalled.

> The stoves were of the primitive type and, as far as I knew, nobody used coal. The municipal sanitation service was entrusted to a group of volunteer sweepers who buried the corpses and the carcasses of animals, kept the streets clean and took away household waste. We had moved to the new villa: the house plan was square, with a veranda that ran on all four sides. The kitchen, according to local custom, was separate from the house, a few meters away. No cooking smells in the house, therefore, but rain and dust in the soup when it was brought from the kitchen to the house under the beautiful sky.[52]

An appreciation for the look, texture, flavors, smells, and sounds of food inscribed a colonial world in Ethiopian bodies and identities. However, clear racial hierarchies were complicated by an increasingly shared language of food and taste, so vividly seen in the case of the Askaris, Ethiopian servants in Italian households, and the wives of *insabbiati*. The need for Europeans to share social space with the Africans who built and operated their food systems created opportunities for Ethiopians, many of whom became tastemakers in the domestic and social life of Italians. "Interacting with colonial power" in the arena of food and taste, Ethiopians "experienced processes of modernization and elevation of their social status," just as they were being disciplined as subjects.[53] As Homi Bhabha has emphasized, daily contact with Italians raised them to the rank of "indigenous elite," forcing them to alternate strategies of imitation and mimicry and resolve the tension between the impossibility of assimilation and the conditions imposed on their bodies. Such a political, psychological, and emotional subalternity could only be healed through resistance, insurrection, and the reclamation of an indigenous land, its foods, and its kitchens.[54] The anti-colonial struggle began and ended with the senses.

The Taste of the Empire

Over the years, the taste of the empire changed and evolved. The first contact with the body and food of the other typically resulted in aversion, disgust, and suspicion. In time, in a slow process of education about the empire and its landscapes, plants, animals, human bodies, and foods, Ethiopians and Italians began experiencing the food of the other within familiar culinary metaphors. "Injera, or indigenous bread, is a kind of mucilage that looks like tripe," explained Poggiali.[55] An Italian traveler of the late nineteenth century, Pellegrino Matteucci (1850–1881), dismissed Abyssinian cuisine as an "indescribable mess"—describing starches, meats, and sauces (*injera* and *wat*, spiced with *berbere* and seasoned with *niter kibbeh*) as coarse and malodorous mixtures. Matteucci had nonetheless explored that cuisine and judged it carefully against the culinary patterns he was familiar with.[56] Ethiopian women expressed their aversion to Italian foods in much the same fashion: to many Ethiopian women, spaghetti seemed like hookworms. Faced with what seemed strange, dry biscuits distributed in rations by the Italian Colonial Army, they simply used them in the ways they knew, crumbled finely into the spicy sauces they used for seasoning.[57]

For Italians, acknowledging the food of the other encouraged feelings of tolerance, appreciation, and even pleasure. The settler Palmiro Forzini initially found Ethiopian food repulsive, but after a while he began to educate himself about the "smells of spices and perhaps dirt, in any instance odors new to my sense of smell, sometimes too penetrating and offensive," of the market in Addis Ababa. Instead of disgust, he felt "almost a sense of relaxation."[58] Masotti blended bodies and food in his sensorium: "As for the characteristic smells of Ethiopians, first among them red pepper and spices, I had quickly become accustomed to them and found them almost pleasant."[59] Masotti's highly seasoned tastes of *berbere* and *niter kibbeh* moved in clouds across the colonial sky, inviting Italians to experience new sensations.

Italian settlers internalized the taste of Ethiopian food and eating habits against their image of primordial landscapes and unchanging ways of life. As strange as it was, this image resonated with an Italian nostalgia for a direct connection to the land and for the authentic human relationships that marked their own "past" (even if imagined and imaginary). Italian settlers seemed to feel that Ethiopian gastronomy was also "close to nature."

Settlers particularly appreciated African food when it was transformed by Italian hands in an evolving Ethiopian-Italian/Italian-Ethiopian cuisine. "In our trip we tasted the fruit of the mango, squeezed the green berry of coffee between our teeth, passed our tongue over the sweet pulp of the papaya," Vergani commented on visiting a farm Italians had created in the late nineteenth century.

> These fruits were the wonders of a plantation where one must make a stop, to pay homage to a masterpiece of [Italian] ingenuity and integrity. The first plants in the farmstead were born forty-six years ago and since then the loving gardener never left, in adoration of the tropical fruits and the blue Madonna [statue] who watches over the fruit orchard and protects the old farm. That taste of tropical fruits remained on my palate all day.[60]

The picture of the Madonna watching over these fields testified to the sacredness of traditional knowledge and expert work that Italian farmers had transplanted to the African frontier. The image was a founding discourse of gastrofascism.

Vergani enthusiastically supported the creation of an original Ethiopian-Italian/Italian-Ethiopian cuisine by Italian cooks:

> In Korem. A young man entered my room. He came to Africa early on to work in road construction. He worked in the lowlands at 125°F in the shade. "Believe me,"

he says, "I couldn't even swallow a piece of bread." And yet his looks are enviable. How did he survive? He was one of the best workers, and engineer Rocca—who got killed in the Gondrand massacre—did not want to lose him, and gave him a special permit so that, instead of the food ration, he could get two bottles of wine a day from the camp's grocery store. "So," he says modestly, "I was able to get by … A sip every now and then." Now he is the supervisor and cook in a truck transport company's camp. His latest masterpiece is a soup that he brought me half an hour ago, holding the tureen between his big, caring, and diesel-smelling hands. Rice, canned peas, and wild guinea fowl liver from Lake Hashenge. "You can't expect all food to arrive intact from Italy to Korem! It would be too easy."[61]

The African-flavored foods "smelling of diesel," as Vergani remembered, that nourished truck drivers and construction workers were hybrid creations. Masotti commented on this hybridity, insisting that "Italian food" produced in Africa was a sad imitation of the "authentic" food imported from Italy: "Along the road to Gondar, many wooden shacks had sprung up: small mechanic's shops, humble grocery stores, and primitive restaurants. Rudimentary places catering to drivers who contented themselves with the Eritrean-made pasta and the Chianti wine—God forgive the bottler—bottled in Massawa on sale there."[62]

However, despite nativist criticism, for settlers far from segregated cities and exposed to the cultural and biodiversity of Ethiopia, creolized Italian-Ethiopian cuisine was a pleasingly adaptive and resilient culinary creation: "As far as food was concerned, as long as I had to provide only for the few compatriots of the settlements, I managed to supply myself quite easily with local resources," wrote colonial official Calabrò from the Jimma region in 1940.

> I had one ton of wheat, from a sowing I had done a few months before. With the flour obtained by pounding the wheat in a wooden mortar, the doctor, who was in charge of the cafeteria, made bread and pasta. I had replaced wine with mead and indigenous beer. From crushed sunflower seeds immersed in boiling water, I got modest but sufficient quantities of cooking oil. Chickens and eggs could be easily found, and hunting provided a good dietary complement.[63]

"Baco, April 1938. Dearest Mom," wrote Roman official Ambrosio, "Baco is banana paradise: I make myself a banana salad, with a little cognac, like I made in Rome with oranges. You want to try too: bananas cost a penny each; and chickens two or three lire each. Veal brains is one lira for two pounds, liver is free."[64]

In the sea of letters they sent home to Italy, settlers created a vast translational imaginary of the new cuisine of the empire, its tastes and its dietary values. Ambrosio's letters, in their expression of emotions through the senses connected a political love for the empire with affection for distant loved ones. Ambrosio constantly wrote "home" in a gustatory grammar that transcended the simple emotion of nostalgia:

> Jimma, Friday, November 26, 1937. Dearest Mom, I'm doing great, much better, healthier than in Rome. Imagine that I eat boiled chicken every night and always

watch out carefully for the bones as you taught me. For eggs, I have chickens (five) that give me two or three a day. For fruit here I have bananas, which they bring me fresh from the surroundings of Jimma. We have tomatoes, zucchini, different varieties of lettuce, green beans, and lots of other vegetables: everything grows in every season. Do you know that coffee grows in front of my house? It doesn't cost anything. I drink cups of it like the ones we used to drink together when no one was watching. I prepare it slowly and dip bread crusts in it. I wish you could taste how good and fragrant it is![65]

Settlers shared everyday life in Africa vicariously with their family in Italy, often writing of local foods:

Baco, December 3, 1938. Dear old [mother], I'm doing great here: you wouldn't believe how well we eat! The honey is so genuine that I extract it myself from the wax-filled mass from the hive. Bananas all year round. Vegetables like in Rome, except for red peppers; very fresh shallots, lettuce and plenty of small potatoes that go perfectly with roast meat. There's no fruit from Italy: no grapes, figs, apples, or oranges. There are no mini pastries from Rosati's Pastry Shop, but I don't miss them: you yourself said they're not worth anything.[66]

The photographs settlers sent home were even more convincing proof of their well-being: their robust, even overweight, bodies signified good health in the peasant and working-class traditions of 1930s Italy. The larger space occupied by the settler's body was also a persuasive metaphor for the expansion of colonial White power. The mother and sisters of the Venetian settler Edoardo Costantini were comforted by the photos he sent of himself. "We were so pleased to see the seven photos you sent us; I immediately tell you that they were beautiful and that you also looked very good in them, for the first time. You seem happy, fat and that's enough for us."[67] Similarly, the truck driver Guerino used food to reassure his wife in Bologna of his successful "acclimatization": "Dear Uciona, I tolerate the climate very well, I have a good appetite and I don't skimp on food and drink."[68]

Imperial Food Anthropologies

Italian settlers used sensory perception to understand the empire, immersing themselves in "the nature" of East Africa. The immersion could be terrifying and monstrous; just as often, though, it evoked nostalgia for an idyllic world in which Ethiopians stood as wild, authentic figures rooted in nature, reminding Italians "of how they used to be."

The various Ethiopian ethnic groups with their different religions, languages, and cultures were an integral part of the empire. Italians identified every ethnic group as "indigenous" or "native," although group migrations and contacts were common throughout East Africa. Settlers explored Ethiopian foodways and modes of consumption and conviviality in different ethnic communities. Calabrò, for example, wrote about the diet of the Oromo people in the Bunno region of western Ethiopia:

In early March, a locust swarm, one of the most feared calamities by the natives, hit the region. A cloud that obscured the sun advanced, devouring crops and leaving behind a barren desert. The total destruction of the crops forced the indigenous people to use locusts in their diet. They collected them in sacks, tore off their wings, toasted them, and pounded them in mortars, obtaining a grayish powder that, mixed with corn or teff flour, was used to prepare flatbreads. I tasted this mixture and I must say that the taste was not bad and resembled that of roasted chickpea flour.[69]

In a language often sharpened by hunger, settlers-ethnographers revealed entire gastronomies in their recording of everyday habits. "We are industriously trying to cope with the supply situation," explained settler Costantini in a 1940 letter.

> Searching for indigenous cereals that former slaves [Somalis] ground with stones to save on [imported] flour; intensifying the making of butter and the production of vegetables from the garden: now I even await a recipe for making cheese with goat milk using the pounded bones of the same animal as rennet: if it is true and it works, it is really a beautiful tradition![70]

Local foodways were often considered interesting because they were "simple," "spontaneous," and "authentic." "The Somali natives of the Shebelle valley never think about tomorrow, they have had the good fortune to be born in a land that produces wheat all year round, and their needs are few," Costantini noted.

> Their ration consists of a little roasted corn, or polenta. They ground the grain daily with a crude mill made of two stones operated by hand. They also consume their tea daily, as for them tea is indispensable. For clothing they have a kind of wrap-around skirt called *futa*. For home they have a hut made of twigs plastered with a special lime (animal manure with dirt).[71]

These settlers-as-ethnographers often reflected on the sacredness of many Ethiopian foodways and the transcendent powers of their rituals. They frequently expressed a certain envy for a religious-spiritual dimension that had been lost or greatly diluted in their own lives.[72] Calabrò respected the religious dimension of food among Ethiopians. After a hunting trip, he noted that

> the antelope to the Muslim Askaris and the gazelle to the Coptic Christians, as the two religions use different slaughter systems. For Muslims, animals must always be slaughtered so that they die bled out, as it is not allowed to consume their meat with blood "because the soul is in the blood and it is not lawful to eat the soul with the body."[73]

For the settlers, organized events such as religious festivals were special opportunities to engage their senses in understanding the cultures around them. Calabrò remembered:

In October, I attended the *Butta*, a traditional pagan festival celebrated by the Oromo, even though they were of Christian Coptic or Muslim religion. The *Butta* ceremony culminated in the sacrifice of a bovine, with whose blood the officiant and his helpers smeared their heads and faces. The sacrificer wore its skin, masked himself by placing the emptied head of the animal on his head, and imitated its mooing while dancing. Immediately afterwards, he went to a nearby watercourse for a purifying bath. The meat was distributed and consumed raw, seasoned with berbere.[74]

The farther they moved away from large cities and the dominating culture of the Abyssinian highlands, the more Italians felt—breathed—the diversity of the countryside. Trying to describe these new sensations, they associated the "primitive" peoples they met with those from their own peasant past; Africans did things the way their own ancestors did, and ate as their own ancestors ate. Exploring a new land by means of the senses, the settlers found a way to "visit" their own foreign past.[75] "Towards mid-November, I organized an excursion to the Sai forest, about thirty miles from Bedele," wrote Calabrò.

On the edges of this immense and largely unexplored forest lived a special ethnic group consisting of a few thousand individuals. Very small in stature, very black, very thin, extremely diffident and timid, they lived in a primordial way, did not cultivate fields, did not raise animals. Their favorite food was monkey, which they hunted with a spear and bow. They lived in small and rudimentary huts, camouflaged among the trees. Making contact with this tribe was not easy, but thanks to an Oromo merchant I was able to enter the area and meet their chief and some of the most curious members of the tribe. I was amazed to see how human beings could exist in conditions that, I believe, were identical to those of cavemen. Their needs were minimal and limited to ensuring nothing more than survival.[76]

Hunting, as a ritual communal activity, also pointed to a preagricultural, tribal past. Calabrò again remembered:

During one of my travels, I had the opportunity to witness the *adamo*, a hunting party conducted by the Oromo with their traditional weapons: spears and sturdy clubs. The male population of the village, including boys, surrounded a wooded area, advancing slowly, beating long poles, drums, and metal containers. At a certain moment, the trapped animals tried to escape the surrounded area. I was amazed to see so many gazelles, antelopes, wild boars, hares, and all were hit and killed. The hunt ended with a lavish banquet during which the meat was roasted and eaten accompanied by abundant libations of *tej* and *tella*.[77]

Echoing fascist propaganda, Calabrò embraced the empire as a primordial place of creation, feeling its ancient breath:

In the plain, the landscape was characterized by the absolute absence of human life, contrasting with the triumphant forces of nature. The incandescent globe of the sun, the flat savannah dotted with thorny bushes, the imposing mass of water of the river that appeared almost motionless, the silence that reigned supreme, brought the imagination back to the beginnings of creation, to a time when man was in constant struggle for his [sic] survival.[78]

African soundscapes also reinforced the visual, olfactory, tactile, and gustatory perception of Ethiopian food as a place of primordiality. Calabrò deciphered the sounds of Ethiopians as if immersed in a timeless past, colored by a dreamlike eroticism:

> I was reading an old magazine in my tent, when I was intrigued by some songs, accompanied by the sound of a flute and the rhythm of a drum, bearing an unusual sweetness. The women of the village were celebrating the Atete festival, a deity who presided over sowing and harvesting. Something similar to the homage that the ancient Romans paid to Ceres, the goddess of agriculture. A fantastic image, in the moonlit night, appeared before my eyes with the grace and elegance of simple and mysterious movements. In the center of a group of women, wrapped in white shawls, there was one who directed the dance. Around her were the other young dancers, so slow, precise, and graceful as to give the image of a white, large rose that was moved by a magical force.[79]

Italians also experienced the medicinal use of wild plants unknown to Europeans.[80] "Ethiopia possesses almost all the medicinal plants known to Western therapy and it cannot be denied that the natives derive curative benefits from them," Poggiali argued. "The Italian pharmacopoeia has already set its sights on the Ethiopian flora, today to study it thoroughly, tomorrow to supply its laboratories."[81] Italian scientists were also interested. A report from the military hospital in Massawa, for example, focused on the therapeutic value of herbs used by the "natives" and

> all the applications of those remedies known [in Ethiopia], such as miswak [a twig from *Salvadora persica*, or toothbrush tree] to clean teeth, which placed on the tongue would have purgative virtues; henna [a powder from *Lawsonia inermis*, or henna tree], which taken in infusion would induce sweat and cure rheumatism; and an unnamed fatty plant that, mixed with water, is used to smear the bodies of feverish people to refresh them.[82]

Colonizers were particularly attracted to the traditional knowledge and natural remedies that Ethiopians used against the endemic diseases and infections, which afflicted Europeans as "Africa's revenge." One was tapeworm: "I was amazed at the speed with which this operation took place without the knife injuring the face and, in particular, the nose of the diners, as well as the amount of meat that each one managed to devour," Calabrò recalled about the skill with which his Ethiopian dining companions cut pieces of just killed beef and brought them to their mouths. "The only disturbance that resulted from it—I later learned—was tapeworm, which, transmitted by raw meat, had to be periodically eliminated by means of a special mixture of medicinal herbs called *kosso* [*Hagenia abyssinica*]."[83] Italians were understandably more curious about the traditional remedies for syphilis, the universal disease of the empire.

Against syphilis, which they call the disease of whites because they say it was imported by the Portuguese, [Ethiopians] adopt several curative methods. The most popular and effective is that of *usciva*, the roots of a plant, a kind of sarsaparilla. They close themselves in a tiny house, wear heavy woolen clothes, cover doors and cracks; they light a fire, burn small pieces of *usciva* root, and inhale the vapors. Some crush the root, and mix it with white honey that they swallow. Others put crushed *usciva* root in hot water and honey, drinking four cups in the morning and four in the evening. The cure and the confinement last at least forty days, and whoever interrupts is sure to die (!). The cost [of the dose] is five or six lire. After twenty days, [the sick person] goes to the hot springs. Hot baths are effective and widely used. Even Europeans sometimes go there to seek relief.[84]

Feeling that Ethiopians were "close to nature" and its most mysterious workings, Italian settlers were keenly interested in local magical-ritual practices. Costantini wrote to Italy that

I am also sending two photos. One photo was taken on a boat on the river at Afgoye. The second Ethiopian from the right in the photo is the chief of the river, called in the native language *bahar*, which means the "exorcist of crocodiles." I asked him why he is not afraid of crocodiles, he replied that he has a leather belt with a small bag sewn onto his right arm, as you see in the photo, containing powdered crocodile blood and other substances, and thus the crocodiles do not approach him. True or not, we depend on the *bahar* to pass ropes from one end of the river to the other.[85]

By the mid-1930s, Fascism had implemented a range of environmental policies, including the creation of national parks managed by the state.[86] Building on the fascist idea that nature equaled nation, Mussolini made environmental protection a political priority: "It is imperative that we create; we, people from this epoch and this generation, because we have the duty to remake the face of the Fatherland both spiritually and materially. In ten years, comrades, we will have made a new [Italy]."[87] In Italian East Africa, the environmental program was carried out mainly from the bottom up. Settlers, enthusiastic creators of their own home gardens, transformed the landscape of the empire—as Mussolini had urged—while harvesting a rich variety of products for a cuisine that was both colonial and diasporic.

Settlers were offered horticulture courses by the Fascist Colonial Institute and the Women's Groups of the Fascist Party. "Given the enormous difference in climate in our colonies, it will be necessary, in order not to have unpleasant surprises, to obtain the necessary information on site, before starting the various crops, both for choosing what to plant and the individual crop's cultivation instructions," one manual recommended.[88] By becoming self-sufficient gardeners, settlers could reconnect to nature and its products—especially the vegetables, legumes, herbs, and other foods most popular in Italian kitchens.

The program for remaking local agriculture was basic to achieving food autarchy, which was, after all, the premise—as well as the unfulfilled promise—of the entire imperial adventure. The Fascist Party's local envoy for agricultural "valorization," Davide Fossa, while underlining difficulties posed by the lack of irrigation, acknowledged the failure of demographic colonization. At the same time, he praised the efforts of settlers. "In order to ensure the supply of vegetables to Addis Ababa and all the main centers of the Empire, numerous gardens have sprung up, through the interest of Government Offices and Military Commands, as well as through the initiative and goodwill of workers. Truck gardens are scattered everywhere they work, all over Ethiopia."[89] Fossa attributed the success of these largely spontaneous and small-scale initiatives to settlers' careful application of production, management, and resource protection policies.

> The *Milizia Forestale* (Forestry Militia, the voluntary unit in charge of Italy's forestry resources and parks), which has already given its valuable contribution to the African conquest, is now tackling the forest problem of the Empire. The land, previously uncultivated, transformed into a seedbed by the Forestry Militia, is now rich in young seedlings destined for the next and wider reforestation, and countless quantities of seedlings have been planted.[90]

Seeds and seedlings filled the pockets and suitcases of Italians headed for Ethiopia. Poggiali commented, "In Addis Ababa, in the summer of 1936, signs of *Italianità* flourished even in utter chaos: the gardens that the settlers planted around their homes."[91] Ambrosio wrote:

> Baco, September 2, 1938. Dearest Papa, I sowed potatoes and onions on about 2,300 square feet: harvested in December. The abundance of vegetables is one of the advantages of these areas. We have all our varieties, except artichokes. We consume a lot of produce: therefore, apart from the tropical diseases, everyone's health is good: mine is wonderfully fine. I was never so well in Rome.[92]

"Africa Eats Us": The Animal and Cannibal Empire

Equally significant in the empire's ecology was the relationship between Italian settlers and nonhuman animals. Historians have pointed out that animals, wild or domesticated, were critical to European colonialism: from their environmental, economic, and cultural impact and their labor in military and economic projects to the conquest of animal bodies—in zoos, circuses, or in natural history museums—as a demonstration of European technological and scientific power. Europeans included indigenous people and nonhuman animals in the same wilderness they, as colonizers, had to confront, domesticate, oppress, and civilize.[93]

Fanon noted that in the colonizers' Manichean view,

> [the native] is reduced to the state of an animal. And consequently, when the colonist speaks of the colonized he [sic] uses zoological terms. Allusion is made of to the slithery movements of the yellow race, the odors for the "native" quarters, to the hordes, the stink, the swarming, the seething, and the gesticulations. In his

endeavors at description and finding the right word, the colonist refers constantly to the bestiary.[94]

In his description of everyday life in Addis Ababa, Poggiali confirms Fanon's argument:

> Alongside the most attractive nature, the city brims with mud and straw tukuls, huts made with rusty corrugated iron, and any kind of squalid sheds, swarming like parasites. Everywhere there is garbage, waste, the remains of slaughtered livestock. When it gets dark and women and children have laid down to sleep on the earthen floor covered only by a tanned skin, the head of the household pushes into the tukul the chickens, the goat, and the heifer.[95]

The writer Sem Benelli (1877–1949) remarked that in Abyssinia there was "not a vegetable garden, not a cultivated flower, not a tree planted and loved. These poor people have the soul of a goat: they wait for heaven to send them the sprout; and as soon as the bud sprouts, they eat it."[96]

Italian settlers, especially those who migrated from rural areas, had daily contact with animals. Their African experience was a sensory return to a traditional Italy on the brink of disappearance, filled with nostalgia for a premodern world the rarefied air and low sun of the empire only amplified. From Merca, Somalia, the farmer-settler Costantini sent his family in the Veneto vivid descriptions of animals: "The only hotel in Merca is run by a man from Padua. In the bedrooms, toads and certain insects that look like crabs roam undisturbed. Here you have to get used to insects because there are a lot of them everywhere."[97] A few days later, he encountered larger creatures:

> The animals that come to visit us are: lynxes, some monkeys, wild boars, and other beasts that would take too long to list. Tonight, even jackals (they're harmless, like dogs) entered the camp and stole some game hanging on the tent. I am a little far from Merca, the area is good and healthy. I'm out of the malaria zone and have no fever. It's comfortable; game is never lacking.[98]

Costantini's family responded favorably to the mementos he sent home—turtle shells and python skins, and photographs of himself with Africans:

> Good, you explain everything so well to us that we feel like we are living a little bit in your environment too. How dark are your Somalis! I would like very much to get to know them a little bit too. What a surprise was to receive your pythons, dear Edoardo, I would have never believed that such huge beasts existed, please be very careful.[99]

Hunting—the oldest means of survival—was for many colonizers a purifying retreat from modernity to a fresh state of nature. Perhaps prefiguring Fanon's argument that indigenous animals and people were seen as a single wildness, Italians usually hunted with Ethiopians (Figure 26). "The waters, so calm as to appear almost motionless, were literally sprinkled with wild ducks and I took advantage of that to hunt a good number of them. Those ducks, together with a dozen large fish, which the native driving the boat gave me, procured a rich dinner for me and my Askari," Calabrò recalled.

> In the afternoon, accompanied by some Askaris, I went hunting to supply the men with meat. The area was rich in every species: antelopes, gazelles, zebras, wild boars, hares, guinea fowl, ducks, partridges, but also leopards, cheetahs, leopards, hyenas, jackals, and vultures …. Hunting in Ethiopia was very easy because game was abundant, not afraid of man, and therefore not a difficult target. Returning to camp, I met a female wild boar, with seven or eight piglets in tow. I let them go: the scene was one of moving maternity.[100]

With concerns similar to those expressed by Calabrò and now in possession of African landscapes, the regime sought to control all forms of life. "It should be borne in mind that the rigorous provisions on hunting issued by the Italian Government will prevent the destruction of such a rich wildlife heritage," the Fascist Colonial Institute warned migrants about to leave for Ethiopia.[101]

Animals were omnipresent in the sensory landscapes of empire:

> We were evicted from the little hill where we had settled because an elegant residential district (which never materialized) was to be built there, and we took refuge in a grove near an old, abandoned Coptic church in the company of squirrels and hyenas. Those animals served as the country's sanitation service, but were a great nuisance when they howled at night interrupting our well-deserved sleep.[102]

The sounds of animals were not always disturbing: "In the lake I often took a bath, which, it may be said in passing, did not involve any risk as hippos are vegetarian, timid and harmless animals, despite their imposing size and the noisy blarings they launched to intimidate and drive away the intruder."[103]

Living with animals meant returning to the past, even if it was another people's past:

> In the evening, after dinner, preceded by [the Askari helper] Zelleca who illuminated my path with a kerosene lantern, I went to my lodging away from the mess building, I always stopped at the stables. And I remember with nostalgia the sense of calm and serenity that the sight of the horses resting or chewing the hay gave me; the acrid smell and warmth of the environment; the dim light that illuminated the long shed, the silent and vigilant presence of the Askari guards.[104]

> Despite its drawbacks, the rain season had a special charm. Everything surrendered to a peaceful lethargy and the noises of the forest, the cries of the animals, and the voices of the travelers came faint and muffled in the diffuse silence that enveloped everything. This sleepy atmosphere made the so-called civilized world, so harsh and tormented, appear more distant than ever.[105]

Living with animals, settlers found that time passed according to the flow of days and seasons instead of the rhythm of machine and clock: "The deputy allowed us to sleep in the warehouse so at the first light of dawn we would already be outside breathing the balsamic air of the African morning," Masotti recalled. "The company of the chickens in the warehouse was not annoying, albeit not exactly hygienic, at night, and was useful as a noisy wake-up call at sunrise."[106]

The natural world could be a source of nostalgia and peace, but also one of fear and terror. On the day he left Africa, the soldier Sergio Botta bid a sensory farewell: "Goodbye to the muddy swamps that quenched parched throats; treacherous thickets; torrential rains without shelter; malarial climates; insidious insects; dangerous animals and reptiles; bread with worms; soup with flies; Abyssinians in guerrilla warfare."[107] The animal voices that triggered affection could also cause anguish and anxiety:

> With the intensity of the rains diminished, I was finally attached to a convoy of trucks that, escorted by a company of Askaris, headed to Jimma. We traveled for four days and quickly set up the tents. After sunset, conversations continued late into the night in the silence broken by the distant howling of hyenas, the laughter of jackals, and a thousand other mysterious noises.[108]

As much as Italian colonizers embraced Africa's nature, they also feared that, in return, it would unleash its primal forces and, like an awakened Golem, devour them all.

Italians had come to Ethiopia to establish an Empire of Food, to eat Africa. They were aware enough to suspect that at in any hidden corner, under any unpredictable guise, Africa might chew, swallow, and eat *them*. The Ethiopians and nonhuman animals the Italians had idealized and violently suppressed could explode at any moment in anger and resentment. Italians knew that at the first sign of weakness, the same Ethiopian nature they had come to conquer would devour them. They frequently experienced the damage nature could do, whether swarms of locusts periodically destroying wheat fields or wild animals ravaging crops. "The wildlife that constituted an important source of food also represented a constant danger to crops that could be irreparably damaged or destroyed in a few minutes," remembered Calabrò.

> Monkeys, in particular, were hated and feared for the damage they caused. An invasion of them in a field was a disaster. They devoured what they needed and destroyed what they could not eat, as if animated by a malignant spirit of hatred and revenge. It was not uncommon to see farmers sowing and groups of monkeys, keeping a safe distance, collecting and eating the seeds, indifferent to the shouts and throwing of stones and sticks that they skillfully managed to avoid.[109]

Rivers and lakes, sources of life and a prized attraction in the imperial landscape, could hide deadly dangers:

> The locality of Wech'e was about ten kilometers from a river, the Gibe of Ennarea, populated not only by fish that provided delicious food, but also by crocodiles. Despite their presence, I stopped on its banks to take a bath with the Askaris. On these occasions, half of the unit would position on both sides of the river where

the other half took a bath and, with long fronded poles, beat the water to keep the crocodiles away.[110]

"I had an adventure that could have ended tragically," Calabrò recalled.

> Having noticed a strange movement in a bush and believing that there were hidden guinea fowl in it, I approached with the shotgun. Behind the bush, lying peacefully, was a magnificent leopard who, annoyed by the intrusion, snorted in irritation. Following the advice whispered to me by Zelleca, I remained still. In turn, the leopard got up and, with a bored air, slowly walked away. I breathed a sigh of relief and, mounted on horseback, quickly reached the camp where I drank a double whiskey in one gulp. The Askaris, informed by Zelleca that my gaze and charisma had intimidated the leopard, improvised a dance in my honor.[111]

Tales of the strangeness, the unknowability, and the daily horrors of the empire were collected in a growing narrative of constant insecurity:

> After twelve days in the hot plains, I moved to the highland in the country of Dimma. The village chief brought me a long python skin as a gift and told me that these amphibious reptiles lived in the area. I asked him how they caught them and he replied that he could show me snake hunting the next day. At dawn, he took me to the lake where a native sat motionless on the shore, crouched on one leg, the other leg immersed in the water up to his groin, with a long knife beside him. After an hour my guide pointed out that the water was stirring and the hunt would soon begin. As the man remained motionless, a large python, now clearly visible, slowly approached and began to swallow his leg. When, after about twenty minutes, the head of the python emerged from the water, the man cut its throat cleanly with his razor-sharp knife. As the python's blood reddened the water, the hunter and two assistants extracted the leg from its throat. I was told that this type of hunting could be practiced because that class of pythons, being toothless, could only swallow the prey. The hunter had the advantage and could strike it fatally.[112]

In the strange, harsh life of the empire, colonizers could feel as if they were being slowly eaten every day, swallowed by the ravines (in Italian *gole*, throats) of the highlands, or lost in the desert, their flesh torn by African "prickles."

> After passing the village of Nefasit, our trucks stopped to refuel at a military building. We all jumped out, and since our hunger had reached its maximum, we immediately attacked the prickly pears that were everywhere. Those who knew took them delicately and, with a cloth, removed the thorns. But I, who had never seen them, used my bare hands, and I confess that, stimulated by hunger, I ate the first ones skin and all. I felt stung all over my body. I don't know how many thorns I had in my hands, but the ones on my tongue were the worst, almost preventing me from speaking. I swore to myself that next time I would rather die of hunger, but I would never eat that kind of figs again.[113]

Feeling that the land was eating them alive and facing dangers at every turn—like the attacks of Ethiopian guerrillas—settlers expressed their fears in morbid tales of real or imagined cases of cannibalism.

One evening, during one of the feasts in the nearby village, we became curious and went to see. We knew that the day before the Daasanach had brought to their village two Turkana mortally wounded in a fight; we wanted to know what was happening. Suddenly we heard a cry near us, then another further away, then another, and suddenly, in the village where the celebration was in full swing there was absolute silence. We realized they discovered us, and we ran back to avoid incidents. As soon as we set foot in our garrison, the village party resumed. Afterward, the Daasanach looked like they had stuffed themselves well. A dog came with a bone in its mouth. That bone looked suspicious, so we took it to the doctor who said it was a calf's shin. But I would swear that it wasn't a beef bone ... right, doctor? We know what a beef bone looks like and the Daasanach do not eat cattle. They are too precious. They eat donkeys. If they have nothing else, they make an incision on a cow's leg and suck a little blood, but they do not kill the animal. In short, no one has ever seen them eat human flesh, but we are all certain that the Daasanach are cannibals.[114]

Such stories traveled freely as warnings across Ethiopia: in this Empire of Food, at any moment, Italians could become food for the empire. In the end, one way or another, Africa would eat them alive.

Conclusion: Fascist Colonial Crops and the Legacies of the Empire of Food

In the 2022 general election, the victory of the right-wing coalition led by the Brothers of Italy (Fratelli d'Italia) party marked the ascent to power of the first non-antifascist government since the fall of Mussolini's regime. The Brothers of Italy party originates from the Italian Social Movement (Movimento Sociale Italiano, MSI), the party that in 1946 inherited the ideological legacy of fascism. For that reason, during the Cold War years—or during the First Republic—MSI was blocked from any governing role, but that changed in 1993 with the collapse of traditional Christian Democrat, Socialist, and Communist parties and the political emergence of TV tycoon Silvio Berlusconi (1936–2023). Berlusconi, prime minister from 1994 to 1995, 2001 to 2006, and 2008 to 2011, helped legitimize the neofascist MSI until 1995, followed by the Alleanza Nazionale (AN—National Alliance) from 1995 to 2009, and Fratelli d'Italia in 2012. The leader of Brothers of Italy, Giorgia Meloni, elected in 2022 as Italy's first woman prime minister, was a member of the youth organization of MSI, the Youth Front (Fronte della Gioventù), and a minister in one of Berlusconi's cabinets for AN.[1] For her loud and aggressive style, some opponents nicknamed Meloni "the fishmonger." In response, she recorded a video in which she appeared with fish, yelled "Fish! Fresh fish! We've got fresh fish!" and proclaimed it a compliment to be called "one of the people."

The Return of Gastrofascism?

Not surprisingly in light of the history that *Gastrofascism and Empire* has explored, the most right-wing Italian government since Mussolini aggressively stressed that the agricultural sector and food policy would play a key role in its political agenda. In fact, much of the ideology that made food the core of fascist nationalism, and by the mid-1930s precipitated the invasion of Ethiopia, live on today in Italy and the world.

At her swearing-in in 2022, Meloni unexpectedly renamed the Ministry of Agriculture the "Ministry of Food Sovereignty." The progressive press saw in the appropriation by postfascists of the notion of food sovereignty—normally associated with the Left in its support for self-determination by indigenous communities—a grotesque echo of Mussolini's plan for food autarchy, which required Italy to rely exclusively on food it grew and introduced isolationist policies like the Battle for Wheat. In response, the newly appointed Minister of Food Sovereignty Francesco Lollobrigida explained, "What autarchy? Food sovereignty is not a fascist concept, but a principle that even countries ruled by socialists, such as Ecuador and Venezuela, included in their constitutions. It's about defending national interests." Lollobrigida claimed his administration had no intention of banning the import of "foreign foods," but rather of protecting "Made in Italy" foods from copies and imitations and "declaring war" on "Italian-sounding" foods named "Parmesan" or "Prosec" produced abroad that profited from a counterfeit Italian identity.[2] The minister envisioned a "task force" that would police self-described Italian restaurants abroad to make sure they used Italian ingredients, followed "correct recipes," and employed Italian staff.[3] For Lollobrigida, taste was political. "Food sovereignty," he argued,

> means supporting the national economy by re-establishing a strong relationship with farmers, not only in order to protect the national food chain, but our rural culture. It's about defending our citizens, farmers, and consumers from the degenerations of globalization. Italian food is the best in the world and the bond between the food and the land where it comes from is of primary importance.[4]

Despite Lollobrigida's disavowal, it's clear that Meloni's strategies for food sovereignty in a democratic society link directly back to interwar gastrofascism, reworked for twenty-first-century far-right populism.[5] Recalling 1930s fascist environmentalism, Lollobrigida insisted that an autonomous national diet must be achieved sustainably by consuming Italian-grown and Italian-processed food in season—at the same time that export of Italian food and wine be vigorously promoted regardless of any environmental effects. The minister of food sovereignty argued that "in Italy, poor people eat better than the rich." In contrast to the United States, Lollobrigida explained, Italy operates an egalitarian food system, where individuals of modest means "buy high-quality food at low cost directly from the producers."[6] (In response, political opponents argued that food insecurity and unhealthy diets among the poor were indeed on the rise in Italy.[7])

In another return to gastrofascism, contemporary food nationalism suggests that external enemies threaten national autonomy by determining what Italians eat (and do not eat) and by jeopardizing distinctive culinary traditions. Right-wing nationalist food policy is portrayed as a shield against foreign and supranational powers said to endanger Italian foodways, when, for example, the European Union legalized the commercialization of insect-derived flour. Protesting that the EU was "sneaking" a foreign ingredient onto the plates of unaware Italian eaters, Lollobrigida introduced decrees controlling the sale of insect meal so that "Italians could retain their right to choose what to eat."[8]

A more vivid legacy of classic gastrofascism is the way reactionary anti-modernism exalts farmers and landscapes in a yearning for an ordered past at the same time as it supports the cult of technology to feed the nation. Like Mussolini, today's food nationalists alternatively praise modernity and anti-modernity according to the issues that food is mobilized to support. Lollobrigida drafted a law that will not only ban the commercialization of cultured meat but also prohibit research on any food grown in laboratories. The minister described the ban as a vital measure to "protect the nation's food heritage."[9] Confronting the EU's argument that laboratory-grown meat would help meet sustainability goals, he stressed environmental and food safety concerns. By banning cultured meat, "Italy can be the first country not to produce, commercialize or import these 'agglomerations of cells'—I struggle to even call it meat—that could pose a health and environmental risk and would certainly wipe out our economy: a veritable suicide for a country like ours, for which quality is of the utmost importance."[10]

At the same time, however, Lollobrigida highlighted Italy's investment in agricultural research to boost production. "Italy will be one of the first countries in Europe to push for New Genomic Techniques, to strengthen, thanks to our research, our plants, to increase yield."[11] Echoing 1930s gastrofascist narratives about advanced food science, he claimed, "Today, to be a farmer means operating in a top-notch advanced sector. It's not about plow and sweat, but technology, research, and modernity."[12] Lollobrigida also praised the fascists' godfather of genetic grain science, Nazareno Strampelli: "Strampelli is widely recognized as the forerunner of the Green Revolution. Applying groundbreaking theories to genetics he managed to double the production of wheat per acre."[13] At the second UN Food Systems Summit, Meloni neatly summarized her party's plan: "Italy will continue to invest in agrotechnology. I believe that innovation should go hand in hand with identity and tradition."[14]

Finally, the gastrofascism of the 1930s lives on in current discourses of food and race. In his most controversial public appearance, Lollobrigida referred to the Great Replacement theory, popular among White nationalists worldwide, that claimed to identify a secret scheme by global elites to increase their power by manipulating the White birthrate and encouraging mass migrations from the non-White Global South. Responding to the pleas of farmers' associations for higher quotas of legal immigrants to perform the agricultural work that Italians shunned, Lollobrigida used the Great Replacement theory to argue that unemployed Italians on welfare, not migrants, should work fields, farms, and feedlots. While he later defended his position—"I'm not racist; I respect music or ethnic dishes regardless of the skin color of the person playing or cooking"—his words faithfully echoed "the way forward" theme that 1930s gastrofascism used to link cuisine and taste with demography and race. Italian food was grown and produced by White Italian hands, and the project of feeding the nation required an invasion of Ethiopia and the creation of an Italian Empire of Food in East Africa.

Today, the shadow of gastrofascism continues to fall on Italian culture, society, and politics—on issues of population, nutrition, race, rural culture, land use, culinary identity, and taste. But what were the consequences of food imperialism that gastrofascism created? In the 1930s, the idea of the nation as an organic society based on blood and sustained by unique foodways "naturally" led to an imperialism motivated by agriculture. The Empire of Food in East Africa perfectly reproduced the balance between the cult of rural tradition and the fascination for modernity, technology, and speed that shaped gastrofascism. In the twenty years of its reign, Italian gastrofascism, which glorified the bond between people and landscape, food self-sufficiency, and agricultural and culinary civilization, provided the main ideological impetus for the invasion of the last independent state in Africa.[15]

The history of the major crops that the Italian Empire was created to produce—European favorites like wheat and beef, and tropical bananas and coffee—sheds light on the structural dynamics of the fascist adventure and its long-term consequences. Despite its short duration and total military defeat, the Italian Empire of Food in East Africa produced as many environmental, political, and cultural long-term effects as its British, French, Belgian, Portuguese, German, or Dutch colonial counterparts.

Fascist Wheat and Beef: Taste and the Environmental Consequences of the Empire of Food

In *Diet for a Large Planet*, Chris Otter traced the origins of today's unsustainable global food system to the British Empire's craving for beef, wheat, and sugar. From the late eighteenth century, Otter argues, Britain decided that a diet based heavily on meat and wheat reflected the racial distinctiveness of its population. A diet rich in animal proteins and refined carbohydrates made taller and stronger British bodies, in sharp contrast to the weaker bodies fed by rice, corn, and vegetables that the empire was subjugating around the world. A "power cuisine" of meat and wheat—aspirational symbols of wealth, luxury, and dominance—fueled Britain's rapid growth in the nineteenth century. For many Britons, food preferences shifted from locally sourced plant-based nutrition. This new diet demanded significantly more farm and pasture land than Britain possessed, and beef and wheat were inefficient converters of soil resources into calories. The solution was territorial expansion, first to Ireland, with historically deadly results. The hunger for beef and white bread was so intense that Britain began installing food systems extending as far as Argentina, India, Canada, and Australia, until by century's end these countries swelled with British-owned wheat fields, pastures, and slaughterhouses. Otter identifies the source of the current unhealthful and unsustainable global food system to the nineteenth-century popularity of red meat, white bread, and sugar and the consequent establishment of a British meat-and-wheat empire.[16]

Despite Mussolini's criticism of British plantation colonialism, his invasion of Ethiopia in 1935 drew inspiration from the British model of food imperialism, especially the foods the new colony should produce. Supported by fascist scientists, Mussolini agreed with the British that wheat bread and beef were the most important nutrients for improving the bodies of Italians, whose frailty and short stature had long been a national embarrassment. The diet of rural Italians, including the young men drafted by the regime, seemed to pale in comparison with their British, German, and French counterparts. Italians of that era were noted for consuming the smallest amount of animal protein in Europe. Peasants survived almost entirely on cornmeal polenta in the north and "black bread"—made of any flour except wheat—in the south. To eat white bread and beef was the great dream of Italian peasants; fulfilling it was the fascist mission on which its biopolitical project of racial regeneration and international power was based.[17]

Presented with the same geographic challenge Britain had met more a century earlier Mussolini deemed Ethiopia to be the source of the foods that would power the new fascist nation. He based his plans for the "economic valorization" of Ethiopia on basic crops plus the cash crops of coffee and the exotic banana. Ernesto Massi, the inspector of the Ministry of Italian Africa for the economic development of Ethiopia, explained: "The basis of demographic colonization must be the production of grains and fodder, so that to avoid dangerous crop monocultures and contribute to the autarchy of the Empire."[18] As the historian of Ethiopian agriculture James McCann put it,

> Italy's imperial plans included ambitious schemes for agricultural autarchy, the *"panificazione"* [bread-making] of the rural economy, which they envisioned would not only provision Ethiopia's cities with wheat, but also feed the metropolitan Italian Empire as well. These plans had a strong empirical thrust, including national cropping surveys, experiment stations for wheat and livestock production, building on three decades of crop experimentation in Eritrea.[19]

As did nineteenth-century Britain, Italy in the 1930s used its colonies to develop the intensive and unsustainable farming required to satisfy its new dietary preferences, participating, as Otter and others have noted, in the ruthless extraction of human, animal, vegetable, and fossil resources at the basis of today's ecological crises.[20]

Armed with the notion that the Ethiopian highlands were one of the historic "centers of origin" of wheat and that the high-yield, pest-resistant "elite" wheat cultivars developed by Strampelli would thrive there, Italians expected the region to become their breadbasket. But they overlooked a key local reality: in Ethiopia the cultivation of wheat was very limited, as farmers widely preferred to grow other grains.[21] Furthermore, the highlands that Abyssinian wheat farmers cultivated were not hospitable for Strampelli's elite cultivars, yielding instead a grain low in gluten and thus poorly fit for bread and pasta-making. As McCann noted, the Italian disregard for local agricultural knowledge and conditions not only doomed their plans to create an Abyssinian breadbasket, but also had severe human and environmental consequences that persisted long after Italians left in 1941. "Wheat, [in East Africa], rose in importance in the twentieth century with urban growth and the strong Italian interest, overcoming its limited ecological range and poor rust resistance."[22]

In the early years of occupation and the state investment in demographic colonization, fascist planners followed racist ideology in shaping policies and programs. Once they grasped that Ethiopian agriculture valued indigenous grains such as sorghum (durra), barley, corn, and teff over wheat they demarcated the production of food for Italians from that for "indigenous subjects" on the basis of irreconcilably different nutritional needs and tastes. Next, they blamed Abyssinian farmers for not understanding the advantages of Italian genetically developed wheat varieties. Planners saw that the teff and sorghum cultivated in the highlands (as well as other "plants of civilization" like ensete in the south) were useless for making white bread or pasta and of no interest as an export commodity but they were a zero-cost source of calories for the Ethiopian labor force, just as the British had seen in the "Irish" potato). "Indigenous agriculture," Massi argued, can be oriented towards food products that are in high demand among the indigenous people. To better implement the separation between agricultural practices, the removal of indigenous populations and land swaps can be considered, a system that has already been followed with successful results in the colonization settlements of *Opera Nazionale Combattenti* in Holetta and Bishoftu.[23]

Italians began to grab from Ethiopian communities what they thought were the best farmlands for growing the "elite cultivars" of wheat that had already been tested in Italy in its Battle for Wheat. They believed there was little to learn from Ethiopian farmers, and nothing to benefit from local varieties of wheat, let alone sorghum, barley, or teff. "The in-depth examination of Abyssinian agricultural production has led to this observation: all products are of poor quality," summarized Poggiali. "No Abyssinian land, despite the favorable appearance of the soil, has ever produced more than 0.3 ton of wheat per acre. The short, rapid, and forced vegetation yields hay that is unsuitable for livestock feed. The cereal species sown are still those from the time of the Pharaohs."[24]

However, by 1938 Italian agronomists were admitting that the elite wheat varieties that were the pride of Italian genetics had given disappointing results in farmlands cultivated by the Regional Colonization Agencies and the National Veteran Association. After experimentation at an agrarian research center in 1937, agronomists concluded that the prized varietals *Mentana* and *Quaderna* "have achieved a lower level of development compared to what they normally reach in Italy: shorter plants, shorter spikes with fewer grains, and these grains are smaller."[25] Their findings came just as Mussolini decreed that the East African Empire must achieve food independence by July 1, 1938.

The appointment in 1937 of the pragmatic Prince Amedeo Duke of Aosta as viceroy in place of the hated General Graziani opened a dialogue between Italian agrarian experts and local landlords about recovering indigenous agricultural knowledge to provide at least the wheat needed to make enough bread and pasta to satisfy settlers' appetites.[26] Italian agronomists realized, "The variety and unique behavior of Ethiopian wheat landraces [make them] an optimal genetic reservoir from which plant breeders could draw in engineering new 'elite' cultivars."[27]

The theory that the Italian Battle for Wheat could be won in Ethiopia by interbreeding Italian wheat cultivars with local varietals was proposed by Raffaele Ciferri (1897–1964), a professor of botany in Florence.[28] Ciferri promoted the hybridization of Italian and Ethiopian cultivars, but since these "imperial hybrids" took years to yield a harvest he recommended that wheat produced by Ethiopians be used to meet Italian needs. Ciferri noted that the Ethiopian practice of cultivating different types of grains in the same field, which Italians had dismissed as irrational, best fit highland soil and climate. The colonial government established a hub for wheat experimentation in Ethiopia's principal grain-producing regions at the Crop and Livestock Experimentation Center (Centro Sperimentale Agrario e Zootecnico) in Addis Ababa.[29] Responding to the *Duce*'s call for self-sufficiency, agrarian services turned Italian farming settlements into a wheat monoculture and through aggressive "campaigns" forced Ethiopian farmers to work as sharecroppers and sow *Mentana* wheat in their own plots. Despite a lack of coordination, in 1938–9 these efforts resulted in the first satisfactory harvests since the occupation, close to the goal of making Italian Ethiopia self-sufficient in wheat.[30]

Soon after, however, stem rust, a disease caused by the fungus *Puccinia graminis*, destroyed the last colonial harvests (1940–1). "Our wheat crops seemed in a state of grace, then rust suddenly appeared," lamented Mario Pavirani, head agronomist for Società Italiana Importazione Banane (SIMBA—Italian Company for Banana Imports), which had started a program of intensive wheat farming in Aselle, Oromia. "The disease developed sneakily and dramatically, it immediately looked uncontrollable. We can and could do nothing against this plague that has turned our crops into barren lands."[31] Strampelli's high-yield hybrid wheat cultivars, developed to resist pests in the rust-prone regions of central and northern Italy, could not thrive elsewhere. Ethiopian farmers—and the Ethiopian resistance that mobilized them against the occupiers—were proven right in their distrust of any collaboration with the Italians. Only the import of Kenya 1 wheat seeds from the British colony in 1939 guaranteed some sort of supplies to Italian settlers.[32]

Notwithstanding this fiasco, when British troops arrived in Ethiopia in 1941 they found that wheat had become an export commodity widely cultivated regardless of soil sustainability (wheat remained Ethiopia's most important export crop until it was surpassed by coffee in 1956).[33] Even with the adjustments Ciferri and other agronomists made to official policy, the determination to transform Ethiopia into a breadbasket reflected the regime's ultimately futile faith in the superiority of Italian taste.

The fascist desire for beef created similarly disruptive environmental and social problems. Fascist food policies linked wheat and beef because the focus on grains during the Battle for Wheat depressed the amount of meat Italians consumed. Between 1931 and 1937, while the population of the country grew from 41 to 43.5 million, meat consumption declined from 41 pounds per capita in to less than 32 pounds, causing meat imports from abroad to rise and "the imperative necessity to acquire meat resources from Italian East Africa."[34]

In Ethiopia, many ethnic groups were pastoralists—tending livestock, using oxen as draft animals, and putting beef from zebus, local humped back cattle, at the top of their dietary preferences. Livestock production, often combined with cereal cultivation, played a vital role for thousands of years. In the northeast,

> the scarce unit of production was neither land nor labor but capital in the form of oxen. Far more than the acquisition of land—readily available to the vast majority of households—the breeding, buying, borrowing, and maintaining of oxen determined the allocation of land and labor, affected cropping decisions, and cemented vertical patterns of dependency and stratification.[35]

In the Abyssinian highlands dominated by teff and durra, cattle and pastures were essential components of the agricultural landscape into the twentieth century. As seen in Chapter 6, even in the predominantly ensete (false banana) cultivating region in the south, cattle were important for food and for soil fertility.[36]

At first sight, Ethiopia's bovine stock (zebus of the *Dawara*, *Begait*, *Arado*, and *Boran* breeds) looked like a solution to the hunger for beef.[37] In his survey of the earliest phases of colonization, Davide Fossa declared "cattle to be the most valuable item in Ethiopian economy [and] zootechnics to be a sure source of wealth" for Italians in East Africa.[38] Italian efforts at developing substantial beef production in Ethiopia were supposed to concentrate on the creation of breeding centers for the "rational" selection of breeds; the regulation of pastures and grazing lands providing livestock with a balanced diet based on high-yield plants and cereals; and, finally, the fight against epizootics—the livestock plague that could undermine any chance of turning Ethiopia into an enormous cattle ranch.[39]

By the end of 1938, however, colonizers could claim that operations in Addis Alem and the Gulele district of Addis Ababa were helping meet the need for beef in the capital city, while another cattle ranch was provisioning Harar and Dire Dawa, but few other successes.[40] Establishing an effective production and distribution system for Ethiopian beef to the Motherland and across the empire remained elusive. Reporting for *Corriere della Sera*, Poggiali could only offer open questions:

> It is not yet known if the abundant zootechnical heritage of the Empire will be able to meet our needs for beef, because the enormous distance [between Ethiopia and Italy] is not conducive to the transport of live animals; but it is certain that when suitable industrial facilities are ready, Ethiopia will supply Italy with canned meat and extracts that we currently import from the Americas.[41]

In their ambitious campaigns to increase beef and wheat production, Italians virtually guaranteed failure by setting goals unreasonably high. They also completely disregarded the environmental and social challenges that Ethiopia presented. Italians blamed Ethiopia's limited production capacity for beef on the racial inferiority of both Ethiopian herders and Ethiopian cattle (in Italian, "race" and "breed" both translate as *razza*). Colonial agriculturalists also ignored or dismissed the reality that Ethiopian practices were shaped by traditional pastoralist knowledge and a deep awareness of sustainability.[42]

Poggiali faced a difficult task: how to tell the Italian public a convincing story about the opportunities for developing a modern meat industry in Ethiopia while at the same time explaining why there was yet no Ethiopian beef in shops or on their tables? His answer was to blame the conundrum on the clash between state-of-the-art Italian zootechnics and the rudimentary state of Ethiopian agropastoralism. While Poggiali admitted that the Italian appetite for beef could not be satisfied by the local pastoralist system, he assured his readers that the application of advanced genetics would soon expand production.

> Livestock farming is one of the main resources of Italian East Africa, estimated at fifteen million head of cattle (zebu). It is a considerable asset, though widely overstated because of certain descriptions by visitors to Ethiopia who are regularly amazed by the numerous herds. We have inflicted considerable damage to this asset, both during and after the [1935–6] war. The indigenous people willingly consume raw zebu meat, but they do so with much restraint, mainly due to the annual two hundred days of fasting that everybody observes. As soldiers

and settlers, we consume zebu beef every day, primarily because in a country devoid of vegetarian resources it constituted the most effective and economical food. Some colonial experts even went so far as to predict that [at these levels of consumption] we would run out of meat if remedies were not found. National zootechnics has indeed stepped in to recommend new breeding practices, cross-breeding, and breed selections; and above all, a rational approach to livestock farming that Ethiopia has never known. In early 1938, sperm was collected from selected breeders by an institute in Milan and sent by plane to Italian East Africa, greatly expanding the possibility of reproduction. Italy had been fighting livestock diseases by sending its experts around Ethiopia. They sold and gave away vaccines and this immunizing effort is getting expanded and perfected. In early 1937, to boost the confidence of indigenous producers, the first livestock exhibition was organized in Addis Ababa. We will never forget the attitude of the local herders and cattle owners. They participated in the exhibition only because the village elders urged them, convinced that the exhibition concealed a trap, and that the "Italian Government," imitating the Negus' regime of the past, would either seize from them or purchase at ridiculously low prices whatever it liked.[43]

Not only did Poggiali describe Ethiopian practices as inferior, he went on to blame beef shortages on Ethiopian consumption practices and culinary culture:

In Ethiopia, minimal quantities of milk are available for human consumption and the dairy industry. The cows, not forced to produce, only produce enough milk for the nourishment of the calf, averaging three to four quarts per day. This leads to supplying our troops and settlers with milk and butter in cans, even imported from Holland. However, Ethiopia is rich in excellent pastures, and thus, the possibility of increasing production is one of the certainties of our conquest.[44]

Italians were in fact only marginally interested in the production of milk, which would have required a large and difficult importation of European cows as well as the establishment of dairy farms and a distribution system of cold storage rooms and refrigerated trucks. When experiments in dairy production were made, the disappointing results were typically blamed on the poor quality of Ethiopian forage grasses.

Italians seemed unaware that by 1935, when they invaded Ethiopia and started tapping into beef resources, Ethiopian livestock production and the acreage it needed had been shrinking for four decades, particularly in the highlands where farmers had for centuries combined livestock and crops. As historian Getnet Bekele showed, from the early 1890s on there was a significant shift in agricultural practices from livestock to food crops. This transformation seems to have coincided with the outbreak in 1889–90 of rinderpest, or cattle plague (*pestis bovina*), but it later gained momentum when it was learned that dedicating more land to crops benefited farmers and landowners alike. The changes in land use, resource entitlement rights, and the spread of pathogens had a significant impact on the Shewan highlands: former cattle herders began to raise crops at a faster rate as the twentieth century progressed and caused a significant decline in pastureland, per capita livestock possession, and caloric intake from beef (even in the lowlands and the heavily pastoralist south).[45] Italian raids only aggravated this preexisting decline. Cows began to be more prized for their milk than for their meat, and, for the vast majority of the population, eating beef became a ritualized, special-occasion indulgence. "I had breakfast at noon, and dinner at eight," remembered Italian official Lino Calabrò about his experience in southern Ethiopia. "When the weather allowed it, I would go hunting to vary the usual dishes. Pharaohs, francolins, wild ducks, gazelles, warthogs, and hares were not lacking and provided a pleasant alternative to the usual chicken we regularly consumed. We could only have beef when these animals [zebus] were slaughtered during local festivities."[46]

Colonial authorities responded to complaints about the failing Ethiopian beef program by blaming the panzootic rinderpest that every year killed a large portion of the Ethiopian livestock population.

> It was a terribly devastating disease, which ran its course in an infected animal over a period of a week or so. The animal initially manifests discharges around the nose, mouth, and eyes; these early symptoms are succeeded by astonishing stench, recurrent debilitating and explosive diarrhea (with subsequent dehydration), and, perhaps most arresting, tenesmus—the painful struggle of the beast to defecate even when nothing remains to be voided. Death is followed by very rapid putrefaction.[47]

Italian colonizers blamed the apparently uncontrollable spread of rinderpest on Ethiopia's ecological and biological conditions: "The tropical environment determines, on the one hand, a lower organic resistance of livestock, making them more prone to diseases, while on the other hand, the hot and humid conditions enhance the virulence of many pathogenic microorganisms. Wild animals, feeding on the putrefying carcasses of infected dead animals, carry and transmit the virus over long distances." They also blamed Ethiopians for their "dietary misery" and "total lack of sanitary knowledge."[48] Because beef was central to the entire colonization project, the fight against cattle plague became a priority. The Ministry of Italian Africa established research centers (Istituti Vaccinogeni Zooprofilattici—Institutes for Zooprophylaxis and Vaccines) in every Governorate of Ethiopia, Eritrea, and Somalia. These institutes experimented with refrigeration as a means of killing the virus in infected meat, as well as in the development of vaccines.[49]

Ethiopian cattle owners fiercely resisted these containments. They opposed both the killing of animals thought to be infected but which were asymptomatic, and the vaccines, which even Italian zootechnicians admitted were still far from being safe and effective.[50] Calabrò boasted of an exceptional instance in which he managed to win the trust of local cattle owners and prove the effectiveness of Italian vaccines:

> Very rich was the local livestock heritage which, however, suffered heavy losses due to recurring outbreaks of cattle plague. To overcome this scourge, I obtained a veterinarian to carry out a vaccination campaign. Gathering the leaders and notables, I explained to them the methods and purpose of this operation.

I convinced the leaders and notables to set an example by vaccinating their own cattle first. Within a couple of days, about a hundred bovines were vaccinated. As a result, a couple of weeks later, the veterinarian was able to carry out the vaccination of a large part of the livestock in the area without any difficulty, and was warmly welcomed by the population. The fame of the achieved results spread rapidly and the populations of neighboring regions requested a similar treatment for their livestock.[51]

The reputation of Italian livestock experts was poor enough that Ethiopians widely believed that Italians were responsible for introducing the rinderpest epidemic that had ravaged first Eritrea, then Ethiopia, then Sudan, Kenya, and Uganda down to South Africa, by smuggling infected cattle from India into Eritrea in 1887. During the Great Ethiopian Famine of 1888–92, the plague killed almost 90 percent of all cattle. As the diplomat Count Pietro Antonelli (1853–1901) reported, by 1890 the loss of plowing oxen, combined with drought and locusts, had completely devastated the northern and central highlands: "Previously the country [between Harar and Addis Ababa] was inhabited; there were very beautiful fields of durra and barley, numerous herds of cattle, sheep and goats, and the whole area had an atmosphere of abundance and prosperity. But now the country was one continuous desolation, absolutely a desert; no more inhabitants, no more cultivation, no more flocks."[52] All evidence suggests that the famine of 1888–92, one of the deadliest in Ethiopia's history, began with an outbreak of cattle plague in the north, in Italian Eritrea, and rapidly advanced south. According to Richard Pankhurst, the Italian merchant Lamberto Andreoli imported diseased cattle from India, where rinderpest was endemic, to feed the expedition of General Alessandro Asinari di San Marzano (1830–1906) that landed at the Eritrean port of Massawa on November 8, 1887. A more popular narrative in Ethiopian oral tradition suggested that Italians deliberately inoculated their cattle with the deadly virus, knowing it would spread into Abyssinia.[53] In either account, Italians who had invaded Ethiopia for its beef were commonly recognized as the source of the plague.

In the 1930s Italian gastrofascism evolved into a replica of the British food imperialism that Chris Otter identified as the origin of today's dangerous global diet and food system. It introduced unsustainable agroindustrial practices to obtain the "power" products of wheat and beef and disregarded the environmental consequences of those choices, all the while idealizing nature, landscape preservation, and the national ecological heritage "at home," in fascist Italy or in Victorian Britain.[54] Today's food nationalists similarly continue to celebrate "authentic" foodways and food grown on native soils as most the delicious and most sustainable, while at the same time enjoying cheaper (and even "organic") foods from elsewhere, including from postcolonial countries that obediently respond to the markets, tastes, and safety regulations of the Global North.[55] Italy is a deficit country on many fronts regarding food: it produces only 36 percent of the bread wheat it needs, and 51 percent of the beef. Ironically, in January 2023 (after the inauguration of Meloni's government) the imports to Italy of cereals have increased by 13.2 percent in quantity and 248.7 million Euros in value (37.1 percent) compared to the same period of the previous year.[56]

Also in the 1930s, gastrofascists responded to this kind of "problem" by trying to turn the Horn of Africa into Italian farmlands, employ Italian farm labor, and apply Italian culinary knowledge. Because they considered Ethiopia an empty frontier, Italians claimed that taking land was entirely legitimate. In 2023, Minister Lollobrigida's earliest official preoccupation was to make sure that the beef Italians ate came from cows rather than "labs," and that "flour derived from insects such as crickets and locusts [didn't end up] in pizza or pasta."[57] The Meloni government's environmentalism has emphasized short food chains within national borders while agreeing to the delocalization of intensive unsustainable farming elsewhere. Neither 1930s gastrofascism nor today's food nationalism take interest in the biodiversity or foodways of other peoples unless it fosters the goal of national food security and sovereignty. Dietary choices in today's Italy, as in nineteenth-century Britain, seem to be guided by profit and the politicized cult of tradition rather than by concerns about nonrenewable resources, climate change, or hunger.

Italy's colonial past has been largely invisible in discussions by the current right-wing government about reclaiming national food sovereignty. Even the essential contributions of migrant African workers to the making of high-profile food products for export and the significant food trade with African countries have fallen victim to colonial amnesia. This unsurprising silence has prevented a chance to rethink the environmental and social disruption of Ethiopia in 1935–41 as a price paid to create an Empire of Food. That violent adventure is Italy's contribution to the making of a present-day global food system based on both interdependence and inequality.

Mike Davis's *Late Victorian Holocausts: El Niño Famines and the Making of the Third World* discusses the late nineteenth century's most devastating famines by inverting the terms of causation. The famines, while ignited by natural events—such as El Niño—did not cause millions of deaths across the Global South because "backward" societies in India, China, Brazil, Korea, Vietnam, the Philippines, New Caledonia, the Maghreb, and Ethiopia were marginal to Western capitalist industrialization and economic-financial global integration. "Millions died," Davis argued, "not outside the 'modern world system,' but in the very process of being forcibly incorporated into its economic and political structures. They died in the golden age of Liberal Capitalism; indeed, many were murdered by the [colonial governments'] theological application of the sacred principles of [the free-market, laissez-faire, and Malthusian ideology of classical liberal economics]."[58]

Davis noted that colonial India's grain exports to Great Britain continued steadily, and even peaked, in the harshest years when thousands of Indians died of starvation. British rulers tried to suppress reports of the misery of the population, while allowing the market to run its unbridled course. Allowing Indians to starve was a deliberate choice. Indians, Britain felt, would have mismanaged state-supplied resources, produced more children, and disturbed the precarious balance between population and food resources, supply and demand, labor and capital. As a British colony, India was already entangled in the web of international capitalism. In what would be later been called the Third World, Davis argued, rapacious European colonialism made the human costs of the climatic crises, droughts, and failed crops worse not only by seizing valuable crops even in times of famine, but also by demolishing local communities, agricultural organizations, and food systems, including traditional networks of solidarity, redistribution, and mutual aid.

As Karl Polanyi noted, from the late nineteenth century through World War II,

> The actual source of famines was the free marketing of grain combined with the local failure of incomes. The catastrophe of the native community is the direct result of the rapid and violent disruption of [its] basic institutions. These institutions are disrupted by the very fact that a market economy is foisted upon an entirely different organized community. Indian masses in the second half of the nineteenth century did not die of hunger because they were exploited by Lancashire; they perished in large numbers because the Indian village community had been demolished.[59]

Italian colonialism in East Africa was powered by state capitalism, corporatism, and institutional racism rather than the private capitalist initiatives that financed British colonialism. Yet it still caused the same death and destruction. In *Late Victorian Holocausts*, Davis highlights how the Italian imperialist pressure on Menelik II's Abyssinia made the Great Ethiopian Famine of 1888–92 more deadly and devastating than it would have otherwise been by introducing the plague that decimated oxen and cows, the most important source of rural labor and animal protein.[60] Similar to British colonialism in India, fascist imperialism organized the exploitation of Ethiopia around the mobilization of food resources. Italian colonizers made important early distinctions between foods that were valuable/commodifiable/mobile and valueless/noncommodifiable/immobile. "The agricultural landscape that we found in Ethiopia is divided into two main sectors: production for local needs and production for export," summarized Poggiali.[61] There were two categories: food of interest to Italians—whether for settler consumption, export to Italy, or commercialization on global markets; and food which was to be produced by Ethiopian farmers for their own self-consumption. In this latter category was the ensete, the foundational plant of the agriculture and civilization of southern Ethiopia. To make the ensete bread called *kocho*, stems and roots of the plant were mashed and buried underground for up to two years.[62] Successful production of ensete required a long-term community investment in and care for the land, something Italians had no interest in. Italian disinterest in ensete, in a way, left unchallenged and preserved Gurage gastronomic practice.

For the gastrofascism of the 1930s the same politics of taste dear to 2020s right-wing food nationalism guided the search for food sovereignty through imperialism in Africa. The superior Italian taste selected what was "good to eat" and "good to think," while discarding and leaving what Italians didn't want—teff, sorghum, or ensete—for philistine local populations. Maintaining higher national taste required the construction of a costly road system to extract wheat, beef, coffee, and bananas from East Africa; the transformation of Italian settlers in the colony into modern eaters and consumers; and the racialization of culinary culture by opposing healthy and delicious Italian food to disgusting and commercially worthless Ethiopian fare. As Chapter 6 has suggested, the many crossings, borrowings, and hybridizations that involved the food of the Other significantly changed settlers' taste, and pointed to the creation a fully-fledged Ethiopian-Italian/Italian-Ethiopian cuisine. This emergent way of cooking and eating, however, did not last long enough to influence official culture, gastronomy, or propaganda.

Similar to the disruption of local communities described by Davis, fascist settler colonialism proved to be as destructive of Abyssinian society and people as European capitalist-financial colonialisms were in other parts of the Global South. Demographic colonialism, in the model rural settlements Mussolini and his planners had devised, required the use of force to confiscate the best land and displace and resettle the indigenous population. The goal was to form large, contiguous estates in a fully segregated agriculture, rather than a patchwork of small plots farmed alternatively by Italians and Ethiopians. The African defeat of Italy by Britain in 1941 ended the project of appropriation and displacement, but the disastrous effects of building an Empire of Food were already in place. As Chapters 4 and 5 described, the dismantling of village community life by settler colonialism was no less brutal than British "capitalist plundering colonialism," as Mussolini's long-term goal was to replace Ethiopians with the "superior race" of Italian farmers. Viceroy General Graziani proclaimed the exceptional nature of Italian colonialism.

> We will operate with methods that are very different from the traditional ones: our Italian and Roman methods. A new type of colonization will appear in history. We will demonstrate to the natives that we are not exploiters nor distant masters. We will demonstrate to all European nations that the only way to create a sustainable colonization in Africa is by transplanting a superior race there.[63]

As a propaganda poster entitled "Italy's Colonizing Virtue" proudly boasted, as early as 1937 the ratio of Italian settlers to the total population of Italian colonies in Africa was twenty-two Italians for every 1,000 inhabitants, in contrast to five French, three British, and one Belgian settler for every 1,000 inhabitants in their respective African colonies. The "ethnic replacement" in reverse that Lollobrigida evoked as a dystopic danger for twenty-first-century Italy was actually in the plans and began to be implemented in Italian East Africa.

Fascist Bananas and Coffee: Taste and the Cultural Consequences of the Empire of Food

Italians looked forward to producing wheat and beef in Ethiopia by grabbing enough land to feed Italians in the colonies and at home. But Italians also expected their agricultural domain to deliver the tropical foods symbolic of other European empires—bananas, coffee, chocolate, tea, and cane sugar. Unlike wheat and beef, which were to be produced by transplanted Italian farmers with transplanted Italian varietals and breeds, bananas and coffee were produced in large part by local labor.

In 1930s Italian consumer culture, bananas and coffee were anchored in a colonial discourse about the Black Other that lives today in Italian (and European) culture and food nationalism. An unprecedented set of cultural artifacts on the Empire of Food in

Italian East Africa was generated by a range of media. The fascist regime used the turn-of-the-twentieth-century tradition of colonial expositions to create fairs such as the Triennial Exhibition of the Italian Overseas Lands (*Triennale d'Oltremare* or *Mostra d'Oltremare*) in 1940 in Naples, presenting the cultures of African peoples (sometimes in "living villages"), plans for demographic colonization, and the products—the foods—that the fascist conquest promised to deliver.[64] Documentary photography, films, and newsreels celebrated the potential abundance of African food that an advanced Italian agriculture would create once traditional practices were replaced. Propaganda showed African women grinding grains in crude mortars and men sitting in the dust munching on bloody raw meat in a scenario that embodied prehistoric foodways.[65] In the Luce documentary *In giro per il mondo: Abissinia* (Around the World: Abyssinia), for example,

> although the commentary repeatedly claims that some Ethiopian sceneries may remind the viewer of the splendid Italian landscapes, these spaces are defined as repellent. Mocking the "civilization" of the so-called Ethiopian "empire," the commentary continues to illustrate the "inhuman" customs of the Ethiopians, while the film shows a series of short scenes that could only disgust the Italian audience. The Ethiopians, described as "a mass of clamorous and unclean humanity," are portrayed in perfect harmony with the surrounding nature, once again like animals.[66]

Textbooks taught Italian schoolchildren about the civilizing mission in Ethiopia, the barbarian ways of Abyssinians, and the abundant wheat, meat, bananas, and coffee that colonialism promised.[67] Comics, cartoons, trading cards, and board games portrayed brave Italian men as conquering a dangerous world and extracting its wealth, which often meant its food.[68] In addition, postcards, stamps, and maps helped locate a desirable Ethiopian imaginary. "On the twenty-first of April [1937], the three hundred and fiftieth day since the victory [over Ethiopia], the miracle of a self-propelled railcar carrying passengers to Massawa was seen on its inaugural journey from the capital of the Empire to the Red Sea," recalled Poggiali. "The self-propelled railcar comes with a radio, a small telegraph room, the counter for dispensing cocktails and cold soda, comfortable armchairs to enjoy a nap when tired of seeing too much. A delight."[69] Despite the breakdown of the engine, Poggiali's journey continued:

> Hidden in the woods, there is a trading post that provides supplies for a radius of thirty miles; and attracted by the fame of the luxury vehicle, which quickly spreads, here come women and children offering eggs, chickens, mead, and beer. The unexpected interruption of the journey turns into a countryside excursion rich in rustic resources, joyful like a preordained holiday. We go hunting and roast the prey on the fire of dried euphorbia shrubs, take a bath in the swift-flowing stream under the roaring waterfalls, amidst dense coffee plantations. It's a vigorous dive into primitive life, nature truly enjoyed in its purest aspects, a fullness of serene enjoyment. Now we traverse the Weldiya plain cultivated like a garden, and

Figure 27 Oromo farmers harvesting coffee in a plantation, while an Italian man looks on, southwestern Ethiopia, 1937. Courtesy of Archivio Luce.

In contrast to the fascist plans for the development of two separate agricultures (Italian settlers-run agriculture: modern, mechanized, producing European-preferred foods; and "native" subsistence agriculture: backward and primitive, aimed at providing the colonized with their bare necessities), Italian colonizers heavily depended on Ethiopian farmers to produce Ethiopia's most valuable export crop, as they totally lacked the knowledge and skills for coffee cultivation.

Weldiya itself is a prosperous workers' village resembling the Far West, with large stores in wooden shacks, where the shimmer of a modern espresso coffee machine has a curious effect after so many visions of wild simplicity.[70]

In the 1930s, though, the principal introduction to the empire's food came from cookbooks, food magazines, and food advertising. Under fascism, the sudden ubiquity of cookbooks, home economics manuals, and food columns reflected the centrality of cooking and food in the politics of the regime as it imposed rationing in the face of severe shortages. Recipes became political tools, directing women to use more "autarkic foods," such as grains and substitutes for oil, butter, coffee, sugar, and other groceries, and less of everything else, especially meat. Women were taught to make satisfying meals with poor ingredients, to preserve food, to waste nothing and reuse everything. These same principles would become vital to the far-right food nationalists of the 2020s, especially in their campaigns to "Buy Italian." By becoming autarkic cooks, women at home could fight for the Motherland just like men on the warfront, in Ethiopia and later in Europe.[71]

Figure 28 Bar Impero in Addis Ababa, 1938. Collection of the Author.

Cafes, bars, restaurants, and hotels, which represented the terminals of the complex system of food mobility and distribution Italians implemented in Ethiopia, were racially segregated.

While gastronomic propaganda was suggesting an unlimited abundance of food from East Africa, cookbooks and food magazines were careful in introducing it to Italian cooks. The most important and widely distributed magazine, *La Cucina Italiana*, became fully politicized in 1935 when the League of Nations, Great Britain, and France issued an embargo against Italy for its invasion of Ethiopia. In the January 1936 issue, *La Cucina Italiana* declared that from then on it would focus on an "anti-sanctionist," self-sufficient cuisine, with "recipes that allow economizing, recipes that teach us not to feel the adversities that the sanctionists delude themselves to have caused us."[72] Still, between 1935 and 1940 *La Cucina Italiana* rarely covered the cuisines or specialty products of Italian East Africa. Only on one occasion did the magazine describe Ethiopian cuisine as rich in flavors and ingredients, in an article entitled "Cucina etiopica: Zighinè" (Ethiopian Cuisine: *Zighinè*) by Maria Paris. The national dish of the occupied country, the article claimed, was "zighinè" (meaning *zig'ni*), which was characteristic of both aristocratic and popular cuisine. It was prepared with meat and vegetables cooked slowly in a handmade clay pot. The "surprising feature" of the dish was that the "focaccia" (meaning *injera*) accompanying the dish was left to rise on the table and was eaten raw. After the housewife served the head of the family a portion of *injera* "stained" with meat and sauce did the other diners start. The dish was eaten by hand in a "hunt for meat: everyone plunges their hands into the pot, withdrawing them with noisy sounds of pleasure when they manage to grab a piece of meat."[73]

Unsurprisingly, depicting Ethiopian foodways and manners in such degrading tones was hardly an effective introduction to "authentic" East African food. In the

November 1937 issue, Amedeo Pettini (1865–1948), *chef de cuisine* of King Victor Emmanuel III (1869–1947), presented a recipe for "Past'asciutta all'A.O.I." (Pasta à la Italian East Africa) in an imagined encounter between the quintessential Italian food, pasta, and ingredients or preparations inspired—if only in name—by eastern African cuisine and the cuisine of its Italian settlers. The preparation began with a sauté of vegetables, mushrooms, or seafood in one container, stressing that "nothing should be wasted, not only to avoid unnecessary waste but also to improve the taste of our food. But I don't want to abuse your attention any further on the topic of autarkic cuisine."[74]

For the most part, however, *La Cucina Italiana* dismissed the value of foods of the colony, whether coming from settlers or Ethiopians. By deeming Ethiopian foods such as *injera* and *wat* inferior to (and unfit for) for Italian cooking, the magazine reproduced the racial segregation of eating places and cuisines in Italian East Africa. Unlike the British colonial embrace of Indian curry, *La Cucina Italiana* found no place for "ethnic cuisines" in the Italian diet, even when skillfully adapted by Italian cooks and even in times of sheer necessity.[75]

The magazine also suggested that it was difficult to make traditional Italian dishes in East Africa. In a June 1937 article, "Fioriscano le culle, si celebrino le nozze d'oro, si colonizzino le terre dell'Impero" (Let Cradles Flourish, Golden Weddings Be Celebrated, the Lands of the Empire Be Colonized), Fanny Dini responded to a letter from a friend who had moved to Addis Ababa with her husband and children. Dini addressed her friend's problem—that pasta tended to overcook in Addis Ababa. She explained that Ethiopian highland altitudes made it harder to keep water boiling strongly enough to make it *al dente*. Dini suggested using "glutinated" spaghetti as a solution.[76] Another article explained that the addition of gluten to pasta "makes it firmer and more resistant to cooking in Italian East Africa, where regular pasta tends to overcook."[77]

Given the generally depressing state of Italian cuisine in East Africa, *La Cucina* limited its coverage of Ethiopia's raw food resources to only useful to the magazine's mission to promote nationalistic foodways because they were familiar to Italians. An article entitled "Una nuova conquista della cucina italiana" (A New Conquest by Italian Cuisine) observed that while lamb, sheep, and goat meat was not widely appreciated in Italy, "in the new Italy of Africa, we found numerous flocks" not raised for their wool but for milk and meat.[78] A later article, "Per l'autarchia alimentare: Come allestire le carni di agnello castrato, capretto e capra" (For Food Self-Sufficiency: How to Prepare the Meats of Castrated Lamb, Kid, and Goat) showed how every part of the animal should be used, "the muscle or meat and the offal." Italian housewives were encouraged to "cook and promote the use of this type of meat, to dispel the notion that the use of ovine meat at one's table is too plebeian."[79] The June 1938 issue presented various lamb-based recipes: "Costolettine di capretto con passato di piselli" (Baby Goat Chops with Pea Puree), "Grillettato d'agnello con piselli" (Grilled Lamb with Peas), and "Animelle d'Agnello alla Margherita" (Lamb Sweetbreads Margherita).[80] Hostesses were invited to offer guests "a cup of tea (Italian, the monopoly's tea) or *karkade* [Ethiopian hibiscus tea]," instead of coffee and milk or hot chocolate. One article emphasized the importance of replacing English tea with "*karkade*, which is the tea of our Eritrean Colony," preferably without milk.[81] For almost every occasion, homemakers were encouraged to serve exclusively national products, even those as humble as cooked apples and chestnuts.[82]

No food from Italian East Africa was more popular in the pages of *La Cucina Italiana* than the banana, despite a widespread distrust by Italians of anything edible coming from the other shores of the Mediterranean. In July 1937, the magazine published a recipe for "Gelato di banane" (Banana Ice Cream). In August, two banana-based recipes appeared in the same article: "Bavarese di mele e banane" (Bavarian Cream with Apples and Bananas) and "Banane alla crema" (Bananas with Cream). The latter recipe appeared again in the October issue in the section "Dolci casalinghi" (Homemade desserts).[83] In January 1939, there were more banana-based recipes, "Soffiato di banane" (Banana Soufflé).[84] In October 1940, Italian cooks could find "Banane fritte" (Fried Bananas), "Dolce di Banane al cacao" (Banana Dessert with Chocolate) and "Dolce di banane e panna" (Banana Dessert with Cream).[85]

La Cucina Italiana presented bananas as a versatile ingredient easily incorporated in Italian dishes. Although the project of creating an Italian banana industry had begun in the prefascist Somalia of the early 1920s, for the regime and its imperial ambitions bananas were the only commodity—food or nonfood—produced on an industrial scale, thanks to the colony's massive transport infrastructure. Bananas were an ideal food, appealing to children, adults, and the elderly. However, with a shorter shelf-life than other "dry" tropical crops such as coffee, chocolate, and sugar, they needed to be marketed quickly after harvest. When growers, shippers, and distributors, all financially controlled by the state, finally figured out how to safely ship bananas from Somalia to Italy, they delivered for the first time a truly colonial "fresh" product back to the homeland.[86]

For the duration of the colony, Ethiopian banana production remained minimal in the fascist "demographic settlements." Italians managed to grow commercially only the *Giuba* (Jubba) varietal—and only in Somalia's Shebelle River Valley, a narrow strip of marshy land in the desert between the Indian Ocean and the fertile central areas of Ethiopia. Africans did the labor-intensive work of growing, harvesting, and packing the fruits, often contracted out to Italian planters by tribal chiefs and religious leaders.[87] The sweet, pulpy Jubba, named after its native region, was almost identical to the Canary Islands banana that dominated Italian markets before the invasion of Ethiopia, but which were affordable only to middle-class families. Giuba bananas were "less showy than those from Honduras and the Canary Islands, but able to hold their ground in the competition, despite the higher selling price, due to their taste and subtle fragrance."[88] They also had the advantage of being a fruit of the nascent empire, and now could emancipate consumers from the hated dependence on the global Anglo-American monopoly of such capitalist giants as the United Fruit Company.[89]

Before the proclamation of the empire in 1936, production of Somalia's bananas had been limited and problematic. In 1929, fewer than one thousand acres were cultivated with the fruit, whose total export value amounted to a meager 186,000 lire. Technical issues and transportation costs limited production and crippled trade. Renting one cubic meter (35 cubic feet) of storage on the passenger ships of Compagnia Italiana Transatlantica (CITRA—Italian Transatlantic Company) could cost 325 lire, not including customs duty paid at the British-controlled Suez Canal. In transit, some

40 percent of the cargo was regularly spoiled from poor packing or by exposure to salt air and water, while the 60 percent that did arrive sound sparked widespread speculation by merchants and exorbitant prices for consumers.[90]

On December 2, 1935, in the heat of the war in Ethiopia, Mussolini created the Regia Azienda Monopolio Banane (RAMB—Royal Banana Monopoly Agency) as the state agency in charge of optimizing and boosting production, trade, and consumption. RAMB was

> to realize transportation [of bananas] under the best and most favorable conditions in order to ensure products of impeccable quality; to implement a sales organization as widespread as possible; to carry out a policy of decreasing prices in order to make bananas accessible to the working classes and the less affluent and in every field and social class. These objectives were to be guided not by profit but autarkic principles and the interests of the nation.[91]

RAMB was charged to achieve the core political goal of national food sovereignty through advanced food technology and marketing. "Without food sovereignty, a nation cannot live, cannot expand, cannot have a voice in the international arena," RAMB's president Enrico Cibelli said in 1938. "It is destined to be subject to the will of others and to suffer the dominance of the powerful."[92]

The establishment of RAMB marked the intervention of the state in the banana food chain from private-capital plantations in Somalia and the creation of modern systems of fertilization, irrigation, and pest management to transport, distribution, and commercialization. By 1938–9, improvements in the ports of Merca and Kismayo meant that a maximum 35,000 tons of bananas could be shipped, still short of the 50,000 grown on the combined plantations of Janale and Village Duke of Abruzzi. RAMB improved logistics and launched four new fast banana boats, *RAMB I, II, III*, and *IV*, while also converting and modernizing three older ships, *Duca degli Abruzzi*, *Capitano Bottego*, and *Capitano Cecchi*, managed by the private Società Anonima Navigazione Italo-Somala (SANIS—Italian-Somali Navigation Company).[93] As a result of state investment in the *Giuba* and the efforts of RAMB, banana exports from Somalia to Italy (and to a lesser extent elsewhere) grew significantly, from five tons in 1927 to 20,000 tons in 1936.[94] The increased export capacity expanded Somali lands devoted to bananas to almost ten thousand acres in 1939 or 1,000 percent larger than a decade before.[95]

The Royal Banana Monopoly Agency's work was even more intense on the consumer side. RAMB organized fifty-four wholesale distributors in thirteen districts across Italy. They were chosen from "politically and morally virtuous" merchants who could offer modern cold storage warehouses and ripening chambers. With the support of the Fascist Party, RAMB promoted the consumption of bananas, sponsoring the most popular sporting event in Italy, the bicycle race *Giro d'Italia*, which reached almost every corner of the country. Bananas were supplied at a special price to kindergartens, elementary schools, orphanages, hospitals, and factory cafeterias, spreading the taste to all classes of society, especially among mothers and children.[96] "When consumed fresh," the banana was "the most delicious fruit that nature offers us," Dr. Giuseppe

Fabriani of the Istituto Nazionale di Biologia (National Institute of Biology) claimed.[97] Nutrition experts presented *Giuba* as healthy and desirable because of its digestibility and high content of sugars, potassium, sodium, calcium, and magnesium. Bananas, Italians were told, were not only a great source of calories and vitamins, but also safe because its impermeable skin resisted insects and germs (important for such an exotic fruit).[98] Filippo Bottazzi (1867–1941), a prominent biochemist and a signatory of *The Manifesto of Race*, wrote *Le banane frutto di alto valore nutrizionale* (Banana: A Fruit of High Nutritional Value) to celebrate the virtues of the new Italian fruit.[99]

These efforts at making the Somali banana the exemplary product of the Empire of Food had only limited success, however. In 1938–9, Italian banana consumption was still one tenth of France's and a fraction of US consumption. Despite elaborate plans for making the *Giuba* popular across social class and regional divides, its market remained limited mainly to the large cities, more in the north than in the south and the islands, where it was almost unavailable. Somalia continued to account for most of the production, with no sign of development elsewhere in Italian East Africa.[100] Because of the nature of the crop, colonizers never seriously tried to establish it in the "demographic settlements." It was instead the exclusive product of agroindustrial plantations owned by state-supported private companies, a system similar to Britain's despised "colonial capitalism." Like their British counterparts, Italian plantations only survived as a monopoly employing low-wage, semi-enslaved local labor—not the idealized Italian farmer-soldiers who would have never accepted such degrading conditions.[101] Finally, the start of World War II "harshly and directly hit the whole Italian banana food chain, causing the cessation of all profitable activity."[102] Still, despite many failures, RAMB boasted that, "regardless of the disruptions of war, the state monopoly, which turned this nutritious and exquisite fruit into a product of national relevance and interest, represented without a doubt one of the most significant achievements of the fascist regime."[103]

Even though bananas and coffee were meant to be the most valuable of colonial crops, *La Cucina Italiana* treated the two very differently. Articles celebrated the former but dismissed the latter. The April 1936 issue advised "rookie homemakers" to make their "coffee" by toasting inexpensive barley and mixing it with just a little ground coffee: coffee alone was too expensive to use by itself.[104] In June 1939, another article, "Vini tipici e frutta invece di caffè" (Let's Eat Fruit and Drink Local Wines Rather than Coffee), predicted that coffee consumption, especially among professionals and white-collar workers, "will gradually disappear, not only because abstaining from drinking coffee is an Italian and fascist virtue, but because the new consciousness of work as a social duty excludes this continuous and ridiculous crutch of coffee during the working day." Manual workers, "who are ultimately the strongest and healthiest," typically drank little coffee, preferring instead wine "red like their generous blood, acutely fragrant like their land." In particular, *La Cucina Italiana* argued, middle-class women would benefit from eliminating coffee, not just because of its cost, but also because coffee "after the initial relief leads to inevitable depression."[105]

Coffee was, in the 1930s like it is today, the world's most widely consumed hot drink and one of the most traded commodities. Although the most popular species of the *Coffea* plant originated in Africa (*Coffea arabica* in the Kaffa area in southwestern

Ethiopia, and *Coffea canephora*—known as *Robusta* —in central and western Africa), coffee production spans the Global South, and its source largely determines its commercial value.[106] A powerful stimulant, coffee provides no energy from calories (unless mixed with sugar, another scarce commodity in 1930s Italy) and Italians came to enjoy it, or, more likely, aspired to enjoy it as a pleasing, social complement to the everyday diet—as a stimulant, not as a staple. In some ways, the emerging espresso coffee culture of the 1930s reflected certain fascist values, including the cult of modernity, speed, energy, and vitality. These values materialized in the Victoria Arduino chrome-plated espresso machines and trapezoidal Bialetti aluminum (the preferred fascist metal) *moka* coffee pots, both of which were patented in those years.[107] For the most part, though, foamy espresso and cappuccino drinks were connected to the life of luxury, frivolity, and self-indulgence that marked the urban bourgeoisie; and with cosmopolitan liberalism, rather than conservative nationalism. It was not until the economic boom and the rise of mass consumerism in the mid-1950s to mid-1960s that the espresso bars and cafes and the *moka* pot at home became the national nonalcoholic drink.[108]

Ethiopian coffee fit into fascism's imperial as well as nationalistic ambitions in a kind of transnational circle: wheat from the breadbasket in Ethiopia was to sustain the labor of empire and make it profitable by trading its coffee for gold and other hard currencies. Fascist planners firmly believed that selling Ethiopian coffee on the European and global markets would be substantially more profitable than limiting it to the domestic market. Here again, the British plantation system was both the most important competitor and source of inspiration: Italian economists studied how Britain mastered the international marketing of its Kenyan, Ugandan, and Tanzanian coffee.[109] Of course, diverting "Italian" coffee from Ethiopian plantations to world markets dealt a blow to autarkic food sovereignty, since coffee imports would have to meet Italy's own demands, as they always did. But the greatest potential value of Ethiopian coffee lay in the successful export trade that preinvasion Ethiopia had developed under Menelik II and Haile Selassie I to replace the declining trade in ivory: coffee became the country's most valuable commodity.[110] Italians understandably expected to take over a successful international enterprise, but such was not to happen.[111]

Furthermore, the Italians had to consider the overall impact on trade relations with the countries whose coffee Italy imported. First was Brazil. Brazil's role in the fulfillment of fascist autarchy was especially important after the dictatorial government of Getúlio Vargas (1882–1954) refused to participate in the League of Nations trade sanctions against Italy. As a result, after 1935 Brazil became, along with Nazi Germany, Mussolini's most valued commercial partner. The Brazilian connection was also strengthened by the northern Italian migrants who replaced slaves on coffee plantations after abolition in 1888. By the 1930s, many of the *colonos*—owners and managers of coffee plantations around São Paulo—were the children and grandchildren of these immigrants.[112] Replacing Brazilian and other international coffee imports with coffee from Ethiopia would have caused coffee-exporting countries to reduce their imports of Italian goods, enlarging Italy's trade deficit and endangering its goal of self-sufficiency.[113]

The Italian government's campaign to discourage coffee consumption—paradoxically, "Italian" coffee from Ethiopia—was meant to avoid endangering Italy's trade balance and, ultimately, its self-sufficiency.[114] In fact, when on August 24, 1937 Italy removed all tariffs from commodities imported from Italian East Africa in order to stimulate the consumption of domestic products, Ethiopian coffee was excluded and taxed at the same level of the highest-grade coffee imported from elsewhere.[115] By September 1937, Ethiopian coffee "exporting firms were allowed to send to the metropolis consignments equivalent to a maximum of thirty percent of their exports to other countries."[116] Because of these measures, shipments of Ethiopian coffee into Italy declined from 3,300 tons in 1930 to 2,500 in 1936 and 1937, and 1,500 in 1938.[117] If coffee could not be Italian—if it was more convenient to export abroad coffee the Ethiopian colony while importing it from Brazil for home use—Italians would have to drink less of it. Ciferri, the botanist of the Agricultural Institute for Italian Africa praised

> the sobriety of Italians, which is one more time confirmed as far as coffee consumption is concerned. The daily requirement of coffee in Italy amounts to 110 tons a day, very modest proportions when one considers that it equals to *less than a cup a day every three residents*; that is, 1.7 pounds per capita a year, as compared to 13.2 pounds for a Belgian or an American, and 17.6 pounds for a Suede or a Dane.[118]

Italian coffee consumption at home plummeted during the imperial period, dwindling from a total of 44,533 tons in 1935 to 551 in 1941.[119] The case of coffee was perhaps the clearest paradox of Italian designs on Ethiopia: the occupied country's best crop could not be used to build Italian self-sufficiency—autarchy—because it would threaten Italy's overall international economic position. In the end, fascist ideals had to give in to economic realities, dooming the goal of demographic settler colonization that regime fought to achieve. By promoting bananas as patriotic and denouncing coffee as anti-Italian, *La Cucina Italiana* supported those economic interests, as conflicted as they were, in a propaganda of taste.

Against these political and economic realities, Italian planners threw themselves enthusiastically in the work of extracting the most revenue from occupied Ethiopia. Unlike wheat—which was supposed to feed an invading Italian army, millions of settlers, farmers, and workers, and even more millions of Italians at home—Ethiopian coffee became instead the key fulfilling the dream of wealth through currency and gold: Italy's advanced agricultural systems would generate untold riches from *Coffea arabica*, the most important variety in the world. As late as 1940, five years after the invasion, Ciferri still believed that despite land, labor and cost problems, "Even if the current production of coffee in Ethiopia has declined to about 22,000 tons, there is indeed potential to more than triple today's production with the full certainty of a secure capital investment: indeed, the safest among all the investments in agricultural enterprises in Italian East Africa."[120]

Developing a viable industry that shipped Ethiopian coffee around the world could have made the empire thrive. However, just as with wheat, and despite vigorous efforts at "modernizing" production, Italian scientists and planners were faced with a coffee agriculture more challenging than they had expected. As Poggiali reported, Ethiopian coffee grew in diverse ecologies supporting a range of varieties, yielding crops of varying commercial value: "Of coffee there are as many varieties as there are regions in which it grows and bears fruit. Many of these varieties exist in a spontaneous state, in patches of scrubland where the proximity of a river and dense undergrowth provide shade and warm humidity."[121]

As Poggiali anticipated, fascist rural experts first had to standardize Ethiopian coffee production and deal with its very rich biodiversity. Although all Ethiopian coffee plants originated in and belonged to the *Coffea arabica* species, they had developed many varieties in the two main coffee production regions of Harar and southwestern Oromia. Adding to the challenges, the world of Ethiopian coffee was marked by deep social, organizational, economic, and production differences.

By 1935, the prevalently Muslim region of Harar produced approximately one-third of the Ethiopian coffee exported abroad (7,500 tons). Part of the crop came from a few large plantations owned by Europeans that predated the occupation and were dependent on Ethiopian wage labor.[122] Surrounding these large capitalist plantations, though, were some thousand small family-owned farms.[123] Italian agronomists noted that in the Harar highlands coffee cultivation complemented annual grain cropping, just as in the forested areas of the southwest. "The Muslims of Harar take great care of the cultivation of this aromatic plant from sowing to harvesting, thoroughly clearing the land from invasive weeds and working deeply into the soil to ensure a healthy development of individual plants."[124] This may have been because Harar coffee originated from plantings by Arabs of wild trees from the original birthplace of Arabica coffee in the southwest of Ethiopia. Arab planters later developed a trade that would extend into Yemen and the Arabian Peninsula, where it was well established by the fifteenth century. Harar coffee evolved into having characteristically large, long, flat beans with a slightly green/blue color and a full-bodied aroma.[125] Because it was so highly aromatic, Harar coffee didn't meet the European taste when consumed alone, but represented "a prized product for blends, to be used to impart aroma to coffee of other [lesser] qualities, sought after and listed on the stock exchanges of Amsterdam and Le Havre."[126] By the 1920s, Harar coffee was well known in Northern Europe and the United States for its high quality.[127] For agronomists, Harar coffee production needed to be "guided by the preservation of the esteemed quality already recognized in international markets."[128]

In the southwest, in the ancestral coffee regions of Oromia incorporated, conditions were very different. Coffee-farming there was described more as an informal foraging activity that capitalized on the abundance of wild plants. Even so, by the time Italians arrived in 1936, coffee from the southwest represented as much as two-thirds of total exports (18,200 tons).[129] Italian planners noted that

> [in the southwest] the majority of the production comes from coffee forests. The plants receive no assistance, and their propagation is ensured by seeds that sprout in the vicinity of the mother plant: human intervention occurs only for occasional basic soil clearing and for harvesting the product. This insufficient and irrational management results in both quantitative and qualitative deficiencies in the product.[130]

As in Harar, changing sociopolitical and economic conditions affected the cultivation of coffee. During the Oromo war of resistance against the Abyssinian invaders at the end of the nineteenth century, coffee-farming had been virtually abandoned. The later resurgence in coffee production in the area was due to an effective Abyssinian administration, the desire of Abyssinian rulers to reap wealth from conquered lands, and the ongoing export demand. By the 1920s, varieties from all over southwestern Ethiopia would be traded on international markets as a single "Abyssinian coffee."[131] The export of Abyssinian (or southwestern) coffee jumped from fewer than 320 tons in 1921 to 6,500 tons in 1925 and 10,370 in 1935, while between 2,750 and 5,000 tons were exported to Sudan.[132] (All coffee exports —Harar and Abyssinian—grew from 4,523 tons in 1921 to 17,440 in 1935.)[133] Italians described the coffee growing regions of Jimma, Limmu-Ennarea, and Kaffa as "a system of beautiful and highly fertile valleys, the territory where coffee has its homeland, and the plant, without any care, yields its fruits across 125 square miles that forms the most beautiful coffee park in the world."[134] Ironically, growing conditions were so ideal that farming demanded minimal effort.[135] Unlike in Harar, the problem in this more remote and wild area was not to "maintain quality," but to reeducate, train, and put native farmers to work for Italians. In general, the diversity of coffee culture was so stunning that the prospect of organizing it to the "European" standards of quality and quantity seemed to many a task of colossal proportions.

Adding to the complexity of the task, coffee was produced under both types of colonial systems discussed in Chapter 2—the "demographic" settler colonization of impoverished rural Italians cultivating small parcels in collective settlements; and capitalist plantations of varying sizes where Africans worked as low-cost labor. Unlike wheat and beef, however, coffee was a long-standing specialty of Ethiopian farmers, but not of the new settlers. These skilled indigenous farmers were of varying ethnicities and followed their own ways, from foraging "wild" beans to tending plants in small plots. Against their racist ideology, Italians were forced to convince local farmers to cultivate their crops for cash, as part of the imperial economy (Figure 27).

Italian agronomists and economists still blamed local farmers and their "primitive" practices for the roadblocks to a profitable coffee industry. In the spring of 1938, a mission of the Compagnia Italiana Importatori Caffé (Italian Company of Coffee Importers, designed to bring coffee into Italy) detailed the shortcomings of indigenous farmers and recommended interventions to improve their productivity. Their report covered every step of the local production system, starting with cultivation, particularly in the southwest where

> the extraordinary fertility of the soil allows for lush plant growth. Because the plants are placed too closely together, they tend to meet each other and form a dense thicket that obstructs the passage of light and air. The plants then grow very tall. Only the upper branches, exposed to light, bear fruit. The indigenous people do not even carry out the most basic pruning. Consequently, the plants, left to their own devices, become almost wild. The average life of the plant is only about twenty years and its annual productivity is much lower than it could be.[136]

The mission also found serious drawbacks in the drying, cleaning, and sorting of the beans.

> The indigenous people lack even the most basic rational criteria in this operation. In fact, they collect the coffee partly from the plants and partly from the dirty ground, and they even let it fall onto goat skins spread on the ground. They then leave the mixed berries like this for a few days before laying them out in the poorly cleaned sun-exposed ground. After a few days, they store them in small tukuls, where the coffee can get wet from rain or absorb moisture from the soil. All of this inevitably leads to a significant deterioration of the product.[137]

The report then noted that

> the indigenous people start the peeling process by placing the berries in a wooden mortar. Then, two of them, armed with a stick, pound the mortar with rhythmic and alternating blows until they believe that the peeling has occurred. It is clear that peeling with this system is not complete. Evidently, with this rudimentary system, the product ends up containing many impurities, to the extent that for coffee from some regions, impurities can reach a very high percentage of eighteen percent.[138]

Agronomist Fabrizio Cortesi (1879–1949) reported on a Brazilian investigation that determined that while Ethiopian coffee was generally of excellent quality, it presented an exceptional number of defects due to inferior harvesting, drying, and sorting.[139] Poggiali, as usual, translated this data into the popular language of racism:

> The capital Addis Ababa channels ninety percent of the production from various plantations brought there by *nagadi* [Amharic for traveling traders] from late December to early June. The *nagadi* sell to Arab intermediaries who, in turn, sell to European agents. The main export firms are in Djibouti and in Dire Dawa, where selection and cleaning create up to thirty percent of waste. It is noteworthy that attempts to carry out the cleaning in Addis Ababa have always failed due to the difficulty of finding female labor in the capital, as Ethiopian women consistently oppose systematic and even well-paying work.[140]

Italian experts were quick to blame the Negus and his administration for the problems with coffee production, part of a broader divide-and-rule strategy.[141] "The Harar region," Cortesi pointed out, "is particularly suitable for coffee cultivation. However, the lack of knowledge of the Abyssinians became once again evident when, after the annexation of this territory, they destroyed many coffee plantations to replace them with barley and sorghum, thus exchanging a rich product for very poor ones, all for the sake of ... firewood!"[142] Poggiali hinted at another important challenge: the Abyssinians' "irrational" concern about expanding production in an international market where supply exceeded demand.[143] "At the time of our conquest, the total production of Ethiopian coffee represented 0.1 percent of the world's coffee production," he wrote.

A large part of Ethiopian territory, otherwise uncultivated, represented an immense opportunity to expand cultivation and production. The Negus regime had always been opposed to this. In reality, the cultivation of Ethiopian coffee, faced with formidable American competition—so abundant that in certain years coffee was used as locomotive fuel in Brazil—never allowed for substantial profits. The local *Ras* (governors) and regional leaders who also took their share of profits feared that increased production would lead to an unbearable price depreciation, difficulty in selling, and would ultimately jeopardize their interests.[144]

Armed with their advanced technologies, Italian experts were primarily driven to "correct" native mistakes and take control of a system still firmly in Ethiopian hands. The final report of the Italian Company of Coffee Importers mission included such rubrics as "How the Indigenous People Carry Out Coffee Drying—Tips for Improvement," or "Peeling and Initial Cleaning of Coffee Practiced by the Indigenous People—Inconveniences and Defects."[145]

In 1939, the Istituto Agronomico per l'Africa Italiana designated agronomist Edoardo Carlo Branzanti to develop a coffee research center in southwestern Ethiopia in the Kaffa region. Branzanti immediately identified the causes of the limited coffee production in Ethiopia in the native practice of little or no pruning, which caused erratic growth. The casual methods used to dry the berries and extract the beans caused impurities and irregularities that degraded the crop's value.[146] And the Oromo farmers' practice of growing plants taken directly from the forest or with seeds collected randomly was the most pernicious, since the diversity of fields and flora compromised productivity. The research center's most important task was to develop standardized plants in its nurseries by selecting and cross-breeding elite varietals for hardiness and productivity and to redistribute them to farmers. In 1940, the nursery provided approximately 300,000 Italian-bred seedlings to Oromo farmers with which who replace their plants. The strategy of establishing model coffee plantations demanded collaboration with local leaders, controlled the local distribution of the new plants.[147]

The experimental work in Kaffa was interrupted in 1940 by start of World War II and the arrival of British colonial armies a year later.[148] Data collected during the previous years of occupation suggested that the plan to make Ethiopian coffee a lucrative cash crop had failed miserably. As it was for wheat and beef, the coffee failure was an agricultural, environmental, and political one and bore long-term consequences for Italian Africa. Perhaps even more so than for wheat and beef, the failure illustrated the reasons why the Empire of Food itself was a disaster—from its unsustainable design and blind disregard of key ecological and social variables to the racist violence that spawned armed resistance. In the end, its principal failing was the inability to attract Italian farmers to its model settlements—opportunities so few found appealing.

Early on, embarrassed colonial authorities were already aware that Ethiopia exported much more coffee under Haile Selassie I's administration than their own. The Minister of Italian Africa Lessona acknowledged in 1937 that "under the rule of the Negus, a quantity of the product was exported, along with a corresponding income in precious currency, much greater than today, and this constitutes a severe critique of the unhappy results of imperial economic activities."[149] Between 1931–4 Ethiopia's coffee exports averaged 17,000 tons per year. By 1939 the number fell to a mere 2,000 tons.[150] In the last year of the empire, 1941, 6,500 tons of coffee were produced in all of Italian East Africa—well below what was needed just to meet local demand, estimated at 26,375 tons.[151]

As *Gastrofascism and Empire* has shown, the regime's plans meant "scientifically" controlling all forms of life, from human biology to natural ecosystems. Lessona's "disappointing results of imperial economic activities" exemplified the mismanaged application of Italian technoscience in reshaping an entire society. By the 1930s all signs suggested that the dream of a profitable coffee based on massive transformations was doomed. Ethiopian coffee, however delicious it was, was no Somali banana.

And along the way, Italian experts faced still another unintended consequence of their adventures: rationalizing farming at the expense of Ethiopian biodiversity simply encouraged the spread of coffee plant pests. The transplanting of coffee trees from forests to monocropped farms, as Italians encouraged Ethiopians to do, removed natural barriers to fungal diseases. The devastating *Hemileia vastatrix*, or coffee rust, destroyed new plantation crops so much that agronomists considered importing a pest-resistant varietal from the Belgian Congo.[152]

The debacle was also a political one. The Galla and Sidama Governorate, Ethiopia's best coffee region and the birthplace of Arabica coffee, was inexplicably the most undeveloped. Of the first three model "mass settlements" of the Regional Colonization Agencies, the one in Galla and Sidama (Oromia)—*Ente Veneto d'Etiopia*—had not even been started by the time the empire dissolved.[153] In Oromia, the arable land needed for Italian coffee agriculture was both too scarce and too densely populated. In 1941, the number of commercial-agroindustrial and demographic concessions in the Galla and Sidama Governorate was 112, compared to 229 in the much smaller Shewa. The land acquired and granted to Italian farmers amounted to just 52,000 acres, compared to 160,000 in Harar, and 82,000 in Shewa; of the 52,000 acres only 16,000 were cultivated, mostly with coffee.[154] In the best coffee regions of Sidamo and Kaffa Italian farming was almost completely limited to two large commercial operations while the farms of "transplanted" Italian peasants were small in size and number.[155] Far from Red Sea ports, coffee-rich southwestern Ethiopia also lacked roads, and was the last region to be linked by highway to Addis Ababa.[156]

There were other reasons for the isolation of Italians in Oromia. The Ethiopian resistance terrorized settlers who ventured outside their garrisons and towns.[157] Apart from rebel attacks, the land was difficult for Europeans to farm and then could be theirs only after repaying long-term loans from the state colonization agency. Other, better-paying "imperial jobs" in truck driving and construction work were also easily available. Southwestern Ethiopia was indeed the most promising coffee region, but also the least accessible and most poorly protected by the Italian military. Ultimately, most of the area's native coffee forests and farms remained under Ethiopian control, forcing Italians to rely on indigenous growers, whether the occupiers wanted to or not.

Cooperation with local farmers was also deeply problematic. Cortesi, Branzanti, and the agronomists of the Italian Company of Coffee Importers all assumed that Ethiopian sharecroppers would continue farming, largely unconcerned about whether they were paying rent or handing their coffee harvests to Ethiopian landlords or Italian settlers.¹⁵⁸ Italian officials were soon proven wrong. Opposition from local farmers was widespread and manifested in different forms: the refusal to work for Italians and to be paid in Italian lire, on top of a general disinterest in wage labor. Many simply preferred to work in other better-paid or higher-status occupations, such road construction or service in the colonial army.

Colonization planners not only failed to grow Ethiopia's robust preoccupation coffee export market, they were unable even to maintain it. "The quotations for Ethiopian coffee take place in Djibouti," reported Poggiali in 1938,

> and its price in the last fifteen years varied from eight to ten Maria Theresa thalers (four Italian lire) for just under 34 pounds, an average of 5.30 lire per pound. The transportation costs by railroad, loading onto the ship, cleaning, export duties, and government tax, slightly exceeded, as a whole, the price of the commodity.¹⁵⁹

The Compagnia Italiana Importatori Caffè struggled both to promote Ethiopian coffee in Italy or build an international market for it. "There is the Italian Company of Coffee Importers in Rome," Cortesi complained, "but it is completely lacking an organization to handle the distribution and placement of the product in foreign markets, especially the United States, Canada, Great Britain, Belgium, etc."¹⁶⁰ The result was a great loss in hard and foreign currencies, just as domestic consumption dropped dramatically as prices increased: "At the dawn of the Empire, we did not change the situation. We continued to keep the coffee exports from Ethiopia alive, which brought gold to our trade balance. Because of treaties, we had to acquire coffee for ourselves in Brazil, so that no advantage has come to the Italian consumers from this side." "Italians," Poggiali sarcastically concluded, "can proudly enjoy the aromatic drink at a price so high that perhaps has no parallel anywhere else in the world."¹⁶¹

Colonial planners did identify one surprising obstacle to the development of a successful coffee industry: the skyrocketing growth in coffee drinking by Italian settlers, who consumed great quantities of imported but also local coffee, shrinking the stock available for export. As discussed in Chapter 3 about other consumables (bottled water, packaged pasta, and canned food), Italians learned to love coffee when they landed in Africa. Taking advantage of the easy availability of food imported from Italy, they could also comfortably enjoy a desirable product scarcely enjoyed at home. The migrants who ran on caffeine—whether from Ethiopia or Brazil—helped East Africa become associated with coffee in the Italian imagination, despite the very small quantity of Ethiopian coffee exported to Italy between 1935 and 1941. Ironically, the largesse of the caffeinated empire was perhaps the most unexpected reason for the failure of the Empire of Food. Colonization planners had forged strategies to monetize Ethiopian goods, but spent far less energy learning how to turn settlers into active local consumers.

The "problem" of the settlers' consumption of coffee looked even worse when compared to the coffee economy of preinvasion Abyssinia. At the time of the invasion, Ethiopians consumed only about 20 percent of their total coffee production, exporting the rest.¹⁶² This simple fact undermined a fundamental rationale for creating an Italian Empire: the fascist government could hardly assert its "civilizing" mission if their modern plantation system did not compete successfully with traditional Ethiopian. Felice Guarneri (1882–1955), Mussolini's Minister for International Trade and Currencies, explained:

> The export streams, primarily fueled by coffee from Harar, which once sufficed to balance the values of imported goods, were stranded [between Haile Selassie I's and the Italian rule of Ethiopia]. The influx of large contingents of White population and the increased standard of living of indigenous populations also led to a significant increase in domestic consumption of these products, particularly coffee.[163]

Poggiali identified the lifestyles and consumer culture of Italian settlers as an issue.

> In the second semester of 1936 our Ethiopian Empire had exported to the world goods for a total value of twelve million lire, two million of those to Italy. Under the Negus regime, in the first half of 1935, exports amounted to 25 million Italian lire. Unspecified but substantial quantities of Ethiopian products that were previously exported were absorbed by the Italians, who numbered around half a million. Take, for instance, coffee, which each Italian settler consumes on average five grams per day. This means that 27.5 tons of coffee were withdrawn from export trade daily. And this is a product that Italians themselves would have consumed regardless if they were in Italy, from the mass imported from Brazil and hence paid for in gold. Such saved gold, therefore, remains in our country; which is as if we had acquired it by selling our own goods abroad.[164]

Meanwhile, Italians in Ethiopia made the drinking of coffee that everyday signaled one of their most tangible "conquests." In the invasion army, almost every soldier enjoyed coffee often, whether from their rations, purchased at *spacci*, or acquired directly from Ethiopians. "We were starving," a soldier wrote. "Even when we got coffee, it was two beans for one, two beans for another, and so on. So, our whole squad would get together and put everything in a mess tin. We'd pound it with rocks, and that's how we made coffee."[165]

Settlers would also recall the sight of a shining, chrome-plated espresso machine in a café or in an isolated roadside restaurant—reassuring signs of "modernity" in the middle of "Africa." Sipping espresso from an unblemished China cup, seated outside a segregated café and being noticed by passing Ethiopians was a clear expression of superiority. So, too, was the ability to drink the prized local coffee *in situ*, an experience that could only be dreamt of in Europe. "Jimma, Friday, November 26, 1937," wrote a settler from the heart of the coffee region. "Dearest Mom, I am doing very well, much better health-wise than in Rome. Imagine that coffee grows right in front of my house here. It doesn't cost a thing. I brew myself big cups of it, just like the ones we used to have together. You should taste how good and fragrant it is!"[166] Coffee drinking tales were messages of well-being and success in Africa, so much so that Ethiopian coffee, snuck back home, became a prized gift. "Jimma, June 25, 1939. Dearest Father, I have consigned some coffee for you to several people who are returning home. Some of it will reach you. Tomorrow, my dear fellow Carlo Luna is leaving. He'll be bringing six pounds of it."[167]

For settlers, their vigorous daily intake of caffeine made them appear dynamic and high performing, unlike their compatriots in the homeland. Also, as seen in Chapters 5 and 6, the shared taste for coffee in Ethiopia provided a tool for cross-cultural conviviality. Different coffee rituals were regularly mentioned by observers, whether it was the interest of Ethiopians in machine-made espresso or the curiosity of Italians about Ethiopian practices of adding salt or rue to their coffee. "We made some gifts," remembered an Italian official on meeting with an Ethiopian delegation. "Sugar, chewing tobacco, coffee with the husk, which they eat raw, just as it is."[168]

The Italian thirst for coffee had significant consequences for post-World War II Ethiopian agriculture.[169] James McCann found that "oral evidence from community elders recalls Gera's expansion of coffee production as being linked to an overall resurgence of the coffee trade at the end of the Italian occupation when Italian-built roads promoted the use of motorized transport from coffee collection centers."[170] The caffeinated Italian Empire had an impact on postwar Ethiopia's position in international markets through its most prized commodity, and by the mid-1950, coffee was once again the largest export cash crop for Ethiopia.[171]

Advertising the Empire of Food: Taste and the Making of Italian Racial Consumer Identity

In the Age of Empire, *La Cucina Italiana* and other cultural gatekeepers described Ethiopian cuisine as inferior, useless even in times of food emergencies like those in the late 1930s. Exceptionally, *La Cucina Italiana* did deem some African foods like bananas fit for Italian diets, clearly conforming to official dictates about food sovereignty. The language of advertisement took a different, more ambitious, and more diversified approach to "colonial food." Working to help clients sell their coffee and chocolate in a hyper politicized environment, marketers, art directors, and graphic designers framed an entire commercial culture around these exotic products. Their goal was to create a mass taste for "colonial food," and, more subtly, connect the consumption of colonial food to the metaphorical consumption of colonized bodies.

The development of modern advertising is closely connected to European colonialism in Africa, especially in the 1930s. After World War I, in Italy as well as in Great Britain, France, and Germany, advertising changed significantly. A new commercial style marked by strikingly simple, aesthetically adventurous designs replaced the elaborate prewar Art Nouveau style that centered on the product and an elaborate description of its quality. With a more assertive approach suited to the modern city, advertising became a form of capitalist communication. Employing new techniques in branding and consumer psychology, professional advertisers made creative use of various avantgarde styles, from Cubism to Dadaism, adapting modern art to everyday commercial objects. By the 1930s, minimalist advertisements were creating a symbolic aura around ordinary products and talking to the inner emotions of "love, fear, and angriness" of mass consumers.[172]

Advertising reflected other pivotal changes in European culture. In Italy, the press changed from a "journalism of ideas" to a business that relied almost completely on advertising for revenues. New technologies made reproducing images cheaper and easier. And as the media sector expanded, so did advertising: alongside *La Cucina Italiana*, new women's weekly magazines such as *Lei* (1933), later renamed *Annabella*, and *Gioia* (1937) began advertising colonial food products. Logos, brand names and placards, posters, and billboards transformed the urban landscape. Fin-de-siècle upper-class department stores like *Rinascente* in Milan (established in 1917) began courting the middle class, and five-and-dime stores like *Upim* (1928) and *Standa* (1930) drew a large audience. These transformations paralleled the introduction of mass-produced goods, such as canned foods, soaps, toothpaste, and—during the nationalist response to foreign "sanctions"—domestic food substitutes such as ersatz coffee and chocolate.[173]

The growing middle class living in the "industrial triangle" of Milan, Turin, and Genoa was the direct target of the new consumerism that created a dynamic public culture of "symbols, language, and communication." The advertising of standardized, branded goods, and colonial products was one of the most powerful of those creations.[174] The nascent middle class was generally supportive of fascism, as were large strata of rural society, and for Italians coming of age in the 1930s, the successful war in Ethiopia and the conquest of the empire represented the most exciting event of their lives. Images of Africa and Africans had been popular objects of consumption for all classes of Italians since the late nineteenth century, such as the *art nègre* that inspired many interwar artists.[175] But the invasion of Ethiopia and the foundation of Italian East Africa went further—they brought the fascination for the "Black Continent," its riches and its peoples, to unprecedented heights of popularity. Advertising both created and capitalized on such allure.[176]

For advertisers, the representation of Black bodies in campaigns for "black foods" often depended upon images created by the most accomplished artists. In promoting the products of the empire, advertisers were not simply marketing commodities; rather, they were influencing individual thoughts, feelings, and behaviors about the idea of empire itself. Adopting the rhetoric of persuasion developed by their American counterparts, Italian advertisers sought to embed consumer desires and lifestyles in a larger fascist agenda promoting a well-ordered national culture centered on the state, and expressing a new "fascist spirit."[177] Advertising and consumer culture were crucial to the building of a distinctive Italian national character and the creation of a Great Italy (by branding products as uniquely Italian, for example).[178] In the "imperial" 1930s, Italian advertising drew inspiration from the strategies and techniques in play in the United States, put to more local use exploiting the "primitiveness" of Africa: the Italian "interwar advertising empire was built on the advertising of the Empire."[179]

Despite the ongoing violence in Ethiopia and East Africa, the widespread use of caricatured Black bodies in advertising seemed to suggest that Italy had "finally" won its colonial crown. Reflecting a popular culture now defined by racial identity and active racism, images of Black bodies were used to advertised products with

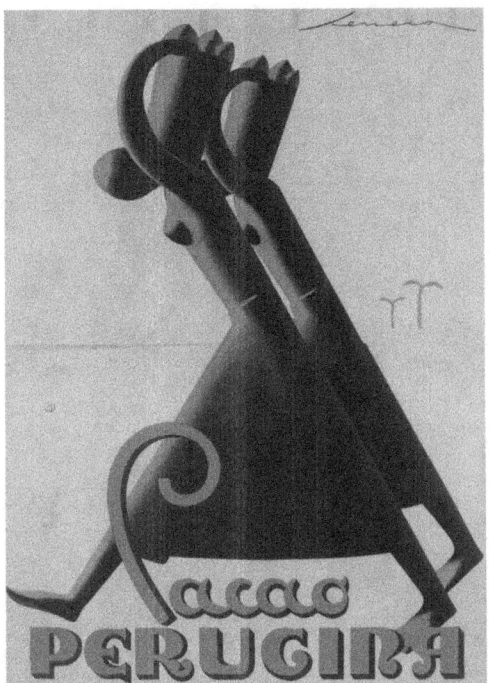

Figure 29 Ad for Cacao Perugina chocolate powder, Federico Seneca, c.1930. Courtesy of Collezione Salce, Catalogo generale dei Beni Culturali.

no real or even imagined African provenance. A 1937 advertisement by the famed illustrator Gino Boccasile for Amaro Ramazzotti foregrounded the iconic bottle of the bitter liqueur, a seltzer bottle, and a half-full glass, promoting Ramazzotti as *aperitivo* before dinner rather than as an after-dinner *digestive* (Figure 22). The advertisement conveys a carefree version of the empire, "with its racial and national identities both, not just imagined, but materially imaged—in color."[180] In it, an Italian/White woman in khaki attire and a safari helmet smiles as she proudly gazes into the sunlight. In the background, a bare-breasted Black female figure holds a tray carrying the Ramazzotti set up, ostensibly to serve her master. She is so dark that only her silhouette is visible, her traits almost undistinguishable. Only because her white teeth glisten against her deep black skin can the viewer tell she smiles as she serves. In perfect opposition to the Italian's pith helmet, she sports a big head of frizzy hair, likely fashioned with the spicy cultured butter, *niter kibbeh*, whose smell nauseated so many settlers.

Boccasile himself was a central figure of the new profession, whose work appeared on covers of the well-known fashion magazine *Le Grandi Firme*; and, during World War II, as fascist propaganda, including a poster of an apelike African American soldier grabbing a white Venus statue in what it looks like an Italian museum, and a poster entitled *Ritorneremo!* (We Will Return!) portraying settlers leaving their defeated colony in 1941. The Ramazzotti ad conflated racial entitlement with

Figure 30 Ad for Banane Perugina chocolates, Federico Seneca, c.1930. Courtesy of Collezione Salce, Catalogo generale dei Beni Culturali.

consumer pleasure, a trope that still inflects Italian taste and identity. If it weren't for its role in subtly enforcing racial categories, the racialized Ramazzotti ad would have been both unrealistic and unnecessary. Ramazzotti was already heavily promoted in ads reflecting an urban petit-bourgeois lifestyle. In real life, the cheerful Ethiopian woman and her elaborate hairstyle would have never ended up in Italy, nor served her master while naked. Similarly, the Italian woman of the ad would not likely find herself in Ethiopia, where only a small number lived. Rather, advertisements like the Ramazzotti introduced Italians to a consumer culture born of the triumphs of fascism in the conquest of empire. In 1937, public preoccupation with the genocidal Second Italo-Ethiopian War of 1935–6 needed to be replaced by an enjoyment of pleasures in—or coming from—the conquered "place in the sun." The "everyday empire" was to be savored as if it were a refreshing *aperitivo*.

More broadly, advertisements mirrored the political economy of Italian colonialism in East Africa. The presence of Black figures like Boccasile's naked server signified the legacy of European plantation slavery that Italians were preparing to install in Ethiopia. Black bodies in food advertisements represented the racial hierarchies of food-producing European colonies around the world and the fascist fascination with the "science" of race. Taken together, these engaging depictions accentuated "racial boundaries as sharp as the silhouettes of the graphic forms themselves in an advertisement that sells 'class' and 'style' as inextricable from whiteness."[181]

Finally, in 1930s Italian advertisements of food products ("colonial" or not), representations of African bodies fed the fantasy of an Other with clear sexual, erotic, and libidinous appeal, a style still present in Italian consumer and popular culture. In Boccasile's advertisement, the two soda bottles' prominently penile taps aiming at the Black woman's body can be associated with masculinity and male erotism. The display evokes the conquest of Ethiopia as the sexual conquest of its women (the *bella Abissina* of the *Faccetta Nera* song discussed in Chapter 6). A culture of consumption based on Black labor entitled Italian women to enjoy an unprecedented right to pleasure and to being served. It also gave Italian men the unprecedented power to perform sexual acts on colonized subjects, extinguishing the flame of desire like the Ramazzotti and soda that "disseta e tonifica," or quenched thirst and invigorated sexuality.[182]

In the later 1930s, images of Black bodies and references to Blackness at large promoted a wide array of products, including those obviously European, that made Italians aware of their privileged taste and power. However, advertisements for distinctly colonial products like bananas, chocolate, and coffee did more than evoke a Black identity; instead, they established a complete identification between the product and Blackness.

Given the common association of Black bodies with disgusting, polluting culinary practices, advertisers had to convince consumers that colonial foods were not just safe but also a source of exotic pleasure. In one solution, advertising for bananas took on a distinctly institutional tone, stressing the benefits of the banana plantation while erasing the Blackness of its workers. In a poster for Società Anonima Banane Italiane (SABI—Italian Bananas Company) in Genoa—the monopoly distributor of Somali bananas between 1933 and 1935—a plantation manager in a white shirt and safari helmet smiles cheerfully while holding in one hand a bunch of bananas that fills the center of the illustration (Figure 10).[183] His other hand leans forward in an offering that echoes the caption "Ecco la banana somala! Frutto squisito e nutriente" (Here's the Somali Banana! A Delicious and Nutritious Fruit!). In the background a white banana boat navigates the coast of Somalia, its characteristic Arabic white buildings scattered across a green landscape. The shining yellow of the bananas dominates the image, but Black, the color of "Africa," is nowhere seen, and neither are the Africans who farmed, harvested, packed, and loaded the golden fruit on ships bound for Europe. For Italian consumers, such use of color was meant to assure freshness, familiarity, and pleasure, while yellow was associated with wheat fields, corn, lemons, gold, and the sun. In one advertisement, bananas benefited from these associations in the construction of their "Whiteness" and their welcome as an Italian taste.[184]

Another of SABI's 1934 posters, *La banana somala: Il frutto della salute!* (The Somali Banana: The Fruit of Health), cautiously acknowledged the blackness of bananas by depicting a plantation house at night in an oasis (Figure 11). While palm trees confirmed the scene as African, the darkness of the image is brightened by a large bunch of bananas shining like the sun, and by a half-moon suggesting the "oriental" flavor of Muslim Somalia, seeming to distance it from its Black, sub-Saharan reality.

By 1937, some advertisements began to at least acknowledge an African provenance. One for RAMB displayed a globe on which only East Africa, the Arabian Peninsula, and Italy were visible. A bright line on the map connected the seaports of Kismayo,

Merca, Mogadishu, Assab, Massawa, Suez, Port Said, Bari, Ancona, Rijeka, Trieste, Venice, Genoa, and Naples in the journey of the Somali banana, with the bundled axe of fascism above it all. The line drawn from port to port resembled a hydra with its head in Italy and its tentacles in Africa, as if sucking the wealth of the Black Continent.

Having dropped the "R" for Royal, the Azienda Monopolio Banane (AMB— Banana Monopoly Agency) operated a few years after World War II, when Italy temporarily regained administrative control of Somalia.[185] A 1950 AMB advertisement firmly identified the fruit of colonization with Blackness (Figure 12). In the ad, "A banana grows as a tassel from the fez of a Somali Black head. A Black head is formed by, and its very shape defined by, the banana that surrounds it, constituting nothing less than the entire ethos from which Blackness emerges."[186] In this last imperial assertion of the Africanness of the banana, AMB managed to reclaim its place in a postwar food trade that continued the inequalities created by prewar colonialism. Biting into a Somali banana, Italians were also supposed to bite into Somali bodies, feel their taste, and enjoy it. Not coincidentally, in the 1930s Somali women were often rated as the most attractive female subjects of the empire in the racist rankings that appeared in travel literature and pornography as well as in "scientific" journals.[187]

In the 1930s, almost every sign of consumable Blackness was contained in Federico Seneca's advertisement for Banane Perugina, small chocolate candies shaped in the form of bananas, wrapped in yellow foil, and produced by the leading candy company, Perugina (Figure 30). Like Boccasile, Seneca was among the most popular advertising artists of the era, equally infatuated with Black bodies and themes. Unlike the figurative work of Boccasile, though, Seneca's direct, abstract art was inspired by Cubism, Purism, and Futurism, particularly by the work of Fortunato Depero (1892–1960), another leading graphic designer. The first notable feature of the Perugina poster was the absence of the product. Seneca showed instead a naked, athletic young Black man with a broad smile exaggerated to the point of clownishness playfully clutching a massive banana. The image immediately conjured Black inferiority and animality. The Black figure swung on the giant banana like an ape on a tree. The size and shape of the Black body and the banana were exactly the same, both indistinguishable fruits of the empire. Finally, the phallic banana of hyperbolic proportions offered its own suggestions. These innuendoes imparted an ironic, humorous approach to the delicious fantasy of the never-shown Banane Perugina. The letter "B" in "Banana" mirrored the famous "B" in *Baci* Perugina (Perugina Kisses)—its most popular product then and now. The lettering suggested that the exotic Banane be eaten just like the familiar *Baci*, in one sensual bite. After all, the creation of Perugina's chocolate bananas in 1925 was a response to the desire for real bananas and real chocolate, whose high prices put them beyond the reach of most Italians.[188] Two desirable colonial food products came together in Banane Perugina, and the consumable Black body represented them both at once.

Seneca designed another colonial-themed poster, this time for the chocolate powder Cacao Perugina (Figure 29). The product was again absent, and Seneca created an essentialized Black body in a "geometrization of Blackness." Here, two identical Black women carried baskets of cocoa nuts on their heads, looking like "animated robots with their towering head baskets and iconic breasts."[189] "Seneca's 'chocolate' women

Conclusion   235

Figure 31 "I Am Coffee!" Ad for Bricco brand coffee blend, Gino Boccasile, 1939. Courtesy of Collezione Salce, Catalogo generale dei Beni Culturali.

are small steel machines; their breasts are gyrating cogs, delivering their cargo with robotic rhythm."[190] Unlike the lascivious Black figure in the advertisement for Banane Perugina, these striding, serious women lacked any subjectivity, not even one Italian consumers could mock or sexualize: they were simply the labor bringing colonial food to Italian tables, small wheels in the machinery of empire. Seneca's anonymous Black women trekking through the desert with their cargo of cocoa affirmed the violent modern history of European expansion and oppression, making Perugina customers part of it.

The most extreme identification of a colonial food or drink with the Black bodies who produced it was in the posters that Boccasile designed for coffee products. Boccasile worked for a Tuscan company—Luzio Crastan's Sons—that made the surrogate product that almost completely replaced real coffee during the embargo from 1936 to 1940. Boccasile's use of Black bodies to represent coffee made commercial sense as it gave the ersatz drink an authenticity it lacked by showing the Africans who produced real coffee, and making them "drinkable." The advertisement also had a political value

Figure 32 "The Best Coffee Surrogate." Ad for Moretto brand coffee blend, Gino Boccasile, c.1939. Courtesy of Collezione Salce, Catalogo generale dei Beni Culturali.

for the regime, excusing it for failing to supply the African coffee it promised, claiming that foreign enemies had prevented it. However, the empire had enabled Italians to consume Black bodies, their labor, and their exotic taste. In his advertisement for Miscela Marca Bricco (Bricco Brand Blend) under the caption *Il caffè sono io!* (I Am Coffee!), Boccasile conveyed this theme by linking Black skin to the dark brown color of coffee (Figure 31). Viewers discovered that the Black head dominating the ad, peering over two black hands stirring a dark drink in a white porcelain cup, was, in fact, an enlarged coffee bean. "There was no longer any distance between Blackness and the products that its very subjection may yield for an Italian public on the brink of being-conscious-of-Blackness," Karen Pinkus has argued.

> Boccasile exploited this, brilliantly, in his iconic conflation of the product and the laborer. [The advertisement] represented a very significant moment in the history of cultural persuasion in Italy, the selling of racial identity along with the brand name of a product as two inseparable events [and interpellating] the Italian public as a national racial consumer.[191]

Boccasile further explored the identification of Black food and body with his campaign for another coffee stand-in produced by Luzio Crastan's sons, the Moretto brand (Figure 32). Here, in an ad captioned *Il migliore surrogato del caffè* (The Best Coffee Surrogate), Boccasile designed a smiling Black boy wrapped in a shawl and crouched on the floor, holding two boxes of the product on his lap and lifting another to the sky. The association of a dark body and a dark product echoed the name of the brand: *moretto* meant "little Black boy." Boccasile's work illustrated the gustatory pleasures of both a dark dessert drink and a young Black body. The smiling *moretto* represented a generation of young colonized subjects born and raised under the Italian flag. But the image could not erase the many parentless Ethiopian boys used by Italians for their domestic and sexual services. As seen in Chapter 5, Italian army officers and soldiers had young Ethiopian boys serve them coffee in bed, addressing them typically as "my little chocolate."

Altogether, advertising was crucial in the "invention" of racially entitled Italian consumers. Today, as in Mussolini's times, Italy does not produce enough food to meet the need for its distinctive products, durum wheat for pasta being the most controversial example. These racially conscious consumers, offspring of the Empire of Food, also inherited unrealistic expectations about the labor it took to bring food grown in Italy to market. Claiming to preserve the Whiteness of Italian culture, consumers opposed to immigration from the Global South are either unaware or unconcerned that immigrants are indispensable to Italian agriculture, and always have been. In this they replay the fascist colonial agenda of the 1930s that looked to transplanting millions of Italian farmers to a new Empire of Food that could completely satisfy the hungers of the nation.

Conclusion

Across disciplines, a rich literature explores the impact of European food imperialism in Africa, Asia, and Latina America. *Gastrofascism and Empire* uses a food history approach—concentrating on food production, exchange, and consumption practices, the material and symbolic meanings of food, and taste in historical perspective—to illuminate how the imperial architecture of Italian East Africa was founded on food and the central role played by food in the birth, life, death, and afterlife of the fascist Empire of Food, Senses, and Taste. The individual histories of wheat, meat, banana, and coffee in Italian East Africa shed light on the consequences of Italy's colonial adventure. On the one hand, Italians claimed East Africa as national lands where Italian farmers using modern means could grow the staples—wheat and meat—to feed a new, aggressive, and expanding nation. On the other hand, Italians created an imaginary of Ethiopian food that categorized it as either an exotic, pleasurable addition to Italian cuisine when prepared by Italian hands, or as inferior, unclean, and disgusting, fit only for "indigenous consumption" and the reproduction of laboring "indigenous bodies."

Gastrofascism and Empire has presented the Italian Empire of Food in East Africa in its infrastructure. All modern empires were built to move food, commodities, people, weapons, technologies, ideas, images, and tastes. Empires were not just political organizations but also physical networks that connected distant places, by ports and roads or through the circulation of material cultures. In its biopolitical frenzy, the Italian Empire attempted to create this circulation of bodies, crops, agricultural technologies, foods, and culinary practices. Its massive undertakings were intended to support the demographic expansion and racial perfection of the "new" fascist Italian nation. Its most celebrated legacy, particularly in the nostalgic and forgiving narratives of Italian colonialism, is the extraordinary system of roads built in Ethiopia. Ironically, the financial and human costs of building Mussolini's highways diverted vital resources away from rural colonization and the development of model settlements. Infrastructure may well have caused the failure of the entire imperial dream.

In its history of technological and biological transfers, the Empire of Food anticipated in many ways the manifold effects of the first Green Revolution—the introduction from 1950 to 1980 in Africa, South Asia, and Latin America of advanced agrofood technologies for feeding the growing populations of many postcolonial societies. A decade before the launch of the Green Revolution, however, the Empire of Food provided tools for the modernization of food production in East Africa, making it possible to feed more mouths from the same fields. Those tools also helped establish a local agriculture at the mercy of European markets, Italy's included, and the decisions made in the Global North. In East Africa, Italians tried to replace sustainable farming for self-sufficiency with a mechanized agriculture of specialized crops dependent on oil and other nonrenewable resources. Italy's legacy would also include deforestation, desertification, diffusion of pests, appropriation of land, and displacement and impoverishment of entire communities. In the late 1930s, Italian settlers in East Africa enjoyed a much better and more varied diet than their compatriots in Italy. Political developments in 2020s Italy suggest that the sense of racially conscious entitlement that the Empire of Food created among Italian consumers, both in Ethiopia and Italy, may have helped make Italian eaters increasingly nationalistic in their tastes and less concerned about the impact of the global food system on environmental sustainability and climate change.

Living under the racist asymmetries of the Empire of Food, Ethiopians actively observed, resisted, and selectively accepted Italian foodways. Taste informed their opposition to the exploitation of their land and bodies as well as to the programs of Italian colonization, and *Gastrofascism and Empire* illustrates the many culinary forms that opposition assumed. At the start of the Italian invasion, Ethiopia was a newly created multiethnic empire, in which the formation of national cuisine—orchestrated in the capital of Addis Ababa but engaging many regional and ethnic foodways—represented the most powerful discourse of an identity in the making. The richness, complexity, and diversity of Ethiopian cuisine contradicted the Italian narrative of a "civilizing mission," built on superior agricultural knowledge, taste, and table manners. Second, realizing that the Italian occupation rested on the success of settler colonization, the Ethiopian armed resistance focused their tactics on destroying the imperial food system—truck convoys, depots, freight trains, and warehouses—as well as poisoning water and starving the occupiers however possible. Women were a central presence among the Ethiopian patriots, fighting Italians and feeding themselves and guerrilla men, procuring food, and acting as spies as they disguised themselves in open markets selling food to Italians. They also performed multiple acts of resistance in their everyday cooking (including, when in an interracial relationship, the food they served to their Italian men) by maintaining traditional foodways and culinary knowledge as a statement of identity. Adaptation as resistance constituted the third and final mode of Ethiopians' culinary anti-colonialism and reclamation of their agriculture and cuisine. The culinary triangle—of *injera*; *wats* spiced with *berbere*, greased with butter, and accompanied with legumes and pulses; and *tej*, *tella*, and coffee drinks, perhaps with the selective incorporation of Italian food (like canned tomatoes or ration biscuits)—solidified a robust national cuisine. The Ethiopian lasagna—popular today in the Ethiopian diaspora, a fusion dish with roots in the tradition of *injera*, minced meat, and *berbere* that also adds Italian tomato sauce and melted cheese—is a vivid and lasting celebration of resilience.

The violent, segregated, and interrupted Empire of Food of Italian East Africa is in fact a telling historical example of how cuisines are made. By 1941, Ethiopian-Italian/Italian-Ethiopian cuisine was emerging from unequal relations of power, and from the mobility of food, people, and ideas that led to exchange and hybridization. Italian ingredients, recipes, meal structures, and forms of conviviality influenced Ethiopian food culture at the same time that Italian settlers adapted to local foodways in contact with local landscapes, markets, cooks, techniques, and products, most notably spices. The long-term results of the short-lived imperial encounter were many: the creation of a new shared foodscape and sensescape; the transformation of the Ethiopian landscape, agriculture, and biodiversity and Italian taste and foodways; and the movements of culinary and dining practices across the empire and into diasporas, both materially—as Ethiopian lasagna suggests—and in countless imaginaries.

Notes

Introduction

1. Tom Kington, "'Fascist' Pasta Condemned for Referring to Abyssinia," *The Times*, January 9, 2021; Nick Squires, "Italian Pasta Company Apologises for 'Fascist' Rigatoni Named after Abyssinia: Pasta Company Says It Will Now Change the Name of the Rigatoni to 'Conchiglie'—Shells," *The Telegraph*, January 6, 2021; "And Finally … Basta Pasta: An Italian Pasta Maker Has Apologised after Naming a Product in Apparent Tribute to Mussolini's Military Campaign in Ethiopia," *Irish Legal Times*, January 11, 2021.
2. Paola Suraci, "Decostruire il colonialismo, le 'Abissine' de La Molisana e lo storytelling di cui avremmo fatto volentieri a meno," *Immezcla*, January 5, 2021.
3. Angelo Del Boca, *Italiani brava gente? Un mito duro a morire* (Vicenza: Neri Pozza, 2011); Francesco Filippi, *Noi però gli abbiamo fatto le strade: Le colonie italiane tra bugie, razzismi e amnesie* (Turin: Bollati Boringhieri, 2021).
4. Massimiliano Tonelli, "La Molisana e i formati di pasta fascisti: Storia di un'aggressione incredibile," *Gambero Rosso*, January 6, 2021; Roberto Vivaldelli, "'Quella pasta è fascista': Il solito doppiopesismo colpisce La Molisana," *Il Giornale*, January 6, 2021; Angelo Bruscino, "Caso La Molisana: Contro la cancel culture all'amatriciana: Il pedigree di sinistra dell'azienda, difesa pure dall'ANPI, non le è bastato per sopravvivere alla furia iconoclasta," *Huffington Post Italia*, January 6, 2021.
5. Arnaldo Cortesi, "Italy Is Receiving Fruit of Conquest: Ethiopian Coffee, Now on the Market, Is First Product from New Empire," *New York Times*, March 7, 1937.
6. Leo Longanesi, *In piedi e seduti* (Milan: Longanesi, 1948), 137.
7. Anne McClintock, *Imperial Leather: Race, Gender, and Sexuality in the Colonial Contest* (New York: Routledge, 1995); Ann Laura Stoler, *Carnal Knowledge and Imperial Power: Race and the Intimate in Colonial Rule* (Berkeley: University of California Press, 2002); Barbara Sòrgoni, "'Defending the Race': The Italian Reinvention of the Hottentot Venus during Fascism," *Journal of Modern Italian Studies*, Vol. 8, No. 3 (2003): 411–24.
8. Karen Pinkus, *Bodily Regimes: Italian Advertising under Fascism* (Minneapolis: University of Minnesota Press, 1995), 22–81; Karen Pinkus, "Shades of Black in Advertising and Popular Culture," in *Revisioning Italy: National Identity and Global Culture*, ed. Beverly Allen and Mary Russo (Minneapolis: University of Minnesota Press, 1997), 134–55.
9. Frantz Fanon, *The Wretched of the Earth* (New York: Grove Press, 1963), 39–40.
10. Alexander Abad-Santos, "Barilla Pasta Doesn't Want Gay People in Their Ads," *The Atlantic*, September 26, 2013; Eric Sasson, "Why Did Barilla Pasta Cook Up Trouble with Gay Rights Groups?" *Wall Street Journal*, September 30, 2013; Lizzy Davies, "Pasta Firm Barilla Boycotted over 'Classic Family' Remarks," *The Guardian*, September 26, 2013.

11. Neelam Srivastava, *Italian Colonialism and Resistances to Empire, 1930–1970* (London: Palgrave Macmillan, 2018), 65–99; James Hunter Meriwether, *Proudly We Can Be Africans: Black Americans and Africa, 1935–1961* (Chapel Hill: University of North Carolina Press, 2002), 27–56.
12. Craig Claiborne, "It May Be a Bit Far to Go for Pasta, but Italian Cooking Is Popular in Ethiopia," *New York Times*, December 12, 1970; Henok Reta, "Pasta: From Colonial Legacy to Major National Food," *The Reporter Ethiopia*, December 13, 2014, 16–19.
13. Emanuele Bompan, "From Wheat to Pasta: A Very Italian Solution to Ethiopian Poverty," *La Stampa*, May 3, 2015.
14. Hannah Giorgis, "Ethiopia and Eritrea's Long History with Lasagna," *Taste*, May 4, 2018.
15. Minale Adugna, "Women and Warfare in Ethiopia: A Case Study of Their Role during the Campaign of Adwa, 1895–96, and the Italo-Ethiopian War, 1935–41," *Organization for Social Science Research in Eastern and Southern Africa: Gender Issues Research Report Series*, No. 13 (2001): 1–41.
16. In her ethnography of Italian migrant foodways to post-World War II Belgium, Leen Beyers contrasts the recipe of Bolognese (urban, middle-class, northern Italian) lasagna—whose defining ingredient is the bland, creamy, white, French béchamel sauce, adopted by northern Italian immigrants and acceptable to Belgian palates—to the richer, spicier version made by first-generation southern Italian rural immigrants, featuring small meatballs and thick tomato sauce, pungent grated Pecorino cheese instead of Parmesan, hard-boiled eggs and peas and no béchamel. The beloved dish celebrated family Sundays and special occasions, a break from the *cucina povera* (simple rural cooking) that dominated the southern Italian everyday diet. Leen Beyers, "Creating Home: Food, Ethnicity and Gender among Italians in Belgium since 1946," *Food, Culture & Society*, Vol. 11, No. 1 (2008): 7–27.
17. James C. McCann, *Stirring the Pot: A History of African Cuisine* (Athens: Ohio University Press, 2010), 6.
18. Arjun Appadurai, "Gastro-politics in Hindu South Asia," *American Ethnologist*, Vol. 8, No. 3 (1981): 494–511.
19. Fabio De Ninno, "L'Oceano Indiano e la grande strategia italiana," in *Italy on the Rimland: Storia militare di una penisola eurasiatica. Vol. 2: Suez*, ed. Virgilio Ilari (Rome: Nadir Media, 2019), 105–16.
20. Contrary to fascist colonization plans, almost 90 percent of Italian settlers in Ethiopia ended up living in one of the six main urban centers, giving Italian colonialism a strong urban character. By 1940, a full 50 percent of the settlers lived in Addis Ababa. The second city in Ethiopia, Jimma, had 10,611 settlers, followed by Gondar with 5,944 Italians, then Harar with 4,802, and Dire Dawa and Dessie with 4,556 and 4,033 settlers, respectively. Emanuele Ertola, *In terra d'Africa: Gli italiani che colonizzarono l'impero* (Rome: Laterza, 2017), 16.
21. Susanne Freidberg, *French Beans and Food Scares: Culture and Commerce in an Anxious Age* (New York: Oxford University Press, 2004); Parama Roy, *Alimentary Tracts: Appetites, Aversions, and the Postcolonial* (Durham, NC: Duke University Press, 2010).
22. Sidney Mintz, *Sweetness and Power: The Place of Sugar in Modern History* (New York: Penguin Books, 1985); Alfred Crosby, *The Columbian Exchange: Biological and Cultural Consequences of 1492* (Westport, CT: Greenwood Press, 1972); Alfred Crosby, *Ecological Imperialism: The Biological Expansion of Europe, 900–1900* (New York: Cambridge University Press, 1986).

23. Elizabeth M. Collingham, *The Taste of Empire: How Britain's Quest for Food Shaped the Modern World* (New York: Basic Books, 2017); Lauren Janes, *Colonial Food in Interwar Paris: The Taste of Empire* (New York: Bloomsbury Academic, 2016); Cecilia Leong-Salobir, *Food Culture in Colonial Asia: A Taste of Empire* (New York: Routledge, 2011); Priscilla Mary Işın, *Bountiful Empire: A History of Ottoman Cuisine* (New York: Reaktion Books, 2018).
24. Jayeeta Sharma, "Food and Empire," in *The Oxford Handbook of Food History*, ed. Jeffrey M. Pilcher (New York: Oxford University Press, 2012), 241–57.
25. Tiago Saraiva, *Fascist Pigs: Technoscientific Organisms and the History of Fascism* (Cambridge, MA: MIT Press, 2016).
26. Patrick Bernhard, "Borrowing from Mussolini: Nazi Germany's Colonial Aspirations in the Shadow of Italian Expansionism," *Journal of Imperial and Commonwealth History*, Vol. 41, No. 4 (2013): 617–43; Patrick Bernhard, "Hitler's Africa in the East: Italian Colonialism as a Model for German Planning in Eastern Europe," *Journal of Contemporary History*, Vol. 51, No. 1 (2016): 61–90.
27. Carol Helstosky, "Fascist Food Politics: Mussolini's Policy of Alimentary Sovereignty," *Journal of Modern Italian Studies*, Vol. 9, No. 1 (2004): 1–26.
28. Umberto Eco, "Ur-Fascism," *New York Review of Books*, June 22, 1995, 12–15.
29. Lauren E. Forcucci, "Battle for Births: The Fascist Pronatalist Campaign in Italy, 1925 to 1938," *Journal of the Society for the Anthropology of Europe*, Vol. 10, No. 1 (2010): 4–13; G. Bruce Strang, "'Places in the African Sun': Social Darwinism, Demographics and the Italian Invasion of Ethiopia," in *Collision of Empires: Italy's Invasion of Ethiopia and Its International Impact*, ed. G. Bruce Strang (New York: Routledge, 2013), 11–32. Mussolini's quote is from "Marcia funebre," *Il Popolo d'Italia* (June 9, 1934).
30. Federico D'Onofrio, "The Microfoundations of Italian Agrarianism: Italian Agricultural Economists and Fascism," *Agricultural History*, Vol. 91, No. 3 (2017): 369–96.
31. Antonio Gramsci, *Selections from Cultural Writings* (Cambridge, MA: Harvard University Press, 1985), 189–91.
32. Touring Club Italiano, *Guida Gastronomica d'Italia* (Milan: Touring Club Italiano, 1931).
33. Agnese Portincasa, "Il Touring Club Italiano e la *Guida Gastronomica d'Italia*: Creazione, circolazione del modello e tracce della sua evoluzione (1931–1984)," *Food and History*, Vol. 6, No. 1 (2008): 83–119; Marco Armiero and Wilko Graf von Hardenberg, "Green Rhetoric in Blackshirts: Italian Fascism and the Environment," *Environment and History*, Vol. 19, No. 3 (2013): 283–311.
34. Consociazione Turistica Italiana, *Guida dell'Africa Orientale Italiana* (Milan: Consociazione Turistica Italiana, 1938). On Italian tourism of the empire, Stephanie Malia Hom, "Empires of Tourism: Travel and Rhetoric in Italian Colonial Libya and Albania, 1911–1943," *Journal of Tourism History*, Vol. 4, No. 3 (2012): 281–300.
35. Victoria de Grazia, *How Fascism Ruled Women: Italy, 1922–1945* (Berkeley: University of California Press, 1992); Perry R. Willson, "Cooking the Patriotic Omelette: Women and the Italian Fascist Ruralization Campaign," *European History Quarterly*, Vol. 27, No. 4 (1997): 531–47; Barbara Spadaro, "Intrepide massaie: Genere, imperialismo e totalitarismo nella preparazione coloniale femminile durante il fascismo (1937–1943)," *Contemporanea*, Vol. 13, No. 1 (2010): 27–52; "I corsi di preparazione della donna alla vita coloniale," *Africa Italiana*, Vol. 3, Nos. 2–3 (1940): 19–24.

36. Ruth Ben-Ghiat, "Modernity Is Just over There: Colonialism and Italian National Identity," *interventions*, Vol. 8, No. 3 (2006): 380–93.
37. Helstosky, "Fascist Food Politics."
38. Michele Sollai, "The Fascist Green Revolution," *Plants People Planet* (2023): 1–10; Sergio Salvi, Oriana Porfiri, and Salvatore Ceccarelli, "Nazareno Strampelli, the 'Prophet' of the Green Revolution," *Journal of Agricultural Science*, Vol. 151, No. 1 (2013): 1–5.
39. Saraiva, *Fascist Pigs*.
40. Ferdinando Bigi, "Il Prof. Armando Maugini: Un maestro indimenticabile," *Africa*, Vol. 32, No. 1 (1977): 117–34.
41. Irma Taddia, *L'Eritrea-colonia 1890–1952: Paesaggi, strutture, uomini del colonialismo* (Milan: Angeli, 1986); Angelo Matteo Caglioti, "'In This Country, Water Means Life': Eritrea's Erratic Rivers and Italian Irrigation Projects between Adwa and Mussolini (1897–1934)," *Contemporanea*, Vol. 25, No. 2 (2022): 265–91.
42. Federico Cresti, *Non desiderare la terra d'altri: La colonizzazione italiana in Libia* (Rome: Carocci, 2011).
43. Nicola Labanca, *Oltremare: Storia dell'espansione coloniale italiana* (Bologna: Il Mulino, 2007); Roberta Pergher, *Mussolini's Nation-Empire: Sovereignty and Settlement in Italy's Borderlands, 1922–1943* (New York: Cambridge University Press, 2017).
44. Alessandro Volterra, *Sudditi coloniali ascari eritrei, 1935–1941* (Milan: Angeli, 2005).
45. Haile Selassie, "Appeal to the League of Nations," June 30, 1936, cited in Matteo Dominioni, *Lo sfascio dell'impero: Gli italiani in Etiopia (1936–1941)* (Rome: Laterza, 2008).
46. Del Boca, *Italiani brava gente*, 197.
47. Peter D'Agostino, "Craniums, Criminals and the 'Cursed Race': Italian Anthropology in American Racial Thought, 1861–1924," *Comparative Studies in Society and History*, Vol. 44, No. 2 (2002): 319–43.
48. Luigi Preti, *Impero fascista, africani ed ebrei* (Milan: Mursia, 2004), 290.
49. Giorgio Almirante, "La nuova razza nell'Agro Redento," *La difesa della razza*, No. 12 (1940): 15.
50. Richard Pankhurst, "Fascist Racial Policies in Ethiopia, 1922–1941," *Ethiopia Observer* Vol. 12, No. 4 (1969): 270–86.
51. Carlo Conti-Rossini, "L'Etiopia è incapace di progresso civile," *Nuova Antologia*, Vol. 13 (1935): 171–7.
52. Lidio Cipriani, "La decadenza razziale delle genti negre e la necessità di una protezione degli Etiopici," *Africa Italiana*, Vol. 3, No. 1 (1940): 21. On Cipriani and his racist elaborations on Ethiopians, Gianni Dore, "Antropologia e colonialismo italiano nell'epoca fascista: Il razzismo biologico di Lidio Cipriani," *Annali della Facoltà di Lettere e Filosofia dell'Università di Cagliari*, Vol. 2 (1981): 285–313.
53. Ciro Poggiali, *Agli albori dell'Impero: L'Etiopia com'è e come sarà* (Milan: Fratelli Treves, 1938), 196–7.
54. Ibid., 197.
55. Alba Sartori Felter, *Vagabondaggi, soste, avventure negli albori di un impero* (Brescia: Tip. F.lli Geroldi, 1940), 136.
56. Haile M. Larebo, *The Building of an Empire: Italian Land Policy and Practice in Ethiopia, 1935–1941* (Oxford: Clarendon Press, 1994), 69–71.
57. Haile Larebo, "Empire Building and Its Limitations: Ethiopia (1935–1941)," in *Italian Colonialism*, ed. Ruth Ben-Ghiat and Mia Fuller (New York: Palgrave Macmillan, 2005), 83–94; Alberto Sbacchi, "Italian Colonization in Ethiopia: Plans and Projects,

1936–1940," *Africa*, Vol. 32, No. 4 (1977): 503–16; Emilio Conforti, *Impressioni agrarie su alcuni itinerari dell'altopiano etiopico* (Florence: Regio Istituto Agronomico per l'Africa Italiana, 1941); Roberto Asinari di San Marzano, *Le terre del nostro impero. Vol. 2: Dalla piana somala all'altipiano etiopico* (Rome: La Voce della Stampa, 1937); Vito Cosimo Basile, *Uebi Scebeli: Diario di tenda e cammino della spedizione del Duca degli Abruzzi in Etiopia, 1928–1929* (Bari: Stilo, 2010); Ferruccio Canali, "Giuseppe Tassinari e la Relazione al Duce del viaggio attraverso i territori dell'Impero: Paesaggi e territori nella prospettiva della colonizzazione dell'Africa Orientale Italiana (gennaio-febbraio 1937)," *Annuario di Storia dell'Urbanistica e del Paesaggio* No. 1 (2013): 206–14; Enrico Bartolozzi, "Missione di studio in AOI," *Agricoltura Coloniale*, Vol. 33, No. 3 (1939): 126–31.

58. Emanuele Ertola, "White Slaves: Labor, Whiteness, and Settler Colonialism in Italian East Africa (1935–1941)," *Labor History*, Vol. 61, Nos. 5–6 (2020): 551–67.
59. "Speaking of protecting our workers: I learned that many of them have been treated so harshly and worked in such demanding occupations that Ethiopians would comment: 'The Italians brought White slaves over with them.'" Ciro Poggiali, *Diario AOI (15 giugno 1936–4 ottobre 1937): Gli appunti segreti dell'inviato del Corriere della Sera* (Milan: Longanesi, 1971), 34. For more of the same kind of commentaries, Richard Pankhurst, "Italian and 'Native' Labor during the Italian Fascist Occupation of Ethiopia, 1935–41," *Ghana Social Science Journal*, Vol. 2, No. 2 (1973): 56; Francesco Pierotti, *Vita in Etiopia, 1940–41* (Bologna: Cappelli, 1959), 20.
60. G. M. Sangiorgi, "Il meticciato: Un problema da evitare," in *Atti del Terzo Congresso di Studi Coloniali. Vol. 2*, ed. Centro di Studi Coloniali, Istituto Coloniale Fascista (Florence: Tipografia giuntina di Leo Olschki, 1937), 134.
61. Cited in Giulia Barrera, "Colonial Affairs: Italian Men, Eritrean Women, and the Construction of Racial Hierarchies in Colonial Eritrea (1885–1941)" (PhD Diss., Northwestern University, 2002), 311.
62. Mussolini's speech to the Fascist Party National Council of October 25, 1938, reprinted in Luigi Preti, *Impero fascista, africani ed ebrei* (Milan: Mursia, 2004), 290.
63. Poggiali, *Agli albori dell'Impero*, 208–9.
64. Ibid., 218–19.
65. Elizabeth M. Collingham, *The Taste of Empire: How Britain's Quest for Food Shaped the Modern World* (New York: Basic Books, 2017); Lauren Janes, *Colonial Food in Interwar Paris: The Taste of Empire* (New York: Bloomsbury Academic, 2016); Cecilia Leong-Salobir, *Food Culture in Colonial Asia: A Taste of Empire* (New York: Routledge, 2011); Priscilla Mary Işın, *Bountiful Empire: A History of Ottoman Cuisine* (New York: Reaktion Books, 2018); Sarah Gibson, "Food Mobilities: Traveling, Dwelling, and Eating Cultures," *Space and Culture*, Vol. 10, No. 1 (2007): 4–21; Jennie Germann Molz, "The Cosmopolitan Mobilities of Culinary Tourism," *Space and Culture*, Vol. 10, No. 1 (2007): 77–93.
66. Barbara Sòrgoni, *Parole e corpi: Antropologia, discorso giuridico e politiche sessuali interrazziali nella colonia Eritrea (1890–1941)* (Naples: Liguori, 1998), 234–5; Giulia Barrera, "Dangerous Liaisons: Colonial Concubinage in Eritrea, 1890–1941," *Northwestern University PAS Working Papers*, No. 1 (1996): 34–49; Giulia Barrera, "Mussolini's Colonial Race Laws and State-Settler Relations in Africa Orientale Italiana (1935–1941)," *Journal of Modern Italian Studies*, Vol. 8, No. 3 (2003): 425–43; Sandra Ponzanesi, "The Color of Love: Madamismo and Interracial Relationships in the Italian Colonies," *Research in African Literatures*, Vol. 2, No. 2 (2012): 155–72;

Nicoletta Poidimani, *Difendere la razza: Identità razziale e politiche sessuali nel progetto imperiale di Mussolini* (Rome: Sensibili alle foglie, 2009).
67. Gianluca Gabrielli, "Colpevole di leso razzismo: Una sentenza per il reato di unione di indole coniugale tra cittadini e sudditi," *ANUAC: Rivista della Società Italiana di Antropologia Culturale*, Vol. 1, No. 1 (2012): 12–13.
68. Mia Fuller, "Wherever You Go, There You Are: Fascist Plans for the Colonial City of Addis Ababa and the Colonizing Suburb of EUR '42," *Journal of Contemporary History* Vol. 31, No. 2 (1996): 397–418; Diana Garvin, "Black Markets: Fascist Constructions of Race in East African Marketplace Newsreels," *Journal of Modern European History*, Vol. 19, No. 1 (2021): 103–24.
69. Ertola, *White Slaves*, 551–67.
70. Fabienne Le Houérou, "Gender and Sexual Abuses during the Italian Colonization of Ethiopia and Eritrea: The Insabbiatti Thirty Years After," *Sociology Mind*, Vol. 5, No. 4 (2015): 255–67.
71. Giulia Barrera, "Patrilinearità, razza e identità: L'educazione degli italo-eritrei durante il colonialismo italiano (1885–1934)," *Quaderni Storici*, Vol. 37, No. 1 (2002): 21–54.
72. Michele Strazza, "Faccetta nera dell'Abissinia: Madame e meticci dopo la conquista dell'Etiopia," *Humanities*, Vol. 1, No. 2 (2012): 129.
73. Yonas Seifu, "A Historical Survey of Jimma Town (1936–1974)" (MA thesis, Addis Ababa University, 2002), 23; Laketch Dirasse, *The Commoditization of Female Sexuality: Prostitution and Socio-economic Relations in Addis Ababa, Ethiopia* (New York: AMS Press, 1991), 21–41; Bethlehem Tekola, *Narratives of Three Prostitutes in Addis Ababa* (Addis Ababa: CERTWID, 2002).
74. Ruth Ben-Ghiat, *Fascist Modernities: Italy, 1922–1945* (Berkeley: University of California Press, 2001); Gianmarco Mancosu, *Vedere l'impero: L'Istituto Luce e il colonialismo fascista* (Milan: Mimesis, 2022).
75. Ruth Ben-Ghiat, *Italian Fascism's Empire Cinema* (Bloomington: Indiana University Press, 2015), 68, 80, 85, 118, 123; Marie-France Courriol, "Documentary Strategies and Aspects of Realism in Italian Cinema (1935–1939)," *The Italianist*, Vol. 34, No. 2 (2014): 122–41; Immacolata Amodeo, "In the Empire's Eyes: Africa in Italian Colonial Cinema between Imperial Fantasies and Blind Spots," in *Empires and Boundaries: Race, Class, and Gender in Colonial Settings*, ed. Harald Fischer-Tiné and Susanne Gehrmann (New York: Routledge, 2009), 166–78; Gabriele Proglio, "Il cammino degli eroi: The Empire as a Mark of Modernity—Representations of Colonial Power in a Famous Regime Documentary," *Modern Italy*, Vol. 21, No. 3 (2016): 289–303; Valeria Deplano, *L'Africa in casa: Propaganda e cultura coloniale nell'Italia fascista* (Milan: Mondadori, 2015); Giuseppe Fidotta, "Un impero cinematografico: Il documentario in Africa Orientale Italiana (1935–1941)" (PhD Diss., Università di Udine, 2015).
76. Anandi Ramamurthy, *Imperial Persuaders: Images of Africa and Asia in British Advertising* (Manchester: Manchester University Press, 2003.
77. Fanon, *The Wretched of the Earth*, 39.
78. Silke Hackenesch, *Chocolate and Blackness: A Cultural History* (Berlin: Campus Verlag), 2017.
79. bell hooks, "Eating the Other: Desire and Resistance," in *Black Looks: Race and Representation* (Boston: South End Press, 1992), 21–39.
80. Cynthia Enloe, *Bananas, Beaches and Bases: Making Feminist Sense of International Politics* (Berkeley: University of California Press, 2014), 211–49.

81. On the civilizing project as foundational to European modern identity, Norbert Elias, *The Civilizing Process: Sociogenetic and Psychogenetic Investigations* (Oxford: Blackwell, 2000).
82. McClintock, *Imperial Leather*.
83. Fanon, *Black Skin, White Masks*.
84. Fanon, *The Wretched of the Earth*, 135, 44.
85. Maaza Mengiste, *The Shadow King* (New York: W.W. Norton, 2019).

1 Ethiopian Foodways and Italian Foodways: Frameworks of an Imperial Culinary Encounter

1. McCann, *Stirring the Pot*, 78–106.
2. Taddesse Tamrat, *Church and State in Ethiopia, 1270–1527* (Oxford: Clarendon Press, 1972).
3. Alberto Capatti and Massimo Montanari, *Italian Cuisine: A Cultural History* (New York: Columbia University Press, 2003).
4. McCann, *Stirring the Pot*, 32–61.
5. Capatti and Montanari, *Italian Cuisine*.
6. McCann, *Stirring the Pot*, 65–100; Jack Goody, *Cooking, Cuisine, and Class: A Study in Comparative Sociology* (New York: Cambridge University Press, 1982).
7. Piero Camporesi, "Introduction," in *La scienza in cucina e l'arte di mangiar bene*, ed. Pellegrino Artusi (Turin: Einaudi, 1970), lv.
8. McCann, *Stirring the Pot*, 65–100.
9. Gianni Dore, "Per un repertorio degli stili alimentari nell'altopiano etiopico: Note su commensalità, divisione, spartizione e gerarchie sociali," *Ethnorema*, No. 2 (2006): 3–4.
10. McCann, *Stirring the Pot*, 65–7.
11. Abbebe Kifleyesus, "The Construction of Ethiopian National Cuisine," *Ethnorema*, No. 2 (2006): 39.
12. Kifleyesus, "The Construction," 27–48; McCann, *Stirring the Pot*, 65–100; Dore, "Per un repertorio," 3–4.
13. Dore, "Per un repertorio"; Kifleyesus, "The Construction."
14. Giovanni Rebora, *Culture of the Fork: A Brief History of Everyday Food and Haute Cuisine in Europe* (New York: Columbia University Press, 2001); Marzio Barbagli, *Sotto lo stesso tetto: Mutamenti della famiglia in Italia dal XV al XX secolo* (Bologna: Il Mulino, 1984), 440–4.
15. Richard Pankhurst, "Hierarchy at the Feast: The Partition of the Ox in Traditional Ethiopia," in *Proceedings of the Ninth International Congress of Ethiopian Studies*, ed. Anatoliĭ Andreevich Gromyko (Moscow: USSR Academy of Sciences Africa Institute, 1988), 173–89; Dore, "Per un repertorio," 10–14.
16. Visco, "L'alimentazione nelle colonie," 516.
17. Kifleyesus, "The Construction," 37; Dore, "Per un repertorio," 10, 16; McCann, *Stirring the Pot*, 89.
18. McCann, *Stirring the Pot*, 65, 73.
19. P. C. M. Jansen, *Spices, Condiments and Medicinal Plants in Ethiopia, Their Taxonomy and Agricultural Significance* (Wageningen: Center for Agricultural Publishing and Documentation, 1981).
20. Kifleyesus, "The Construction," 38–9; Dore, "Per un repertorio," 5.

21. Kifleyesus, "The Construction," 37.
22. Dore, "Per un repertorio," 4–5.
23. Mooha Lee, Meron Regu, and Semeneh Seleshe, "Uniqueness of Ethiopian Traditional Alcoholic Beverage of Plant Origin, Tella," *Journal of Ethnic Foods*, Vol. 2, No. 3 (2015): 110–14.
24. McCann, *Stirring the Pot*, 73; Gianni Dore, "Etnografia del miele nelle fonti coloniali italiane su Eritrea e Etiopia," *Ethnorema*, No. 5 (2010): 51–60.
25. Pier Marcello Masotti, *Ricordi d'Etiopia di un funzionario coloniale* (Milan: Pan, 1981), 184.
26. The exoticizing fascination of Europeans for the cosmetic practices involving the use of *niter kibbeh* on African bodies continues today. Sarah Bridges and Ruth Styles, "The Ethiopian Tribes Who Use Butter to Style Their Hair: Incredible Photos Reveal the Elaborate Curled Creations of the Afar People, and the Hamer Who Mix Ghee with Red Ochre to Spectacular Effect," *Daily Mail*, February 12, 2014.
27. Gianni Dore, *Scritture di colonia: Lettere di Pia Maria Pezzoli dall'Africa Orientale a Bologna (1936–1943)* (Bologna: Patron, 2004), 21; Vincenzo Ambrosio, *Tre anni fra i Galla e i Sidama* (Rome: Ministero dell'Africa Italiana, 1942), 83–4.
28. Kifleyesus, "The Construction," 38; Dore, "Per un repertorio," 12; Znabu Hadush, Zewdie Birhanu, Mulugeta Chaka, and Haylay Gebreyesus, "Foods Tabooed for Pregnant Women in Abala District of Afar Region, Ethiopia: An Inductive Qualitative Study," *BMC Nutrition*, Vol. 3, No. 40 (2017): 1–9.
29. Yaqob Beyene, "I tabù alimentari e il Cristianesimo etiopico," *Rassegna di Studi Etiopici*, Vol. 38, No. (1994): 209–32; Tilahun Bejitual Zellelew, "The Semiotics of the 'Christian/Muslim Knife': Meat and Knife as Markers of Religious Identity in Ethiopia," *Signs and Society*, Vol. 3, No. 1 (2015): 44–70; Tilahun Bejitual Zellelew, "Meat Abstinence and Its Positive Environmental Effect: Examining the Fasting Etiquettes of the Ethiopian Orthodox Church," *Critical Research on Religion*, Vol. 2, No. 2 (2014): 134–46; Semeneh Seleshe, Cheorun Jo, and Mooha Lee, "Meat Consumption Culture in Ethiopia," *Korean Journal for Food Science of Animal Resources*, Vol. 34, No. 1 (2013): 7–13.
30. Valentina Peveri, *The Edible Gardens of Ethiopia: An Ethnographic Journey into Beauty and Hunger* (Tucson: University of Arizona Press, 2020); William Shack, *The Gurage: A People of the Ensete Culture* (New York: Oxford University Press, 1966); McCann, *Stirring the Pot*, 88–9, 99; Visco, "L'alimentazione nelle colonie," 514.

2 Fascist Bioimperialism in East Africa: Mass Colonization as Transplantation of Seeds, Breeds, and Farming Hands

1. Sbacchi, "Italian Colonization in Ethiopia," 503.
2. Alessandro Lessona, *L'Africa italiana nel primo anno dell'Impero* (Rome: Edizioni della Rassegna Economica dell'Africa Italiana, 1937), 18, cited in Del Boca, *Gli italiani in Africa Orientale. Vol. 3: La caduta dell'Impero* (Milan: Mondadori, 2014), 173.
3. Alessandro Lessona, *Memorie* (Rome: Edizioni della Rassegna Economica dell'Africa Italiana, 1937), 356–7.
4. Chiudero and Rocchetti, "L'avvaloramento in Etiopia," 265–411; Raffaele Ciferri, "Potenzialità agricola dell'Impero," *Africa Italiana*, Vol. 2, No. 5 (1939): 18–22;

Vincenzo Rivera, *Prospettive di colonizzazione dell'Africa Orientale Italiana* (Rome: Edizioni della Rassegna Economica dell'Africa Italiana, 1939); Giulio Gennari, *L'agricoltura nell'Africa Orientale Italiana* (Rome: Edizioni della Rassegna Economica dell'Africa Italiana, 1938); "La valorizzazione agraria e colonizzazione," *Annali dell'Africa Italiana*, Vol. 2, No. 1 (1939): 259–69.

5. Riccardo De Robertis, "From Colonialism to Cooperation: The Training of Tropical Agricultural Experts in Florence (1908-1968)," *Journal of Agriculture and Environment for International Development*, Vol. 113, No. 2 (2019): 253–71.
6. Franco Cardini and Isabella Gagliardi, "Towards a New Empire," in *L'Istituto Agronomico per l'Oltremare: La sua storia* (Florence: Masso delle Fate, 2007), 78–111.
7. Arrigo Chiudero and Giuseppe Rocchetti, "L'avvaloramento in Etiopia," in *L'avvaloramento e la colonizzazione. Vol. 2. L'opera di avvaloramento agricolo e zootecnico in Eritrea, in Somalia e in Etiopia*, ed. Ministero degli Affari Esteri. Comitato per la Documentazione delle Attività Italiane in Africa (Rome: Soc. Abete, 1970), 369.
8. Roberto Maiocchi, *Scienza italiana e razzismo fascista* (Florence: La Nuova Italia, 1999).
9. Haile M. Larebo, *The Building of an Empire*. On the relations between Italian and Ethiopian farmers, Michele Sollai, "Microcosms of Colonial Development: Italian and Ethiopian Farmers at the Crossroads of Fascist Empire Building (1937–1941)," *Contemporanea*, Vol. 24, No. 1 (2021): 79–101.
10. A list of Ethiopian notables whose lands were confiscated is in Enrico Brotto, *Il regime delle terre nel Governo dell'Harar* (Addis Ababa: Servizio tipografico del Governo Centrale AOI, 1939), 108–14, cited in Del Boca, *Gli italiani in Africa Orientale*, 196.
11. Donald Crummey, *Land and Society in the Christian Kingdom of Ethiopia: From the Thirteenth to the Twentieth Century* (Urbana: University of Illinois Press, 2000), 198–234; Larebo, *The Building of an Empire*, 28–50.
12. James McCann, *People of the Plow: An Agricultural History of Ethiopia, 1800–1990* (Madison: University of Wisconsin Press, 1995), 211.
13. Ibid.
14. David Forgacs, *Italy's Margins: Social Exclusion and Nation Formation since 1861* (New York: Cambridge University Press, 2014), 87.
15. Larebo, "Empire Building and Its Limitations," 83–4.
16. Sbacchi, "Italian Colonization in Ethiopia," 34.
17. Poggiali, *Agli albori dell'Impero*, 193.
18. Ibid., 206.
19. Curzio Malaparte, *Viaggio in Etiopia e altri scritti africani* (Florence: Vallecchi, 2006), 46.
20. Giuseppe Sangiorgi, *Elementi di igiene coloniale: Per la coscienza igienica dei colonizzatori dell'Impero* (Bari: Laterza, 1939), 17.
21. Alessandro Melchiori, *Il nostro Impero coloniale* (Rome: Italia Maestra, 1938), 14.
22. Poggiali, *Agli albori dell'Impero*, 222.
23. Gian Luca Podestà, "Il lavoro in Africa Orientale Italiana (1935–1939)," in *Il lavoro come fattore produttivo e come risorsa nella storia economia italiana: Atti del Convegno di studi, Roma, 24 novembre 2000*, ed. Sergio Zaninelli and Mario Taccolini (Milan: Vita e Pensiero, 2002), 124–7.
24. Davide Fossa, *Lavoro italiano nell'Impero* (Milan: Mondadori, 1938), 472–90; Ernesto Massi, "Economia dell'Africa Italiana," *Rivista Internazionale di Scienze Sociali*, Vol. 11, No. 3 (1940): 424–39; Del Boca, *Gli italiani in Africa Orientale*, 199–211.

25. Benito Mussolini, "La necessità di espansione dell'Italia in Africa (8 ottobre 1935)," in *Opera omnia di Benito Mussolini. Vol. 27: Dall'inaugurazione della provincia di Littoria alla proclamazione dell'impero (19 dicembre 1934-9 maggio 1936)* (Florence: La Fenice, 1959), 162.
26. Sbacchi, "Italian Colonization in Ethiopia," 510-12.
27. Fossa, *Lavoro italiano*, 472-3.
28. Alfio Berretta, *Con Amedeo d'Aosta in Africa Orientale Italiana in pace e in guerra* (Milan: Ceschina, 1952), 258-9.
29. Italians dismantled Ethiopia into the four governorates of Amhara, Shewa (with the empire's capital city of Addis Ababa), Harar, and Galla and Sidama, which were added to those of the *colonia primigenia* (eldest colony) of Eritrea (est. 1890) and Somalia (colonized by Italy at the beginning of the twentieth century) to create Italian East Africa (Africa Orientale Italiana, AOI).
30. Del Boca, *Gli italiani in Africa Orientale*, 200-5; Richard Pankhurst, "A Page of Ethiopian History: Italian Settlement Plans during the Fascist Occupation of 1936-1941," *Ethiopia Observer*, Vol. 13, No. 2 (1970): 148-50; Virgilio C. Galati, "Saverio Dioguardi e il Piano Regolatore dei Villaggi Agricoli Nazionali di Oletta e Biscioftù nell'Etiopia Italiana (1936-1940)," *Annali di Storia dell'Urbanistica e del Paesaggio*, No. 1 (2013): 111-58; Alberto Sbacchi, *Ethiopia under Mussolini: Fascism and the Colonial Experience* (London: Zed Books, 1985), 109.
31. Podestà, "Il lavoro in Africa Orientale Italiana," 134.
32. Ibid., 141.
33. Carlo Giglio, *La colonizzazione demografica dell'Impero* (Rome: Edizioni Rassegna Economica dell'Africa Italiana, 1939); Fossa, *Lavoro italiano*, 479-90; Sbacchi, "Italian Colonization in Ethiopia," 515-16; Del Boca, *Gli italiani in Africa Orientale*, 205-7.
34. Curzio Malaparte, "Nella Romagna d'Etiopia," *Corriere della Sera*, August 1, 1939, cited in Forgacs, *Italy's Margins*, 85. On *Romagna d'Etiopia*, G. B. Lusignani, "L'Ente di Colonizzazione Romagna d'Etiopia," *Autarchia Alimentare*, Vol. 1, No. 7 (1938): 35-7; Enrico Paolini and Davide Saporetti, *La Romagna in Etiopia: Sogni e speranze in Africa* (Cesena: Il Ponte Vecchio, 1999).
35. Pankhurst, "A Page of Ethiopian History," 150-2; Larebo, *Building of an Empire*, 144-5; Poggiali, *Agli albori dell'Impero*, 218-19; Giornale Luce B1241, "La partenza del primo nucleo di rurali per l'Africa Orientale," January 26, 1938, Archivio Storico Luce; Virgilio C. Galati, "Bari d'Etiopia (Harar): Le vicende della fondazione del centro urbano e l'utopia della colonizzazione agricola," *Annali di Storia dell'Urbanistica e del Paesaggio*, No. 1 (2013): 127-61.
36. Enrico Cerulli, "La colonizzazione del Harar," *Annali dell'Africa Italiana*, Vol. 6, No. 1 (1943): 71-2.
37. Fossa, *Lavoro italiano*, 494, 492.
38. Emanuele Ertola, "L'Impero immaginario: I coloni italiani in Etiopia, 1936-1941" (PhD Diss., Università di Firenze, 2014), 75-6.
39. Sbacchi, *Ethiopia under Mussolini*, 107-14.
40. Larebo, *The Building of an Empire*, 177-237; Chiudero and Rocchetti, "L'avvaloramento in Etiopia," 399-406.
41. I. M. Lewis, *A Modern History of Somalia: Nation and State in the Horn of Africa* (London: Longman 1980), 92-5; Renzo Meregazzi, "La Società Agricola Italo-Somala," *Rivista delle Colonie Italiane*, No. 5 (1928): 665-86; Ernesto Milanese, "La

Società Agricola Italo-Somala e l'opera del Duca degli Abruzzi in Somalia tra il 1920 e il 1933," *Miscellanea di storia delle esplorazioni*, Vol. 24 (1999): 235–58; Società Agricola Italo-Somala, "Il contributo dato dalla SAIS durante la guerra italo-abissina," in *Atti del Terzo Congresso di Studi Coloniali, Firenze-Roma, 12-17 aprile 1937*, ed. Istituto Coloniale Fascista, Centro di Studi Coloniali (Florence: Sansoni, 1937), 582–6.

42. Ernesto Quadrone, *Pionieri, donne e belve: Uebi Scelebi, Giuba* (Milan: Agnelli, 1934), 34–5.
43. Del Boca, *Italiani brava gente?*
44. Lewis, *A Modern History of Somalia*, 95–7; Ferrante Paveri-Fontana, "Note sul comprensorio di bonifica di Genale nella Somalia Italiana," in *Atti del Terzo Congresso di Studi Coloniali*, 587–92.
45. Regia Azienda Monopolio Banane, "Il monopolio delle banane nel quadro della autarchia economica e dei trasporti nazionali," *Annali dell'Africa Italiana*, Vol. 5, No. 2 (1942): 977–92; Labanca, *Oltremare*, 318–20.
46. Larebo, *The Building of an Empire*, 223.
47. Ibid., 243.
48. Ibid., 217.
49. Ibid., 221.
50. Ibid., 212–23.
51. Ibid., 184.
52. *Il Popolo d'Italia*, April 3, 1940, cited in Del Boca, *Gli italiani in Africa Orientale*, 213.
53. Raffaele Ciasca, *Storia coloniale dell'Italia contemporanea* (Milan: Hoepli, 1940), 728.
54. The figure compared very unfavorably to the faster capital-returning commercial (1,436) and industrial (1,225) firms Italians opened in Ethiopia between 1935 and 1940. Sbacchi, *Ethiopia under Mussolini*, 111.
55. Raffaele Di Lauro, "L'impero può bastare a sé stesso?" *Autarchia Alimentare*, Vol. 2, No. 2 (1939): 10. As early as May 1936, in a dispatch to the Viceroy Rodolfo Graziani in Addis Ababa, Mussolini ordered to "adopt all the practical measures needed for local life and ask the motherland only what is strictly necessary." Mussolini to Graziani, May 26, 1936, Archivio Storico del Ministero dell'Africa Italiana, Archivio Segreto di Gabinetto, b. 160, cited in Podestà, "Il lavoro in Africa Orientale Italiana," 125–6. Less than a year later, on April 13, 1937, a disappointed Mussolini will send Graziani an even more ultimate telegram: "From July 1, 1938, the Empire must be self-sufficient as per its food supply and the motherland won't send anything. Get prepared accordingly." Del Boca, *Gli italiani in Africa Orientale*, 180.
56. General Guglielmo Nasi, governor of Harar between 1936 and 1939 and Shewa between 1939 and 1940, provided the figure of 338 tractors (148 made in Italy, 190 made by foreign manufacturers). Guglielmo Nasi, *Noi Italiani in Etiopia* (Rome: Attività Editrice Internazionale, 1950), 6. The organ newspaper of the Fascist Party, *Il Popolo d'Italia*, mentioned a total of 379 tractors (April 3, 1940), cited in Del Boca, *Gli italiani in Africa Orientale*, 210n.
57. Richard Pankhurst, "Italian and Native Labor," 42–73.
58. Sbacchi, *Ethiopia under Mussolini*, 97.
59. Pierotti, *Vita in Etiopia*, 36.
60. Sbacchi, *Ethiopia under Mussolini*, 111.
61. Del Boca, *Gli italiani in Africa Orientale*, 178–85; Massi, "Economia dell'Africa Italiana," 437.

3 Establishing the Fascist Food System in East Africa: The Imperial Mobility of Italian Food and the Ethiopian Struggle for Food Sovereignty

1. Gian Luca Podestà, "Building the Empire: Public Works in Italian East Africa (1936–1941)," *Enterprises et Histoire*, No. 70 (2013): 37–53; Richard Pankhurst, "Road Building during the Italian Fascist Occupation of Ethiopia, 1935–1941," *Africa Quarterly*, Vol. 15, No. 3 (1968): 21–62; Mattia C. Bertazzini, "The Long-Term Impact of Italian Colonial Roads in the Horn of Africa, 1935–2000," *London School of Economics Economic History Working Papers*, No. 272 (2018): 1–55; Louise Diel, *Behold Our New Empire: Mussolini* (London: Hurst and Blackett, 1939), 74–8; Getahun Benti, *Urban Growth in Ethiopia, 1887–1974: From the Foundation of Finfinnee to the Demise of the First Imperial Era* (Lanham, MD: Lexington Books, 2016), 81–120; "Le opere stradali," *Annali dell'Africa Italiana*, Vol. 2, No. 4 (1939): 321–64; Corrado Masi, "Gli italiani e la ferrovia Gibuti-Addis Abeba," *Africa Italiana*, No. 3 (1943): 32–4.
2. Poggiali, *Agli albori dell'Impero*, 153.
3. Ibid., 162, 173.
4. Guardia di Finanza, "Relazione sull'attività della R. Guardia di finanza dell'Impero durante l'esercizio finanziario 1938–39," *Bollettino d'Archivio*, Vol. 1, No. 1 (2005): 38–40, 58–9, 65; Podestà, "Il lavoro in Africa Orientale Italiana," 137.
5. Canali, "Giuseppe Tassinari e la Relazione al Duce del viaggio attraverso i territori dell'Impero."
6. S.P., in Irma Taddia, *La memoria dell'Impero: Autobiografie d'Africa Orientale* (Bari: Lacaita, 1988), 124–5.
7. Dante Galeazzi, *Il violino di Addis Abeba: L'uomo sulla soglia* (Milan: Gastaldi, 1959), 108.
8. Archivio Storico del Ministero dell'Africa Italiana, Gabinetto, Archivio Segreto, b. 23, f. 4, Segnalazioni OVRA, "Africa Orientale Italiana," Milan, October 7, 1937, cited in Ertola, *L'Impero immaginario*, 205.
9. Del Boca, *Gli italiani in Africa Orientale*, 186.
10. Ibid., 186, 180. The quote is by Italian Undersecretary of Exchange and Foreign Currencies Felice Guarneri (1882–1955).
11. Podestà, "Il lavoro in Africa Orientale Italiana," 142; Emanuele Ertola, "The Italian Fascist Settler Empire in Ethiopia, 1936–1941," in *The Routledge Handbook of the History of Settler Colonialism*, ed. Edward Cavanagh and Lorenzo Veracini (New York: Routledge, 2016), 263–76; Stefano Bellucci, "Italian Transnational Fluxes of Labour and Changing Labour Relations in the Horn of Africa," *Workers of the World*, Vol. 1, No. 3 (2013): 1–14; Chiara Giorgi, "Soggetti e politiche della mobilità coloniale," in *Votare con i piedi: Mobilità degli individui nell'Africa coloniale italiana*, ed. Isabella Rosoni and Chelati Dirar (Macerata: EUM, 2012), 199–230.
12. Fossa, *Lavoro italiano*, 238–9.
13. On the social value of food imported from the metropole in colonial settings, Richard Wilk, *Home Cooking in the Global Village: Caribbean Food from Buccaneers to Ecotourists* (New York: Berg, 2006).
14. Massi, "Economia dell'Africa Italiana"; Saraiva, *Fascist Pigs*, 22–42; Richard Pankhurst, "A Chapter in Ethiopia's Commercial History: Developments during the Fascist Occupation of Ethiopia, 1936–1941," *Ethiopia Observer*, Vol. 14, No. 1 (1971): 47–67.

15. Adriana Sciubba, "Il Commercio dell'Italia con l'AOI," *Rassegna Sociale dell'Africa Italiana*, Vol. 3, No. 1 (1940): 57–62; Sbacchi, *Ethiopia under Mussolini*, 99–100.
16. Del Boca, *Gli italiani in Africa Orientale*, 180.
17. Poggiali, *Agli albori dell'Impero*, 289.
18. Orio Vergani, *La via nera: Viaggio in Etiopia da Massaua a Mogadiscio* (Milan: Garzanti, 1949), 91–3.
19. "Il lavoro e l'assistenza sociale," *Annnali dell'Africa Italiana*, Vol. 3, No. 2 (1940): 1067.
20. Carlo Morengo, in Filippo Colombara, *Raccontare l'impero: Una storia orale della conquista d'Etiopia (1935–1941)* (Milan: Mimesis, 2019), 32.
21. Vittorio Pallotti, "'Ti scrivo dall'Abissinia': Lettere di Guerrino, camionista bolognese, alla moglie Derna dall'Africa Orientale Italiana," *I Sentieri della Ricerca*, No. 3 (2006): 189, 185.
22. Silvia Camilotti, "'Tutto ciò risponde alle mie irrequiete aspirazioni': I viaggi di Alba Felter Sartori nella colonia italiana," in *La detection della critica: Studi in onore di Ilaria Crotti*, ed. Ricciarda Ricorda and Alberto Zava (Venice: Edizioni Ca' Foscari, 2020), 191.
23. Marianna Scarfone, "La nevrastenia sotto i tropici: I disturbi mentali dei bianchi in colonia," in *Quel che resta dell'Impero: La cultura coloniale degli italiani*, ed. Valeria Deplano and Alessandro Pes (Milan: Mimesis, 2014), 31–2.
24. Ian Campbell, *The Addis Ababa Massacre: Italy's National Shame* (New York: Oxford University Press, 2017), 132, 157, 199; Angelo Del Boca, "I crimini del colonialismo fascista," in *Le guerre coloniali del fascismo*, ed. Angelo Del Boca (Rome: Laterza, 2008), 232–55.
25. Pierotti, *Vita in Etiopia*, 17.
26. Poggiali, *Diario AOI*, 142.
27. On the ideals of sobriety in fascist consumer culture, Brian J. Griffith, "Bacchus among the Blackshirts: Wine Making, Consumerism and Identity in Fascist Italy, 1919-1937," *Contemporary European History*, Vol. 29, No. 4 (2020): 394–415.
28. Alfredo Gonzales-Ruibal, "Fascist Colonialism: The Archaeology of Italian Outposts in Western Ethiopia (1936–41)," *International Journal of Historical Archaeology*, Vol. 37, No. 4 (2010): 566.
29. Ibid., 566.
30. Ibid.
31. Simone Fari, "Una fatica dimenticata: Operai modenesi in Africa orientale 1936–1941," in *Sognando l'impero: Modena-Addis Abeba (1935–1941)*, ed. Paolo Bertella Farnetti (Milan: Mimesis, 2007), 163–214.
32. Ertola, *L'impero immaginario*, 62.
33. Pallotti, "Ti scrivo dall'Abissinia," 189.
34. Ibid., 194, 202.
35. Ibid., 187.
36. Poggiali, *Agli albori dell'Impero*, 198.
37. Pierino Bertinotti, in Colombara, *Raccontare l'impero*, 110.
38. Poggiali, *Agli albori dell'Impero*, 163.
39. E.P., in Taddia, *La memoria dell'Impero*, 82.
40. Poggiali, *Agli albori dell'Impero*, 292–3.
41. "Testimony of Michael Tessema: Extract from Affidavit No. 32," in *Documents on Italian War Crimes Submitted to the United Nations War Crimes Commission by the Imperial Ethiopian Government. Vol. 2: Affidavits and Published Documents*, ed. Command of His Imperial Majesty (Addis Ababa: Ministry of Justice, 1950), 11–13.

42. Poggiali, *Agli albori dell'Impero*, 217.
43. Vincenzo Ambrosio, *Tre anni fra i Galla e i Sidama, 1937–1940: Lettere di un funzionario coloniale e testimonianze della sua morte sul campo* (Rome: Signorelli, 1942), 75.
44. Capatti and Montanari, *Italian Cuisine*, 252–7; David Gentilcore, *Pomodoro: A History of the Tomato in Italy* (New York: Columbia University Press, 2010), 99–170; Elizabeth Zanoni, *Migrant Marketplaces: Food and Italians in North and South America* (Urbana: University of Illinois Press, 2018).
45. Perry R. Wilson, "Cooking the Patriotic Omelette: Women and the Italian Fascist Ruralization Campaign," *European History Quarterly*, Vol. 27, No. 4 (1993): 351–47; Paul Corner, "Women in Fascist Italy: Changing Family Roles in the Transition from an Agricultural to an Industrial Society," *European History Quarterly*, Vol. 23, No. 1 (1997): 51–68; Kate Ferris, "Fare di ogni famiglia un fortilizio: The League of Nations' Economic Sanctions and Everyday Life in Venice," *Journal of Modern Italian Studies*, Vol. 11, No. 2 (2006): 117–42.
46. Colombara, *Raccontare l'impero*, 108–9.
47. Francesco Chiapparino and Renato Covino, *Consumi e industria alimentare in Italia dall'Unità a oggi: Lineamenti per una storia* (Perugia: Giada, 2002), 39–42, 52–8.
48. Poggiali, *Agli albori dell'Impero*, 215.
49. Purnima Mankekar, "India Shopping: Indian Grocery Stores and Transnational Configurations of Belonging," *Ethnos*, Vol. 67, No. 1 (2002): 75–97; Tulasi Srinivas, "As Mother Made It: The Cosmopolitan Indian Family, Authentic Food, and the Construction of Cultural Utopia," *International Journal of Sociology of the Family*, Vol. 32, No. 2 (2006): 191–221.
50. Francesco Bolongaro, in Colombara, *Raccontare l'impero*, 112–13.
51. Vergani, *La via nera*, 40.
52. Masotti, *Ricordi d'Etiopia*, 72.
53. Laura Nicoli, "La casa in Africa," in *Africa come un mattino*, ed. Fabio Roversi Monaco (Bologna: Tamari, 1969), 249.
54. Dicodimos Tesfamikel, in Volterra, *Sudditi coloniali*, 143.
55. T.T., in Irma Taddia, *Autobiografie africane: Il colonialismo nelle memorie orali* (Milan: Angeli, 1996), 85.
56. Adolfo Mignemi, *Lo sguardo e l'immagine: La fotografia come documento storico* (Turin: Bollati Boringhieri, 2003), ill. inset, photographs 13–17. For a visual culture discussion, Forgacs, *Italy's Margins*, 120–2. On Hailu Chebbede and the anti-Italian peasant revolt he led in northern Ethiopia in the summer of 1937, Gabriele Zorzetto, *La resistenza etiopica nel Lasta: Dalla rivolta anti-italiana di Hailu Chebbede del 1937 alle operazioni della primavera 1939* (Udine: Gaspari, 2019).
57. Mary Douglas and Baron C. Isherwood, *The World of Goods: Towards an Anthropology of Consumption* (New York: Routledge, 1996).
58. Diana Garvin, "Building Pasta's Empire: Barilla in Italian East Africa," *Modern Italy*, Vol. 28, No. 2 (2023): 97–126.
59. Egidio Antonioli, in Colombara, *Raccontare l'impero*, 31–2.
60. Pierino Bertinotti, in Colombara, *Raccontare l'impero*, 110.
61. Carlo Morengo, in Colombara, *Raccontare l'impero*, 111.
62. Francesco Bolongaro, in Colombara, *Raccontare l'impero*, 111.
63. "Il lavoro e l'assistenza sociale," 1067.
64. Ertola, *L'impero immaginario*, 72.
65. Fossa, *Lavoro italiano*, 245, 247.
66. Ertola, *L'impero immaginario*, 65n.
67. Sbacchi, *Ethiopia under Mussolini*, 100.

68. Franco La Cecla, *Pasta and Pizza* (Chicago: Prickly Paradigm Press, 2007).
69. Carol Helstosky, "Recipe for the Nation: Reading Italian History Through *La Scienza in Cucina* and *La Cucina Futurista*," *Food and Foodways*, Vol. 11, No. 2 (2003): 113–40.
70. Pierotti, *Vita in Etiopia*, 17.
71. Pallotti, "Ti scrivo dall'Abissinia," 188, 214.
72. Bahru Zewde, *History of Modern Ethiopia, 1855–1991* (Athens: Ohio University Press, 2001), 165, 171; Andrew Hilton, *The Ethiopian Patriots: Forgotten Voices of the Italo-Abyssinian War 1935–1941* (Chalford Stroud: Spellmount, 2008); Salome G. Egziabher, "The Ethiopian Patriots, 1936–1941," *The Ethiopian Observer* Vol. 12, no. 2 (1968): 63–91; Richard Pankhurst, "The Ethiopian Patriots: The Lone Struggle, 1936–1940," *The Ethiopian Observer* Vol. 13, no. 1 (1970): 40–56.
73. Del Boca, *Gli italiani in Africa Orientale*, 180n151.
74. O.G., in Taddia, *La memoria dell'Impero*, 138.
75. A.F., in Taddia, *La memoria dell'Impero*, 132.
76. Luigi Pilosio, "Grandi operazioni di polizia coloniale," in *Posti al sole: Diari e memorie di vita e di lavoro dalle colonie d'Africa*, ed. Nicola Labanca (Rovereto: Museo Storico Italiano della Guerra, 2001), 78.
77. Poggiali, *Diario AOI*, 70.
78. Ibid., 190.
79. Sbacchi, *Ethiopia under Mussolini*, 100–2.
80. Michele Sollai, "How to Feed an Empire? Agrarian Science, Indigenous Farming, and Wheat Autarchy in Italian-Occupied Ethiopia, 1937–1941," *Agricultural History*, Vol. 96, No. 3 (2022): 379–416.
81. Federica Saini Fasanotti, *Vincere: The Italian Royal Army's Counterinsurgency Operations in Africa, 1922–1940* (Annapolis, MD: Naval Institute Press, 2020), 126, 121.
82. A. J. Barker, *The Rape of Ethiopia 1936* (New York: Ballantine Books, 1971), 159.
83. Richard Pankhurst, "L'occupazione fascista nella letteratura etiopica," *Studi Piacentini*, No. 13 (1993): 135–48.
84. Richard Pankhurst, "Come il popolo etiopico resistette all'occupazione e alla repressione da parte dell'Italia fascista," in *Le guerre coloniali del fascismo*, ed. Angelo Del Boca (Rome: Laterza, 1991), 277.
85. "Letter signed 'a numerous group of workers' sent to Starace on March 5, 1937, forwarded by Lessona to Nasi on April 7, 1937," cited in Ertola, "White Slaves," 557, and Ertola, *L'Impero immaginario*, 53–4.
86. Charles Schaefer, "Serendipitous Resistance in Fascist-Occupied Ethiopia, 1936–1941," *Northeast African Studies*, Vol. 3, No. 1 (1996): 102.
87. Richard Pankhurst, "The Perpetuation of the Maria Theresa Dollar and Currency Problems in Italian-Occupied Ethiopia, 1936–1941," *Journal of Ethiopian Studies*, Vol. 8, No. 2 (1970): 96.
88. Schaefer, "Serendipitous Resistance," 99.
89. Sbacchi, *Ethiopia under Mussolini*, 100.
90. Tekalign Wolde-Mariam, "A City and Its Hinterlands: The Political Economy of Land Tenure, Agriculture, and Food Supply for Addis Ababa, Ethiopia (1887–1974)" (PhD Diss., Boston University, 1995), 229.
91. Fasanotti, *Vincere*, 125.
92. Ibid., 86.
93. Aregawi Berhe, "Revisiting Resistance in Italian-Occupied Ethiopia: The Patriots' Movement (1936–1941) and the Redefinition of Post-War Ethiopia," in *Rethinking Resistance Revolt and Violence in African History*, ed. Jon Abbink, Klaas van Walraven, and Mirjam de Bruijn (Leiden: Brill, 2003), 110.

94. Caroline Waldron Merithew, "'O Mother Race': Race, Italian Colonialism and the Fight to Keep Ethiopia Independent," *Zapruder World* Vol. 4 (2017): 1–31.
95. Adugna, "Women and Warfare," 19.
96. Ibid., 31–5.
97. Masotti, *Ricordi d'Etiopia*, 192.
98. Anthony Mockler, *Haile Selassie's War: The Italian-Ethiopian Campaign, 1935–1941* (New York: Random House, 1984), 364.
99. Masotti, *Ricordi d'Etiopia*, 214.
100. *Corriere dell'Impero*, September 10, 1939, cited in Ertola, *L'impero immaginario*, 46.
101. *Corriere dell'Impero*, June 13, 1940; *Corriere dell'Impero*, June 29, 1940, cited in Ertola, *L'impero immaginario*, 46.
102. Ertola, *L'Impero immaginario*, 212.
103. Jolanda Rapaccini, "Strade fiorite e filo spinato," in *Le italiane in Africa Orientale: Storie di donne in colonia*, ed. Fabrizio Di Lalla (Chieti: Solfanelli, 2014), 188–9.

4 Forbidden Commensality in a Supremacist Society: Food and Racial Segregation in Italian Ethiopia

1. Michel Foucault, *Power/Knowledge: Selected Interviews and Other Writings, 1972–1977* (New York: Vintage, 1980).
2. Francesco Cassata, *La difesa della razza: Politica, ideologia e immagine del razzismo fascista* (Turin: Einaudi, 2008).
3. Silvana Patriarca, *Il colore della Repubblica: "Figli della guerra" e razzismo nell'Italia postfascista* (Turin: Einaudi, 2021); Gianluca Gabrielli, "Un aspetto della politica razzista nell'impero: Il 'problema' dei meticci," *Passato e Presente* Vol. 15, No. 41 (1997): 77–105; Sòrgoni, *Parole e corpi*.
4. Richard Pankhurst, "Fascist Racial Policies in Ethiopia: 1922–1941," *Ethiopia Observer* Vol. 12, No. 4 (1969): 270–86; Ponzanesi, "The Color of Love"; Barrera, "Mussolini's Colonial Race Laws"; Giulietta Stefani, *Colonia per maschi: Italiani in Africa Orientale: Una storia di genere* (Verona: Ombre Corte, 2007); Angelica Pesarini, "'Blood Is Thicker Than Water': The Materialization of the Racial Body in Fascist East Africa," *Zapruder World: An International Journal for the History of Social Conflict*, Vol. 4 (2017): 1–15; Daniela Baratieri, "Itay's Sexual El Dorado in Africa," in *Imperial Expectations and Realities: El Dorados, Utopias and Dystopias*, ed. Andrekos Varnava (Manchester: Manchester University Press, 2015), 166–90; Giovanna Trento, "Madamato and Colonial Concubinage in Ethiopia: A Comparative Perspective," *Aethiopica*, Vol. 14, No. 1 (2011): 184–205.
5. "Direttive del Governo fascista per l'organizzazione dell'Impero, 5 agosto 1936," cited in Giorgio Rochat, *Il colonialismo italiano* (Turin: Loescher, 1973), 188–91.
6. Stoler, *Carnal Knowledge and Imperial Power*; Angela Woollacott, *Gender and Empire* (New York: Bloomsbury, 2006).
7. Camera dei Fasci e delle Corporazioni, "Atti della Commissione Legislativa degli Affari dell'Africa Italiana," *Discussione* (June 15, 1939): 27. Mussolini inquired about some episodes of relationships between Italian women and Ethiopian men he had heard of with a letter to the Undersecretary to Italian Africa Attilio Teruzzi

in the spring of 1938. Teruzzi replied that he excluded "the possibility that there are Italian women who mingle with Ethiopians. That kind of incident happened almost two years ago and was promptly terminated with the expulsion of those shameful, ignoble compatriots of ours." Cited in Del Boca, *Gli italiani in Africa Orientale*. In an October 1937 conversation with the German diplomat Vicco von Bülow-Schwante (1891–1970), the *Duce* had insisted that "the racial issue of the relations between White and Black people [in East Africa] was becoming urgent. After a long and accurate postal survey, he felt reassured to discover only three cases of Italian women in Africa who had forgotten who they were. He ordered that they be beaten, as a warning to others, and sent to a concentration camp for five years." Giulia Barrera, "Sessualità e segregazione nelle terre dell'Impero," in *L'Impero fascista: Italia ed Etiopia (1935–1941)*, ed. Riccardo Bottoni (Bologna: Il Mulino, 2008), 408.

8. Gabriella Campassi, "Il madamato in Africa Orientale: Relazioni tra italiani e indigene come forma di aggressione coloniale," *Miscellanea di storia delle esplorazioni*, Vol. 12 (1987): 219–60.
9. Michel Foucault, *Discipline and Punish: The Birth of the Prison* (New York: Vintage, 1995), 25.
10. "Tribunale di Addis Ababa, Udienza 13 gennaio 1938, Pres. Buongiorno, Imp. Puccinelli e Ascalè," *Il Foro Italiano*, Vol. 63 (1938): 278–9.
11. "Sentenza 3 gennaio 1939, imputato Manca, Corte d'Appello di Addis Abeba," cited in Gabrielli, "Colpevole di leso razzismo," 12.
12. "Sentenza 7 febbraio 1939, imputato Venturiello," *Razza e civiltà*, Vol. 1, No. 5 (1940), cited in Gabrielli, "Colpevole di leso razzismo," 12.
13. "R. Tribunale Penale di Gondar, Udienza 19 novembre 1938, Madamismo. Estremi. Qualità di 'sciarmutta' dell'indigena. Irrilevanza," *Rivista di Diritto Coloniale*, Vol. 2 (1939): 98.
14. Francesca Locatelli, "Migrating to the Colonies and Building the Myth of 'Italiani Brava Gente': The Rise, Demise, and Legacy of Italian Settler Colonialism," in *Italian Mobilities*, ed. Ruth Ben-Ghiat and S. Hom (New York: Routledge, 2015), 140–1.
15. Ruth Iyob, "Madamismo and Beyond: The Construction of Eritrean Women," *Nineteenth-Century Contexts*, Vol. 22, No. 2 (2000): 228–9.
16. Giorgio Rigotti, *L'edilizia nell'Africa Orientale Italiana: La zona di Addis Abeba* (Turin: Editrice Libraria Italiana, 1939), 126, cited in Mia Fuller, *Moderns Abroad: Architecture, Cities and Italian Imperialism* (New York: Routledge, 2006), 211.
17. Rigotti, *L'edilizia*, 128, cited in Fuller, *Moderns Abroad*, 211.
18. Rigotti, *L'edilizia*, 129–30, cited in Fuller, *Moderns Abroad*, 211–12.
19. Mark M. Smith, *How Race Is Made: Slavery, Segregation, and the Senses* (Chapel Hill: University of North Carolina Press, 2008); Dane Keith Kennedy, *Islands of White: Settler Society and Culture in Kenya and Southern Rhodesia, 1890–1939* (Durham, NC: Duke University Press, 1987); George M. Fredrickson, *White Supremacy: A Comparative Study in American and South African History* (New York: Oxford University Press, 1981); Angela Jill Cooley, "'Eating with Negroes': Food and Racial Taboo in the Twentieth-Century South," *Southern Quarterly*, Vol. 52, No. 2 (2015): 69–89; Elizabeth Guffey, "Knowing Their Space: Signs of Jim Crow in the Segregated South," *Design Issues*, Vol. 28, No. 2 (2012): 41–60; Chin Jou, "Neither Welcomed, Nor Refused: Race and Restaurants in Postwar New York City," *Journal of Urban History*, Vol. 40, No. 2 (2014): 232–51.
20. Jock McCulloch, *Black Peril, White Virtue: Sexual Crimes in Southern Rhodesia, 1902–1935* (Bloomington: Indiana University Press, 2000).

21. "Telegramma di Lessona a Graziani, n. 6759, 12 giugno 1936," cited in Barrera, *Colonial Affairs*, 311.
22. "Telespresso di Teruzzi al Governatore Generale dell'AOI, n. 15741, 26 dicembre 1937," cited in Barrera, *Colonial Affairs*, 311.
23. Ertola, *White Slaves*, 551.
24. Cited in Luca Acquarelli, *Il fascismo e l'immagine dell'impero: Retoriche e culture visuali* (Rome: Donzelli, 2022).
25. "Direttive per l'organizzazione e l'avvaloramento dell'AOI. Lessona a Graziani, 2 agosto 1936," cited in Dominioni, *Lo sfascio dell'impero*.
26. Angelo Del Boca, "Le leggi razziali nell'impero di Mussolini," in *Il regime fascista: Storia e storiografia*, ed. Angelo Del Boca, Massimo Legnani, and Mario G. Rossi (Rome: Laterza, 1995), 337–8.
27. Taddia, *Autobiografie africane*, 98, 100.
28. Ibid., 54.
29. Asfaha Chasai, in Volterra, *Sudditi coloniali*, 196.
30. Paulos Tesfemariam, in Volterra, *Sudditi coloniali*, 144.
31. Consociazione Turistica Italiana, *Guida*, 20.
32. Malaparte, *Viaggio in Etiopia*, 63.
33. Consociazione Turistica Italiana, *Guida*, 20.
34. Antonia Bellencin, "Abitazioni non così diverse," in Labanca, *Posti al sole*, 126.
35. Poggiali, *Diario AOI*, 206.
36. Vergani, *La via nera*, 11.
37. Ibid., 65–6. In a note from his private diary, Poggiali also reflected on the salvific effect of the experience of modernity brought about by technologically advanced objects of material culture for the transformation of food imported from Italy and sold in the *spacci*: "April 28, 1937. Stop on the plain of Weldiya. Large worker camp reminiscent of the Far West. Shacks equipped with everything; you can see that we are approaching Asmara, the source of the supply. It's quite something to see the gleam of an espresso coffee machine among all this wildness." Poggiali, *Diario AOI*, 214.
38. Vergani, *La via nera*, 66.
39. Ibid., 68.
40. On transnational grocery stores as spaces of socialization and belonging for diaspora consumers, Purnima Mankekar, "'India Shopping': Indian Grocery Stores and Transnational Configurations of Belonging," *Ethnos*, Vol. 67, No. 1 (2002): 75–98; Helen Vallianatos and Kim Raine, "Consuming Food and Constructing Identities among Arabic and South Asian Immigrant Women," *Food, Culture and Society*, Vol. 11, No. 3 (2008): 355–73.
41. Vergani, *La via nera*, 70–2.
42. Volterra, *Sudditi coloniali*, 196.
43. Jeff Forret, *Race Relations at the Margins: Slaves and Poor Whites in the Antebellum Southern Countryside* (Baton Rouge: Louisiana State University, 2010); Keri Leigh Merritt, *Masterless Men: Poor Whites and Slavery in the Antebellum South* (New York: Cambridge University Press, 2017).
44. W. E. B. Du Bois, *Black Reconstruction in America, 1860–1880* (New York: Free Press, 1998).
45. Francesca Locatelli, "La comunità italiana di Asmara negli anni Trenta tra propaganda, leggi razziali e realtà sociale," in Bottoni, *L'impero fascista*, 383–4.
46. Poggiali, *Diario AOI*, 56–7.
47. Ibid., 60.

48. Consociazione Turistica Italiana, *Guida*, 20.
49. Malaparte, *Viaggio in Etiopia*, 73.
50. Ibid.
51. Alda Brunelli, "Il ristoratore," in Labanca, *Posti al sole*, 207–8.
52. Brunelli, "Il ristoratore," 208–9.
53. Ibid., 209–10.
54. E.M., in Taddia, *La memoria dell'Impero*, 129.
55. Pallotti, "Ti scrivo dall'Abissinia," 212–13.
56. F.M., in Taddia, *La memoria dell'Impero*, 140.
57. Pallotti, "Ti scrivo dall'Abissinia," 205.
58. Ertola, *White Slaves*, 555.
59. Vergani, *La via nera*, 51.
60. Ibid., 57–8.
61. Carmine Conelli, "Razza, colonialità, nazione: Il progetto coloniale italiano tra Mezzogiorno e Africa," in Deplano and Pes, *Quel che resta dell'Impero*, 149–67; Vito Teti, *La razza maledetta: origini del pregiudizio antimeridionale* (Milan: Manifestolibri, 2011); D'Agostino, "Craniums, Criminals, and the Cursed Race."
62. Labanca, *Oltremare*, 391.
63. Dore, *Scritture di colonia*, 37.
64. Vittorio Natali-Morosow, "Memorie inopportune," Archivio Diaristico Nazionale, MP/08.
65. Poggiali, *Diario AOI*, 127, 208.
66. A.P., in Taddia, *La memoria dell'Impero*, 142.
67. Pallotti, "Ti scrivo dall'Abissinia," 212.
68. R.G., in Taddia, *La memoria dell'Impero*, 143.
69. Dicodimos Tesfamikel, in Volterra, *Sudditi coloniali*, 143.
70. Berhane Ghebregherghis, in Volterra, *Sudditi coloniali*, 142.
71. T.T., in Taddia, *La memoria dell'Impero*, 85.
72. Ghebremicael (Gherenchiel) Feseha, in Volterra, *Sudditi coloniali*, 145.
73. Berachi Menghescia Hailu, in Volterra, *Sudditi coloniali*, 145.
74. Mia Fuller, "Building Power: Italy's Colonial Architecture and Urbanism, 1923–1940," *Cultural Anthropology*, Vol. 3, No. 4 (1988): 455–87.
75. G. M. Angioi, "Idee sulla colonizzazione fascista," *Etiopia Latina*, Vol. 2, Nos. 11–12 (1938): 44, cited in Olindo De Napoli, "Disciplinare i coloni: Sessualità e razzismo in *Etiopia Latina*," *S-nodi*, Nos. 15–16 (2017): 217.
76. Marco Antonsich, "Segni del potere sul territorio: Iconografie urbane in Etiopia, 1936–1941" (PhD Diss., Università di Trieste, 1997), 3.
77. "Città di Addis Abeba. Relazione dell'attività svolta dagli uffici dell'amministrazione municipale dal gennaio 1939 all'aprile 1940," cited in Gian Luca Podestà, "Le città dell'Impero: La fondazione di una nuova civiltà italiana in Africa Orientale," *Città e Storia*, Vol. 4, No. 1 (2009): 129.
78. Fossa, *Lavoro italiano*, 245–6.
79. Ertola, *L'Impero immaginario*, 65n395.
80. Consociazione Turistica Italiana, *Guida*, 20.
81. Ibid.
82. *Corriere dell'Impero*, January 23, 1938, cited in Ertola, *In terra d'Africa*, 51.
83. *Corriere dell'Impero*, January 12, 1939, cited in Ertola, *In terra d'Africa*, 51.
84. Giuseppe Serra, "Il pittore di Ras," in Labanca, *Posti al sole*, 204.
85. *Il Giornale di Addis Abeba*, June 16, 1936, cited in Ertola, *In terra d'Africa*, 50.

86. *Corriere dell'Impero*, July 7, 1937; November 21, 1937; October 31, 1937, cited in Ertola, *In terra d'Africa*, 51–2.
87. *Corriere dell'Impero*, December 20, 1936; January 26, 1937, cited in Ertola, *In terra d'Africa*, 63n374.
88. At the end of the first complete year of occupation (1936), "437 business licenses [including restaurants] [were issued] to Italians, while only 316 had been given to foreigners (128 stateless person of Armenian origin, 129 Greeks, fifteen Germans, ten Lebanese, nine French, six Russians, four Syrians, four Hungarians, four English, three Indians, one Albanian, one Egyptian, one Swiss, one Austrian). 138 licenses were denied to Italian applicants; as many as 248 were rejected from foreign applicants (146 for insufficient capital, eighty-one for political reasons, fifty-two for incompetence and inadequacy, fifty-two for an excess number of establishments in the same trade, fifteen for sanitary reasons)." *Corriere dell'Impero*, January 26, 1937, cited in Ertola, *L'Impero immaginario*, 63n378.
89. Podestà, "Le città dell'Impero," 130.
90. Gherardo Bosio, "Future città dell'Impero," *Architettura*, Vol. 16, No. 2 (1937): 427, cited in Fuller, *Moderns Abroad*, 206.
91. Fuller, *Moderns Abroad*, 206.
92. Contardo Bonicelli, "L'urbanistica nell'impero italiano e il piano regolatore di Addis Abeba," in *Opere per l'organizzazione civile in Africa Orientale Italiana* (Addis Ababa: Servizio Tipografico del Governo Generale A.O.I., 1939), 257, cited in Antonsich, *Segni del potere sul territorio*, 150–1.
93. Bahru Zewde, *A History of Modern Ethiopia, 1855–1991* (Oxford: James Currey, 2002), 163–4, 196–7; Kibur Kassie and Daniel Lirebo, "The Impact of Multi-Story Commercial Buildings on the Heritage Values of Open Market in Addis Ababa," *Journal of Architectural Engineering Technology*, Vol. 10, No. 9 (2021): 1–7.
94. Diana Garvin, "Constructing Race through Commercial Space: Merkato Ketema under Fascist Urban Planning," *Journal of Modern Italian Studies*, Vol. 25, No. 2 (2020): 118–48.
95. *Corriere dell'Impero*, September 23, 1938, cited in Pankhurst, "Fascist Racial Policies in Ethiopia," 279.
96. Giornale Luce B0974, *Il mercato di Addis Abeba*, October 14, 1936, Archivio Storico Luce.
97. Cristina Lombardi-Diop, "Spotless Italy: Hygiene, Domesticity, and the Ubiquity of Whiteness in Fascist and Postwar Consumer Culture," *California Italian Studies*, Vol. 2, No. 1 (2011): 1–22.
98. Catherine Cocks, *Doing the Town: The Rise of Urban Tourism in the United States, 1850–1915* (Berkeley: University of California Press, 2001); Seth Koven, *Slumming: Sexual and Social Politics in Victorian London* (Princeton: Princeton University Press, 2005); Chad Heap, *Slumming: Sexual and Racial Encounters in American Nightlife, 1885–1940* (Chicago: University of Chicago Press, 2009); Johannes Novy, "Urban Ethnic Tourism in New York's Neighborhoods: Then and Now," in *Selling Ethnic Neighborhoods: The Rise of Neighborhoods as Places of Leisure and Consumption*, ed. Volkan Aytar and Jan Rath (New York: Routledge, 2013), 16–33.
99. Manlio La Sorsa, "Etnografie e nik nik," in Labanca, *Posti al sole*, 123.

100. Enrico Bartolozzi, "I mercati indigeni dell'Etiopia e la loro funzione nel quadro dell'economia indigena," *Agricoltura Coloniale*, Vol. 37, No. 2 (1943): 44.
101. Ibid., 44–5.
102. Ibid., 46, 48.
103. Zewde, *A History of Modern Ethiopia*, 170–3.
104. Maria Giaconia Landi, *Crocerossina in Africa Orientale* (Milan: Treves, 1938), 123, cited in Ertola, *In terra d'Africa*, 132.
105. Wolde-Mariam, *A City and Its Hinterlands*, 214–17.
106. Poggiali, *Agli albori dell'Impero*, 337–8.
107. Wolde-Mariam, *A City and Its Hinterlands*, 216–17.
108. Richard Pankhurst, "A Chapter in Ethiopia's Commercial History: Developments during the Fascist Occupation, 1936–41," *Ethiopia Observer*, Vol. 14, No. 1 (1971): 48.
109. Evelyn Waugh, *Waugh in Abyssinia* (Baton Rouge: Louisiana State University Press, 2007), 232.
110. Ladislas Sava [Sáska László], "Ethiopia under Mussolini's Rule," *New Times and Ethiopia News*, December 7, 1940, cited in Pankhurst, "A Chapter in Ethiopia's Commercial History," 47.
111. Wolde-Mariam, *A City and Its Hinterlands*, 218–34; Larebo, "Empire Building and Its Limitations."
112. Poggiali, *Agli albori dell'Impero*, 346, 348.
113. Kassie and Lirebo, "The Impact of Multi-Story Commercial Buildings."
114. A landscape view of the new Merkato is in the photograph *Veduta dall'alto del mercato indigeno di Addis Abeba affollato di persone* (View from above of the Indigenous Market of Addis Ababa Crowded with People), Reparto Africa Orientale Italiana (1935–1938), codice foto AO00005661, 1936–1937, Archivio Storico Luce.
115. Masotti, *Ricordi d'Etiopia*, 119.
116. Benti, *Urban Growth in Ethiopia*, 81–120.
117. Poggiali, *Agli albori dell'Impero*, 206.
118. Vergani, *La via nera*, 81–2.
119. Quaranta, *Ethiopia*, 16.
120. Lino Calabrò, *Intermezzo africano: Ricordi di un Residente di Governo in Etiopia (1937–1941)* (Rome: Bonacci, 1988), 43–4.
121. Calabrò, *Intermezzo africano*, 54.
122. Poggiali, *Agli albori dell'Impero*, 300–1.
123. Ibid., 51.
124. Ertola, *L'Impero immaginario*, 231.
125. Barrera, *Colonial Affairs*, 338–9.
126. Massi, "Economia dell'Africa Italiana," 424.
127. A.L., in Taddia, *La memoria dell'Impero*, 127.
128. Barrera, "Mussolini's Colonial Race Laws," 430.
129. bell hooks, "Eating the Other"; Iyob, "Madamismo and Beyond"; Barrera, "Dangerous Liaisons"; Barrera, "Sessualità e segregazione"; Sòrgoni, *Parole e corpi*.
130. Y.H., in Taddia, *Autobiografie africane*, 128.
131. Barrera, *Colonial Affairs*, 304.
132. Ibid., 322–3.

5 Liminal Colonial Gastronomies: Ethiopian-Italian Food Encounters in the Interstices of Segregation

1. Bhabha, *The Location of Culture*.
2. Ferruccio Botti, *La logistica dell'esercito italiano (1831–1981). Vol. 3: Dalla guerra totale alla guerra integrale (1919–1940)* (Rome: Ufficio Storico dell'Esercito Italiano, 1994), 602–5.
3. A.F., in Taddia, *La memoria dell'Impero*, 132.
4. Giuseppe Barbera, *L'Africa non fa paura* (Rome: Unione editoriale d'Italia, 1937), 44, cited in Nicola Labanca, "Constructing Mussolini's New Man in Africa? Italian Memories of the Fascist War on Ethiopia," *Italian Studies*, Vol. 41, No. 2 (2006): 229.
5. Sergio Botta, "Valeva la pena?" in Labanca, *Posti al sole*, 144.
6. Botta, "Valeva la pena?" 148–9.
7. Ilvo Piccone, "Quello che il cronista vede," in Labanca, *Posti al sole*, 211.
8. Giovanni Di Modica, *Cinghia: Scarpe in A.O.* (Turin: R. Mariano, 1937), 58.
9. Poggiali, *Agli albori dell'Impero*, 205.
10. Luigi Marini, "La paura del combattimento," in Labanca, *Posti al sole*, 50–1.
11. Sergio Botta, "Nuovi cibi," in Labanca, *Posti al sole*, 121.
12. Botta, "Nuovi cibi," 121–2.
13. Giuseppe Morettini, "La fatica della conquista," in Labanca, *Posti al sole*, 143.
14. Luigi Pilosio, "Grandi operazioni di polizia coloniale," in Labanca, *Posti al sole*, 150–1.
15. Pilosio, "Grandi operazioni di polizia coloniale," 80.
16. Masotti, *Ricordi d'Etiopia*, 205.
17. Ibid., 205–6.
18. Ibid., 200.
19. Giulietta Stefani, "Italiani e ascari: Percezioni e rappresentazioni dei colonizzati nell'Africa Orientale Italiana," *Italian Studies*, Vol. 41, No. 2 (2006): 207–23; Uoldelul Chelati Dirar, "From Warriors to Urban Dwellers: Ascari and the Military Factor in the Urban Development of Colonial Eritrea," *Cahiers d'études africaines*, No. 175 (2004): 533–74.
20. On the feminization of the male colonized subject, Mrinalini Sinha, *Colonial Masculinity: The "Manly Englishman" and the "Effeminate Bengali" in the Late Nineteenth Century* (Manchester: Manchester University Press, 1995).
21. Unno Bellagamba, "Quattordici luglio," in Labanca, *Posti al sole*, 90; Masotti, *Ricordi d'Etiopia*, 105.
22. Lino Calabrò, *Intermezzo africano: Ricordi di un Residente di Governo in Etiopia (1937–1941)* (Rome: Bonacci, 1988), 106.
23. Malaparte, *Viaggio in Etiopia*, 173–4. Emphases are original.
24. Ibid., 117, 106. Emphases are original.
25. Elizabeth Pleck, "The Making of the Domestic Occasion: The History of Thanksgiving in the United States," *Journal of Social History*, Vol. 32, No. 4 (1999): 773–89; Janet Siskind, "The Invention of Thanksgiving: A Ritual of American Nationality," *Critique of Anthropology*, Vol. 12, No. 2 (1992): 167–91.
26. Calabró, *Intermezzo africano*, 83–5.
27. Giuseppe Berto, *Un po' di successo* (Milan: Longanesi, 1963), 11–28.
28. Vittorio Gorresio, *La vita ingenua* (Milan: Rizzoli, 1980), 127.
29. Manlio La Sorsa, "Il mio viaggio in Africa," Archivio Diaristico Nazionale, DG/95, cited in Stefani, "Italiani e ascari," 218.

30. Aldo Polcri, "Il soldato e il negretto," in Labanca, *Posti al sole*, 252.
31. Barrera, *Colonial Affairs*, 339–40.
32. On the colonial origins of the discourse on the superiority of European cuisines, Rebecca Earle, *The Body of the Conquistador: Food, Race and the Colonial Experience in Spanish America, 1492–1700* (New York: Cambridge University Press, 2012); Alison Blunt, "Imperial Geographies of Home: British Domesticity in India, 1886-1925," *Transactions of the Institute of British Geographers*, Vol. 24, No. 4 (1999): 421–40; Richard Wilk, "A Taste of Home: The Cultural and Economic Significance of European Food Exports to the Colonies," in *Food and Globalization: Consumption, Markets and Politics in the Modern World*, ed. Alexander Nuetzenadel and Frank Trentmann (New York: Bloomsbury, 2008), 93–108; Rachel Laudan, *Cuisine and Empire: Cooking in World History* (Berkeley: University of California Press, 2015).
33. Istituto Coloniale Fascista, *Elementi pratici di vita coloniale per le organizzazioni femminili del Partito Nazionale Fascista* (Rome: Castaldi, 1938); Istituto Coloniale Fascista, *Nozioni coloniali per le organizzazioni femminili del Partito Nazionale Fascista* (Rome: Castaldi, 1938), 71–166; Dario Poggiali, "La donna italiana in A.O.," *Almanacco della donna italiana*, Vol. 20 (1939): 53–73; Silvia Benedettini, "La donna italiana in Africa Orientale," *Almanacco della donna italiana*, Vol. 18 (1937): 399–402; Barbara Spadaro, "Intrepide massaie: Genere, imperialismo e totalitarismo nella preparazione coloniale femminile durante il fascismo (1937–1943)," *Contemporanea*, Vol. 13, No. 1 (2010): 27–52.
34. Antonella Cagnolati, "Dreaming of Distant Lands: How Fascism Built Colonial Women (1937–1941)," *Historia y Memoria de la Educación*, Vol. 17 (2023): 205–33.
35. Prospector, "I corsi di preparazione della donna alla vita coloniale," *Africa Italiana*, Vol. 3, Nos. 2–3 (1940): 19–24. The emphasis is original.
36. Giuseppe Acanfora, "Consigli di igiene coloniale per le donne," *Africa Italiana*, Vol. 3, Nos. 2–3 (1940): 46.
37. Acanfora, "Consigli di igiene coloniale per le donne," 46.
38. Istituto Coloniale Fascista, *Nozioni coloniali*, 127.
39. Ibid., 128–9.
40. Istituto Coloniale Fascista, *Elementi pratici*, 41.
41. Luigi Piccinato, "La donna e la casa in colonia," *Africa Italiana*, Vol. 3, Nos. 2–3 (1940): 50.
42. Ibid., 50–1. On early twentieth-century European domestic architecture, reflecting middle-class family ideologies, mentalities, and behaviors, Philippe Ariès, Michelle Perrot, and Georges Duby, *A History of Private Life: From the Fires of Revolution to the Great War* (Cambridge, MA: Belknap Press, 1994).
43. Piccinato, "La donna e la casa in colonia," 51.
44. Alex Butchart, *The Anatomy of Power: European Constructions of the African Body* (New York: Zed Books, 1998).
45. Barrera, *Colonial Affairs*, 342.
46. Alberto Sbacchi, *Il colonialismo italiano in Etiopia, 1936–1940* (Milan: Mursia, 2009), 227.
47. Vergani, *La via nera*, 86.
48. Dore, *Scritture di colonia*. Some of Pezzoli's letters are also reproduced and cited in the history of food in unified Italy, Emanuela Scarpellini, *A tavola! Gli italiani in 7 pranzi* (Rome: Laterza, 2012).
49. Dore, *Scritture di colonia*, 21.
50. Ibid.

51. Ann Laura Stoler, *Race and the Education of Desire: Foucault's History of Sexuality and the Colonial Order of Things* (Durham, NC: Duke University Press, 2000).
52. Dore, *Scritture di colonia*, 22.
53. Vergani, *La via nera*, 94.
54. de Grazia, *How Fascism Ruled Women*.
55. Dore, *Scritture di colonia*, 11, 13.
56. Ibid., 21.
57. Ibid., 15.
58. Scarpellini, *A tavola!* 130–1.
59. Ibid., 131; Dore, *Scritture di colonia*, 21.
60. Scarpellini, *A tavola!* 130; Dore, *Scritture di colonia*, 20–1.
61. Rapaccini, "Strade fiorite," 168–9, 207.
62. Calabrò, *Intermezzo africano*, 17.
63. Pallotti, "Ti scrivo dall'Abissinia," 194.
64. Masotti, *Ricordi d'Etiopia*, 111–12.
65. Ibid., 37–8.
66. Ambrosio, *Tre anni*, 56.
67. Calabrò, *Intermezzo africano*, 60.
68. Masotti, *Ricordi d'Etiopia*, 84.
69. Psyche A. Williams-Forson, *Building Houses out of Chicken Legs: Black Women, Food, and Power* (Chapel Hill: University of North Carolina Press, 2006); Frederick Douglass Opie, *Hog and Hominy: Soul Food from Africa to America* (New York: Columbia University Press, 2010); Adrian Miller, *Soul Food: The Surprising Story of an American Cuisine, One Plate at a Time* (Chapel Hill: University of North Carolina Press, 2017); Rafia Zafar, *Recipes for Respect: African American Meals and Meaning* (Athens: University of Georgia Press, 2019).
70. Diana Garvin, "Imperial Wet-Nursing in Italian East Africa," in *The Routledge Companion to Sexuality and Colonialism*, ed. Chelsea Schields and Dagmar Herzog (New York: Routledge, 2021), 145–58.
71. Francesco Cassata, *Building the New Man: Eugenics, Racial Science and Genetics in Twentieth-Century Italy* (Budapest: Central European University Press, 2011), 223–84; Alexander De Grand, "Women under Italian Fascism," *Historical Journal*, Vol. 19, No. 4 (1976): 947–68.
72. Giuseppe Lucidi, "L'alimentazione del bambino in colonia," *La difesa della razza*, Vol. 2, No. 11 (1939): 15–16. Emphasis (capitalization of words) is original.
73. Ibid., 16.
74. Haile M. Larebo, "The Myth and Reality of Empire Building Italian Land Policy and Practice in Ethiopia, 1935–1941" (PhD Diss., University of London School of Oriental and African Studies, 1990), 181.
75. Rapaccini, "Strade fiorite," 182, 192.
76. Chiara Volpato, "La violenza contro le donne nelle colonie italiane: Prospettive psicosociali di analisi," *DEP: Deportate esuli profughe*, Vol. 10 (2009): 110–31. On prostitution and colonialism, Stoler, *Carnal Knowledge and Imperial Power*; Philippa Levine, *Prostitution, Race and Politics: Policing Venereal Disease in the British Empire* (New York: Routledge, 2003); Julie Peakman, *Licentious Worlds: Sex and Exploitation in Global Empires* (New York: Reaktion Books, 2019); Luise White, *The Comforts of Home: Prostitution in Colonial Nairobi* (Chicago: University of Chicago Press, 1990).
77. Malaparte, *Viaggio in Etiopia*, 63–4.
78. Seifu, *A Historical Survey of Jimma Town*, 23.

79. Tekola, *Narratives of Three Prostitutes in Addis Ababa*.
80. Seifu, *A Historical Survey of Jimma Town*, 23.
81. Richard Parkhurst, "The History of Prostitution in Ethiopia," *Journal of Ethiopian Studies*, Vol. 12, No. 2 (1974): 159–78.
82. On White women brothels in Ethiopia, the settler-painter Giuseppe Serra wrote in his diary: "The bars, cafes, and hotels of Addis Ababa would make those in Italy jealous. There are even different types of brothels: for fifteen, ten, and five lire. There is one as cheap as three lire. The women who work in these brothels are almost all Italians who came here from every Italian city, and some from abroad. The [fascist] regime wants these brothels to operate to serve the military who are here single." Serra, "Il pittore di Ras," in Labanca, *Posti al sole*, 204.
83. Barrera, *Colonial Affairs*, 344–5.
84. Diel, *Behold Our New Empire*, 91.
85. Manlio La Sorsa, "Etnografie e nik nik," in Labanca, *Posti al sole*, 123–4.
86. La Sorsa, "Etnografie e nik nik," 124.
87. Poggiali, *Diaro AOI*, 219–20.
88. Berto, *Un po' di successo*, 11–28.
89. Dirasse, *The Commoditization of Female Sexuality*.
90. Poggiali, *Diario AOI*, 248.
91. Sam Chapple-Sokol, "Culinary Diplomacy: Breaking Bread to Win Hearts and Minds," *Hague Journal of Diplomacy*, Vol. 8 (2013): 161–83; Fatin Mahirah Solleh, "Gastrodiplomacy as a Soft Power Tool to Enhance Nation Brand," *Journal of Media and Information Warfare*, Vol. 7 (2015): 161–99; Đana Luša and Ružica Jakešević, "The Role of Food in Diplomacy: Communicating and 'Winning Hearts and Minds' through Food," *Media Studies*, Vol. 8, No. 16 (2017): 99–119; Paul S. Rockower, "Recipes for Gastrodiplomacy," *Place Branding and Public Diplomacy*, Vol. 8 (2012): 235–46.
92. Luigi Goglia, ed., *Colonialismo e fotografia: Il caso italiano* (Messina: Sicania, 1990).
93. Scarpellini, *A tavola!* 131.
94. Dore, *Scritture di colonia*, 14.
95. Luigi Pignatelli Della Leonessa, "Tre generazioni," in Roversi Monaco, *Africa come un mattino*, 267–8.
96. Poggiali, *Diario AOI*, 72–3.
97. Fanon, *Black Skin, White Masks*.
98. On the Gramscian concept of cultural hegemony, David Forgacs, ed., *The Antonio Gramsci Reader: Selected Writings 1916–1935* (New York: New York University Press, 2000).
99. Poggiali, *Agli albori dell'Impero*, 202–3.
100. Masotti, *Ricordi d'Etiopia*, 105–6.
101. Ariès et al., *A History of Private Life*, 271–4.
102. Kifleyesus, "The Construction"; McCann, *Stirring the Pot*, 94–6.
103. Masotti, *Ricordi d'Etiopia*, 177.
104. Ibid., 104–5.
105. Pierre Bourdieu, *Distinction: A Social Critique of the Judgement of Taste* (Cambridge, MA: Harvard University Press, 1984).
106. Dore, *Scritture di colonia*, 17.
107. Ibid., 28.
108. Malaparte, *Viaggio in Etiopia*, 134.

109. Calabrò, *Intermezzo africano*, 24–5. On Oromo–Italian relations, Alessia Alvisini, "I rapporti politico-economici fra gli oromo e l'Italia: Alleanze e ambiguità," *Africa*, Vol. 55, No. 4 (2000): 489–521; Ezekiel Gebissa, "The Italian Invasion, the Ethiopian Empire, and Oromo Nationalism: The Significance of the Western Oromo Confederation of 1936," *Northeast African Studies*, Vol. 9, No. 3 (2002): 75–96; Fekede Sileshi Fufa and Ketebo Abdiyo, "The Reactions of Limmu Oromo of Western Ethiopia during and after the Italian Occupation (1936–41)," *Research on Humanities and Social Sciences*, Vol. 8, No. 21 (2018): 38–44; Ahmed Hassen Omer, "The Italian Impact on Ethnic Relations: A Case Study of a Regional Policy in Northern Shoa (Ethiopia), 1936–1941," *Annales d'Éthiopie*, Vol. 16 (2000): 147–59.
110. E. P. Thompson, "The Moral Economy of the English Crowd in the Eighteenth Century," *Past and Present*, No. 50 (1971): 76–136.
111. Calabrò, *Intermezzo africano*, 75.
112. Ibid., 29–30.
113. Ibid., 30.
114. Ibid., 39–40.
115. Poggiali, *Diario AOI*, 131.
116. Ibid., 125.
117. Dore, *Scritture di colonia*, 28.
118. Masotti, *Ricordi d'Etiopia*, 181.
119. Poggiali, *Diario AOI*, 81–2.
120. Ibid., 237–8.
121. Serra, "Il pittore di Ras," 205–6.
122. Ibid., 207.
123. Barrera, *Colonial Affairs*, 322–3.
124. Ertola, *L'Impero immaginario*, 62. The definition of "mechanized peddling" to describe this business is from Gian Luca Podestà, *Il mito dell'impero: Economia, politica e lavoro nelle colonie italiane dell'Africa orientale 1898–1941* (Turin: Giappichelli, 2004), 312.
125. Franco Ciarlantini, *Seconda guerra* (Milan: Mondadori, 1938), 65.
126. Barrera, *Colonial Affairs*, 225–6.
127. Ibid., 226.
128. Le Houérou, "Gender and Sexual Abuses."
129. Ibid., 258. Emphases are original.
130. Simone Cinotto, *The Italian American Table: Food, Family, and Community in New York City* (Urbana: University of Illinois Press, 2013).
131. Le Houérou, "Gender and Sexual Abuses," 261.
132. Hannah Arendt, *Eichmann in Jerusalem: A Report on the Banality of Evil* (New York: Penguin Books, 2006).
133. Le Houérou, "Gender and Sexual Abuses," 265.
134. Marie Louise Pratt, *Imperial Eyes: Travel Writing and Transculturation* (New York: Routledge, 1992), 3.
135. Ambrosio, *Tre anni*, 80.
136. Dore, *Scritture di colonia*, 6.
137. Calabrò, *Intermezzo africano*, 103–4.
138. Vergani, *La via nera*, 37.
139. Pallotti, "Ti scrivo dall'Abissinia," 205.
140. Vergani, *La via nera*, 84–5.

141. Masotti, *Ricordi d'Etiopia*, 34.
142. Giuseppe Bottai, *Diario 1935–1944* (Milan: Rizzoli, 1982), 115.
143. Masotti, *Ricordi d'Etiopia*, 82.
144. Rapaccini, "Strade fiorite," 220–1.
145. Baudendistel, *Between Bombs and Good Intentions*, 233.
146. Ibid., 242.
147. Ibid., 227.
148. Giornale Luce B0925, "La liberazione dei prigionieri di guerra," July 22, 1936, Archivio Storico Luce.
149. Bob Moore and Kent Fedorowich, *The British Empire and Its Italian Prisoners of War, 1940–1947* (New York: Palgrave Macmillan, 2002); Bob Moore, "Enforced Diaspora: The Fate of Italian Prisoners of War during the Second World War," *War in History* Vol. 22, No. 2 (2015): 174–90; Elena Bellina, "Space and Violence in WWII Italian Captivity in Africa," *Italian Studies*, Vol. 75, No. 4 (2020): 426–40; H. A. P. Smit, "Italian Prisoners of War in South Africa during the Second World War: Circumstances and Contributions," in *Military Geoscience: A Multifaceted Approach to the Study of Warfare*, ed. Aldino Bondesan and Judy Ehlen (Cham: Springer, 2022), 165–82; Laura Ruberto, "Creative Expression and the Material Culture of Italian POWs in the United States during World War II," *Material Culture Review/Revue de la culture matérielle*, Vol. 92 (2022): 3–32.
150. Emanuele Ertola, "Navi bianche: Il rimpatrio dei civili italiani dall'Africa Orientale," *Passato e presente*, No. 91 (2014): 127–43.
151. Masotti, *Ricordi d'Etiopia*, 228.
152. Mario Cassisa, *Le mie memorie di guerra e di prigionia, 1940–1946* (Trapani: Monitor, s.d.), 90–1.
153. Calabró, *Intermezzo africano*, 138, 140–1.
154. Rapaccini, "Strade fiorite," 222.
155. Felice Benuzzi, "Preparativi segreti," in Roversi Monaco, *Africa come un mattino*, 21.
156. Cassisa, *Le mie memorie di guerra e di prigionia*, 96.
157. Campbell, *The Addis Ababa Massacre*.
158. Matteo Dominioni, "La repressione di ribellismo e dissentismo in Etiopia, 1936–1941," in *Crimini di guerra: Il mito del bravo italiano tra repressione del ribellismo e guerra ai civili nei territori occupati*, ed. Luigi Borgomaneri (Milan: Guerini e Associati, 2006), 1–18.
159. Baudendistel, *Between Bombs and Good Intentions*, 233.
160. On the Ethiopian War Crimes Commission (1946–9), Richard Pankhurst, "Italian Fascist War Crimes in Ethiopia: A History of Their Discussion, from the League of Nations to the United Nations (1936–1949)," *Northeast African Studies*, Vol. 6, Nos. 1–2 (1999): 83–140.
161. Michael Blatta Bekele Hapte, "Extract from Affidavit No. 18," in *Documents on Italian War Crimes Submitted to the United Nations War Crimes Commission by the Imperial Ethiopian Government. Vol. 2: Affidavits and Published Documents* (Addis Ababa: Ministry of Justice of Ethiopia, 1950), 8.
162. Ibid., 9.
163. Imru Zelleke, "My Collection of Fascist Italy's Occupation of Ethiopia," *Ethiopian Review: Ethiopian News and Opinion Journal*, February 22, 2012.
164. Tessema, "Extract from Affidavit No. 32," 11–13.

6 The Empire of the Senses: Food Tastes, Disgusts, and Identities in Italian Ethiopia

1. David Howes, ed., *Empire of the Senses: The Sensual Culture Reader* (New York: Routledge, 2020); Andrew J. Rotter, *Empires of the Senses: Bodily Encounters in Imperial India and the Philippines* (New York: Oxford University Press, 2019); Daniela Hacke and Paul Musselwhite, eds., *Empire of the Senses: Sensory Practices of Colonialism in Early America* (Leiden: Brill, 2017). The quote from Mussolini is in Bottai, *Diario 1935–1944*, 115.
2. Mark M. Smith, *Sensing the Past: Seeing, Hearing, Smelling, Tasting and Touching in History* (Berkeley: University of California Press, 2007).
3. Marshall McLuhan, *The Gutenberg Galaxy: The Making of Typographic Man* (Toronto: University of Toronto Press, 1967).
4. Alain Corbin, *The Foul and the Fragrant: Odor and the French Social Imagination* (Cambridge, MA: Harvard University Press, 1986).
5. Rotter, *Empires of the Senses*, 233.
6. David Sutton, "Food and the Senses," *Annual Review of Anthropology*, Vol. 39 (2011): 209–23.
7. Wolfgang Schivelbusch, *Tastes of Paradise: A Social History of Spices, Stimulants and Intoxicants* (New York: Vintage Books, 1993).
8. Paul Freedman, ed., *Food: The History of Taste* (Berkeley: University of California Press, 2007), 22.
9. Bourdieu, *Distinction*.
10. Botta, "Nuovi cibi," 121.
11. Ferdinando Martini, *Nell'Affrica Italiana* (Milan: Touring Editore, 1998), 106–7.
12. Vittorio Beonio Bricchieri, *Cieli d'Etiopia: Avventure di un pilota di guerra* (Milan: Mondadori, 1936), 238.
13. Poggiali, *Agli albori dell'Impero*, 211.
14. Dore, *Scritture di colonia*, 20.
15. Nino Dolfin, *Solo col mio cuore: Diario di guerra di un legionario in A.O.* (Vicenza: Arti Grafiche delle Venezie, 1936), 37.
16. Emilio Ceretti, *Con l'esercito italiano in AOI: Dal passaggio del Mareb alla battaglia di Scirè* (Milan: Mondadori, 1937), 88.
17. Ibid., 88; Salvatore Farfaglio, *Le bande autocarrate dei fedelissimi da Roma ad Addis Ababa* (Pisa: Nistri-Lischi, 1937), 84.
18. Silvio Meloni, *Il redivivo dell'Adì-Abò: Diario di nove mesi di prigionia nella guerra dell'impero* (Grottaferrata: Scuola Tipografica Italo-Orientale S. Nilo, 1939), 62.
19. Bellencin, "Abitazioni non così diverse," 125.
20. Warwick Anderson, "Excremental Colonialism: Public Health and the Poetics of Pollution," *Critical Inquiry*, Vol. 21, No. 3 (1996): 640–99.
21. Masotti, *Ricordi d'Etiopia*, 184.
22. Ibid., 175–6.
23. *Collins English Dictionary*, 13th ed. (New York: HarperCollins, 2018).
24. Taddia, *Autobiografie africane*.
25. Masotti, *Ricordi d'Etiopia*, 25, 28, 36.
26. E.P., in Taddia, *La memoria dell'Impero*, 82.
27. Nicoli, "La casa in Africa," 248.
28. Maria Luisa Astaldi, *Voci sull'altipiano* (Milan: Mondadori, 1943), 226.

29. bell hooks, "Eating the Other"; Smith, *How Race Is Made*.
30. McClintock, *Imperial Leather*; Stoler, *Carnal Knowledge and Imperial Power*.
31. Sòrgoni, "Defending the Race."
32. Nicoletta Poidimani, "'Faccetta Nera': I crimini sessuali del colonialismo fascista nel Corno d'Africa," in *Crimini di guerra: Il mito del bravo italiano tra repressione del ribellismo e guerra ai civili nei territori occupati*, ed. Luigi Borgomaneri (Milan: Guerini e Associati, 2006).
33. Lidio Cipriani, *Un assurdo etnico: L'impero etiopico* (Florence: Bemporad, 1935), 181.
34. Paolo Monelli, "Moglie e buoi dei paesi tuoi," *Gazzetta del Popolo*, June 13, 1936.
35. Carlo Domenici, "Le parole … e i fatti," *Il 420*, July 5, 1936. On political cartoons' contribution to the racist discourse about Italian East Africa, Mirco Dondi, "Il razzismo coloniale del fascismo e i suoi riflessi alla radio e sulla stampa (1935–36)," *I sentieri della ricerca*, Vols. 7–8 (2008): 281–331.
36. Lidio Cipriani, "Riti e superstizioni," *La difesa della razza*, Vol. 4, No. 10 (1941): 18–21.
37. L.B., in Taddia, *La memoria dell'Impero*, 85–6.
38. Consociazione Turistica Italiana, *Guida*, 21.
39. Masotti, *Ricordi d'Etiopia*, 170–1.
40. Poggiali, *Agli albori dell'Impero*, 334–5.
41. Ambrosio, *Tre anni*, 67.
42. R.G., in Taddia, *La memoria dell'Impero*, 110.
43. Costanza Bonelli, "Clima, razza, colonizzazione: Nascita e sviluppo della medicina tropicale in Italia" (PhD Diss., Università di Roma Sapienza, 2019), 289.
44. Ambrosio, *Tre anni*, 83–4.
45. Gianni Dore, "Vi dirò qualcosa di questa gente nera: Un bellunese in Somalia (1934–1936)," *Un bellunese in Somalia: Lettere di Edoardo Costantini a Polpet (1934–1936)*, ed. Istituto Storico Bellunese della Resistenza e dell'Età Contemporanea (Padua: CLUEP, 2001), 17.
46. Scarfone, "La nevrastenia sotto i tropici."
47. Consociazione Turistica Italiana, *Guida*, 21.
48. Masotti, *Ricordi d'Etiopia*, 112–13.
49. Gonzales-Ruibal, "Fascist Colonialism," 565–6.
50. Ibid., 564. On the disciplination of the body through the practices of everyday life, Michel de Certeau, *The Practice of Everyday Life* (Berkeley: University of California Press, 1984).
51. Rapaccini, "Strade fiorite," 177.
52. Masotti, *Ricordi d'Etiopia*, 175.
53. Antonio M. Morone, "Amministrazione, confini e mobilità nello spazio coloniale italiano: Il caso della Somalia," in Rosoni and Chelati Dirar, *Votare con i piedi*, 270.
54. Bhabha, *The Location of Culture*, 121–31.
55. Poggiali, *Agli albori dell'Impero*, 211.
56. Pellegrino Matteucci, *In Abissinia: Viaggio* (Milan: F.lli Treves, 1880), cited in Dore, "Per un repertorio," 9–10.
57. Aida Edemariam, *The Wife's Tale: A Personal History* (London: 4th Estate, 2014), 76.
58. Palmiro Forzini, "Avventura africana," Archivio Diaristico Nazionale, MG/88, 26.
59. Masotti, *Ricordi d'Etiopia*, 105.
60. Vergani, *La via nera*, 14–15.
61. Ibid., 45–6.
62. Masotti, *Ricordi d'Etiopia*, 33.
63. Calabró, *Intermezzo africano*, 118.

64. Ambrosio, *Tre anni*, 93.
65. Ibid., 50.
66. Ibid., 188.
67. Dore, "Vi dirò qualcosa," 11. For a social history of the fat body, Peter N. Stearns, *Fat History: Bodies and Beauty in the Modern West* (New York: New York University Press, 2002).
68. Pallotti, "Ti scrivo dall'Abissinia," 187.
69. Calabrò, *Intermezzo africano*, 75.
70. Dore, "Vi dirò qualcosa," 43.
71. Ibid., 11–12.
72. Barrera, "Patrilinearità, razza e identità."
73. Calabrò, *Intermezzo africano*, 80.
74. Ibid., 101–2.
75. David Lowenthal, *The Past Is a Foreign Country* (New York: Cambridge University Press, 2015).
76. Calabró, *Intermezzo africano*, 63–4.
77. Ibid., 71–2.
78. Ibid., 80–1.
79. Ibid., 72–3.
80. Pratik Chakrabarti, *Medicine and Empire: 1600–1960* (New York: Palgrave Macmillan, 2013).
81. Poggiali, *Agli albori dell'Impero*, 287.
82. Panfilo Panara, "L'ospedale da campo in Massaua e le vicende sanitarie del corpo di spedizione dal febbraio al settembre 1885," *Giornale medico del R. Esercito e della R. Marina*, Nos. 4–5 (1886): 447.
83. Calabró, *Intermezzo africano*, 40.
84. Carlo Annaratone, "Le condizioni igieniche dell'Eritrea," in *L'Eritrea economica: Prima serie di conferenze tenute in Firenze sotto gli auspici della Società di Studi Geografici e Coloniali* (Novara: Istituto Geografico De Agostini, 1913), 449–50.
85. Dore, "Vi dirò qualcosa," 12.
86. Armiero and Graf von Hardenberg, "Green Rhetoric in Blackshirts."
87. Speech by Benito Mussolini to the people of Reggio Emilia, October 30, 1926, cited in Armiero and Graf von Hardenberg, "Green Rhetoric in Blackshirts," 284.
88. Istituto Coloniale Fascista, *Elementi pratici*, 30.
89. Fossa, *Lavoro italiano*, 455.
90. Ibid., 468.
91. Poggiali, *Agli albori dell'Impero*, 345.
92. Ambrosio, *Tre anni*, 51.
93. Jonathan Saha, *Colonizing Animals* (New York: Cambridge University Press, 2021; James L. Hevia, *Animal Labor and Colonial Warfare* (Chicago: University of Chicago Press, 2018); John Miller, *Empire and the Animal Body: Violence, Identity and Ecology in Victorian Adventure Fiction* (London: Anthem Press, 2012); Saheed Aderinto, *Animality and Colonial Subjecthood in Africa: The Human and Nonhuman Creatures of Nigeria* (Athens: Ohio University Press, 2022).
94. Fanon, *The Wretched of the Earth*, 42.
95. Poggiali, *Agli albori dell'Impero*, 334.
96. Sem Benelli, *Io in Africa: Con una conclusione politica* (Milan: Mondadori, 1936), 51.
97. Dore, "Vi dirò qualcosa," 5–6.
98. Ibid., 7.

99. Ibid.
100. Calabró, *Intermezzo africano*, 78–9.
101. Istituto Coloniale Fascista, *Nozioni coloniali*, 77–8.
102. Masotti, *Ricordi d'Etiopia*, 41.
103. Calabró, *Intermezzo africano*, 28.
104. Ibid., 95.
105. Ibid., 93.
106. Masotti, *Ricordi d'Etiopia*, 36–7.
107. Sergio Botta, "Addio Etiopia," Archivio Diaristico Nazionale, MG/90.
108. Calabró, *Intermezzo africano*, 16–17.
109. Ibid., 67.
110. Ibid., 32.
111. Ibid., 80.
112. Ibid., 81–3.
113. Gino Bernardini, "Novità tristi e paurose," in Labanca, *Posti al sole*, 137–8.
114. Masotti, *Ricordi d'Etiopia*, 70–1.

Conclusion: Fascist Colonial Crops and the Legacies of the Empire of Food

1. Alessia Donà, "The Rise of the Radical Right in Italy: The Case of *Fratelli d'Italia*," *Journal of Modern Italian Studies*, Vol. 27, No. 5 (2022): 775–94.
2. Virginia Picolillo, "Lollobrigida: 'Difenderò le nostre eccellenze: La sovranità alimentare non è un concetto fascista,' " *Corriere della Sera*, October 23, 2022.
3. Andrea Bulleri, "Ristoranti italiani all'estero, dagli ingredienti alle ricette fino al personale: Il ministro Lollobrigida annuncia un disciplinare," *Il Messaggero*, March 6, 2023.
4. Picolillo, "Lollobrigida."
5. Dani Rodrik, "Why Does Globalization Fuel Populism? Economics, Culture, and the Rise of Right-Wing Populism," *Annual Review of Economics*, Vol. 13 (2021): 133–70.
6. Giulia Carbonaro, " 'Poor Eat Better Than Rich': Italy's Food Sovereignty Minister Sparks Outrage with Shock Statement," *Euronews*, August 25, 2023.
7. James Imam, "Let Them Eat Pasta! Poor Italians 'Have Better Diet,' " *The Times*, August 28, 2023; "Farm Minister Spurs Ire for Saying Poor Eat Better Than Rich: 'Hope Lollobrigida Becomes Poor' Says Opposition," *Ansa News*, August 24, 2023.
8. Luisa Mosello, "Mai più mangiare insetti senza saperlo: Arrivano i decreti Lollobrigida," *La Repubblica*, March 23, 2023.
9. Lela London, "Italy Proposes a Ban on Lab-Grown Meats to Protect Its Food Heritage," *Forbes*, March 29, 2023; Angela Giuffrida, "Italian Plan to Ban Lab-Grown Food Criticized as Misguided," *The Guardian*, March 29, 2023.
10. Stef Bottinelli, "Cultured Meat Is 'a Veritable Suicide for a Country Like Ours,' Says Italy Minister of Agriculture Francesco Lollobrigida," *Food Matters*, April 28, 2023.
11. Ibid.
12. Francesco Lollobrigida, post on Facebook, June 11, 2023.
13. Francesco Lollobrigida, post on Facebook, May 29, 2023.

14. "Food Summit: Meloni: 'Russia riconsideri sua decisione': Il presidente del Consiglio interviene al vertice dei sistemi alimentari ONU, ospitato dalla FAO," *European Food Agency News*, July 24, 2023.
15. Ben-Ghiat, *Fascist Modernities*, 123–70.
16. Chris Otter, *Diet for a Large Planet: Industrial Britain, Food Systems, and World Ecology* (Chicago: University of Chicago Press, 2020).
17. D'Onofrio, "The Microfoundations of Italian Agrarianism"; Paolo Sorcinelli, "Identification Process at Work: Virtues of the Italian Working-Class Diet in the First Half of the Twentieth Century," in *Food, Drink and Identity: Cooking, Eating and Drinking in Europe since the Middle Ages*, ed. Peter Scholliers (New York: Berg, 2001), 81–98; Helstosky, "Recipe for the Nation."
18. Massi, "Economia dell'Africa Italiana," 425.
19. McCann, *People of the Plow*, 210.
20. Otter, *Diet for a Large Planet*.
21. Donald Crummey, "Ethiopian Plow Agriculture in the Nineteenth Century," *Journal of Ethiopian Studies*, Vol. 16 (1983): 1–23.
22. McCann, *People of the Plow*, 100, 102.
23. Massi, "Economia dell'Africa Italiana," 425–6.
24. Poggiali, *Agli albori dell'Impero*, 221.
25. Sergio Boninsegni, "Esperimenti di coltivazione di frumenti italiani ad Ugri nel 1937," *Agricoltura Coloniale*, Vol. 32, No. 5 (1938): 205–10.
26. Getnet Bekele, *Ploughing New Ground: Food, Farming and Environmental Change in Ethiopia* (Rochester, NY: Boydell & Brewer, 2017), 58–9.
27. Sollai, "How to Feed an Empire," 390.
28. Raffaele Ciferri and Guido R. Giglioli, "I frumenti duri e piramidali dell'Etiopia" *Autarchia Alimentare*, Vol. 2, No. 1 (1939): 16–18; Raffaele Ciferri and Guido R. Giglioli, "Considerazioni pratiche sul problema della produzione frumentaria nell'AOI," *Agricoltura Coloniale*, Vol. 33, No. 12 (1939): 660–5; Raffaele Ciferri and Enrico Bartolozzi, "La produzione cerealicola dell'AOI nel 1938," *Agricoltura Coloniale*, Vol. 34, No. 11 (1940): 441–50; Raffaele Ciferri and Enrico Bartolozzi, "La produzione cerealicola dell'AOI nel 1938," *Agricoltura Coloniale*, Vol. 34, No. 12 (1940): 502–15; Raffaele Ciferri, "I cereali dell'Africa Italiana," *Rassegna Economica dell'Africa Italiana*, Vol. 30, No. 1 (1942): 10–27.
29. Chiudero and Rocchetti, "L'avvaloramento in Etiopia," 365–6.
30. Larebo, *The Building of an Empire*, 253–9.
31. Cited in Sollai, "How to Feed an Empire," 399.
32. Bekele, *Ploughing New Ground*, 58.
33. Sollai, "How to Feed an Empire," 403–4.
34. Sabato Visco, "Autarchia alimentare," *Autarchia Alimentare*, Vol. 1, No. 5 (1938): 3–12.
35. James McCann, *From Poverty to Famine in Northeast Ethiopia: A Rural History, 1900–1935* (Philadelphia: University of Pennsylvania Press, 1987), 73–4.
36. Getnet Bekele, "Contingent Variables and Discerning Farmers: Marginalizing Cattle in Ethiopia's Historically Crop-Livestock Integrated Agriculture (1840–1941)," *Northeast African Studies*, Vol. 9, No. 2 (2002): 83–100.
37. Chiudero and Rocchetti, "L'avvaloramento in Etiopia," 314–19.
38. Fossa, *Lavoro italiano nell'Impero*, 464.
39. Tito M. Bettini, *Il problema del miglioramento del bestiame bovino indigeno nell'Africa Orientale Italiana* (Florence: Istituto agricolo coloniale italiano, 1938).
40. Massi, "Economia dell'Africa Italiana," 430.

41. Poggiali, *Agli albori dell'Impero*, 287.
42. Kristin Hoganson, "Meat in the Middle: Converging Borderlands in the U.S. Midwest, 1865–1900," *Journal of American History*, Vol. 98, No. 4 (2012): 1025–51.
43. Poggiali, *Agli albori dell'Impero*, 215–16.
44. Ibid., 217.
45. Getnet Bekele, "Contingent Variables."
46. Calabrò, *Intermezzo africano*, 94.
47. Holger Weiss, "'Dying Cattle': Some Remarks on the Impact of Cattle Epizootics in the Central Sudan during the Nineteenth Century," *African Economic History*, Vol. 26 (1998): 182.
48. Francesco Valori, "Il problema zootecnico in AOI," *Annali dell'Africa Italiana*, Vol. 1, Nos. 3–4 (1938): 1043.
49. Vittorio Cilli, "La bonifica antipestosa nell'Impero ed il problema biologico delle carni africane conservate col freddo ai fini dell'autarchia alimentare," *Società italiana per il progresso delle scienze*, Vol. 28, No. 3 (1938): 259–72.
50. Valori, "Il problema zootecnico," 1042–45.
51. Calabrò, *Intermezzo africano*, 55.
52. Richard Pankhurst, "The Great Ethiopian Famine, 1888–1892: A New Assessment," *Journal of the History Applied Sciences*, Vol. 21, No. 2 (1966): 109.
53. John A. Rowe and Kjell Hødnebø, "Rinderpest in the Sudan, 1888–1890: The Mystery of the Missing Panzootic," *Sudanic Africa*, Vol. 5 (1994): 153–7.
54. Armiero and Graf von Hardenberg, "Green Rhetoric in Blackshirts"; Peder Anker, *Imperial Ecology: Environmental Order in the British Empire, 1895–1945* (Cambridge, MA: Harvard University Press, 2001).
55. Freidberg, *French Beans and Food Scares*; Laura T. Raynolds, "The Globalization of Organic Agro-Food Networks," *World Development*, Vol. 32, No. 5 (2004): 725–43.
56. Associazione Nazionale Cerealisti, "Import/export cerealicolo in Italia nel primo mese del 2023," press release, April 20, 2023.
57. Paul Kirby, "Italy Moves to Ban Lab-Grown Meat to Protect Food Heritage," *BBC News*, March 29, 2023.
58. Mike Davis, *Late Victorian Holocausts: El Niño Famines and the Making of the Third World* (London: Verso, 2001), 9.
59. Karl Polanyi, *The Great Transformation* (Boston: Beacon Press, 1957), 159–60.
60. Davis, *Late Victorian Holocausts*, 128.
61. Poggiali, *Agli albori dell'Impero*, 210.
62. Peveri, *The Edible Gardens of Ethiopia*, 65.
63. Rodolfo Graziani, *La giornata coloniale dell'anno XVI in Roma: Parole pronunciate da S.E. il Maresciallo d'Italia Rodolfo Graziani il 22 maggio 1938 al Teatro Adriano* (Roma: Istituto Fascista dell'Africa Italiana, 1938), 14.
64. Guido Abbattista, *Umanità in mostra: Esposizioni etniche e invenzioni esotiche in Italia (1880–1940)* (Trieste: Edizioni Università di Trieste, 2013); Nicola Labanca, ed., *L'Africa in vetrina: Storie di musei e di esposizioni coloniali in Italia* (Treviso: Pagus, 1992); Giuliana Tomasella, *Esporre l'Italia coloniale: Interpretazioni dell'alterità* (Padua: Il Poligrafo, 2017); Giovanni Arena, "The Last Exhibition of the Italian Colonial Empire: Naples 1938–40," in *Cultures of International Exhibitions 1840–1940: Great Exhibitions in the Margins*, ed. Marta Filipová (New York: Routledge, 2016), 313–32.
65. Julia Adeney Thomas and Geoff Eley, eds., *Visualizing Fascism: The Twentieth-Century Rise of the Global Right* (Durham, NC: Duke University Press, 2020).

66. Filmato Luce D029902, *In giro per il mondo: Abissinia*, 1932–1937, Archivio Storico Luce; Fidotta, *Un impero cinematografico*, 98. Other Istituto Luce's newsreels describing Ethiopian foodways are Giornale Luce B0833, *Gondar antica capitale etiopica*, 1936; Cronache dell'Impero CI003, *Harar, Baccà*, 1937; Giornale Luce B0603, *La coltivazione delle banane*, 1935; Cronache dell'Impero CI004, *Galla e Sidamo, Uondo*, 1937.
67. Alessandro Pes, "Becoming Imperialist: Italian Colonies in Fascist Textbooks for Primary Schools," *Journal of Modern Italian Studies*, Vol. 18, No. 5 (2013): 599–614.
68. Priscilla Manfren, *Icone d'Oltremare nell'Italia fascista: Artisti, illustratori e vignettisti alla conquista dell'Africa* (Trieste: Edizioni Università di Trieste, 2019).
69. Poggiali, *Agli albori dell'Impero*, 179.
70. Ibid., 180, 185–6.
71. Diana Garvin, *Feeding Fascism: The Politics of Women's Food Work* (Toronto: University of Toronto Press, 2021); Patrizia Caccia, "Libri, cucina e sanzioni," *La fabbrica del libro*, Vol. 15, No. 2 (2009): 21–7.
72. Nina, "Quattro chiacchiere con le lettrici," *La Cucina Italiana*, Vol. 8, No. 1 (1936): 3.
73. Maria Paris, "Cucina etiopica: Zighiné," *La Cucina Italiana*, Vol. 8, No. 9 (1936): 32.
74. Amedeo Pettini, "Le cronache della cucina: Piccolo contributo ad una grande soluzione," *La Cucina Italiana*, Vol. 9, No. 11 (1937): 20–1.
75. Ravi Arvind Palat, "Empire, Food and the Diaspora: Indian Restaurants in Britain," *South Asia: Journal of South Asian Studies*, Vol. 38, No. 2 (2015): 171–86.
76. Fanny Dini, "Fioriscano le culle, si celebrano le nozze d'oro, si colonizzano le terre dell'Impero," *La Cucina Italiana*, Vol. 8, No. 6 (1937): 3.
77. U. C. Monti, "Elogio scientifico al pepperoncino," *La Cucina Italiana*, Vol. 9, No. 1 (1938): 29.
78. Amalia Piscel, "Una nuova conquista della cucina italiana," *La Cucina Italiana*, Vol. 9, No. 9 (1937): 21.
79. Amalia Piscel, "Per l'autarchia alimentare: Come allestire le carni di agnello castrato, capretto e capra," *La Cucina Italiana*, Vol. 9, No. 10 (1937): 20–1.
80. Amedeo Pettini, "Le cronache della cucina," *La Cucina Italiana*, Vol. 10, No. 6 (1938): 20–1.
81. Frida, "L'A.B.C. della cucina: Corrispondenza delle abbonate," *La Cucina Italiana*, Vol. 7, No. 2 (1936): 8.
82. Elena Morozzo della Rocca, "Signorilità in tempo di guerra," *La Cucina Italiana*, Vol. 6, No. 12 (1935): 12–13.
83. Giuliana, "Gelati di frutta," *La Cucina Italiana*, Vol. 8, No. 7 (1937): 28; Amedeo Pettini, "Dolci casalinghi," *La Cucina Italiana*, Vol. 8, No. 8 (1937): 30; Amedeo Pettini, "Dolci casalinghi," *La Cucina Italiana*, Vol. 8, No. 10 (1937): 31.
84. Frida, "L'A.B.C. della cucina," *La Cucina Italiana*, Vol. 10, No. 1 (1939): 20.
85. Amedeo Pettini, "L'articolo del maestro," *La Cucina Italiana*, Vol. 11, No. 3 (1940): 53; L'Innominata, "Dolci senza zucchero," *La Cucina Italiana*, Vol. 11, No. 10 (1940): 225.
86. Roderick Abbott, "A Socio-Economic History of the International Banana Trade, 1870–1930," *European University Institute Working Papers* No. 22 (2009); Raffaele Ciferri, "Le razze di banane coltivate nella Somalia," *Rivista di biologia coloniale*, Vol. 1, No. 3 (1938): 171–81.
87. Labanca, *Oltremare*, 275, 277–8.
88. Regia Azienda Monopolio Banane, "Il monopolio delle banana," 987.
89. Enrico Cibelli, "Le banane della Somalia," *L'Illustrazione Italiana*, Vol. 65, No. 41 (1938): 552–5; Enloe, *Bananas, Beaches and Bases*, 211–49.

90. A. Camposanpiero, "L'industria delle banana in Somalia," *Rivista delle colonie italiane*, Vol. 7, No. 12 (1933): 971–7.
91. Regia Azienda Monopolio Banane, "Il monopolio delle banana," 990.
92. Cibelli, "Le banane della Somalia," 552.
93. Ibid., 555.
94. Luigi Fioresi, "L'industria del banano in Somalia," in *Atti del Terzo Congresso di Studi Coloniali (Firenze-Roma 12–17 aprile 1937)*, ed. Centro di Studi Coloniali, Istituto Coloniale Fascista (Firenze: Sansoni, 1937), 663.
95. Giuseppe Fabriani, "Le banane della Somalia," *Autarchia alimentare*, Vol. 2, No. 2 (1939): 20.
96. Enrico Cibelli, "La Regia Azienda Monopolio Banane, creazione fascista," *Rassegna Economica dell'Africa Italiana*, Vol. 25, No. 11 (1937): 1705.
97. Fabriani, "Le banane della Somalia": 21.
98. Ibid.
99. Filippo Bottazzi, *Le banane frutto di alto valore nutrizionale* (Rome: Societa Anonima Italiana Arti Grafiche, 1936).
100. Cibelli, "Le banane della Somalia," 552–5.
101. Emilio Conforti, *L'esportazione delle banane dalla Somalia italiana dagli inizi ad oggi e i suoi futuri sviluppi* (Florence: Istituto Agronomico per l'Africa italiana, 1939).
102. Regia Azienda Monopolio Banane, "Il monopolio delle banana," 992.
103. Ibid.
104. Frida, "Consigli a Rosetta: Ancora per le massaie inesperte," *La Cucina Italiana*, Vol. 7, No. 4 (1936): 8–9.
105. Eleonora della Pura, "Vini tipici e frutta invece di caffè," *La Cucina Italiana*, Vol. 10, No. 6 (1939): 164.
106. Frederick G. Meyer, "Notes on Wild Coffee Arabica from Southwestern Ethiopia, with Some Historical Considerations," *Economic Botany*, Vol. 19, No. 2 (1965): 136–51.
107. Jeffrey T. Schnapp, "The Romance of Caffeine and Aluminum," *Critical Inquiry*, Vol. 28, No. 1 (2001): 244–69.
108. Jonathan Morris, "Making Italian Espresso, Making Espresso Italian," *Food & History*, Vol. 8, No. 2 (2010): 155–84.
109. Francesco Weigelsperg di Caneva, "La valorizzazione del caffè etiopico," *Rassegna economica dell'Africa Italiana*, Vol. 15, No. 12 (1937): 1731–42; Rivera, *Prospettive di colonizzazione*, 75–108.
110. Merid W. Aregay, "The Early History of Ethiopia's Coffee Trade and the Rise of Shawa," *Journal of African History*, Vol. 29, No. 1 (1988): 19–25.
111. Enrico Bartolozzi, "Il commercio del caffè nell'AOI," *Agricoltura Coloniale*, Vol. 32, No. 7 (1938): 316–19.
112. Diana Garvin, "The Italian Coffee Triangle: From Brazilian *Colonos* to Ethiopian *Colonialisti*," *Modern Italy*, Vol. 26, No. 3 (2021): 291–312.
113. Fabrizio Cortesi, "Il caffè etiopico," *Annali dell'Africa Italiana*, Vol. 1, Nos. 3–4 (1938): 990.
114. Felice Venezian, Massimo Oblath, Antonio Redondi, and Augusto Valinotti, "Il caffè dell'Impero: Relazione sui lavori svolti dalla missione in A.O.I. dalla Compagnia Italiana Importatori Caffè," *Annali dell'Africa Italiana*, Vol. 1, Nos. 3–4 (1938): 996.
115. Massi, "Economia dell'Africa Italiana," 457.
116. Larebo, *The Myth and Reality*, 210.

117. Raffaele Ciferri, "Problemi del caffé nell'Africa Orientale Italiana," *Agricoltura Coloniale*, Vol. 34, No. 4 (1940): 144.
118. Ibid., 136–7. The emphasis is original.
119. Istituto Centrale di Statistica, *Sommario di statistiche storiche dell'Italia, 1861–1965* (Rome: Istituto Centrale di Statistica, 1968), 135.
120. Ciferri, "Problemi del caffé," 138.
121. Poggiali, *Agli albori dell'Impero*, 212.
122. Venezian et al., "Il caffè dell'Impero," 1016. Formed in 1913, the Belgian Société Belge des Plantations d'Abyssinie was the largest of these, extending over 5,000 acres. In 1935, Société Belge had 1,700,000 coffee plants and employed an African labor force of 2,000. Larebo, *The Myth and Reality*, 260.
123. Venezian et al., "Il caffè dell'Impero," 1002.
124. Cortesi, "Il caffè etiopico," 983.
125. Bartolozzi, "Il commercio del caffè," 316.
126. Cerulli, "La colonizzazione del Harar," 75–6.
127. Ciferri, "Problemi del caffé," 142.
128. Cerulli, "La colonizzazione del Harar," 75–6.
129. Venezian et al., "Il caffè dell'Impero," 1016. Four-fifths of the area's coffee were shipped to Addis Ababa, and then for the most part to Djibouti via railroad; one-fifth to Gambela, and from there to Sudan. Bartolozzi, "Il commercio del caffè," 317.
130. Chiudero and Rocchetti, "L'avvaloramento in Etiopia," 311.
131. According to Cortesi and Bartolozzi, these included the higher-value Kaffa; Ennara; Jimma, high in caffeine; Sidama; and Nekemte, of a quality similar to Harar, also used in blends. Cortesi, "Il caffè etiopico," 984; Bartolozzi, "Il commercio del caffè," 316–17.
132. Guluma Gemeda, "The Rise of Coffee and the Demise of Colonial Autonomy: The Oromo Kingdom of Jimma and Political Centralization in Ethiopia," *Northeast African Studies*, Vol. 9, No. 3 (2002): 58–9.
133. Bartolozzi, "Il commercio del caffè," 317.
134. Cortesi, "Il caffè etiopico," 982.
135. Even in his enchanted description, Cortesi suggested that the task of developing a modern coffee agroindustry in the Oromo region was challenging because "coffee farmers used very imperfect systems and rudimentary methods. One cannot speak of a true coffee culture because they exploited the spontaneous production and, at most, grow a certain number of plants near their homes for convenience." Cortesi, "Il caffè etiopico," 982–3.
136. Venezian et al., "Il caffè dell'Impero," 1002–3.
137. Ibid., 1008.
138. Ibid., 1009. The same complaints are reported in Chiudero and Rocchetti, "L'avvaloramento in Etiopia," 312.
139. Cortesi, "Il caffè etiopico," 987.
140. Poggiali, *Agli albori dell'Impero*, 213–14.
141. Birhanu Bitew Geremew, "The Tragedy of Colonialism in a Non-colonized Society: Italy's Historical Narratives and the Amhara Genocide in Ethiopia," *Journal of Asian and African Studies*, Vol. 58, No. 5 (2023): 1–12.
142. Cortesi, "Il caffè etiopico," 983.
143. Ibid., 988–90.
144. Poggiali, *Agli albori dell'Impero*, 214–15.
145. Venezian et al., "Il caffè dell'Impero," 1008, 1009.

146. Edoardo Carlo Branzanti, "Linee programmatiche per il miglioramento delle colture del caffè nell'Africa orientale Italiana," *Agricoltura Coloniale*, Vol. 34, No. 2 (1940): 60–5; Edoardo Carlo Branzanti, "La coltura del caffè nel Gimma," *Agricoltura Coloniale*, Vol. 36, No. 1 (1942): 1–8.
147. Saraiva, *Fascist Pigs*, 150–3.
148. Chiudero and Rocchetti, "L'avvaloramento in Etiopia," 387–90.
149. Felice Guarneri, *Battaglie economiche tra le due grandi guerre. Vol. 2* (Milan: Garzanti, 1953), 197.
150. Larebo, *The Myth and Reality*, 210.
151. Ibid., 269.
152. Cortesi, "Il caffè etiopico," 981–2.
153. Fossa, *Lavoro italiano*, 509–14.
154. Larebo, *The Myth and Reality*, 269.
155. Ibid., 202.
156. Ibid., 204.
157. Sbacchi, "Italian Colonization in Ethiopia," 510.
158. John M. Cohen, "Effects of Green Revolution Strategies on Tenants and Small-Scale Landowners in the Chilalo Region of Ethiopia," *Journal of Developing Areas*, Vol. 9, No. 3 (1975): 335–58.
159. Poggiali, *Agli albori dell'Impero*, 214.
160. Cortesi, "Il caffè etiopico," 991.
161. Poggiali, *Agli albori dell'Impero*, 215.
162. Bartolozzi, "Il commercio del caffè," 318.
163. Guarneri, *Battaglie economiche*, 197.
164. Poggiali, *Agli albori dell'Impero*, 284.
165. Biagio Borgatta, in Colombara, *Raccontare l'impero*, 110.
166. Ambrosio, *Tre anni*, 50.
167. Ibid., 232.
168. Pierotti, *Vita in Etiopia*, 69.
169. Birhanu Tsegaye Sisay, "Coffee Production and Climate Change in Ethiopia," in *Sustainable Agriculture Reviews 33: Climate Impact on Agriculture*, ed. Eric Lichtfouse (New York: Springer, 2018), 99–113; Joel Iscaro, "The Impact of Climate Change on Coffee Production in Colombia and Ethiopia," *Global Majority*, Vol. 5, No. 1 (2014): 33–43.
170. McCann, *People of the Plow*, 174.
171. Leslie H. Brown, "Coffee, the Main Crop," *Ethiopia Observer*, Vol. 2, No. 7 (1958): 231–2.
172. David Ciarlo, *Advertising Empire: Race and Visual Culture in Imperial Germany* (Cambridge, MA: Harvard University Press, 2011); Ramamurthy, *Imperial Persuaders*; McClintock, *Imperial Leather*, 207–31.
173. Adam Arvidsson, "Between Fascism and the American Dream: Advertising in Interwar Italy," *Social Science History*, Vol. 25, No. 2 (2001): 155–7; Victoria de Grazia, "Nationalizing Women: The Competition between Fascist and Commercial Cultures in Mussolini's Italy," in *The Sex of Things: Gender and Consumption in Historical Perspective*, ed. Victoria de Grazia with Ellen Furlough (Berkeley: University of California Press, 1996), 337–56.
174. Arvidsson, "Between Fascism and the American Dream," 157.
175. Pinkus, "Shades of Black," 135–7; Pinkus, *Bodily Regimes*, 41–6.

176. Pinkus, "Shades of Black," 78; Pinkus, *Bodily Regimes*; Lombardi-Diop, "Spotless Italy."
177. de Grazia, "Nationalizing Women."
178. Arvidsson, "Between Fascism and the American Dream," 161–9; Irene Di Jorio, "Pubblicità e propaganda durante il fascismo: Saperi e transfer di competenze fra mercato e politica," *Italia Contemporanea*, No. 291 (2019): 209–36.
179. Ciarlo, *Advertising Empire*, 4.
180. Ibid., 5.
181. Pinkus, "Shades of Black," 148.
182. Pinkus, *Bodily Regimes*, 76–8; Pinkus, "Shades of Black," 146–8.
183. Fioresi, "L'industria del banano in Somalia," 659.
184. Rebecca Ruth Falkoff, "After Autarchy: Male Subjectivity from Carlo Emilio Gadda to the Gruppo 63" (PhD Diss., University of California Berkeley, 2012), 102–5.
185. The Italian parliament finally disbanded AMB in 1964 when its directors were convicted of corruption. Enrico Gregori, "11 maggio 1964: Chiuso il processo per il business delle banane somale," *Il Messaggero*, May 7, 2015.
186. Pinkus, *Bodily Regimes*, 25.
187. Ibid., 54–5; Pinkus, "Shades of Black," 141–2.
188. Marcello Scalzo and Benedetta Terenzi, "Communication's Strategies and Images: The Case of Federico Seneca in Perugina," in *Proceedings of the 2nd International and Interdisciplinary Conference on Image and Imagination*, ed. Enrico Cicalò (New York: Springer, 2016), 544–8.
189. Pinkus, *Bodily Regimes*, 44.
190. Ibid., 59.
191. Pinkus, "Shades of Black," 144–6.

Bibliography

Abbattista, Guido. *Umanità in mostra: Esposizioni etniche e invenzioni esotiche in Italia (1880–1940)* (Trieste: Edizioni Università di Trieste, 2013).
Abbott, Roderick. "A Socio-economic History of the International Banana Trade, 1870–1930," *European University Institute Working Papers* No. 22 (2009): 1–27.
Acquarelli, Luca. *Il fascismo e l'immagine dell'impero: Retoriche e culture visuali* (Rome: Donzelli, 2022).
Aderinto, Saheed. *Animality and Colonial Subjecthood in Africa: The Human and Nonhuman Creatures of Nigeria* (Athens: Ohio University Press, 2022).
Adugna, Minale. "Women and Warfare in Ethiopia: A Case Study of Their Role during the Campaign of Adwa, 1895–96, and the Italo-Ethiopian War, 1935–41," *Organization for Social Science Research in Eastern and Southern Africa: Gender Issues Research Report Series* No. 13 (2001): 1–41.
Anderson, Warwick. "Excremental Colonialism: Public Health and the Poetics of Pollution," *Critical Inquiry*, Vol. 21, No. 3 (1996): 640–99.
Anker, Peder. *Imperial Ecology: Environmental Order in the British Empire, 1895–1945* (Cambridge, MA: Harvard University Press, 2001).
Antonsich, Marco. "Segni del potere sul territorio: Iconografie urbane in Etiopia, 1936–1941" (PhD Diss., Università di Trieste, 1997).
Aregay, Merid W. "The Early History of Ethiopia's Coffee Trade and the Rise of Shawa," *Journal of African History*, Vol. 29, No. 1 (1988): 19–25.
Arena, Giovanni. "The Last Exhibition of the Italian Colonial Empire: Naples 1938–40," in *Cultures of International Exhibitions 1840–1940: Great Exhibitions in the Margins*, ed. Marta Filipová (New York: Routledge, 2016), 313–32.
Armiero, Marco, and Wilko Graf von Hardenberg. "Green Rhetoric in Blackshirts: Italian Fascism and the Environment," *Environment and History*, Vol. 19, No. 3 (2013): 283–311.
Arvidsson, Adam. "Between Fascism and the American Dream: Advertising in Interwar Italy," *Social Science History*, Vol. 25, No. 2 (2001): 155–7.
Baratieri, Daniela. "Italy's Sexual El Dorado in Africa," in *Imperial Expectations and Realities: El Dorados, Utopias and Dystopias*, ed. Andrekos Varnava (Manchester: Manchester University Press, 2015), 166–90.
Barrera, Giulia. "Colonial Affairs: Italian Men, Eritrean Women, and the Construction of Racial Hierarchies in Colonial Eritrea (1885–1941)" (PhD Diss., Northwestern University, 2002).
Barrera, Giulia. "Dangerous Liaisons: Colonial Concubinage in Eritrea, 1890–1941," *Northwestern University PAS Working Papers* No. 1 (1996): 34–49.
Barrera, Giulia. "Mussolini's Colonial Race Laws and State-Settler Relations in Africa Orientale Italiana (1935–1941)," *Journal of Modern Italian Studies*, Vol. 8, No. 3 (2003): 425–43.
Barrera, Giulia. "Patrilinearità, razza e identità: L'educazione degli italo-eritrei durante il colonialismo italiano (1885–1934)," *Quaderni Storici*, Vol. 37, No. 1 (2002): 21–54.

Barrera, Giulia. "Sessualità e segregazione nelle terre dell'Impero," in *L'Impero fascista: Italia ed Etiopia (1935–1941)*, ed. Riccardo Bottoni (Bologna: Il Mulino, 2008), 393–414.
Baudendistel, Rainer. *Between Bombs and Good Intentions: The International Committee of the Red Cross (ICRC) and the Italo-Ethiopian War, 1935–1936* (New York: Berghahn Books, 2006).
Bekele, Getnet. "Contingent Variables and Discerning Farmers: Marginalizing Cattle in Ethiopia's Historically Crop-Livestock Integrated Agriculture (1840–1941)," *Northeast African Studies*, Vol. 9, No. 2 (2002): 83–100.
Bekele, Getnet. *Ploughing New Ground: Food, Farming and Environmental Change in Ethiopia* (Rochester, NY: Boydell & Brewer, 2017).
Bellina, Elena. "Space and Violence in WWII Italian Captivity in Africa," *Italian Studies*, Vol. 75, No. 4 (2020): 426–40.
Bellucci, Stefano. "Italian Transnational Fluxes of Labour and Changing Labour Relations in the Horn of Africa," *Workers of the World*, Vol. 1, No. 3 (2013): 1–14.
Ben-Ghiat, Ruth. *Fascist Modernities: Italy, 1922–1945* (Berkeley: University of California Press, 2001).
Ben-Ghiat, Ruth. *Italian Fascism's Empire Cinema* (Bloomington: Indiana University Press, 2015).
Ben-Ghiat, Ruth. "Modernity Is Just over There: Colonialism and Italian National Identity," *interventions*, Vol. 8, No. 3 (2006): 380–93.
Benti, Getahun. *Urban Growth in Ethiopia, 1887–1974: From the Foundation of Finfinnee to the Demise of the First Imperial Era* (Lanham, MD: Lexington Books, 2016).
Berhe, Aregawi. "Revisiting Resistance in Italian-Occupied Ethiopia: The Patriots' Movement (1936–1941) and the Redefinition of Post-War Ethiopia," in *Rethinking Resistance Revolt and Violence in African History*, ed. Jon Abbink, Klaas van Walraven, and Mirjam de Bruijn (Leiden: Brill, 2003), 87–113.
Bernhard, Patrick. "Borrowing from Mussolini: Nazi Germany's Colonial Aspirations in the Shadow of Italian Expansionism," *Journal of Imperial and Commonwealth History*, Vol. 41, No. 4 (2013): 617–43.
Bernhard, Patrick. "Hitler's Africa in the East: Italian Colonialism as a Model for German Planning in Eastern Europe," *Journal of Contemporary History*, Vol. 51, No. 1 (2016): 61–90.
Bertazzini, Mattia C. "The Long-Term Impact of Italian Colonial Roads in the Horn of Africa, 1935–2000," *London School of Economics Economic History Working Papers* No. 272 (2018): 1–55.
Bertella Farnetti, Paolo, ed. *Sognando l'impero: Modena-Addis Abeba (1935–1941)* (Milan: Mimesis, 2007).
Beyene, Yaqob. "I tabù alimentari e il Cristianesimo etiopico," *Rassegna di Studi Etiopici* Vol. 38 (1994): 209–32.
Blunt, Alison. "Imperial Geographies of Home: British Domesticity in India, 1886–1925," *Transactions of the Institute of British Geographers*, Vol. 24, No. 4 (1999): 421–40.
Bonelli, Costanza. "Clima, razza, colonizzazione: Nascita e sviluppo della medicina tropicale in Italia" (PhD Diss., Università di Roma Sapienza, 2019).
Butchart, Alex. *The Anatomy of Power: European Constructions of the African Body* (New York: Zed Books, 1998).
Caccia, Patrizia. "Libri, cucina e sanzioni," *La fabbrica del libro*, Vol. 15, No. 2 (2009): 21–7.

Caglioti, Angelo Matteo. "'In This Country, Water Means Life': Eritrea's Erratic Rivers and Italian Irrigation Projects between Adwa and Mussolini (1897–1934)," *Contemporanea*, Vol. 25, No. 2 (2022): 265–91.

Cagnolati, Antonella. "Dreaming of Distant Lands: How Fascism Built Colonial Women (1937–1941)," *Historia y Memoria de la Educación*, Vol. 17 (2023): 205–33.

Campassi, Gabriella. "Il madamato in Africa Orientale: Relazioni tra italiani e indigene come forma di aggressione coloniale," *Miscellanea di storia delle esplorazioni*, Vol. 12 (1987): 219–60.

Campbell, Ian. *The Addis Ababa Massacre: Italy's National Shame* (New York: Oxford University Press, 2017).

Canali, Ferruccio. "Giuseppe Tassinari e la Relazione al Duce del viaggio attraverso i territori dell'Impero: Paesaggi e territori nella prospettiva della colonizzazione dell'Africa Orientale Italiana (gennaio-febbraio 1937)," *ASUP: Annuario di Storia dell'Urbanistica e del Paesaggio* No. 1 (2013): 206–14.

Capatti, Alberto, and Massimo Montanari. *Italian Cuisine: A Cultural History* (New York: Columbia University Press, 2003).

Cardini, Franco, and Isabella Gagliardi. "Towards a New Empire," in *L'Istituto Agronomico per l'Oltremare: La sua storia* (Florence: Masso delle Fate, 2007), 107–18.

Cassata, Francesco. *La difesa della razza: Politica, ideologia e immagine del razzismo fascista* (Turin: Einaudi, 2008).

Chiapparino, Francesco, and Renato Covino. *Consumi e industria alimentare in Italia dall'Unità a oggi: Lineamenti per una storia* (Perugia: Giada, 2002).

Ciarlo, David. *Advertising Empire: Race and Visual Culture in Imperial Germany* (Cambridge, MA: Harvard University Press, 2011).

Collingham, Elizabeth M. *The Taste of Empire: How Britain's Quest for Food Shaped the Modern World* (New York: Basic Books, 2017).

Colombara, Filippo. *Raccontare l'impero: Una storia orale della conquista d'Etiopia (1935–1941)* (Milan: Mimesis, 2019).

Conelli, Carmine. "Razza, colonialità, nazione: Il progetto coloniale italiano tra Mezzogiorno e Africa," in *Quel che resta dell'Impero: La cultura coloniale degli italiani*, ed. Valeria Deplano and Alessandro Pes (Milan: Mimesis, 2014), 149–67.

Cresti, Federico. *Non desiderare la terra d'altri: La colonizzazione italiana in Libia* (Rome: Carocci, 2011).

Crummey, Donald. "Ethiopian Plow Agriculture in the Nineteenth Century," *Journal of Ethiopian Studies*, Vol. 16 (1983): 1–23.

Crummey, Donald. *Land and Society in the Christian Kingdom of Ethiopia: From the Thirteenth to the Twentieth Century* (Urbana: University of Illinois Press, 2000).

D'Onofrio, Federico. "The Microfoundations of Italian Agrarianism: Italian Agricultural Economists and Fascism," *Agricultural History*, Vol. 91, No. 3 (2017): 369–96.

Davis, Mike. *Late Victorian Holocausts: El Niño Famines and the Making of the Third World* (London: Verso, 2001).

de Grazia, Victoria. "Nationalizing Women: The Competition between Fascist and Commercial Cultures in Mussolini's Italy," in *The Sex of Things: Gender and Consumption in Historical Perspective*, ed. Victoria de Grazia with Ellen Furlough (Berkeley: University of California Press, 1996), 337–56.

De Napoli, Olindo. "Disciplinare i coloni: Sessualità e razzismo in *Etiopia Latina*," *S-nodi*, Nos. 15–16 (2017): 209–23.

De Ninno, Fabio. "L'Oceano Indiano e la grande strategia italiana," in *Italy on the Rimland: Storia militare di una penisola eurasiatica. Vol. 2: Suez*, ed. Virgilio Ilari (Rome: Nadir Media, 2019), 105–16.

De Robertis, Riccardo. "From Colonialism to Cooperation: The Training of Tropical Agricultural Experts in Florence (1908–1968)," *Journal of Agriculture and Environment for International Development*, Vol. 113, No. 2 (2019): 253–71.

Del Boca, Angelo. *Gli italiani in Africa Orientale. Vol. 3: La caduta dell'Impero* (Milan: Mondadori, 2014).

Del Boca, Angelo. "I crimini del colonialismo fascista," in *Le guerre coloniali del fascismo*, ed. Angelo Del Boca (Rome: Laterza, 2008), 232–55.

Del Boca, Angelo. *Italiani brava gente? Un mito duro a morire* (Vicenza: Neri Pozza, 2011).

Del Boca, Angelo. "Le leggi razziali nell'impero di Mussolini," in *Il regime fascista: Storia e storiografia*, ed. Angelo Del Boca, Massimo Legnani, and Mario G. Rossi (Rome: Laterza, 1995), 329–51.

Deplano, Valeria. *L'Africa in casa: Propaganda e cultura coloniale nell'Italia fascista* (Milan: Mondadori, 2015).

Di Lalla, Fabrizio, ed. *Le italiane in Africa Orientale: Storie di donne in colonia* (Chieti: Solfanelli, 2014).

Dirar, Uoldelul Chelati. "From Warriors to Urban Dwellers: Ascari and the Military Factor in the Urban Development of Colonial Eritrea," *Cahiers d'études africaines*, No. 175 (2004): 533–74.

Dirasse, Laketch. *The Commoditization of Female Sexuality: Prostitution and Socio-economic Relations in Addis Ababa, Ethiopia* (New York: AMS Press, 1991).

Dogliani, Patrizia. *Il fascismo degli italiani: Una storia sociale* (Turin: UTET, 2022).

Dominioni, Matteo. "La repressione di ribellismo e dissentimo in Etiopia, 1936–1941," in *Crimini di guerra: Il mito del bravo italiano tra repressione del ribellismo e guerra ai civili nei territori occupati*, ed. Luigi Borgomaneri (Milan: Guerini e Associati, 2006), 1–18.

Dominioni, Matteo. *Lo sfascio dell'impero: Gli italiani in Etiopia (1936–1941)* (Rome: Laterza, 2008).

Dondi, Mirco. "Il razzismo coloniale del fascismo e i suoi riflessi alla radio e sulla stampa (1935–36)," *I sentieri della ricerca*, Vols. 7–8 (2008): 281–331.

Dore, Gianni. "Antropologia e colonialismo italiano nell'epoca fascista: Il razzismo biologico di Lidio Cipriani," *Annali della Facoltà di Lettere e Filosofia dell'Università di Cagliari*, Vol. 2 (1981): 285–313.

Dore, Gianni. "Etnografia del miele nelle fonti coloniali italiane su Eritrea e Etiopia," *Ethnorema*, No. 5 (2010): 51–60.

Dore, Gianni. "Per un repertorio degli stili alimentari nell'altopiano etiopico: Note su commensalità, divisione, spartizione e gerarchie sociali," *Ethnorema*, No. 2 (2006): 3–4.

Dore, Gianni. *Scritture di colonia: Lettere di Pia Maria Pezzoli dall'Africa Orientale a Bologna (1936–1943)* (Bologna: Patron, 2004).

Dore, Gianni. "Vi dirò qualcosa di questa gente nera: Un bellunese in Somalia (1934–1936)," *Un bellunese in Somalia: Lettere di Edoardo Costantini a Polpet (1934–1936)*, ed. Istituto Storico Bellunese della Resistenza e dell'Età Contemporanea (Padua: CLUEP, 2001).

Ertola, Emanuele. *In terra d'Africa: Gli italiani che colonizzarono l'impero* (Rome: Laterza, 2017).

Ertola, Emanuele. "The Italian Fascist Settler Empire in Ethiopia, 1936-1941," in *The Routledge Handbook of the History of Settler Colonialism*, ed. Edward Cavanagh and Lorenzo Veracini (New York: Routledge, 2016), 263-76.

Ertola, Emanuele. "L'Impero immaginario: I coloni italiani in Etiopia, 1936-1941" (PhD Diss., Università di Firenze, 2014).

Ertola, Emanuele. "Navi bianche: Il rimpatrio dei civili italiani dall'Africa Orientale," *Passato e presente*, No. 91 (2014): 127-43.

Ertola, Emanuele. "White Slaves: Labor, Whiteness, and Settler Colonialism in Italian East Africa (1935-1941)," *Labor History*, Vol. 61, Nos. 5-6 (2020): 551-67.

Fanon, Frantz. *Black Skin, White Masks* (New York: Grove Press, 1967).

Fanon, Frantz. *The Wretched of the Earth* (New York: Grove Press, 1963).

Ferris, Kate. "*Fare di ogni famiglia un fortilizio*: The League of Nations' Economic Sanctions and Everyday Life in Venice," *Journal of Modern Italian Studies*, Vol. 11, No. 2 (2006): 117-42.

Fidotta, Giuseppe. "Un impero cinematografico: Il documentario in Africa Orientale Italiana (1935-1941)" (PhD Diss., Università di Udine, 2015).

Filippi, Francesco. *Noi però gli abbiamo fatto le strade: Le colonie italiane tra bugie, razzismi e amnesie* (Turin: Bollati Boringhieri, 2021).

Forgacs, David. *Italy's Margins: Social Exclusion and Nation Formation since 1861* (New York: Cambridge University Press, 2014).

Freedman, Paul, ed. *Food: The History of Taste* (Berkeley: University of California Press, 2007).

Freidberg, Susanne. *French Beans and Food Scares: Culture and Commerce in an Anxious Age* (New York: Oxford University Press, 2004).

Fufa, Fekede Sileshi, and Ketebo Abdiyo. "The Reactions of Limmu Oromo of Western Ethiopia during and after the Italian Occupation (1936-41)," *Research on Humanities and Social Sciences*, Vol. 8, No. 21 (2018): 38-44.

Fuller, Mia. "Building Power: Italy's Colonial Architecture and Urbanism, 1923-1940," *Cultural Anthropology* Vol. 3, No. 4 (1988): 455-87.

Fuller, Mia. *Moderns Abroad: Architecture, Cities and Italian Imperialism* (New York: Routledge, 2006).

Fuller, Mia. "Wherever You Go, There You Are: Fascist Plans for the Colonial City of Addis Ababa and the Colonizing Suburb of EUR '42," *Journal of Contemporary History*, Vol. 31, No. 2 (1996): 397-418.

Gabrielli, Gianluca. "Colpevole di leso razzismo: Una sentenza per il reato di unione di indole coniugale tra cittadini e sudditi," *ANUAC: Rivista della Società Italiana di Antropologia Culturale*, Vol. 1, No. 1 (2012): 7-16.

Gabrielli, Gianluca. "Un aspetto della politica razzista nell'impero: Il 'problema' dei meticci," *Passato e Presente*, Vol. 15, No. 41 (1997): 77-105.

Galati, Virgilio C. "Bari d'Etiopia (Harar): Le vicende della fondazione del centro urbano e l'utopia della colonizzazione agricola," *Annali di Storia dell'Urbanistica e del Paesaggio*, No. 1 (2013): 127-61.

Galati, Virgilio C. "Saverio Dioguardi e il Piano Regolatore dei Villaggi Agricoli Nazionali di Oletta e Biscioftù nell'Etiopia Italiana (1936-1940)," *Annali di Storia dell'Urbanistica e del Paesaggio*, No. 1 (2013): 111-58.

Garvin, Diana. "Black Markets: Fascist Constructions of Race in East African Marketplace Newsreels," *Journal of Modern European History* Vol. 19, No. 1 (2021): 103-24.

Garvin, Diana. "Building Pasta's Empire: Barilla in Italian East Africa," *Modern Italy*, Vol. 28, No. 2 (2023): 97-126.

Garvin, Diana. "Constructing Race through Commercial Space: Merkato Ketema under Fascist Urban Planning," *Journal of Modern Italian Studies*, Vol. 25, No. 2 (2020): 118–48.

Garvin, Diana. *Feeding Fascism: The Politics of Women's Food Work* (Toronto: University of Toronto Press, 2021).

Garvin, Diana. "Fruit of Fascist Empire: Bananas and Italian Somaliland," *The Italianist*, Vol. 43, No. 3 (2023): 439–67.

Garvin, Diana. "Imperial Wet-Nursing in Italian East Africa," in *The Routledge Companion to Sexuality and Colonialism*, ed. Chelsea Schields and Dagmar Herzog (New York: Routledge, 2021), 145–58.

Garvin, Diana. "The Italian Coffee Triangle: From Brazilian *Colonos* to Ethiopian *Colonialisti*," *Modern Italy*, Vol. 26, No. 3 (2021): 291–312.

Gebissa, Ezekiel. "The Italian Invasion, the Ethiopian Empire, and Oromo Nationalism: The Significance of the Western Oromo Confederation of 1936," *Northeast African Studies*, Vol. 9, No. 3 (2002): 75–96.

Gemeda, Guluma. "The Rise of Coffee and the Demise of Colonial Autonomy: The Oromo Kingdom of Jimma and Political Centralization in Ethiopia," *Northeast African Studies*, Vol. 9, No. 3 (2002): 51–74.

Geremew, Birhanu Bitew. "The Tragedy of Colonialism in a Non-Colonized Society: Italy's Historical Narratives and the Amhara Genocide in Ethiopia," *Journal of Asian and African Studies* (2023), Vol. 58, No. 8 (2023): 1405–21.

Giorgi, Chiara. "Soggetti e politiche della mobilità coloniale," in *Votare con i piedi: Mobilità degli individui nell'Africa coloniale italiana*, ed. Isabella Rosoni and Chelati Dirar (Macerata: EUM, 2012), 199–230.

Goglia, Luigi, ed. *Colonialismo e fotografia: Il caso italiano* (Messina: Sicania, 1990).

Gonzales-Ruibal, Alfredo. "Fascist Colonialism: The Archaeology of Italian Outposts in Western Ethiopia (1936–41)," *International Journal of Historical Archaeology*, Vol. 37, No. 4 (2010): 547–74.

Griffith, Brian J. "Bacchus among the Blackshirts: Wine Making, Consumerism and Identity in Fascist Italy, 1919–1937," *Contemporary European History*, Vol. 29, No. 4 (2020): 394–415.

Hackenesch, Silke. *Chocolate and Blackness: A Cultural History* (Berlin: Campus Verlag, 2017).

Helstosky, Carol. "Fascist Food Politics: Mussolini's Policy of Alimentary Sovereignty," *Journal of Modern Italian Studies*, Vol. 9, No. 1 (2004): 1–26.

Helstosky, Carol. "Recipe for the Nation: Reading Italian History through *La Scienza in Cucina* and *La Cucina Futurista*," *Food and Foodways* Vol. 11, No. 2 (2003): 113–40.

Iyob, Ruth. "Madamismo and Beyond: The Construction of Eritrean Women," *Nineteenth-Century Contexts*, Vol. 22, No. 2 (2000): 217–38.

Janes, Lauren. *Colonial Food in Interwar Paris: The Taste of Empire* (New York: Bloomsbury Academic, 2016).

Jansen, P. C. M. *Spices, Condiments and Medicinal Plants in Ethiopia, Their Taxonomy and Agricultural Significance* (Wageningen: Center for Agricultural Publishing and Documentation, 1981).

Kassie, Kibur, and Daniel Lirebo. "The Impact of Multi-story Commercial Buildings on the Heritage Values of Open Market in Addis Ababa," *Journal of Architectural Engineering Technology*, Vol. 10, No. 9 (2021): 1–7.

Kifleyesus, Abbebe. "The Construction of Ethiopian National Cuisine," *Ethnorema* No. 2 (2006): 27–48.

Labanca, Nicola. "Constructing Mussolini's New Man in Africa? Italian Memories of the Fascist War on Ethiopia," *Italian Studies*, Vol. 41, No. 2 (2006): 225–32.
Labanca, Nicola, ed. *L'Africa in vetrina: Storie di musei e di esposizioni coloniali in Italia* (Treviso, Pagus, 1992).
Labanca, Nicola. *Oltremare: Storia dell'espansione coloniale italiana* (Bologna: Il Mulino, 2007).
Labanca, Nicola. *Posti al sole: Diari e memorie di vita e di lavoro dalle colonie d'Africa* (Rovereto: Museo Storico Italiano della Guerra, 2001).
Larebo, Haile M. *The Building of an Empire: Italian Land Policy and Practice in Ethiopia, 1935–1941* (Oxford: Clarendon Press, 1994).
Larebo, Haile M. "Empire Building and Its Limitations: Ethiopia (1935–1941)," in *Italian Colonialism*, ed. Ruth Ben-Ghiat and Mia Fuller (New York: Palgrave Macmillan, 2005), 83–94.
Larebo, Haile M. "The Myth and Reality of Empire Building Italian Land Policy and Practice in Ethiopia, 1935–1941" (PhD Diss., University of London School of Oriental and African Studies, 1990).
Le Houérou, Fabienne. "Gender and Sexual Abuses during the Italian Colonization of Ethiopia and Eritrea: The *Insabbiatti* Thirty Years After," *Sociology Mind*, Vol. 5, No. 4 (2015): 255–67.
Lee, Mooha, Meron Regu, and Semeneh Seleshe. "Uniqueness of Ethiopian Traditional Alcoholic Beverage of Plant Origin, Tella," *Journal of Ethnic Foods*, Vol. 2, No. 3 (2015): 110–14.
Levine, Philippa. *Prostitution, Race and Politics: Policing Venereal Disease in the British Empire* (New York: Routledge, 2003).
Lewis, I. M. *A Modern History of Somalia: Nation and State in the Horn of Africa* (London: Longman 1980).
Locatelli, Francesca. "Migrating to the Colonies and Building the Myth of '*Italiani Brava Gente*': The Rise, Demise, and Legacy of Italian Settler Colonialism," in *Italian Mobilities*, ed. Ruth Ben-Ghiat and Stephanie Malia Hom (New York: Routledge, 2015), 133–51.
Lombardi-Diop, Cristina. "Spotless Italy: Hygiene, Domesticity, and the Ubiquity of Whiteness in Fascist and Postwar Consumer Culture," *California Italian Studies*, Vol. 2, No. 1 (2011): 1–22.
Maiocchi, Roberto. *Scienza italiana e razzismo fascista* (Florence: La Nuova Italia, 1999).
Mancosu, Gianmarco. *Vedere l'impero: L'Istituto Luce e il colonialismo fascista* (Milan: Mimesis, 2022).
Manfren, Priscilla. *Icone d'Oltremare nell'Italia fascista: Artisti, illustratori e vignettisti alla conquista dell'Africa* (Trieste: Edizioni Università di Trieste, 2019).
McCann, James C. *From Poverty to Famine in Northeast Ethiopia: A Rural History, 1900–1935* (Philadelphia: University of Pennsylvania Press, 1987).
McCann, James C. *People of the Plow: An Agricultural History of Ethiopia, 1800–1990* (Madison: University of Wisconsin Press, 1995).
McCann, James C. *Stirring the Pot: A History of African Cuisine* (Athens: Ohio University Press, 2010).
McClintock, Anne. *Imperial Leather: Race, Gender, and Sexuality in the Colonial Contest* (New York: Routledge, 1995).
Meyer, Frederick G. "Notes on Wild Coffee Arabica from Southwestern Ethiopia, with Some Historical Considerations," *Economic Botany*, Vol. 19, No. 2 (1965): 136–51.

Milanese, Ernesto. "La Società Agricola Italo-Somala e l'opera del Duca degli Abruzzi in Somalia tra il 1920 e il 1933," *Miscellanea di storia delle esplorazioni*, Vol. 24 (1999): 235–58.

Mockler, Anthony. *Haile Selassie's War: The Italian-Ethiopian Campaign, 1935–1941* (New York: Random House, 1984).

Moore, Bob, and Kent Fedorowich. *The British Empire and Its Italian Prisoners of War, 1940–1947* (New York: Palgrave Macmillan, 2002).

Morris, Jonathan. "Making Italian Espresso, Making Espresso Italian," *Food & History*, Vol. 8, No. 2 (2010): 155–84.

Omer, Ahmed Hassen. "The Italian Impact on Ethnic Relations: A Case Study of a Regional Policy in Northern Shoa (Ethiopia), 1936–1941," *Annales d'Éthiopie*, Vol. 16 (2000): 147–59.

Otter, Chris. *Diet for a Large Planet: Industrial Britain, Food Systems, and World Ecology* (Chicago: University of Chicago Press, 2020).

Pallotti, Vittorio. "'Ti scrivo dall'Abissinia': Lettere di Guerrino, camionista bolognese, alla moglie Derna dall'Africa Orientale Italiana," *I Sentieri della Ricerca*, No. 3 (2006): 169–218.

Pankhurst, Richard. "A Chapter in Ethiopia's Commercial History: Developments during the Fascist Occupation of Ethiopia, 1936–1941," *Ethiopia Observer*, Vol. 14, No. 1 (1971): 47–67.

Pankhurst, Richard. "Come il popolo etiopico resistette all'occupazione e alla repressione da parte dell'Italia fascista," in *Le guerre coloniali del fascismo*, ed. Angelo Del Boca (Rome: Laterza, 1991), 256–87.

Pankhurst, Richard. "Fascist Racial Policies in Ethiopia, 1922–1941," *Ethiopia Observer* Vol. 12, No. 4 (1969): 270–86.

Pankhurst, Richard. "The Great Ethiopian Famine, 1888–1892: A New Assessment," *Journal of the History Applied Sciences*, Vol. 21, No. 2 (1966): 96–124.

Pankhurst, Richard. "Hierarchy at the Feast: The Partition of the Ox in Traditional Ethiopia," in *Proceedings of the Ninth International Congress of Ethiopian Studies*, ed. Anatolii Andreevich Gromyko (Moscow: USSR Academy of Sciences Africa Institute, 1988), 173–89.

Pankhurst, Richard. "The History of Prostitution in Ethiopia," *Journal of Ethiopian Studies*, Vol. 12, No. 2 (1974): 159–78.

Pankhurst, Richard. "Italian and 'Native' Labor during the Italian Fascist Occupation of Ethiopia,1935–41," *Ghana Social Science Journal*, Vol. 2, No. 2 (1973): 42–74.

Pankhurst, Richard. "Italian Fascist War Crimes in Ethiopia: A History of Their Discussion, from the League of Nations to the United Nations (1936–1949)," *Northeast African Studies*, Vol. 6, Nos. 1–2 (1999): 83–140.

Pankhurst, Richard. "L'occupazione fascista nella letteratura etiopica," *Studi Piacentini*, No. 13 (1993): 135–48.

Pankhurst, Richard. "A Page of Ethiopian History: Italian Settlement Plans during the Fascist Occupation of 1936–1941," *Ethiopia Observer*, Vol. 13, No. 2 (1970): 145–56.

Pankhurst, Richard. "The Perpetuation of the Maria Theresa Dollar and Currency Problems in Italian-Occupied Ethiopia, 1936–1941," *Journal of Ethiopian Studies*, Vol. 8, No. 2 (1970): 89–117.

Pankhurst, Richard. "Road Building during the Italian Fascist Occupation of Ethiopia, 1935–1941," *Africa Quarterly*, Vol. 15, No. 3 (1968): 21–62.

Paolini, Enrico, and Davide Saporetti. *La Romagna in Etiopia: Sogni e speranze in Africa* (Cesena: Il Ponte Vecchio, 1999).

Patriarca, Silvana. *Il colore della Repubblica: "Figli della guerra" e razzismo nell'Italia postfascista* (Turin: Einaudi, 2021).
Pergher, Roberta. *Mussolini's Nation-Empire: Sovereignty and Settlement in Italy's Borderlands, 1922–1943* (New York: Cambridge University Press, 2017).
Pes, Alessandro. "Becoming Imperialist: Italian Colonies in Fascist Textbooks for Primary Schools," *Journal of Modern Italian Studies*, Vol. 18, No. 5 (2013): 599–614.
Pesarini, Angelica. "'Blood Is Thicker Than Water': The Materialization of the Racial Body in Fascist East Africa," *Zapruder World: An International Journal for the History of Social Conflict*, Vol. 4 (2017): 1–12.
Peveri, Valentina. *The Edible Gardens of Ethiopia: An Ethnographic Journey into Beauty and Hunger* (Tucson: University of Arizona Press, 2020).
Pinkus, Karen. *Bodily Regimes: Italian Advertising under Fascism* (Minneapolis: University of Minnesota Press, 1995).
Pinkus, Karen. "Shades of Black in Advertising and Popular Culture," in *Revisioning Italy: National Identity and Global Culture*, ed. Beverly Allen and Mary Russo (Minneapolis: University of Minnesota Press, 1997), 134–55.
Podestà, Gian Luca. "Building the Empire: Public Works in Italian East Africa (1936–1941)," *Enterprises et Histoire*, No. 70 (2013): 37–53.
Podestà, Gian Luca. "Il lavoro in Africa Orientale Italiana (1935–1939)," in *Il lavoro come fattore produttivo e come risorsa nella storia economia italiana: Atti del Convegno di studi, Roma, 24 novembre 2000*, ed. Sergio Zaninelli and Mario Taccolini (Milan: Vita e Pensiero, 2002), 123–61.
Podestà, Gian Luca. "Le città dell'Impero: La fondazione di una nuova civiltà italiana in Africa Orientale," *Città e Storia*, Vol. 4, No. 1 (2009): 1–25.
Podestà, Gian Luca. *Il mito dell'impero: Economia, politica e lavoro nelle colonie italiane dell'Africa orientale 1898–1941* (Turin: Giappichelli, 2004).
Poidimani, Nicoletta. *Difendere la razza: Identità razziale e politiche sessuali nel progetto imperiale di Mussolini* (Rome: Sensibili alle foglie, 2009).
Poidimani, Nicoletta. "'Faccetta Nera': I crimini sessuali del colonialismo fascista nel Corno d'Africa," in *Crimini di guerra: Il mito del bravo italiano tra repressione del ribellismo e guerra ai civili nei territori occupati*, ed. Luigi Borgomaneri (Milan: Guerini e Associati, 2006).
Ponzanesi, Sandra. "The Color of Love: *Madamismo* and Interracial Relationships in the Italian Colonies," *Research in African Literatures*, Vol. 2, No. 2 (2012): 155–72.
Portincasa, Agnese. "Il Touring Club Italiano e la *Guida Gastronomica d'Italia*: Creazione, circolazione del modello e tracce della sua evoluzione (1931–1984)," *Food and History*, Vol. 6, No. 1 (2008): 83–119.
Pratt, Marie Louise. *Imperial Eyes: Travel Writing and Transculturation* (New York: Routledge, 1992).
Preti, Luigi. *Impero fascista, africani ed ebrei* (Milan: Mursia, 2004).
Proglio, Gabriele. "Il cammino degli eroi: The Empire as a Mark of Modernity: Representations of Colonial Power in a Famous Regime Documentary," *Modern Italy*, Vol. 21, No. 3 (2016), 289–303.
Ramamurthy, Anandi. *Imperial Persuaders: Images of Africa and Asia in British Advertising* (Manchester: Manchester University Press, 2003).
Roversi Monaco, Fabio, ed. *Africa come un mattino* (Bologna: Tamari, 1969).
Rowe, John A., and Kjell Hødnebø. "Rinderpest in the Sudan, 1888–1890: The Mystery of the Missing Panzootic," *Sudanic Africa*, Vol. 5 (1994): 153–7.

Saini Fasanotti, Federica. *Vincere: The Italian Royal Army's Counterinsurgency Operations in Africa, 1922–1940* (Annapolis, MD: Naval Institute Press, 2020).

Salvi, Sergio, Oriana Porfiri, and Salvatore Ceccarelli. "Nazareno Strampelli, the 'Prophet' of the Green Revolution," *Journal of Agricultural Science*, Vol. 151, No. 1 (2013): 1–5.

Saraiva, Tiago. *Fascist Pigs: Technoscientific Organisms and the History of Fascism* (Cambridge, MA: MIT Press, 2016).

Sbacchi, Alberto. *Ethiopia under Mussolini: Fascism and the Colonial Experience* (London: Zed Books, 1985).

Sbacchi, Alberto. *Il colonialismo italiano in Etiopia, 1936–1940* (Milan: Mursia, 2009).

Sbacchi, Alberto. "Italian Colonization in Ethiopia: Plans and Projects, 1936–1940," *Africa*, Vol. 32, No. 4 (1977): 503–16.

Scarfone, Marianna. "La nevrastenia sotto i tropici: I disturbi mentali dei bianchi in colonia," in *Quel che resta dell'Impero: La cultura coloniale degli italiani*, ed. Valeria Deplano and Alessandro Pes (Milan: Mimesis, 2014), 17–38.

Scarpellini, Emanuela. *Food and Foodways in Italy from 1861 to the Present* (New York: Palgrave Macmillan, 2015).

Scarpellini, Emanuela. *Material Nation: A Consumer's History of Modern Italy* (New York: Oxford University Press, 2011).

Schaefer, Charles. "Serendipitous Resistance in Fascist-Occupied Ethiopia, 1936–1941," *Northeast African Studies*, Vol. 3, No. 1 (1996): 87–115.

Schnapp, Jeffrey T. "The Romance of Caffeine and Aluminum," *Critical Inquiry* Vol. 28, No. 1 (2001): 244–69.

Seifu, Yonas. "A Historical Survey of Jimma Town (1936–1974)" (MA thesis, Addis Ababa University, 2002).

Seleshe, Semeneh, Cheorun Jo, and Mooha Lee. "Meat Consumption Culture in Ethiopia," *Korean Journal for Food Science of Animal Resources*, Vol. 34, No. 1 (2013): 7–13.

Sessa, Ettore, "L'oltremare nel rinnovamento dell'urbanistica italiana," *Storia dell'urbanistica*, Vol. 51, No. 2 (2022): 262–81.

Shack, William. *The Gurage: A People of the Ensete Culture* (New York: Oxford University Press, 1966).

Smith, Mark M. *How Race Is Made: Slavery, Segregation, and the Senses* (Chapel Hill: University of North Carolina Press, 2008).

Sollai, Michele. "The Fascist Green Revolution," *Plants People Planet* (2023): 1–10.

Sollai, Michele. "How to Feed an Empire? Agrarian Science, Indigenous Farming, and Wheat Autarchy in Italian-Occupied Ethiopia, 1937–1941," *Agricultural History*, Vol. 96, No. 3 (2022): 379–416.

Sollai, Michele. "Microcosms of Colonial Development: Italian and Ethiopian Farmers at the Crossroads of Fascist Empire Building (1937–1941)," *Contemporanea*, Vol. 24, No. 1 (2021): 79–101.

Sòrgoni, Barbara. "'Defending the Race': The Italian Reinvention of the Hottentot Venus during Fascism," *Journal of Modern Italian Studies*, Vol. 8, No. 3 (2003): 411–24.

Sòrgoni, Barbara. *Parole e corpi: Antropologia, discorso giuridico e politiche sessuali interrazziali nella colonia Eritrea (1890–1941)* (Naples: Liguori, 1998).

Spadaro, Barbara. "Intrepide massaie: Genere, imperialismo e totalitarismo nella preparazione coloniale femminile durante il fascismo (1937–1943)," *Contemporanea*, Vol. 13, No. 1 (2010): 27–52.

Srivastava, Neelam. *Italian Colonialism and Resistances to Empire, 1930–1970* (London: Palgrave Macmillan, 2018).

Stefani, Giulietta. *Colonia per maschi: Italiani in Africa Orientale: Una storia di genere* (Verona: Ombre Corte, 2007).
Stefani, Giulietta. "Italiani e ascari: Percezioni e rappresentazioni dei colonizzati nell'Africa Orientale Italiana," *Italian Studies*, Vol. 41, No. 2 (2006): 207–23.
Stoler, Ann Laura. *Carnal Knowledge and Imperial Power: Race and the Intimate in Colonial Rule* (Berkeley: University of California Press, 2002).
Stoler, Ann Laura. *Race and the Education of Desire: Foucault's History of Sexuality and the Colonial Order of Things* (Durham, NC: Duke University Press, 2000).
Strang, G. Bruce. "'Places in the African Sun': Social Darwinism, Demographics and the Italian Invasion of Ethiopia," in *Collision of Empires: Italy's Invasion of Ethiopia and its International Impact*, ed. G. Bruce Strang (New York: Routledge, 2013), 11–32.
Strazza, Michele. "Faccetta nera dell'Abissinia: Madame e meticci dopo la conquista dell'Etiopia," *Humanities*, Vol. 1, No. 2 (2012): 116–33.
Taddia, Irma. *Autobiografie africane: Il colonialismo nelle memorie orali* (Milan: Angeli, 1996).
Taddia, Irma. *L'Eritrea-colonia 1890–1952: Paesaggi, strutture, uomini del colonialismo* (Milan: Angeli, 1986).
Taddia, Irma. *La memoria dell'Impero: Autobiografie d'Africa Orientale* (Bari: Lacaita, 1988).
Tekola, Bethlehem. *Narratives of Three Prostitutes in Addis Ababa* (Addis Ababa: CERTWID, 2002).
Tomasella, Giuliana. *Esporre l'Italia coloniale: Interpretazioni dell'alterità* (Padua: Il Poligrafo, 2017).
Trento, Giovanna. "Madamato and Colonial Concubinage in Ethiopia: A Comparative Perspective," *Aethiopica*, Vol. 14, No. 1 (2011): 184–205.
Volpato, Chiara. "La violenza contro le donne nelle colonie italiane: Prospettive psicosociali di analisi," *DEP: Deportate esuli profughe*, Vol. 10 (2009): 110–31.
Volterra, Alessandro. *Sudditi coloniali ascari eritrei, 1935–1941* (Milan: Angeli, 2005).
Waldron Merithew, Caroline. "'O Mother Race': Race, Italian Colonialism and the Fight to Keep Ethiopia Independent," *Zapruder World*, Vol. 4 (2017): 1–31.
Willson, Perry R. "Cooking the Patriotic Omelette: Women and the Italian Fascist Ruralization Campaign," *European History Quarterly*, Vol. 27, No. 4 (1997): 531–47.
Wolde-Mariam, Tekalign. "A City and Its Hinterlands: The Political Economy of Land Tenure, Agriculture, and Food Supply for Addis Ababa, Ethiopia (1887–1974)" (PhD Diss., Boston University, 1995).
Zellelew, Tilahun Bejitual. "Meat Abstinence and Its Positive Environmental Effect: Examining the Fasting Etiquettes of the Ethiopian Orthodox Church," *Critical Research on Religion*, Vol. 2, No. 2 (2014): 134–46.
Zellelew, Tilahun Bejitual. "The Semiotics of the 'Christian/Muslim Knife': Meat and Knife as Markers of Religious Identity in Ethiopia," *Signs and Society*, Vol. 3, No. 1 (2015): 44–70.
Zewde, Bahru. *A History of Modern Ethiopia, 1855–1991* (Oxford: James Currey, 2002).
Zorzetto, Gabriele. *La resistenza etiopica nel Lasta: Dalla rivolta anti-italiana di Hailu Chebbede del 1937 alle operazioni della primavera 1939* (Udine: Gaspari, 2019).

Index

Abate, Lij 156-7
Abaya Lake 157
Abbā Jafar II (Mootii Abbaa Jifaar) 147
Acanfora, Giuseppe 136
Addi Arkay 127
Āddi Qa'yeh 142, 150, 158
Addis Ababa 14, 17-18, 24-5, 29-30, 33, 37, 39, 40, 42, 44, 48, 60, 66-7, 78, 82, 88-9, 92, 98, 100, 104, 106-7, 109-20, 122, 140-1, 146-7, 149, 158-9, 162, 164-6, 169-70, 176-7, 180-1, 185, 192-3, 209, 216, 224, 238, 242 n.20, 250 n. 29, 276 n.129
Addis Ababa massacre 51, 116, 118, 169
Addis Alem 36, 48-9, 117, 206
Adi Keyh 124
Adi Kuala 95
Adi Ugri 115
Adigrat 139-41, 148, 153, 175
advertising 1-2, 15, 19, 44, 47-8, 61-2, 138, 179, 214, 229-37
Adwa 25, 31, 81, 100
Afodo 183
Africa Italiana 13, 34, 136
Africa Orientale Italiana (AOI), *see* Italian East Africa
Agricoltura Coloniale 11, 34
agriculture 7, 10-11, 35-44, 116-18, 185, 191-3
  applied biotechnologies 7, 10-12, 34, 37, 44, 50, 202-8, 226, 238
  blights and famines 50, 155-6, 188, 195, 205, 209-11, 226-7, 238
  Ethiopian 11-12, 23-4, 35, 78-9, 114-20, 131, 141, 146, 155-6, 175, 185, 191-3, 203-9, 213-14, 221-5, 239
  Italian 7, 10-11, 200
    colonial 7, 10-12, 18, 33-44, 47-51, 73-5, 84, 116, 167, 169, 185, 191-2, 203-8, 210, 213-14, 217-25, 238

alcohol and alcoholism, *see also* beer; mead; wine 63-5, 151, 182-3, 186, 196, 231-3
Almirante, Giorgio 12
Amba Aradam 75
Ambo 157
Ambrosio, Vincenzo 144, 163, 182, 186-7, 192
Amedeo, prince Duke of Aosta 79, 106, 118, 167, 204
Anderson, Warwick 176
Andreoli, Lamberto 209
animals 8, 12, 19, 34, 78-9, 112, 114, 117-18, 122, 127-9, 133, 137-8, 150, 156-8, 175-6, 180, 188-9, 192-7, 200, 204-8
Antonelli, Pietro 209
Aregai, Abebe 101
Arendt, Hannah 162
army, Italian 12, 18, 38, 57, 65-6, 70, 73-4, 77-9, 99, 107, 122, 125-34, 137, 180
  colonial, *see askari*
  rations 4, 63, 68, 71, 75, 77, 127-8, 131, 166, 170, 185, 228
  use of chemical weapons 5, 12, 180
Artusi, Pellegrino 25
Aselle 205
Asfaw, Manan Janterar 35
Asinari di San Marzano, Alessandro 209
askari 11, 15, 57, 64-5, 101, 108, 120, 125, 130-5, 137, 144, 150, 152-3, 158, 163-6, 168, 183-5, 188, 194-6
Asmara 57, 67, 90, 98-9, 101, 103, 107, 141, 177, 258 n.37
Assab 69, 234
Astaldi, Maria Luisa 178
Autarchia Alimentare 34
autarchy 9, 50, 62, 82, 122, 169, 191-2, 199-200, 204, 214-17, 220-1
Axum 100, 124
Azienda Monopolio Banane (AMB) 234

Baco 163, 181–2, 187, 192
Badoglio, Pietro 5, 166
Balbo, Italo 11
banana 2, 8, 19, 34, 44–8, 59, 134, 145, 165, 182, 186–7, 202, 211, 217–19, 233–4, 237
Bari d'Etiopia 39, 42–4
Barrera, Giulia 161–2
Bartolozzi, Enrico 115–16, 276 n.131
Battaglia del Grano, *see* Battle for Wheat
Battle for Wheat 2, 10, 73, 200, 204–5
Bedele 144
beer 17, 29, 67, 95, 100–1, 109, 122, 132, 135, 146, 148, 156–7, 161, 182, 186, 189, 213, 239
Bekele, Getnet 207
Belenta 130
Bellagamba, Unno 132
Benelli, Sem 193
Benuzzi, Felice 169
berbere 6, 17, 29–30, 117, 132, 150, 156–7, 176–7, 185, 239
Berhe, Aregawi 81
Berlusconi, Silvio 199
Berretta, Alfio 40
Bertinotti, Pierino 75
Berto, Giuseppe 133, 148
Beyan, Lekyelesh 81
Beyan, Sada 153, 157
Beyers, Leen 242 n.16
Bhabha, Homi 184
biodiversity 7–8, 23
Bishoftu 38, 40, 75, 204
Black diaspora
    anti-Italian mobilization in response to attack to Ethiopia 5
Blatta Bekele Hapte, Michael 170
Boccasile, Gino 3, 15, 61, 138, 231, 234–7
body 72, 92, 102, 106, 112, 133–4, 136, 138, 140, 145–9, 152–3, 174–6, 181–5, 187, 202
    Black, representation of 18–19, 92, 133–4, 174–6, 185, 212–13, 230–7
Boidi, Carlo 111
Boldrini, Laura 1
Bolongaro, Francesco 71
Bonacini, Luciano 179
Bonicelli, Contardo 112
Bonifica Integrale, *see* Integral Reclamation

Bosio, Gherardo 112
Botta, Sergio 127, 129, 174–5, 195
Bottazzi, Filippo 219
Bourdieu, Pierre 152–3
Branzanti, Edoardo Carlo 225
Brazil 2, 210, 220–1, 224–5, 227–8
bread 2, 4, 10, 20, 26–8, 31, 52, 63, 66–7, 73–5, 78, 80, 82–3, 101, 103, 105, 108, 117, 126–7, 130, 132, 136, 143, 148, 150, 152, 162, 164–5, 184, 186–7, 195, 202–4, 209, 211
Brunelli, Alda 101–4
burkutta, *see* bread
butter 28–30, 82, 117–18, 122, 127, 135, 151, 156, 175–81, 185, 207, 214, 231, 239, 248 n.26

Calabrò, Lino 120–1, 132–3, 143–4, 153, 155–6, 164, 168, 186–90, 193–6, 207–8
Camporesi, Piero 25
cannibalism 197
Cassisa, Mario 167–8
cattle plague, *see* rinderpest
cattle, *see* animals
Centro Sperimentale Agrario e Zootecnico (Addis Ababa) 204
Cerulli, Enrico 42
Chasai, Asfaha 94, 99
cheese and dairy, *see also* butter 6, 9, 24, 33, 57, 59, 63, 66, 69, 81–2, 95, 122, 127, 132, 135–6, 141–2, 146, 154, 157, 165–6, 168–9, 171, 176, 182, 207–8, 216, 242 n.16
Chelba 157
Chercher 39, 41, 43
Chiarizia, Ettore 70
Chiavegatti, Arrigo 96
chicken 27–8, 81, 83, 102, 117, 122, 135–6, 150–1, 154, 156, 164–5, 168, 186, 195, 208, 213
children
    Ethiopian 12, 15, 17, 71, 80, 83, 87–8, 90–92, 105–6, 132–4, 139, 142–3, 148–9, 161–2, 178, 183–4, 193, 213, 237
    Italian 20, 28, 79, 96, 167, 217–18
    in Ethiopia 15, 17, 38, 41–2, 44, 87–8, 90, 106, 125, 135, 139, 143–6, 161–2, 165–70, 216, 167, 176

chili pepper, *see also* berbere 17, 24, 29, 156–7, 165–6, 177, 185
chocolate 8, 19, 134, 148–9, 217, 229, 233–5, 237
Ciarlantini, Franco 161
Cibelli, Enrico 218
Ciferri, Raffaele 204–5, 221
Cipriani, Lidio 13, 179–80, 244 n.52
Cirio, Francesco 69
civilization, *see* discipline
coffee 2, 8, 17, 19, 33, 52, 56, 58–9, 63, 116, 121, 126, 132–4, 139–40, 144, 147–8, 162, 170, 185, 187, 202, 211, 213–14, 217, 219–29, 233, 235, 237, 239, 276 nn.131, 135
  espresso coffee machines 214, 220, 228–9, 258 n.37
colonialism, Italian 1–6, 8–9, 19, 23–43, 49–53, 58, 73–5, 79, 84, 93, 105–6, 163–5, 167, 210, 220–9
  capitalist, commercial, and venture farming 44–7, 217–19, 222–3, 226–8
  plans for Ethiopia 7, 10–14, 19, 23–37, 52–3, 58, 167, 203, 220–1, 226–7
  public memory 1–6, 72
  settler, *see also* Enti Regionali di Colonizzazione; Opera Nazionale Combattenti 7, 13–14, 37–45, 49–53, 58, 73–5, 77–9, 93, 105–6, 203–5, 210–14, 217, 219–29
Compagnia Italiana Importatori Caffè (SACIIC) 223, 225–6
Compagnia Italiana Transatlantica (CITRA) 217
Compagnia Italiana Trasporti Africa Orientale (CITAO) 55, 57
Concessione Italiana Alberghi Africa Orientale (CIAAO) 110
Confederazione Fascista degli Agricoltori (CFA) 47–8
consumer culture 5–6, 9–10, 57–9, 62, 65–6, 68, 70–1, 73–6, 82, 84, 134, 140, 155, 162, 219–21, 227–37
  and empire 14, 18–19, 29, 57–61, 70–1, 73–5, 91–2, 97–101, 134, 155, 202, 206–7, 217–21, 227–37
Conti-Rossini, Carlo 13
conviviality, *see* food manners

Coptic Orthodox Church 25, 48–9, 139, 151, 153, 158–9, 189, 194
Corbin, Alain 173
corn 8, 13, 34, 43, 73, 117, 188, 203
Corriere dell'Impero 110–11, 113
Corriere della Sera 13, 36, 41, 60, 100, 118, 206
Cortesi, Fabrizio 224, 226–7, 276 nn.131, 135
Costantini, Edoardo 182, 187–8, 191, 193
Cucina Italiana, La 19, 215–17, 219, 221, 229–30
cuisine 6, 23–31, 58–9, 76, 83–4, 102–7, 111, 124, 128–9, 140–2, 152, 161–2, 185–6, 200–2, 237, 242 n.16
  Ethiopian 6, 20, 23–31, 66, 81, 105, 107, 110, 114–17, 128–30, 132–4, 140–2, 152, 155, 174–7, 184–5, 188, 203, 213, 215–16, 237–9
  Ethiopian-Italian 5–6, 14–15, 17, 19–20, 58–9, 66, 82–4, 104–5, 107, 124–5, 134–46, 155, 161–2, 171, 184–6, 237, 239
  Italian 9, 23–6, 73–6, 83–4, 104–5, 140–2, 186, 200–1, 203, 211, 214–16, 217–19, 237–8, 242 n.16
  regional
    Ethiopian 23, 25–31, 117, 188, 211, 238
    Italian 9–10, 23–5, 60–1, 98, 100–3, 105–7, 200, 211–12, 219, 242 n.16
culinary diplomacy 149–60

Danane 68, 169–71
Davis, Mike 210–12
De Feo, Vincenzo 93
de Medici, Catherine 28
De Vecchi, Cesare Maria 46
Dekemhare 66–7, 71, 107, 123
Del Boca, Angelo 77, 128
Dembi Dolo 81–2, 130–1, 152, 176, 181
Depero, Fortunato 234
Dessie 67, 99, 103–4, 109, 111, 117, 119, 242 n.20
Desta, Agos 89
Desta, Damtew 181
Desta, Lij 159–60
di Crollalanza, Araldo 39–40
di Lauro, Raffaele 50

Diel, Louise 147
Difesa della Razza, La 12, 87, 145, 180
Dini, Fanny 216
Dirasse, Laketch 149
Dire Dawa 76, 106, 120, 169–70, 206, 224, 242 n.20
discipline
    of bodies 18, 28, 65–6, 133–5, 140–4, 152–3, 174–6
    of colonized people 13, 28, 65–6, 71–2, 84, 104–5, 107–8, 133–5, 140–4, 163, 174–6, 182–3, 227–8
    of subaltern settlers 13–14, 28, 65–6, 88–9, 99, 107–9, 135, 143, 160–2, 174–6, 182–3
disease, *see* health
disgust, *see* senses
Djibouti 38, 42, 56, 59, 69, 78, 100, 117, 164, 224, 227, 276 n.129
Dolfo, Angelo 72–3
domestic work 14–16, 83–4, 89–92, 125, 131, 135–46, 162, 183–4, 232, 237
Dongollo 103
DuBois, William Edward Burghardt 99

eggs 28, 57, 60, 81, 83, 102, 114–15, 122, 135–6, 156, 163, 165–6, 176, 186, 213, 242 n.16
Ellero, Giovanni Battista 105, 139, 163–4
empire 173
    and food 2, 8, 14, 23–4, 58–9, 173, 201–2
Enda Sellasie 140–1, 163
ensete 23, 31, 131, 211
Enti Regionali di Colonizzazione 38–45, 51–2, 106, 204, 217, 226
Eritrea 6, 11, 56, 58, 65, 87, 94, 123–4, 126, 131–2, 139, 160, 167, 177, 186, 203, 208–9, 216
European Union 200–1
Ethiopian Americans 5
Ethiopian War Crimes Commission 170–1

Fabriani, Giuseppe 218–19
Faccetta Nera song 3, 99, 178–80, 233
Fanon, Frantz 4, 19–20, 151, 153, 192–3
farmers, *see* agriculture
farming, *see* agriculture
Fasci Femminili del Partito Fascista 10, 135, 181, 191

fascism 10, 38–9, 41–2, 46, 58, 63, 66, 93, 104, 135, 178, 191–2, 199, 213, 218, 230
    environmental policies 191–2, 194, 200, 209
    food policies 8–9, 65–6, 173, 205, 214, 251 n.55
    racism 3, 7–9, 12–14, 18, 65–6, 71–2, 78–9, 87–94, 99, 105, 123–4, 135, 138–9, 160, 178, 213, 230–7
    and women 10, 15–16, 88–90, 92, 101, 135–40, 174, 178, 256–7 n.7
Feseha, Ghebremicael 108
film 16, 18, 114, 166, 213
food aid, *see* culinary diplomacy
food manners 17, 25, 27–8, 30, 64–6, 71–2, 82–4, 92, 104–5, 109, 117, 125, 134–5, 139–42, 149–60, 163, 214–16, 238
food sovereignty 65–6, 70, 199–200, 210, 218, 220, 229
food stores 4, 17, 65, 75, 88, 92, 94–101, 103, 107, 109–10, 123–4, 126, 146, 160, 164, 176, 182, 186, 214, 228, 258 n.37, 260 n.88
food system 64–7, 82, 84, 95–9, 112, 116–17, 126–34, 141, 155, 166, 184–6, 202–3, 213, 217–16, 237–8
    canned 58–60, 69–73, 77–8, 95–9, 108, 110, 118, 121–2, 126–7, 134, 136–7, 145, 155, 164, 186, 206–7, 227, 230
    imperial 7, 34, 38, 45, 50, 53, 55–67, 77–8, 82, 92–3, 95–9, 112, 116–20, 126–34, 155, 166, 181, 184–6, 202–4, 210, 213, 217–26, 237–8, 251 n.55
    segregation 4, 14, 17, 65–6, 71–2, 88, 90–4, 99–101, 104, 107–25, 214
    transport infrastructure 7, 19, 34, 38, 42, 53, 55–61, 65–6, 74–7, 82, 84, 93, 95–101, 112, 116–20, 126–34, 185–6, 213, 237–8
    urban colonial 4, 14, 17, 82, 92–3, 95, 107, 109–24, 141, 181
    urban planning 4, 17, 92–3, 107, 109–12, 116, 118–19, 141, 181
food, *see* individual foods
foodways, *see* cuisine; food manners
Forzini, Palmiro 185

Fossa, Davide 42, 58, 109, 192, 206
Foucault, Michel 87
France 23–4, 56, 59, 115, 215, 229
    French colonialism 8, 88, 93
Franchetti, Leopoldo 11
Fratelli d'Italia party 199
fruits 50, 57, 59, 63, 83, 95, 106, 117–20, 122, 133, 135–6, 141, 145, 154, 166, 175, 182, 185–6, 196, 217
Fuller, Mia 91, 112

Gambela, 276 n.129
Gardula 181
Garibaldi, Giuseppe 25
gastrofascism 8, 20, 24, 200–1, 209–10, 237
Gazzetta del Popolo 179
Gedle, Shewareged 81
Gedo 164
Geneva Convention for the Amelioration of the Condition of the Wounded and Sick in Armies in the Field 166
Gera 229
Germany 167, 220, 229
    German colonialism 8, 202
Ghebregherghis, Berhane 108
Gibe 195–6
Gīnda 101
Giornale d'Italia 87
Giornale di Addis Abeba, Il 110
globalization 5, 200–1, 209, 238
goat, *see* animals
Goglia, Luigi 150
Gondar 24–5, 41, 50, 71, 77, 89, 103, 108–9, 111, 165, 167, 177, 186
Gondrand massacre 77, 128, 186
González-Ruibal, Alfredo 65, 183
Gorresio, Vittorio 133
Gramsci, Antonio 9
Graziani, Rodolfo 5, 48, 51, 57, 59, 78–9, 88, 92–3, 116, 118, 169–70, 204, 212, 251 n.55
Great Britain 59, 115, 210, 215, 227, 229
    British colonialism 8, 11, 37, 44, 88, 93, 202–3, 205, 209–12, 219–20
Green Revolution 201, 238
Guarneri, Felice 228
Guba 183
Guidi, Ignazio 109

Guli, Renato 111
Guzzoni, Alfredo 123–4, 166

Haile Selassie I (Tafari Maconnèn) 5–6, 30, 36, 220, 225, 228
Hailu Chebbede 72–3, 254 n.56
Hailu Tekle Haymanot 151
Harar 16, 42, 75, 82, 111, 119, 151, 154, 170, 206, 209, 222–4, 228, 242 n.20
Hashenge Lake 186
health 44, 63–4, 67, 101, 103, 110, 112–13, 116, 135–6, 140–3, 146–7, 156–7, 166–71, 174–7, 180–7, 190–2, 194–5, 218–19, 233, 238
    and diet
        Ethiopia 135–6, 140–1, 144–6, 156, 174–7, 180–4, 190–1, 238
        Italy 6–7, 63, 73, 200–2, 218–19, 233, 238
        Italian soldiers in Ethiopia 64–5, 76–8, 126–34, 136, 166–7, 182–4
        Italian workers in Ethiopia 56–7, 63, 67, 73, 76–9, 96–7, 103, 122–3, 136, 166, 182–4
    mental 64
Holetta 38, 40, 75, 204
honey, *see also* mead 24, 27, 29–30, 60, 127, 132, 163, 191
household workers, *see* domestic work
housing 90–1, 93, 96, 101–2, 106, 175–6, 192–3, 263 n.42
    Ethiopian 76, 91, 93, 102, 157, 175–6
    Italian colonial homes in Ethiopia 71, 90–3, 135–46, 183–4
hunger 73–5, 77–9, 81–3, 127–34, 166–70
hunting, *see* animals
hygiene, *see* health

Imba Alajeba 81, 167
India 24, 29, 97, 167, 202, 209–11, 216
injera 6, 23, 26, 28, 66, 117, 122, 129, 132, 148, 150, 152, 156, 159, 162, 168, 184, 215–16, 239
insabbiati, *see* settlers, Italian
Integral Reclamation 2, 10, 12, 40–1
Istituto Agronomico per l'Africa Italiana (Florence) 11, 37, 221
Istituto Agronomico per l'Oltremare (Florence) 11

Istituto Coloniale Fascista (Rome) 136–7, 191, 194
Istituto Fascista dell'Africa Italiana (Rome) 10, 23, 34, 135, 181
Istituto Luce (Rome) 18, 114, 166, 213
Istituto Nazionale di Genetica per la Cerealicoltura 10
Italian Americans 162
Italian East Africa 2, 6, 36, 55, 73, 81, 88, 91–2, 132, 147, 173, 204–6, 211–12, 215, 237, 250 n.29

Janale 45–7, 218
Jijiga 165, 168
Jimma 29, 31, 38, 41, 71, 75, 95, 109–11, 117, 122, 144, 147, 153, 176–7, 186–7, 195, 223, 228, 242 n.20
Jiren 95
Jowhar, see Villaggio Duca degli Abruzzi

Kaffa 219, 225
Kassala 153
Kenya 7, 23, 33, 40, 45, 82, 167, 169, 205, 209, 220
Kerem 73
Keren 96
kifto 28–30
Kismayo 182, 218, 233
kocho 31, 131, 211
Korem 104, 185–6

La Sorsa, Manlio 115–16, 134, 147–8
Labanca, Nicola 105
Landi, Maria 116
László, Sáska 118
Le Corbusier (Charles-Édouard Jeanneret) 109
Le Houérou, Fabienne 161–2
League of Nations 5, 7, 70, 215, 220
Lessona, Alessandro 33, 39–40, 49, 59, 88, 91–3, 225
Li Muli, Gianni 48
Lollobrigida, Francesco 200–1, 210, 212
Longanesi, Leo 2
Lucidi, Giuseppe 145
Luigi Amedeo of Savoy, prince Duke of the Abruzzi 45
Lybia 11, 45, 94, 105, 108, 132

Makalle 81
Makonnen, Aleca 153, 157
Malaparte, Curzio 36, 41, 100–1, 132–4, 146, 153
Manzoni, Alessandro 25
Mareb River 77, 128
Marinetti, Tommaso 76
Marini, Luigi 128
markets 17, 92–3, 95, 109, 111–24
  Addis Ababa 92–3, 111–20
  Adigrat 175
  Adi Ugri 115, 147
  Dessie 111–12, 119, 151
  Gondar 111
  Harar 16, 42, 75, 82, 111, 154
  Jimma 111–12, 122
Martini, Ferdinando 11, 175
Marx, Karl 8
Masotti, Pier Marcello 81, 130–2, 143–4, 152, 158, 165, 167, 177, 181–2, 184–6, 194–5
Massawa 56–8, 66–7, 69, 101, 103, 127, 164, 167, 177, 186, 190, 209, 213, 234
Massi, Ernesto 203–4
Matteucci, Pellegrino 184–5
Maugini, Armando 11, 34, 40
McCann, James 203, 229
McClintock, Anne 3
McLuhan, Marshall 173
mead 17, 29, 67, 109, 132, 135, 141, 143, 146, 148–9, 156, 159, 166, 182, 189, 213, 239
meat 25–6, 28, 33, 59–60, 63, 67, 69, 77–9, 82–3, 95, 102, 106, 115, 117, 126–30, 135–7, 155–7, 159, 163–7, 187, 197, 200–11, 214, 239
  beef 27–8, 60, 63, 69–70, 77–9, 126–8, 130, 133, 151, 186, 202, 204–11, 225, 237
  cured meats 9, 17, 24, 59, 95, 97–101, 122, 136, 165
  lab-grown 200–1, 210
  lamb and mutton 25–6, 28, 131, 150, 156, 216
  pork 23, 30, 136
Melchiori, Alessandro 96
Meloni, Giorgia 199–201, 209–10
Meloni, Silvio 166

men
  Ethiopian 19, 91–4, 98–9, 101, 104, 131–46, 158, 183–4, 187–92
    in the Italian colonial army, see *askari*
    labor 35, 39, 56–8, 90–3, 101, 104, 123–5, 131–46, 181, 183–4, 212, 217–19, 233–5
    representation in Italian popular culture 18–19, 28, 72, 114–16, 131, 135, 174–6, 212–13, 230–7
  Italian, *see* army; settlers, Italian
Menelik II (Sahle Maryam) 24–5, 211, 220
Mengesha, Seyoum 153, 158
Mengiste, Maaza 20
Merca 46, 193, 218, 234
migrants, *see* migration and mobility
migration and mobility 8, 13–14, 19, 25, 29, 34, 44, 49–50, 56–7, 62, 66–7, 70–1, 74–8, 84, 95, 97–8, 101–3, 112, 115–17, 119–20, 125, 127, 143, 146–7, 156, 160, 163–5, 184–7, 213–14, 217–26, 237–9
  animals 8, 12, 19, 34, 78–9, 112, 114, 117, 127–8, 206–9
  germs 8, 112–13, 137
  plants 8, 12–13, 19, 34, 44, 73–6, 120, 192
milk, *see* cheese and dairy
Ministry of Agriculture and Food Sovereignty, Italian 199–200
Ministry of Italian Africa, Italian 37, 45, 48–9, 93, 120, 203, 208
Mogadishu 47, 56, 82, 170, 234
Mojo 100
Monelli, Paolo 179–80
Morettini, Giuseppe 129
Mussolini, Benito 2, 9, 12, 14, 18, 37, 39, 40, 44, 49–50, 53, 56, 58, 87, 91, 93, 99, 102, 122–3, 130, 147, 160–1, 165–6, 173, 199–200, 202, 204, 212, 218, 220, 237–8, 251 n.55, 256–7 n.7
Mussolini, Vittorio 12

Nasi, Guglielmo 80, 167, 251 n.56
Natali-Morosow, Vittorio 106
nausea, *see* senses
Nile, River 182
niter kibbeh, *see* butter

Northern Italians 63, 73, 76, 105–6
nostalgia 1, 60, 68, 70, 84, 99, 102–3, 134, 165, 185–7, 193–5
Notari, Umberto 9
nutrition science, *see* health and diet

olive oil 59–60, 63, 82–3, 122, 181, 214
Omhajer 153
Opera Nazionale Combattenti (ONC) 37–40, 44–5, 75, 204
Opera Volontaria di Repressione Antifascista (OVRA) 57
Otter, Chris 202–3, 209

Palazzo, Domenico 166
Pankhurst, Richard 209
Paris, Maria 215
Partito Nazionale Fascista (PNF), *see* fascism
pasta 1–5, 9, 17–18, 20, 24, 52, 57, 63, 67, 70–1, 73–6, 82–3, 95, 102, 104, 106–7, 122, 126, 132, 136, 139–40, 150–1, 161, 168, 181, 186, 204, 210, 216, 227, 239, 242 n.16
Pavirani, Mario 205
Pettini, Amedeo 215
Pezzoli, Pia Maria 105, 139–44, 150, 153, 158, 163
Piccinato, Luigi 137–9
Pierotti, Francesco 76
Pilosio, Luigi 77, 130, 132
pineapple 8, 59
Pinkus, Karen 235
pizza 109, 111, 133, 210
Podestà, Gian Luca 111
Poggiali, Ciro 13–14, 36, 48, 55, 60, 67–9, 78, 96, 100, 106, 109, 117–18, 121–2, 128, 148, 151, 157–9, 175, 181–2, 184, 190, 193, 204, 206–7, 211, 213, 221–2, 224, 227–8, 258 n.37
Polanyi, Karl 211
Polcri, Aldo 134
poor whites, *see* settlers, Italian
Port Said, 234
potato 8, 24, 34, 36, 43, 50, 63, 203, 122, 131, 136, 187, 203
Pratt, Marie Louise 163
prisoners of war (POWs) 68–9, 125, 165–71, 182

detention and concentration camps, British for Italian POWs 165–9, 182
detention and concentration camps, Italian for Ethiopian POWs 68–9, 166, 169–71
prostitution 3, 17, 88, 125, 146–9, 160, 178
Puccinelli, Giuseppe 89
Puglia d'Etiopia, *see* Enti Regionali di Colonizzazione

Quaranta, Ferdinando 120

racism 3, 7–9, 12–14, 35, 50–1, 65–6, 71–2, 79, 87–94, 99–101, 104–6, 108, 111–13, 117, 122–4, 126, 131, 135, 138–9, 145–6, 160–2, 201, 206, 212, 224, 230–7, 256–7 n.7
  in food places 4, 71–2, 88, 91–4, 99–101, 104–13, 117, 122–4, 126, 138–9, 214, 238
  legal 3, 87–94, 99–100, 109, 160, 256–7 n.7
  Manifesto della Razza 12–13, 87, 219
  Racial Laws (1937) 3, 88–9
  Racial Laws (1938) 12
  racial segregation 4, 14, 18, 65–6, 71–2, 87–94, 99–101, 104–13, 118–19, 122–5, 131, 138–9, 147, 214, 256–7 n.7
railroad 38, 42, 56, 59, 78, 100, 117, 177, 227, 276 n.129
Rama 77
Rapaccini, Jolanda 83–4, 142, 146, 165, 168–9, 184
Razza e Civiltà 87
Regia Azienda Monopolio Banane (RAMB) 34, 47, 218–19, 233–4
religion 130, 139, 151, 157–8, 187–91
  and food 10, 24–6, 30, 130, 132, 136, 139, 143–4, 150–1, 157–8, 161–2, 188–9, 191
resistance, Ethiopian 7, 19–20, 38, 51, 56, 66–7, 72–4, 77–84, 100–1, 107–8, 116–18, 120, 126, 128, 130, 134, 139, 155–6, 165–71, 176, 180, 184–6, 195, 205, 226, 238–9
restaurants 4, 17, 65, 71–2, 75, 82, 88, 92, 94–5, 100–11, 123–4, 146, 149, 162, 164, 214, 260 n.88

Rigotti, Giorgio 91
rinderpest 206–9
Romagna d'Etiopia, *see* Enti Regionali di Colonizzazione

Sada, Pietro 69
salt 59, 67, 121, 129–30, 132, 156–7, 166, 218, 229
Santini, Ruggero 94
Sartori Felter, Alba 13, 64
Seka 120, 132, 143, 153
Sekota 130
Senafe 124
Seneca, Federico 3, 231–2, 234
senses 17, 67, 92, 94, 102, 111, 113–16, 119, 128–9, 138, 145–8, 155–7, 161, 164–5, 173–87, 189–90, 210–12
  taste 17, 60, 63–5, 67, 118, 128–9, 155–7, 159, 161, 164–5, 173–87, 210–12, 237–9
Serra, Giuseppe 110, 159–60
settlers, Italian 17, 50–2, 56, 58–9, 62, 73–5, 80–3, 87–94, 97–101, 105–7, 109–11, 118, 125, 135–46, 166–7, 173–97, 206–7, 210–12, 242 n.20
sexuality 12, 87–92, 133–5, 139, 146–9, 178, 190–1, 232–4, 256–7 n.7
  homosexuality 133–4, 143, 237
  Italian men's attraction to African women 2, 17, 19, 87–91, 123, 125, 133, 146–9, 160–2, 174, 177–80, 232–4
  miscegenation 3, 12, 14–15, 87–92, 94, 109, 124–5, 139, 147, 160–2, 174, 178, 256–7 n.7
  reproductive 9, 17, 87–90, 135, 147, 160–2
Seyoum, Kebedech 81
Shebelle River 11, 45–6, 188, 217
sheep, *see* animals
shiro 30, 152
Società Agricola Italo-Somala (SAIS) 45–6
Società Anonima Banane Italiane (SABI) 233
Società Anonima Navigazione Italo-Somala (SANIS) 218
Società Gestione Alberghi Africa Orientale (SGAAO) 110

Società Italiana Importazione Banane (SIMBA) 205
Somalia 6, 11, 44–7, 56, 93–4, 132, 169, 182, 188, 193, 208, 217–19, 233–4
South Africa 33, 92, 108, 167, 209
Southern Italians 2, 73, 76, 105–6, 108
spices 8, 17, 29, 117, 135, 150, 156, 165, 176–7, 185, 242 n.16
Starace, Achille 79
Stirpe, La 87
Stoler, Ann Laura 88
Strampelli, Nazareno 10, 201–3, 205
Sudan 82, 167, 182, 223, 276 n.129
Suez 55, 58–9, 63, 74, 130, 217, 234
sugar and sweets 8, 17, 24, 34, 59–61, 63, 82, 126, 144, 151, 157, 161, 166, 212, 214, 217
Summa, Mario 111
sustainability 189–190, 202–12, 238

table manners, *see* food manners
Taddia, Irma 72, 123, 177
Tana Lake 23, 37, 77, 126, 132
Tanzania 220
Tassinari, Giuseppe 56
taste, *see* senses
Taytu Betul 25–31, 81
tea 8, 33, 67, 111, 115, 126, 132–3, 151, 157, 159, 166, 170, 188, 212, 216
teff 6, 13, 23, 25, 35, 66, 75, 117, 122, 134, 156, 174–5, 188, 203
tej, see mead
Tekeze River 130
tella, see beer
Teruzzi, Attilio 49, 93, 256–7 n.7
Teseney 153
Tesfamikel, Dicodimos 72, 108
Tesfemariam, Paulos 94
Tessema, Michael 68, 171
Thompson, Edward Palmer 155
Tiruneh, Qeleme Worq 81
tomato 8, 24, 50, 69, 156, 181, 187, 239
   canned 17, 60, 63, 65, 69–72, 99, 122, 181
tourism 9–10, 95, 100, 110, 115
   in the empire 18, 95, 110, 114–15, 182, 243 n.34
trade 2, 7, 37, 58–60, 71–2, 74–6, 82, 210, 217–22, 227–9, 234, 266 n.88
   between Ethiopians and Italians 40, 71–2, 122–3, 213–14, 151
   between Italy and Italian East Africa 5, 52–3, 58–60, 74–6, 82, 122, 134, 151, 155, 186, 215, 219–21
travel, *see* migration and mobility, tourism
truck drivers 66–7, 76–7, 102–4, 106, 110–11, 128, 143, 164–5, 186–7

Uganda 209, 220
United Nations 5, 201
United States 5, 92, 97, 115, 132–3, 144, 162, 227, 230

Valle, Cesare 109
Vargas, Getúlio 220
vegetables 9, 24, 34, 36, 59, 69–70, 83, 95, 102, 117–18, 122, 126–7, 131, 135–6, 146, 154, 157, 167, 169–70, 187, 191
Veneto d'Etiopia, *see* Enti Regionali di Colonizzazione
Vergani, Orio 60, 71, 96–8, 104, 119–20, 139–40, 164–5, 185–6
Victor Emmanuel III, King 215
Villaggio Duca degli Abruzzi 45–7, 218
Visco, Sabato 87
Volterra, Alessandro 72
von Bülow-Schwante, Vicco 256–7 n.7

wat 19, 27–8, 117, 132, 141–2, 150–1, 161, 215–16, 239
water 12, 13, 36, 62, 68, 76, 78, 81, 143–6, 164, 166–71, 180–2, 189–90, 193–4
   bottled, mineral 59, 62, 67–9, 81, 95–8, 122, 146, 165, 181, 227
   drinking 57, 62, 68, 81, 143–6, 164, 166–71, 180–2
   drought 209–10
   for irrigation 13, 36, 44
   pollution 12, 180–2
   rain and wet season 12, 40, 44, 46, 60, 67, 101, 114, 165, 184, 194–5, 224
   rivers and lakes 11, 45, 77, 128, 130, 157, 188–90, 193–6
   sea and ocean 7, 12, 24, 46–7, 61, 55–6, 58, 63, 67–8, 73–4, 170–1, 213, 217, 226
Waugh, Evelyn 118
Wech'e 195

Weldiya 213–14, 258 n.37
wheat 2–5, 10–11, 24, 34–5, 43, 50, 52, 56, 59–60, 73–7, 82, 102, 117, 127, 155, 166, 175, 186, 188, 202–5, 211, 221, 225, 237
wine 9–10, 36–7, 57, 59, 63–5, 67, 71, 78, 81–2, 95, 98, 103–4, 110, 119, 126, 141, 143, 151, 161, 165, 182, 186, 219
women
    Ethiopian 13, 17, 20, 25, 80–1, 87–92, 104–5, 114, 122–3, 132, 134, 145–9, 157–8, 177–80, 160–2, 181, 184–5, 187–92, 213, 224
    in anti-colonial resistance 5–6, 20, 80–1, 116, 132, 134, 184–5, 238–9
    representation in Italian popular culture 2, 18–19, 87–8, 114–16, 174–80, 212–13, 230–7

Italian 131, 137–8, 167, 174, 256–7 n.7
    settlers in Ethiopia 13–16, 60–1, 64, 82–4, 88–9, 92, 101–4, 135–46, 155, 167–9, 177–8, 183–4, 231, 238, 256–7 n.7
World War I 47, 53, 70
World War II 5, 7, 18, 40, 53, 79, 82, 84, 118, 130, 167, 176, 183, 211, 219, 225, 231
Wuchale 117

Yekatit 12, *see* Addis Ababa massacre

zebu, *see* animals
Zelleke, Imru 170
Zewde, Ascale 89
zig'ni, *see wat*
Zimelli, Umberto 9

www.ingramcontent.com/pod-product-compliance
Lightning Source LLC
Chambersburg PA
CBHW071803300426
44116CB00009B/1193